MW01592429

The Astute Investor

This book is dedicated to the referenced practitioners, academics, and especially academic-practitioners who are my masters and mentors on stock market investing.

The Astute Investor

Eric L. Prentis, Ph.D.

Prentis Business

Houston

Prentis Business

Houston, Texas
prentisbusiness@earthlink.net
http://home.earthlink.net/~prentisbusiness

Copyright © 2005 by Eric L. Prentis, Ph.D.

All rights reserved
as well as the right of reproduction in entirety or partially in any form,
without the written permission of the copyright owner. Permission or
additional information requests should be submitted to
prentisbusiness@earthlink.net.

The intended purpose of *The Astute Investor* is to present faithful and
useful information on investing. Stock market buy, sell, or hold
recommendations are not made in this book and should not be assumed.
Professional services – such as legal, accounting, tax, insurance, or
registered investment advice, etc. – are not offered in this text. If
professional services are desired, please contact legally-licensed
professionals directly.

Prentis Business is a registered trademark (pending)

Jacket photographs by James Sweet

Publishers Cataloging-in-Publication Data

Prentis, Eric L., 1948-
    The Astute Investor / Eric L. Prentis, Ph.D. – 1st ed.
      p. cm.
    Includes glossary, bibliographical references, and index.
    1. Investments–United States. 2. Stocks–United States.
    3. Discounted Capital Market Theory. I Title.
    ISBN 0-9759660-0-6

Library of Congress Control Number: 2004095593

10 9 8 7 6 5 4 3 2 1

Contents

Introduction 1

Stock Market Success Is Easy: Once You Know How 2
What Is An Astute Investor? 3
Questions Asked 3
Questions Answered 4
Who Should Purchase This Book 7
Website Commands 7
Bull Or Bear Is Not Used 8
The S&P 500 Index As A Proxy 8
Technical Analysis: Less Is More 9
Bibliography 9

PART I

1 Investing Principles And Strategies 13

Investing Defined 13
Seven Principles Of Investing 16
Probabilistic Approach To Investing 19
Investing Foresight 19
Investing Is Not Gambling 22
Diversification Vs. Concentration 23
Investing Pitfalls To Be Avoided 26

2 Theory And Practice 29

Time And Timing 30

Random Walk Theory For Stock Prices 33
Random Walk Theory Paradox 36
Business Cycles 37
Leading Economic Indicator Paradox 38
How American Roulette And The S&P 500 Index Differs 39
Mr. Market 43
The Efficient Capital Market Theory 45
Critique Of The Efficient Capital Market Theory 47
The Random Walk Theory Critique 49
Stock Market Taxonomy 49

3 Equity And Bond Fundamentals 55

Bond Fundamentals 56
Equity Fundamentals 60
Corporate Management's Financial Responsibilities 64
Price-To-Earnings Ratio 65
Price-To-Earnings Standards 66
Price-To-Earnings Ratio Calculation 69
Discounting 69
Forward Price-To-Earnings Ratio 72
Standard & Poor's 72
S&P 500 Estimated Future Reported Earnings 73
Prevailing Interest Rates 77
S&P 500 Index Expected Fair Valuation Model 78

4 Stock Market Technical Analysis 81

Goal Of The Astute Investor 82
Pricing In The Stock Market 83
Inefficient Capital Markets 84
Market Signals To Be Heeded 84
Premise Of Stock Market Cycles 85
Investor Perspective 87
Monthly Data And Moving Averages 87
Share Volume 88
Four Stock Market Stages 90
Stage 1 92
Stage 2 95

Contents

Stage 3 98
Stage 4 99
Stock Market Long-Term Trends 100
Monthly Moving Average (MA) Trend Lines 102
Moving Average Convergence Divergence (MACD) 102
Japanese Candlestick Graphing Techniques 104
Technical Analysis 107
Computer Graphs 109
Custom Graphs 114
Stage 1: Mark-Down - Downtrend 115
Stage 2: Market Bottom - Accumulation 117
Stage 3: Mark-Up - Uptrend 120
Stage 4: Market Top - Distribution 122
Back Testing 124

5 Trading Psychology 127
Basic Human Nature 128
Vanity 131
Greed 134
Will To Believe 135
Types Of Investors 137
Rational Action 144
Non-Rational Emotions 145
Irrational Influences 149

6 Intrinsic, Market, And Bargain Values 155
Graham-Dodd's Margin-of-Safety 156
Margin-of-Safety For Bonds 156
Margin-of-Safety For Stocks 158
Margin-of-Safety Conclusions 161
Fisher's Investing Style 162
Warren Buffett's Investing Style 167
Step 1: Calculating Intrinsic, True, Or Fair Value 170
Step 2: Calculating Market Value Capitalization 179
Step 3: Calculating Bargain Value 180
Step 4: Calculating Margin-of-Safety Multiple 180
Step 5: Additional Crucial Factors 181

Contents

7 Interest Rate Principles 187

Interest Defined 188
Why Interest Rates Adjust Through Time 189
The U.S. Government And Money Supply 190
The Federal Reserve 192
FOMC Organization And Procedures 195
Yield Curve 197
Dynamic Yield Curves 205
Yield Curves In Practice 206
Business Cycle Indicators 209

8 Interpreting The News 213

Discounting The News 214
Expected News 215
Unexpected News 219
What Really Moves The Markets 226
Discounted News Theory 227
Nightly News Investing: A Losing Proposition 228
The News And The Media 230
Inside Information 233
Stock Market Tips 235
Market Newsletters And Advice 237

9 Being Contrarian 241

Contrarian Philosophy 242
Comparing The Contrarian Approach 244
Contrarians Evaluate Financial Experts 246
The Psychology Of Contrarian Investing 249
Contrarian Implementation 252
Contrarian Investing Methodology 257
Contrarian Investing Additional Factors 261

10 The Ten-Step Method For Investing Success 265

March, 2004: Bringing The Parts Together 266
Step # 1: Investing Goals And Strategy 266
Step # 2: Political-Economic Conditions 267

Contents

Step # 3: S&P 500 Index Expected Fair Valuation Model 267
Step # 4: S&P 500 Index Nine Month MA Trend Line 271
Step # 5: Human Nature And Desired Character Traits 273
Step # 6: Intrinsic, Market, And Bargain Values 276
Step # 7: The Yield Curve 286
Step # 8: Discounted News Theory 288
Step # 9: March, 2004: Invest Along With the Crowd 290
Step # 10: March, 2004: Investing Analysis Results 291

PART II

11 Retirement Planning 297

Asset Allocation 298
1: Goal Selection 299
2: Planning Horizon 300
3: Risk Vs. Expected Returns 301
4: Risk Tolerance 303
Risk Vs. Volatility 305
Volatility Tolerance 311
Volatility Vs. Total Return 314
Retirement Planning: 20 Years Vs. 30 Years 316
Pre-Retirement Planning Example 317
At Retirement: The Example Continued 323

12 Discounted Capital Market Theory 329

Mr. Market In Context 330
Stock Market Maps And Territories 334
Life And Happiness Model 336
Discounted Capital Market Theory 346
Discounted Capital Market Theory Formulation 350
Where Have The Random Walk Theorists Gone Wrong? 352
Importance Of The Discounted Capital Market Theory 354
Discounted Capital Market Theory Conclusion 355

Conclusion 359

Practical Benefits 359
Synopsis Of The Efficient Capital Market Theory Critique 360
Paradoxes In The Stock Market 362
Ironies In The Stock Market 366
Discounted Capital Market Theory Summary Conclusions 368
The Astute Investor Firsts 371
Continued Communication 372

Glossary 373

Bibliography 389

Index 393

Graphs

Graph 2 - 1: Irregular Short-Term and Intermediate-Term Movements
    Along a Long-Term Trending Intrinsic, True, Or Fair Value Line 42
Graph 3 - 1: Bond Prices Vs. Prevailing Interest Rates 57
Graph 4 - 1: Four Stock Market Stages 91
Graph 4 - 2: S&P 500 Index V Shaped Bottom Failures 94
Graph 4 - 3: Candlestick Formations 105
Graph 4 - 4: Stage 1: S&P 500 Index Market Mark-Down -
    Downtrend 116
Graph 4 - 5: Stage 2: S&P 500 Index Market Bottom - Accumulation 119
Graph 4 - 6: Stage 3: S&P 500 Index Market Mark-Up - Uptrend 121
Graph 4 - 7: Stage 4: S&P 500 Index Market Top - Distribution 123
Graph 7 - 1: Normal Yield Curve 199
Graph 7 - 2: Steep Yield Curve 201
Graph 7 - 3: Inverted Yield Curve 202
Graph 7 - 4: Flat or Humped Yield Curve 204
Graph 8 - 1: S&P 500 Index - Prior to the Sept. 11th Terrorist Attack 223

Contents

Graph 10 - 1: March, 2004 - Stage 3: S&P 500 Index Mark-Up - Uptrend 274

Graph 10 - 2: March, 2004 - Steep Yield Curve 288

Graph 11 - 1: S&P 500 Index: 1970-1989 Yearly Prices 320

Graph 12 - 1: Mr. Market & Intrinsic, True, Or Fair Value 332

Graph 12 - 2: Life And Happiness Model 345

Tables

Table 2 - 1: Stock Market Taxonomy 51

Table 3 - 1: S&P 500 EARNINGS AND ESTIMATE REPORT 75

Table 3 - 2: S&P 500 Actual & Forward P/E Ratios & Expected Fair Valuation Model 79

Table 5 - 1: Investor Emotions 146

Table 6 - 1: XYZ Corporation - Cash Flow Statement (in millions of dollars) 172

Table 6 - 2: XYZ Corporation - Free Cash Flow (in millions of dollars) 174

Table 6 - 3: Discount Present Worth Factors (P/F) 176

Table 6 - 4: XYZ Corporation - Stage 1: Expected Discounted FCF to Today's Prices 178

Table 7 - 1: Federal Funds & 30-Year T-Bond Rates, and S&P 500 Prices 207

Table 10 - 1: March, 2004 - S&P 500 EARNINGS AND ESTIMATE REPORT 269

Table 10 - 2: March, 2004 - S&P 500 Actual & Forward P/E Ratios & Expected Fair Valuation Model 272

Table 10 - 3: eBay Inc. - Cash Flow Statement (in millions of dollars) 278

Table 10 - 4: eBay Inc. - Free Cash Flow (FCF) (in millions of dollars) 279

Table 10 - 5: eBay Inc. - Sales Revenue & Net Income (in millions of dollars) 280

Table 10 - 6: eBay Inc. - Stage 1: Expected Discounted FCF to Today's Prices 282

Table 11 - 1: Volatility Tolerance, Planning Horizon, & Asset Mix 313

Websites

www.aig.com 325
www.ambest.com 325
http://bigcharts.marketwatch.com 110-115, 273
www.bloomberg.com 238
www.federalreserve.gov/FOMC/ 196, 287

www.fidelity.com 321
http://finance.lycos.com 7
www.fitchratings.com 325
www.globalindicators.org 38, 209
http://home.earthlink.net/~astuteinvestor 372

http://home.earthlink.net/~prentisbusiness iv
www.hulbertdigest.com 238
http://investor.ebay.com 277
www.investors.com 237
www.investorwords.com 373

http://moneycentral.msn.com/investor/home.asp 77, 205
http://money.cnn.com 238
www.moodys.com 325
www.nber.org 37, 124, 209
www.nytimes.com 237

www.outfo.org 175-176
http://www2.standardandpoors.com 73, 325
www.stockcharts.com 205-206
www.thestreet.com 237
www.tiaa-cref.com 325

www.trading-glossary.com 373
www.vanguard.com 321
www.zacks.com 277

Introduction

THE SECRETS OF SUCCESSFUL investing are revealed here for anyone to learn. The information in this book demystifies how to invest in the stock market so that all investors may attain their investing goals of making money in the stock market and achieving a secure retirement.

What is learned here will forever change investors' beliefs about investing. *The Astute Investor* is unique, informative, practical, easy to use, and fun. Beginning and experienced investors alike, requiring practical knowledge of what to look for to be successful when investing, will find this book most helpful.

Is the stock market undervalued or overvalued? Is the market in a long-term upward trend or long-term downward trend? What is the most promising stock to buy? *The Astute Investor* is the first investment book to allow all investors to correctly answer these vital questions, and much more, for themselves. *The Astute Investor* is unique because through the use of correct investment models and current data on the internet, it brings all investors into the twenty-first century.

Fundamental questions are asked and answered here which are vitally important to those investing in the stock market. These crucial investing questions may be easily answered buy reading this book and becoming an astute investor. From beginning investors to financial service professionals, all will find *The Astute Investor* informative and practically useful. A positive approach is used to explain investing that includes a practical ten-step method for investing success.

To find current data to easily run all the models presented in this book, specific Website commands are described in detail. The Standard & Poor's 500 Index is used as a proxy for the overall stock market. The use of a limited number of technical analysis techniques are discussed. *The Astute Investor* is self-empowering, should help individuals feel confident in taking control of their own investment money, and helps to build wealth and a secure future for investors and their families.

Stock Market Success Is Easy: Once You Know How

Unfortunately, the majority of investors find out about the stock market the hard way – simply by doing. Learning by doing, while common in many undertakings, is often a dreadfully expensive approach to learning investing. By reading this book and applying its lessons, investors will avoid many of the pitfalls which await those who begin investing without this requisite knowledge.

Investors will learn that correct investing is not a random activity, nor mere chance or luck; but, an endeavor relying on proper strategy, analysis, evaluation, and judgment. Practical day-to-day solutions to the problems of investing are presented, and internet Websites on where to find the appropriate data for investors to run current models for themselves are specified.

The Astute Investor is distinctive, unique, and superior to any other book on investing; because, it specifically demonstrates where to find the correct information on the internet to run specific investment models to determine whether the stock market is either over or under valued, whether it is in a long-term upward trend or a long-term downward trend, how to use interest rates to determine if the stock market is approaching a long-term market top, and how to calculate intrinsic value to identify the best individual company stocks to purchase. In addition, new investing theories are presented and explained which supports the practical ten-step method for investing success offered here.

The goal is to point all investors to crucial and essential investing knowledge, and to what the knowledge means, so that they may be transformed into astute investors. It is expected that investors will develop a reference for both understanding and feeling comfortable when participating in the United States (U.S.) stock market.

What Is An Astute Investor?

The astute investor may be defined as a person who has foresight and is perceptive, discerning, and keenly aware of what information and facts are the most significant in the field of investing. An astute investor is one who plans and knows where to locate the data necessary to run appropriate investment models and how to interpret these models' results for decision making when investing. The astute investor is a seeker of the truth, a possessor of market vision, investing intelligence, and practical stock market experience.

How investors implement the information presented here and the effort put forth when investing will ultimately establish how successful they will be when investing in the stock market. By knowing what is in this book and applying it well, verses others who are ignorant of what is in this book, will make these knowledgeable individuals investment winners verses those who are naïve and ignorant about investing. The vitally important questions concerning investing are presented next.

Questions Asked

Many millions of Americans invest in the stock market via individual stocks, in mutual funds, or through self-directed retirement accounts (401(k), 403(b), IRA, or Keogh Plans). *The Astute Investor* helps all investors answer, for themselves, the following fundamental investing questions:

PART I

1) What investing principles and strategies are important?
2) What investing theory and practice are fundamental for   investors?
3) Is the stock market currently overvalued or undervalued?
4) Is the stock market in a long-term uptrend or a long-term downtrend?
5) Why do human emotions get in the way of intelligent investing?
6) How are intrinsic, true, or fair value, market value capitalization, bargain value, and margin-of-safety multiples calculated and what do they mean?

7) What interest rates should be monitored that typically indicate a long-term stock market top?

8) Why do stock market prices often respond "illogically" to the news?

9) Being contrarian sounds simple, why is it so difficult to implement?

10) What is the practical ten-step method for investing success?

PART II

11) How can retirement income be safely doubled?

12) What new investing theories are the basis for investing success?

Questions Answered

Each of the chapter topics in *The Astute Investor* will help all investors become astute investors by helping him or her answer the above fundamental investing questions for themselves.

The following chapter synopsis highlights the methodology presented to allow all investors to answer these most crucial investment questions. Ten major investing firsts are presented and explained in *The Astute Investor,* whose goal is accomplished by transforming novice and experienced investors alike into astute investors.

PART I

1) Investing principles are described and strategies of diversification verses concentration are explained. The importance of investing foresight is addressed. Investing pitfalls are presented.

2) The current theory and practice of the stock market are presented to give investors a better perspective on how to view intrinsic, true, and fair value of individual companies in the marketplace. A stock market taxonomy is offered here for the first time which categorizes the stock market for better understanding.

3) Presentation of a step-by-step discounting approach when calculating the forward price-to-earnings (P/E) ratio and the Standard & Poor's (S&P) 500 Index Expected Fair Valuation (EFV) Model are explained. S&P 500 Website data are explicitly identified. Whether the stock market is overvalued or undervalued may be determined. This is the first time that

the S&P 500 Index EFV Model and where to find updated information to run this model are offered in a book on investing.

4) Using the S&P 500 Index Nine Month Moving Average (MA) Trend Line for perspective and using confirming indicators to check on Stage 1 through Stage 4 market cycles are presented. Learning how to determine whether the stock market is either in a long-term upward trend or a long-term downward trend is fully explained. The use of a charting Website is presented and completely described. This is the first time that perspective and the use of monthly S&P 500 Index Trend Lines, with specific confirming indicators to indicate long-term stock market trends, are presented in a book on investing.

5) Basic human nature and the human mind are unchanging. The use of symbols for the things being symbolized, herd mentality, and how an investor's rational, non-rational, and irrational thinking and conduct can undermine and even subvert the most intelligent investors' thoughts and actions are discussed.

6) The Graham-Dodd-Buffett margin-of-safety approach to value investing requires looking for and recognizing corporate bargains. A step-by-step example is used so that all investors may implement the vitally essential intrinsic, true, or fair value methodology for themselves. This is the first time that an explicit step-by-step real-life example is used in a book on investing to calculate intrinsic, true, or fair value using free cash flow, market value capitalization, bargain values, and margin-of-safety multiples.

7) The Federal Reserve Federal Funds Rate of interest and the 30-Year U.S. Treasury Bond interest rate's yield curve may be used to discount an eventual U.S. economic slowdown, and to identify a long-term stock market peak. Learn how this is done. Internet Websites are identified for use. Adding the Federal Funds Rate to yield curves and specifically comparing the Fed Funds Rate to the 30-Year U.S. T-Bond interest rate to forecast stock market peaks are offered here for the first time in an investing book.

8) Interpreting the news requires understanding the expected news discounting process. Being skeptical of both market pundits and conventional wisdom, avoiding stock tips, and why investors should not be swayed by news headlines are all discussed. The new Discounted News Theory is explained, and why it is vitally important to all investors is emphasized. The Discounted News Theory is offered here for the first time as the correct premise to properly explain the sophisticated methods of

professional participants in the stock market, and as the basis for the Discounted Capital Market Theory.

9) Being contrarian is simple in theory but often challenging and disconcerting to implement. The incorrect self-selected market adviser's strategy of being contrarian, which is just another form of taking stock tips, is explained. Why opposing the market and pride of opinion are costly if practiced by investors. The correct approach to being contrarian is offered.

10) The practical ten-step method for investing success brings together all of the previously discussed points in chapters 1 through 9 to form a systematic approach to evaluating the stock market and individual companies for the astute investor. Real examples, as of March, 2004, using S&P 500 Index data, interest rates, and eBay Inc. annual report information are offered. How to calculate the models, and where to find all of the vital data and information on the internet to accomplish each of the ten steps are an investing book first.

PART II

11) Retirement planning, using asset allocation over the super-long-term with dollar-cost-averaging and a buy-and-hold strategy for core investing in the S&P 500 Index verses corporate bonds, is investigated. What beginning investors learn in this chapter could double their income during retirement. The use of volatility tolerance for asset allocation determination in retirement planning is presented here first.

12) A Discounted Capital Market Theory is presented for the first time in a book on investing. The Discounted News Theory follows the expected news discounting process and supports the Discounted Capital Market Theory. These new theories explain the look ahead ability of the S&P 500 Index to help predict coming political-economic conditions and long-term market cycles. The Life and Happiness Model is newly developed and presented here first to support the Discounted Capital Market (DCM) Theory. The DCM Theory gives the theoretical foundation for why the ten-step method for investing success works in practice.

Who Should Purchase This Book

The goal of *The Astute Investor* is accomplished by transforming all investors into astute investors. This book should be purchased by:

1) Financial services professionals who have to fully comprehend the stock market and explain it to their clients.

2) All investors who would like to understand an often ambiguous stock market, and those who desire learning essential investment knowledge obtained from the thirty-seven classic books on investing.

3) Investors who demand more than theory; but, also practical examples from real life, important internet Website addresses, and how to find current data on the internet to run vital investment models for themselves.

4) All those who have self-directed retirement accounts (e.g., 401(k) and Keogh Plans) and would like information on how best to ensure a better retirement for themselves and their loved ones

Website Commands

Current market data are vital for investors to run investment models for themselves. Therefore, Websites with defined commands necessary to find specific current data and information are identified in bold letters. The Website logon address is given first and then, as explained in the brackets, where to look on the computer screen is given, or what to click on, or as sometimes required what to type in is also specified. An example would be:

> **Logon:** http://finance.lycos.com
>
> **Where:** [Where to look on the computer screen (e.g., on the top heading, along the left column, or in the main body) and the name of what to look for]
> **Click:** [What specifically to click on the computer screen to find the next screen or the necessary data]
> **Type:** [Sometimes it is required to type in information]

Many steps may be required; consequently, the **Where**, **Click**, and **Type** instructions may be frequently repeated.

Bull Or Bear Is Not Used

Many investors know that a bull market is a stock market that is trading significantly higher by approximately twenty percent, and that a bear market is one that is trading significantly lower by approximately twenty percent. The terms bull market and bear market are used freely on Wall Street and in the financial media.

A constant string of connected mental images determines an individual's thought process. Unfortunately, the terms bull or bear expressly fixes in the investor's mind either a charging powerful bull or a snarling aggravated bear – neither image which is easy to forget. Investor emotions, discussed in chapter 5, have a way of clouding proper actions in the stock market. Because the terms bull and bear are emotionally charged words, they can create in an investor's frame of mind a mental block that works against proper analysis of the stock market.

Since poise while investing is vitally important, everything that can be done to reduce emotionally charged images and words should be practiced. Therefore, from here on in the terms bull and bear to describe the overall condition of the stock market are not used by *The Astute Investor.* Instead, the stock market is described as being either in a long-term upward trend or in a long-term downward trend.

Flexibility is an important characteristic for investors, and this may be facilitated by staying away from the emotionally charged descriptions of bull market or bear market. Market behavior and corporate results are important, not an investor's fixated mind-set.

The S&P 500 Index As A Proxy

Only the Standard & Poor's (S&P) 500 Index is the recommended average to be used as a proxy for the overall stock market for the purposes of *The Astute Investor*. Other averages, such as the Dow Jones Industrial Average (DJIA), the NASDAQ Composite, the NASDAQ-100 (NDX), the Russell 2000, or the Wilshire 5000 either do not work at all or not nearly as well as the S&P 500 Index.

It is interesting to note that the Wilshire 5000, an average that includes all equities on the NYSE, NASDAQ, and the AMEX exchanges, does not work as well for the purposes of this book as the S&P 500 Index. This could be because the Wilshire 5000 has many smaller more volatile companies in its average than the S&P 500 Index. It is ironic that the S&P 500 Index, which is a proxy for the overall stock market, works better in the models presented here than the overall market itself.

Technical Analysis: Less Is More

Some technical analysis techniques of the overall stock market, as represented by the S&P 500 Index, are recommended in *The Astute Investor*. For example, S&P 500 Index double tops and bottoms, head and shoulders tops and bottoms, and outside reversal days should be looked for to help when identifying changes in long-term stock market trends. In addition, the S&P 500 Index Nine Month Moving Average (MA) Trend Line, and confirming indicators such as the S&P 500 Index Two Month MA Trend Line, the Moving Average Convergence Divergence (MACD), higher-highs and higher-lows, and more are recommended in chapter 4.

Technical analysis for astute investing is recommended for the S&P 500 Index using monthly data only, and it is not to be used for other any other stock market averages or on any specific individual stocks. For example, flags, pennants, price gaps, or the many other assorted techniques are not recommended here and should not be assumed to work for the S&P 500 Index. Technical analysis on individual stocks and other indexes, such as the semiconductor index (SOX), should also not be assumed to work.

It should be emphasized that only a limited number of technical analysis techniques, specifically recommended to be used for the S&P 500 Index in the proper way offered, are recommended. Technical analysis is an enormous area covering scores of techniques used in a myriad of ways, most of which are not suggested for use by *The Astute Investor.*

Bibliography

The essential investing wisdom from the thirty-seven classic books on investing are incorporated into *The Astute Investor*. This should save individuals considerable time when learning how to invest.

The bibliography section presents this comprehensive up-to-date list of the thirty-seven foremost investment books and a financial dictionary of investing words. All of the essential indispensable investing insight from these classic books on investing, and much more, has been included here. Investing principles and strategies are discussed next in Part I – chapter 1.

PART

I

1

Investing Principles And Strategies

Introduction

INVESTING IS DEFINED. Seven investing principles are offered so that the investors may better appreciate what it means to have a sound approach to the field of investing. Why a perfect solution in the stock market is not possible, and why a probabilistic approach for determining when to be in the market is a more appropriate attitude are presented.

Investing foresight is explained as indispensable to successful investing. The many goals of investing are specified. The differences between investing and pure gambling are explained. Diversification in many stocks verses concentration in a limited number of stocks is emphasized and discussed as a strategic decision. The investing pitfalls to be avoided when investing are listed.

Investing Defined

Many items may be invested in – common stocks, bonds, plant & equipment, rare coins, art, real estate, human beings, etc. The idea is that an owner's excess funds are put to work to produce current income or for a superior future financial benefit to the investor. Money may be earned using the following three methods:

1) The first is to be gainfully employed which requires an exchange of one's time for money.

2) The second is to lend one's money with the expectation that it will be returned on time and with interest.

3) The third is to risk one's money – such as in the equity markets – with the expectation that a larger payout will compensate for the expected higher risk.

The last two investment methods, for common stocks and bonds, are explored and discussed in *The Astute Investor.*

Investing requires the most advantageous strategies and analysis leading to proper evaluation and judgment for purchasing or selling common stocks or fixed-income securities for either capital appreciation and/or predictable income over a many year planning horizon. A discussion of a safe or pure investment follows.

A Safe Or Pure Investment

A safe investment may be described as loaning money, backed up by sufficient collateral, so that if payment of interest and repayment of principle on time is not forthcoming – legal action may be taken against the borrower to attach the collateral for eventual sale by the new owner. By performing the proper due diligence, when the protection of the principle and a satisfactory return are fully anticipated, then the contract may be entered into.

A pure investment may be defined as the acquisition of securities based exclusively upon the safety of the principle and the security of income. In this instance, the investor seeks to buy securities based on an assessment of safety and timely repayment of principle and income compensation.

Often it is assumed for safe or pure investments that the payment of interest or dividends are assured over the duration of the investment, and that the securities may be held throughout with investor equanimity. The expectation by the owner is that the principle will be returned on time and with the contracted interest.

Time Dimension

The dimension of time is crucial in the field of investing. Funds are committed with the expectation of being repaid on time and that the money earned will cover any inflation risk, risk of return, and the length of time that the funds are not available to the lender.

Investment is primarily an attempt to secure a rental from the borrowers of funds for a conditional use of the owner's money. Lenders are attempting to stockpile for their forthcoming claims, current surplus spending capacity, with the expectation of a larger total amount of funds when needed in the future. Investing assumes a realistic assessment of income from dividends, interest payments, or rental fees along with any capital appreciation over the term of the investment.

The time periods for investments are normally estimated to match the required return of the funds for any future use by the owner. The need for high predictability of timely replacement of the principle and earnings income over the longer-term separates investing from the more risky and normally shorter-term business of speculating. Investing only on the long side of the market is appropriate and is discussed next.

Investing On The Long Side Of The Market

It is expected that investors will always be invested in equities on the long side of the market, or in other words, always anticipating that stock prices will go up. Individual corporate stocks are expected to be selected based on their projected outperforming of other stocks in its industry, sector, or the market taken as a whole.

An investor may go to a neutral position, into cash or a money market fund, when the long-term prospects of the stock market seem to be poor and are pointing downward.

Going short of the stock market, being on the other side of the market and selling securities one does not own, is too speculative a position and is not considered an appropriate option for an astute investor looking for investments. The following investing principles will help prospective investors set about participating in the field of investing with the proper understanding and attitude about investing.

Seven Principles Of Investing

To better ensure success, an astute investor should approach investing in an intelligent and business-like way. Unfortunately, the investment field is often entered into by those starting out with almost a total indifference of what it takes to function properly when investing.

The typical business or professional person may spend perhaps a decade learning and practicing his or her vocation in order to have money available to invest in the stock market. Yet these same successful individuals may think that the same study and knowledge are not required when entering into a security investment venture. It should be fully appreciated that running a business, or being a doctor, lawyer, engineer, or educator is unlike the occupation of investing on Wall Street.

The following seven investment principles are offered so that prospective investors may better appreciate what it means to have a sensible approach to the field of investing.

1) *Individuals should first understand the nature of investing.* Do not assume outsized profits from securities, be they stocks or bonds. If investors have put forth extensive study and know security valuations then that knowledge may be factored into the equation, but only then.

The study of the stock market and of individual companies, while taking a significant amount of time, is essential. Investing requires intellectual exertion which is much different from pure gambling which is only unsighted luck. To be a consistent winner in the stock market, investors should not simply rely on the kindness of chance; but, they should assess the risk and try to abolish as much risk as feasibly possible.

2) *Purchasing securities should be viewed as having an interest in or having a claim, alongside others, in the expected earnings of a corporation.* When an individual decides to invest in securities, he or she is beginning a commercial undertaking that needs to be treated as any other monetary transaction – with caution and with one's eyes wide open. Expected earnings are a key variable, and corporations without a history of solid earnings are better thought of as speculative and therefore not appropriate for investing.

3) *It is always best for investors to have the correct knowledge and to feel confident in making one's own investment decisions.* Learning, such as reading and understanding this book, and thereby having the confidence to make one's own investment decisions should be the investor's goal. Baring

that, investors may invest along with those they have confidence in and who have demonstrated superior results and the highest integrity in the field of investing. It is assumed that investors will have the capacity to at least understand and oversee their investment manager's performance.

4) *Analysis and calculation are the cornerstone of successful investing.* The decision to invest should not be based on an investor's mere opinion after listening to a market adviser give seemingly cogent reasons why the market is either undervalued or overvalued. Proper investing should not be based simply on the proclamations of a charismatic individual who uses his or her exceptional intellect to offer plausible explanations of what the market may or may not do. Remain skeptical of all free advice.

Proper investing is not based on hopefulness that the market or stock prices will behave a certain way; but, only on studying the uncompromising facts, data, and making the appropriate mathematical calculations. Only when a dependable calculation or technical data indicates a good possibility to secure an acceptable profit should one undertake an investment.

An investor's most powerful advantage over all others participating in the stock market, be they the company's employees or stock market floor traders, is the power to just "say no." Just say no to any scheme with little to earn and the possibility of much to lose. The astute investor's goals are returns that are realistic while at the same time having compelling proof that one's investing capital is not in jeopardy.

5) *Investors should have the courage of their own convictions.* Following one's own judgment is the goal. When investors have the knowledge, have performed the calculations, have reviewed the appropriate technical data, have formed a conclusion based on these data and mathematical facts, and are convinced that their judgment is reliable – investors then should have the courage to act on their convictions.

Astute investors should not vacillate simply because others do not share their resolve. Whether others, be they a few or an entire crowd, agree with one's judgment does not determine whether one is right or wrong in the stock market. Correctness is determined solely on using the right technical data, running appropriate mathematical models, and maintaining sound judgment.

In the world of investing virtues, first comes proper knowledge, then sound judgment, and finally the courage to act. Confidence is only acquired with the experience of actually investing in the stock market. It is expected that after investors comprehend the contents of *The Astute Investor,* they will gain necessary stock market experience only by putting this valuable knowledge into action.

6) *Limit one's investing ambitions and reach to one's area of competence.* If investors do not feel comfortable or proficient in a particular area of investing, by all means stay out. Satisfactory returns are the goal. The expectation of superior returns may initially look attainable in an unfamiliar field, but are often more difficult to achieve than first projected.

Do not feel pressured to jump into the latest hot industry merely because it is receiving copious amounts of press or one's neighbor recently made a killing in it. Staying focused on what the investor knows is paramount.

7) *Successful investing is not accomplished by simply relying on clear-cut facts or rote mathematical formulas, investing judgment is key.* Judgment of what the facts and mathematical formula results mean and the effect this information will have on the stock market and its participants is crucially important. Knowledge, facts, technical data, mathematical models, proper judgment, and the willingness to act on one's convictions separate the successful investors from the merely mediocre.

Investors may discover something vitally significant about a corporation in the marketplace, but the inexperienced do not have the capability to capitalize on this information. It is a long standing truth that simply having the pertinent facts, even if they are critical facts that most investors are unaware of, is not enough to be successful in the stock market. The power of these facts to the investor rests solely with an understanding of what the market will do with the data, and then to act correctly that gives investors the ability to make money from information. Sound judgment will win out, and this acumen is only achieved by careful study of the facts in combination with extensive practical experience.

Along with the proper principles, investing requires a probabilistic approach, foresight, and the most beneficial strategies and analysis leading to proper evaluation and judgment for purchasing or selling common stocks or fixed-income securities for either capital appreciation and/or predictable income over a many year planning horizon. Consequently, a probabilistic approach should be adopted when investing in the stock market which is presented next.

Probabilistic Approach To Investing

A foolproof scientific method for flawless execution in the stock market has never been developed and one will never be discovered. What is offered in this book is knowledge of what is important to observe in the market, what it means, and gaining the practical experience to recognize and take advantage of market signals in a timely manner.

Possessing perfect solutions are impossible when investing. Expecting to participate in the stock market as if one could be judged by an exact standard is absurd and dangerous to an individual's financial health.

A strategy to evaluate and make predictions about the future course of the stock market will never be a mathematical certainty, but may be based on a conceptualized probabilistic basis. Reducing risk as much as possible and having the probability of making money being on the side of the investor are the objectives.

Stressing only the answers when approaching the stock market is often short sighted. Investors repeatedly find it more instructive to be taught the correct questions to be asked rather than to be given only a momentary correct answer, such as in a market newsletter. The right answers are only for specific times and places, while the correct questions and solution methods transcends both dimensions.

Investors quickly learn that the stock market is always changing and that success comes only by balancing market probabilities and not by attaching oneself to one correct answer for all time. Certain universal answers to the stock market will never be found, so it is better to rely on probabilities.

The successful approach offered here is an evaluation method based on correct premises, and observations of past associations that will in all likelihood be to the astute investor's advantage over a many year planning horizon. Knowledge and the experience of working with actual situations are crucial to success when investing in the stock market. The following section emphasizes how important foresight is for investing success.

Investing Foresight

Foresight for investors requires them to envision or imagine what will happen in the future based on all the necessary information available to them, and then to adequately prepare and properly position themselves for the expected consequences. Investing foresight requires proper concepts, being accurately informed, along with looking ahead and making a reasoned inference which adequately anticipates the future.

Financial analysis is probabilistic in nature and not definite, and of course not like making the many more certain calculations in the physical sciences. However, knowing and performing financial analysis are imperative for a systematic investigation of whether to invest in the stock market or in an individual stock. Augmenting the financial analysis, foresight and a projection or estimation of how good business and political conditions will be in the future are also required. Furthermore, determining management's competence, honesty, and energy are mandatory for informed investing judgment.

Financial analysis, business prospects, political conditions, and talented management will all govern the ability to earn an adequate return on an investment and the return of one's principle in a timely manner which ultimately depends on investing foresight to make a correct judgment. Anticipating the future is the stock market's function, and that is what investors with foresight and vision are also striving to estimate and predict.

Investing Vision

The concept of vision requires astute investors to see what others around them do not see. All investors may watch the same things, the difference being that many do not comprehend the significance of what is being observed. To foresee requires ordering or prioritizing images and taking them into consideration beforehand. Foresight and order gives precedence to what should be observed. After reading this book with comprehension, the currently non-seeing unaware investor should be able to see realistic political-economic and stock market conditions and know how best to respond to them.

Looking ahead, vision, and foresight, while certainly not easy, with the help of this book any investor can prioritize what to look for and improve on their foresight capabilities. The ultimate discovery that most investors make in the stock market is that they must examine and interpret political-economic conditions to help them foresee investment probabilities.

Investors with truthful and accurate vision, images, and foresight will be richly rewarded by the stock market. Foresight and vision for investors requires them to imagine what will happen in the future, based on all the information available to them, and to use reasoned inference which is discussed next.

Reasoned Inference

Foresight in investing is the comprehension of past and present facts and actual conditions combined with the correct premises, concepts and reasoning, developed over time, to understand how the future should probably appear. This is called reasoned inference (please see chapter 12 for additional use). It is an investor's foresight concerning expected market conditions prior to their occurrence that is a key factor in intelligent investing. In the main, the development of foresight based on reasoned inference is indispensable to the practice of investing.

Those with the most acute foresight will find the most success in the stock market. A practical example of using investing foresight is presented in chapter 3 for a better understanding of this fundamental investing trait. Those with foresight acquire a preference for looking beyond today to see the probable route that future proceedings are likely to take.

In the short run, stock prices use the exploring-compensating condition to search for the intrinsic, true, or fair value in the marketplace and experience many short-term dips and bulges. It will be discussed in chapter 4 how these short-term dips and bulges normally move around intrinsic, true, or fair value. Astute investors should be looking ahead and striving to understand the truth of the marketplace regardless of these short-term dips and bulges.

The promotion and development of foresight is most indispensable for a successful investor. The individual with the most highly practiced and attuned investing foresight may proceed with confidence. Without foresight, investors are simply hoping that this time their chance in the market will work out. Moving away from merely gambling and taking chances to the more secure position that investing foresight affords will best secure investing success.

Investors Must Not Be Dreamers

Investors must not be dreamers, but appreciate the state of affairs as they are and not simply based the hope of what should be. Hope is merely a belief in that which is desired. Investing should not be based simply on one's hopes or desires; but, only decided upon by proper concepts, the appropriate knowledge, facts, analysis, and sound judgment.

In the short term, the stock market balances investor's opinions and weighs them on the scale of the market. In the long term, however, investor's opinions are proved to be an infinitesimal consequence in the face of facts, truth, and the cold hard reality of market cycles associated with political-economic conditions that ultimately determine stock prices.

The political-economic conditions, over the long term, are stronger than any single person or organization trading in the stock market, and consequently will eventually overwhelm anyone's wrong opinion. That is what is meant by saying that eventually the stock market will go where it wants to go.

Humans beings are known to be superstitious, and often investing errors may be directly linked to one's desire to hold beliefs that are in fact erroneous. In addition, investors may try to will their beliefs to be true – often with disastrous results. Humans are by nature proud which is why when investing belief and reality collide, often the belief is maintained and the reality is ignored.

At stock market long-term bottoms, when reality becomes too painful for the dreamers and those with only plain hope, repeatedly these investments are sold at the wrong time. Over and over again investment dreamers try to bury their mistakes during panic selling so that the their unpleasant losses never have to be faced up to again.

Investing Is Not Gambling

Betting on the flip of a fair coin is a contest of pure chance that requires only luck. This is pure gambling. On the other hand, investing, if performed properly, should not be thought of as pure gambling but as a strategic enterprise. Pure gambling entails no reasoned inference, nor does it presuppose calculation – investing does.

Proper investing demands both correct reasoning and compulsory calculation. Success in investing comes from eliminating risk, as much as possible, from the investing act prior to making the commitment. Winning in the stock market is not achieved merely because one takes a risk, it is accomplish by reducing that risk.

It has been observed with complete wonder how successful business people and professionals who are intelligent, cautious, and extremely experienced in their own fields will make investments without first knowing what they are doing – presumably because it looks so easy. They may straightforwardly pick out a stock on nothing more than a hunch based on outside advice, invest, and then hope to root it on to victory.

The naïve approach to investing is not recommended in *The Astute Investor*. The adage that "it is easier to make money than to keep it" readily applies when discussing the stock market. The investor's intelligence is pitted against all others in the market and the race is won based on a correct assessment of true facts, and then being able to act appropriately on one's judgment. Diversification verses concentration issues are major determinates for investing strategies, a discussion follows.

Diversification Vs. Concentration

The goal of successful investing is safety of principle and security of the expected income, all in a timely manner. A strategy is a plan, scheme, or approach worked out prior to attempting to secure, through a course of action, the intended stated goal.

The means have to be meticulously planned to ensure that the ends are attained. A central decision facing investors is how much of their capital should be invested in how many different stocks. This is the strategic diversification verses concentration issue.

Unsystematic Risks

Individual company stocks have event risks, such as bankruptcy or major lawsuits, that are peculiar to only that specific corporation. These are unique risks associated with individual companies traded on the stock exchange. Risks associated with only one company are described as unsystematic risks.

Putting one's entire life savings in only one company's stock is extremely risky. The individual company may go bankrupt, resulting in the complete loss of one's entire investment. Or the company may suffer a devastating loss, such as a natural disaster or losing a major lawsuit brought by the government or by competitors, which will severely depress earnings over the expected life of the investment. These possibilities for investment losses are called unsystematic risks.

Investing all of one's money in one company's stock may turn out terribly. Based on the definition of investing, buying only one company's stock is not an appropriate strategy for investors. Sufficient diversification of an investment portfolio effectively eliminates the unsystematic risks from individual companies.

Systematic Risk Or Market Risk

The risk that can not be avoided, even if all unsystematic risks could be, is called systematic risk or market risk. Systematic or market risk may be described as the overall political-economic conditions that determine stock prices.

Systematic or market risk uncertainties have a tendency to move most stock prices together, and this risk can not be diversified away regardless of the number of companies or types of stocks in an investment portfolio. Adequate diversification eliminates almost all unsystematic risk, but never the systematic or market risk due to overall political-economic conditions.

Diversification requires adding an adequate number and different type of company stocks together into a portfolio of stocks with the intention of completely reducing the impact of unsystematic risk on the portfolio's returns, as presented next.

Portfolio Diversification

Diversification is an investment management decision, whose goal is to spread the risk among an adequate number of different stock securities and across many different industries which are likely to be vulnerable to different types of unsystematic risks. Diversification associated with a broad selection of common stocks has the added benefit of reducing the variability of the overall portfolio value.

The Standard & Poor's 500 Index is an example of a broadly diversified portfolio that covers many different industries and represents approximately, as this is written, eighty percent of the market capitalization of all companies traded on the three major stock markets. The Standard & Poor's (S&P) 500 Index is recommended as an exceptionally well diversified portfolio suitable for investing purposes. Why investing using the S&P 500 Index, rather than an individual stock, is like being in the insurance industry is presented next.

The S&P 500 Index Acts Much Like The Insurance Industry

Investing in the S&P 500 Index works much like the insurance industry. By collecting publicly traded corporations into a single S&P 500 Index stock market grouping the unsystematic risk associated with an individual company or industry may be effectively eliminated and the portfolio is now diversified.

The S&P 500 Index is a well diversified portfolio across many industries in which the unsystematic risk due to individual corporations is virtually removed. It is assumed that within the S&P 500 Index, one company's failures will be taken advantage of by another company within the stock market grouping and all of these types of pluses and minuses will average out and the stock market average price will be execrably linked to overall political-economic conditions which are systematic in nature.

As with a life insurance policy, as long as the risk is spread among all the policy holders, benefits may be paid out even though the specifics of any actual person at any point in time is unknowable to the company writing the policies.

By taking an S&P 500 Index stock market position, investors are assuming the role of the insurance company and spreading their risk with diversification over many companies and sectors in the economy. The S&P 500 Index now takes on the characteristics of overall political-economic conditions. Which individual corporations win or lose within the stock market grouping is not as important as where the long-term cycles of the political-economic condition are heading.

Diversification is a recognized strategy used when investing. The question of how much diversification is enough may be asked. In general, the more knowledge the investor has the fewer stocks need to be in the portfolio. Warren Buffett, a vastly knowledgeable investor at one time is reported to have had nearly seventy-five percent of the common stock assets of Berkshire Hathaway's stock, the investment company he manages, in only five different companies. This is an example of portfolio concentration which is discussed next.

Portfolio Concentration

Warren Buffett demonstrates his expertise and superior results when investing. His knowhow allows him to concentrate on a limited number of stocks when investing. The better the investor is at financial analysis and possessing investing foresight, the more capable he or she will be in building their own portfolio of fewer stocks that may represent excellent returns.

As one becomes an investing expert, after extensive study and experience, it is a matter of fact that the vast fortunes, such as Warren Buffett's Berkshire Hathaway, are built with a concentration in a relatively fewer number of stocks.

Having only five companies in one's portfolio may not be adequate diversification for almost all other investors however. Selecting a S&P 500 Index fund, rather than limited concentration, for equity investment will ensure an appropriate number of companies and spreading of risk across all major industries.

Diversification rather than concentration in an investment portfolio is especially important and required for all novice investors. For the vast majority of investors, the correct choice for proper diversification is the S&P 500 Index which is assumed here. New investors should be warned against the following easy to fall into investing pitfalls.

Investing Pitfalls To Be Avoided

There are many common investing pitfalls that novice investors are continually drawn to which should be strenuously resisted.

Promotional Stocks

Inexperienced investors may decide to diversify with many promotional stocks that are small and not well known, and are not presently earning profits. These promotional stocks, with especially volatile stock prices, may seem enticing to the unwary.

Particularly during a boom economy and a sky high stock market, new companies are formed and sold to investors through an Initial Public Offering (IPO) that are designed, late in the political-economic upward cycle, primarily to fill the investing public's almost insatiable appetite for equities. Based on the definition of investing, promotional speculative stocks with no earnings would not be appropriate for one's investment portfolio.

New investors should begin investing by purchasing the largest and best known companies that are consistent earners and posses the most liquid stock that may be turned quickly into cash at close to fair value – such as the S&P 500 Index.

Poor Timing

The investing public rarely knows the value of a stock, only its stock price. In general, the investing public's dealings are not determined by what should be done, given the political-economic conditions, but simply on fear alone. The investing public often waits to invest until the stock market advances have been fantastic, because they are fearful of losing their money.

As more and more of the investing public comes into the stock market late in the long-term upward cycle, unaware investors think that the good times and outsized market prices will last forever. Many investors may be astute enough not to continue buying at the absolute long-term market top, but they may unfortunately also neglect to take their profits at this peak time.

The investing public makes the big money during the boom-bubble times, on paper, but neglects to turn large paper profits into cash. The expectation by the investing public here is that the promise is of continued explosive growth and outsized profits. Astute investors should follow the practical ten-step method for investing success for much better long-term timing results

Low-Priced Stocks

In general, all stocks priced less than ten dollars a share should never be purchased for an investment portfolio. The first reason is that low-priced stocks are probably in the portfolios of novice investors who because of less staying power may be forced to sell stocks when times are difficult for whatever price is available. Certainly penny stocks, those priced less than one dollar, should always be avoided since they would never fit the definition of investing.

The second reason is that many institutional mutual funds have covenants in their bylaws that limit purchasing stocks that are under ten dollars a share. As a consequence, this severely restricts the purchasing power necessary to pull low-priced stocks upward after a severe long-term market decline. This could keep unwary investors locked into low-priced stocks which do not demonstrate adequate price recovery, even as the overall stock market responds to newly favorable political-economic conditions.

Summary

Investing requires the most advantageous strategies and analysis leading to proper evaluation and judgment for purchasing or selling common stocks or fixed-income securities for either capital appreciation and/or predictable income over a many year planning horizon. Investors should prefer suitable high-quality securities at proper or reasonable prices which match the investor's scheduled needs, and should believe that all relevant factors or odds are favorable prior to making an investment.

A probabilistic approach and foresight are necessary traits for being a successful investor. What is required is a course of action, a plan, or a specific methodology which has been previously thought out which is projected to achieve the most advantageous investment results. Investing should never be thought of as pure gambling. The program used in *The Astute Investor* is to offer a systematic assembly of significant questions, facts, premises, assumptions, and plans to help investors develop the foresight that they will need to be successful investors. This is the practical ten-step method for investing success.

Individual stocks have unsystematic risks while diversified portfolios, such as the S&P 500 Index, have systematic or market risk. Diversification or concentration are strategic choices for an investment portfolio. Exceedingly knowledgeable investors with widespread experience may concentrate with fewer stocks in their investment portfolio. Promotional and low-priced stock should be avoided. The much safer choice for investors are the largest and best known companies that are consistent earners and posses the most liquidity. The vast majority of investors should select the broadly diversified S&P 500 Index for their investment portfolio.

2

Theory And Practice

Introduction

THE IMPORTANCE OF TIME as a crucial investing factor as well as in our lives is investigated. An explanation of the current theory in finance to describe what is occurring in the stock market, the Random Walk Theory (RWT), is offered for assessment. The RWT and the use of a Leading Economic Indicator leads to paradoxes in the stock market which are discussed. The differences between a true random walk process, such as American roulette, and the stock market are identified.

Mr. Market is a famous fable that is retold here which graphically illustrates the emotional nature of how the investing public on occasion participates in the stock market. How to treat the demonstrative Mr. Market is fully explained.

The Efficient Capital Market Theory, which is based on the Random Walk Theory (RWT), is presented and critiqued. The three versions of the Efficient Capital Market Theory and assumptions are presented and discussed from a practical viewpoint to identify weaknesses.

A Stock Market Taxonomy is presented which categorizes the overall stock market for better investor understanding. One axis of the taxonomy represents the dimension of time, and the other whether the S&P 500 Index or an individual stock is being considered for investment purposes. It is explained that what investing techniques can be correctly utilized in one category of the taxonomy can not necessarily be assumed to work within another category.

Time And Timing

Time is necessary to describe change. Change or fluctuation, particularly in the variability of stock prices, is the nature of the stock market. The flow of time goes from the past, to the present, into the future and is irreversible. A continuous succession of events occurs through time. Understanding time and timing are crucial to comprehending and taking advantage of events in the stock market.

Change or movement is measured by the dimension of time. Material things in space may be described by the three dimensions of height, length, and width. The fourth dimension is time which is non-spatial. Life and matter in motion requires the four dimensions of space-time for adequate description. The vital importance of time to the stock market, beginning with famous maxims to live by, is reviewed.

Famous Maxims To Live By

The famed sayings of the Greek philosophers Socrates (469-399 B.C.) and Aristotle (384-322 B.C.) reveals time's importance by connecting time to their two immortal maxims to live by. Socrates said to know thyself, "The unexamined life is not worth living."

Socrates instructs us not to live life in a fog and simply go along with circumstances as they may direct. Instead, he instructs us to question who we are and what we want in life. We should reflect on what we love, what productive endeavors we are good at, and what achievements will make us happy. This is vitally important because a person' selfhood is their beliefs and values which is the source for their actions, and actions are the source for their happiness.

Aristotle continues Socrates celebrated maxim by explaining the importance of planning in life's pursuit of happiness. Aristotle said, "The unplanned life is not worth examining."

Planning is a course of action or scheme that is determined in advance for which something is to be achieved, or for the realization of a goal. Planning is determining how to get from where we are to where we either want to go or to what we want to be in life. An unplanned life has no bearings or no direction since these individuals do not know how they are going to get to where they want to go.

An unplanned life is often a hodgepodge of unconnected events. Thus, life's disarray makes a close examination impractical. Planning requires the experience of knowing who we are and where we are in life, where we want to go, and the foresight to develop a workable program of action to achieve these selected aims.

Time is vitally important to planning. Only the use of time, and dates – called scheduling – adequately defines a plan. The importance of scheduling is crucial for planning success in life's pursuits. Therefore, adding time to planning is crucial. It should be said, "The unscheduled life is not worth planning."

Scheduling is affixing time and dates to a plan. An allotted amount of time and a date is assigned to each activity or event on the plan to achieve intermediate goals that lead to a final objective of life's pursuits. Many different sub-plans and intermediate objectives may be decided upon, but all should specify a schedule date for their expected accomplishment.

Individuals find it too easy to procrastinate without set dates to compare against and check. A plan without a schedule is only a wish list since it can not be monitored and may drift because the plan has no reference points. Without dates the plan may not be compared with the present and quickly becomes outmoded or even irrelevant. Without a schedule the plan is meaningless, since the activities or events may not happen in our lifetimes. Time is a vital to developing a plan, in knowing thyself, and is also crucial in life as discussed next.

Time Is One's Life

Time is crucial to life as well as for planning purposes. Benjamin Franklin (1706-1790), the brilliant American statesman, United States founding father, and author and publisher of *Poor Richard's Almanac*, may have best recognized the importance of time with regard to life and to one's pursuit of happiness when he made the following observation. Benjamin

Franklin said, "Dost thou love life? Then do not squander time; for that's the stuff life is made of."

Possessions in life, such as land or food, may be put aside for later use. Time in life is different, for time may not be saved. Life must be lived while we are here, in the moment. Therefore it can be said, "Time is one's life." The importance of understanding the essential concept of time in relation to both money and the stock market are investigated next.

Time Is Money

"Remember that time is money," this is the advice Benjamin Franklin gave to a young tradesman. Certainly for those who pay a mortgage or apartment rent on the first of every month know and have a keen appreciation that time is money. Every month on the first, the mortgage or rent money is due without fail.

For those working by the hour or billing by the hour, time is money. Lawyers frequently bill their clients by the hour. Employees such as engineers and accountants may be paid a salary which may be paid once a month on a set date. In these employment instances, time is money.

Bonds have a similar relationship with the payment of interest or principle due at a regular interval of time. Interest may be paid monthly, quarterly, semi-annually, annually, or in the case of zeros (covered in the next chapter) the principle and interest may not be paid until the end of the contract is due. For contractual payment of bond interest on predetermined dates, time is money.

The relationship between time and money changes in the stock market however. Thinking that time is money is not sophisticated or worldly enough for stock market participants. Simply believing that time is money is not enough for investing success which is discussed next.

Timing Is Money

In the complicated and sophisticated stock market, time is not money – timing is money. The difference is significant. Time moves from being regular with specific dates for payment – as with the contractual obligations for employment, interest, rent, or mortgage payments – to being irregular with regard to value and payments.

Professional comedians, publishers, actors, managers, symphony conductors, athletes, ballet dancers, sales personnel, opera singers, and stock traders all recognize the vital importance of timing to being successful in their fields of endeavor. Since an investor has no control over daily stock price movements in the market, he or she has to take advantage of circumstances that the stock market presents as they occur. That requires good timing and recognizing opportunity.

Knowing who you are, where you want to go, what you want, and when are all important concepts and readily applicable in the field of investing. Planning and scheduling of one's life is dependent on one's beliefs and values, plus desires, that result in decisions, leading to actions (more on the Life And Happiness Model in chapter 12). Investment goals may be accomplished based on correct timing over the planning horizon specified.

The strategy that investors use to accomplish specific goals over a set planning horizon using the securities market depends upon the timing that is available to investors. This is more fully explained in the Stock Market Taxonomy section at the end of this chapter, and in chapter 11.

Current research beliefs in the field of investing focus on the random walk process. Daily stock price movements for a company's stock has long been described in the research literature as a random process which is the foundation of the Random Walk Theory discussed next.

Random Walk Theory For Stock Prices

It is reported that the concept of the Random Walk Theory is a result of an investigation into stock price movements in 1953 by Maurice Kendall of the English Royal Statistical Society. His research study purpose was to identify stock price cycles; but, unexpectedly, Kendall could not detect any cycles whatsoever in the data he was investigating. Each daily price series for the company's stock studied seemed to act like a random walk process – no cycles were in evidence.

It was concluded, that day-to-day company stock price movements are seemingly independent from one another and are as random as the flipping of a coin. The idea that stock prices move in a random walk process, much like a pure gambling game, is often presented and discussed in the investment literature and as a consequence is explored here.

Movement of a corporation's stock price in the stock market has long been described in the financial research literature as that of one aimlessly wandering through time as if someone drew by chance a plus or minus number and added that number onto the previous day's closing price. As Burton G. Malkiel explains, the phrase given to this seemingly aimless wandering of corporate stock prices is the random walk process. The game of American roulette is a true random walk process which is explained next for discussion purposes.

American Roulette

A true random walk process may best be understood by looking at the American roulette game of chance. An American roulette wheel has thirty-eight numbered slots on its perimeter. One through thirty-six numbers are evenly divided into red and black colors, and a zero and a double zero are also present which are both green in color. The wheel is spun in one direction and a white ball is rolled in the other direction. The white ball eventually clatters to rest on one of the equally divided thirty-eight slots with a probability of one divided by thirty-eight, or 2.63157 percent.

When playing a fair American roulette game, the numbers that result after each spin of the wheel and roll of the ball are each independent from one another and display no serial correlation whatsoever. Consequently, the numbers that come up in a fair American roulette game are described as a random walk process.

In a random walk process, knowing the last winning number in the American roulette game has no predictive power whatsoever on the next winning number. Each spin of an American roulette wheel is a stand alone process with the numbers produced merely symbolizing what is occurring from the random physical event of spinning the wheel and rolling the ball.

Even if the number seven has not appeared in the last 4,000 spins of the wheel and roll of the ball in American roulette, the likely hood of a seven coming up on the next spin is still only 2.63157 percent. The probabilities on the next spin do not increase merely because the number seven seems to be "due to hit." Thus, the fair American roulette game is a true random walk process with no predictive ability whatsoever based on the outcomes of past numbers. Therefore, looking at its past data is completely immaterial to what will happen in the future. Stock price movements are also described as a random walk process.

Stock Prices And The Random Walk Theory

Stock prices, in the investment research literature, are also described as moving in a random walk process. The Random Walk Theory (RWT), which is based on the random walk process, says that the price of stocks move either up-or-down in a random pattern – and because of that stock prices can not be predicted. It is explained that since prices in the marketplace respond quickly to freely available information, and because that information arrives in a random manner, daily stock prices move in a random walk process.

Random walk theorists have studied day-to-day corporate stock prices and say that knowing what happens to a corporation's stock price today will have no predictive power over its price tomorrow. If stock prices are up today there is no way to know, from prices alone, if stock prices will be up or down tomorrow. Random walk theorists have likened stock prices to an intoxicated partygoer who staggers around on the dance floor – one does not know what direction the inebriated stock-price reveler will step in next.

It is a least tacitly put forth by stating that stock price movement is a random walk process, like the comparison with American roulette gambling, that good luck is a rational strategy for investing in the stock market. After reading *The Astute Investor* it is expected that investors will instead agree that it is correct knowledge, beliefs, and proper strategy that are most important for investing success and not simply dumb luck – such as merely throwing darts at a newspaper listing of common stocks for a suitable selection of investment choices.

A person's correct beliefs, as in life, are paramount to successful investing. Gaining the correct knowledge offered in *The Astute Investor* is demanding work, but it is worthwhile as the acquired confidence will help astute investors feel that they are not simply relying on mere investing luck and adrift on a random wind-swept turbulent sea with no valid signposts in sight. The first indication that a random walk process may not be adequate to model the stock market comes through an investigation of historical market averages.

Historical S&P 500 Index Averages

The Standard & Poor's (S&P) 500 Index average is at 10 in 1941, and as this is written during October, 2003 the S&P 500 Index is at 1,050. From 1941 to 2003, or over approximately sixty-two years, based solely on the price increase alone, which does not include the payment of S&P 500 Index dividends – the S&P 500 Index compounded at approximately an eight percent per year growth rate.

The upward trend in the overall stock market over the super-long-term, i.e., over two decades or more, matches in general the underlying growth of total corporate earnings. Over the super-long-term, this matches the upward trend in the market of approximately on average a little less than one percent per month. This is self-evident for anyone looking at a super-long-term S&P 500 Index stock chart to plainly see.

Over sixty-two years, the trend in the overall stock market is clearly upward and displays a positive serial correlation. The random walk theorists explain this by saying there is a positive drift in the stock market. Stock price changes from day-to-day they say, even with positive drift over the super-long-term, seemingly remain random.

Over the super-long-term, of two decades or more, the overall stock market does have an upward trend. What may be overlooked is that the positive drift is the explanation of why investors should be in the market if their planning horizon is over the super long-term, since day-to-day price changes are immaterial to eventual super-long-term investing success. The random walk process, which supports the Random Walk Theory, produces the following paradox which is not easy for random walk theorists to justify.

Random Walk Theory Paradox

The Random Walk Theory depends on the random walk process. As we have seen in American roulette, a random walk process should never be a positively correlated time series. The stock market as represented by the S&P 500 Index over sixty-two years is a positively correlated time series. The "random walk process" and "prediction," used in the same sentence to describe a stock price course of action is a contradiction in terms. A predictive random walk process is an oxymoron. This is a serious contradiction requiring a theoretical resolution.

It is a paradox that individual corporate stock prices from day-to-day seem to follow a random walk process while the overall stock market, as represented by the S&P 500 Index, over the super-long-term is a positively correlated time series. This is a Random Walk Theory paradox. Random walk theorists, however, concede positive drift of stock market averages over the super-long-term, but do not evaluate the significance for this troubling phenomenon. The significance of this paradox and a theoretical resolution is addressed in this book and presented in chapters 8 and 12.

A super-long-term positively correlated time series is in evidence which is called positive drift. If there is a positively correlated time series over the super-long-term in the S&P 500 Index, why not over the long-term? The long-term is defined as 1, 2, 3, 4, 5 years or more. What is looked for and presented here as a way to identify both long-term positive drift and long-term negative drift for the S&P 500 Index.

The goal in this book is to demonstrate an upward trend or downward trend over the long-term for the S&P 500 Index that may be used to the investor's advantage. Business cycles are important to political-economic conditions and impact the stock market. A discussion follows.

Business Cycles

The National Bureau of Economic Research (NBER), www.nber.org, is the official authority on U.S. business cycle expansions and contractions. NBER's Business Cycle Dating Committee determines the long-term turning points for the U.S. economy. It is reported that from 1854 to 2001 there have been thirty-two business cycles, the most recent recession or contraction during that time period lasted eight months from March, 2001 to November, 2001.

The NBER defines a business recession or contraction as a substantial down-turn throughout the general economy in economic conditions which is ongoing for a few months or more. A recession becomes evident in the contraction of real gross domestic product (GDP), a reduction in total employment, real income, wholesale-retail sales, and industrial production.

Based on NBER statistical averages over thirty-two business cycles – from peak to trough, business contractions last approximately seventeen months. Average business expansions, from prior trough to the next peak, last about thirty-eight months. And on average, from prior peak to the next peak, it takes a little over 4.5 years. In general, overall long-term stock price declines are loosely tied to business contractions and up-trends in the market are loosely coupled with business expansions.

A business cycle only partly controls stock market prices however. The stock market does not move up or down simply based on the business cycle. Political factors also play a central role in determining stock prices.

Political factors may include government lawsuits into stock market or corporate practices, major accounting or business legislation, political unrest in the world, shifting national agendas and revisions to fiscal budgets at all levels of government, and the Federal Reserve changing the Federal Funds Rate (more on fiscal and monetary policy in chapter 7). Thus we can now talk about political-economic conditions that determine overall stock market prices. Leading economic indicators are often used to help predict business cycles, as presented next.

Leading Economic Indicator Index

The Conference Board www.globalindicators.org, a business and research organization founded in 1916, publishes the Business Cycle Indicators which are composite leading, coincident, and lagging Economic Indicator Indexes designed to help identify the peaks and troughs of business cycles. The Economic Indicator Indexes use monthly data and are posted on The Conference Board's Website under latest releases for the United States.

The Leading Economic Indicator Index has traditionally turned either up or down prior to the actual turn in the real economy. The Leading Economic Indicator Index is comprised of ten indicators, one important indicator is for 500 common stock prices.

Economists at The Conference Board recognize that 500 common stock prices reliably project economic prospects because a multitude of experienced and well informed stock market participants form an expert consensus that help accurately forecast economic cycles. The use of 500 common stock prices as a Leading Economic Indicator however leads to a paradox which is discussed next.

Leading Economic Indicator Paradox

A paradoxical and even ironic subject involves economists use of stock market prices as a Leading Economic Indicator. It may be controversial to point out that financial economists believe that individual corporate stock prices from day-to-day seem to follow a random walk process, while Conference Board economists are using aggregate stock prices from 500 common stocks to help predict business cycles and future economic conditions.

Either prices mirror all of the information present in the past performance of prices and predicting future stock prices based on prior stock prices is impossible, as under the Random Walk Theory, or stock prices may be used as a Leading Economic Indicator to predict the future direction of the overall economy. This is more fully discussed in chapter 12.

What is needed is a way to identify the long-term price trend of the Standard & Poor's 500 Index. What is searched for is an investment strategy over the long-term that is not based on or credited to chance or luck. In search of this, lets again look at how a truly physical random American roulette game is vastly different from the process of what happens in the overall stock market as represented by the S&P 500 Index.

How American Roulette And The S&P 500 Index Differs

A fair American roulette game is a stand alone physical random process. American roulette has no ultimate force behind it, if it is fair, that has any influence whatsoever on the numbers that arise during play. The wheel may be spun and the ball rolled in good economic times and bad economic times which will have no influence whatsoever on the independently produced winning numbers.

The fair American roulette game does not change through time as a result of external economic forces, nor does it have anyone's political finger on a button to slow the wheel to influence its prize-winning outcomes. Now compare the game of American roulette with the political-economic conditions that are in place that directly influences the overall stock market.

Political-Economic Conditions

The symbolic physical American fair roulette game is in fact a random process while the symbolic stock market is a consequence of a real political-economic process that is anything but random. It is unrealistic to assume that American roulette is like the overall stock market. The overall stock market is inexorably tied to political-economic conditions. These conditions are defined mainly by long-term business cycles and by politics.

The overall stock market, or its proxy the S&P 500 Index, is not random because unlike American roulette it is not merely a symbolic game; but, the stock market is also a symbolic representation that is moved by actual cyclic events in the real political economy.

If the stock market were not based on the cause and effect of non-random political-economic conditions, then the symbolic stock market would be merely a disconnected game like American roulette. This can not be. The fact that there is a demonstrated cause and effect link between real political-economic conditions and the stock market is self-evident and consequently makes the stock market a vitally important institution in the U.S. financial system. If it were otherwise, the stock market would be irrelevant to the U.S. economy which is clearly not the case.

The search here will be to show a link between the cyclical real political-economic conditions and the S&P 500 Index over the long-term. Stock market upward momentum, matching in general the underlying growth of total corporate earnings, is self-evident over the super-long-term. Stock market upward trends and downward trends may be expected based on corporate earnings and political conditions over the long-term as well. How to view daily stock price movements, while investing for the long term, is investigated next.

Day-to-Day Price Movements Are Immaterial

The next spin-of-the-wheel and roll of the ball outcome in American roulette is vital to know. That's how winners and losers are determined. However, day-to-day movements of stock prices for long term investors are immaterial to long-term success. Studying only the predictive ability of an individual corporation's one day price movement on the next day's price movement may be too narrow a focus. Inquiring simply whether the market will be up or down tomorrow is not be the proper question.

In addition, studying the price movements of only one corporation allows for specific corporate results that are unsystematic, atypical, and may overpower the long-term trend influence in the data being studied. This is a handicap to studying long-term trends in the overall stock market by using data from only one corporation with unsystematic risks.

Random walk theorists may incorrectly extrapolate the predictive power of one day's price movement of an individual stock on the performance of the next day's price movement to make sweeping general statements that all prior actions in all equity prices have no predictive ability whatsoever on all forthcoming market action. As shown previously, this is clearly not the case for the S&P 500 Index over the super-long-term. It is expected that it will be shown that this is not the case for the S&P 500 Index over the long term either.

Long-term investors should not be overly concerned that an individual company's stock price tomorrow may be up or down. The main question needing answering is – over the long-term is now probably the right time to be in the stock market to make money? This should be the proper and fitting concern of long-term investors.

Long-term investors want to know if the stock market is in an upward trend, and that the magnitude of the short-term and intermediate term upward moves are greater than the magnitudes if the short-term and intermediate downward moves. Is the stock market working its way higher, with higher-highs and higher-lows, is the question. Stock price movement, as explained in this paragraph, is an exploring-compensating condition which is more fully described next.

Exploring-Compensating Condition

A long-term upward trending stock market, as represented by the S&P 500 Index, may be expected to have irregular short-term and intermediate term patterns which move, during most of its advance, around an intrinsic, true, or fair valuation. Money is expected to be made by following the stock market's long-term upward trending intrinsic, true, or fair value line. Millions of investor's minds are at work investigating and judging the correctness of the market's valuation and discounting future political-economic conditions. This is described as the exploring-compensating condition.

This is represented in Graph 2 - 1: Figure A, where a long-term upward trending intrinsic, true, or fair value smooth line is shown with the actual prices as a squiggly line that closely matches and moves with the stock market's intrinsic value. The S&P 500 Index is free to move in irregular short-term and intermediate term patterns around a long-term upward trending intrinsic, true, or fair value line. An irregular pattern is in evidence

41

when looking at daily data, but when looking at monthly data it becomes clear that the overall stock market over the long-term is working its way higher.

In Graph 2 - 1: Figure B, the process is repeated for the long-term downtrend. The irregular short-term and intermediate-term squiggly patterns move, during most of the decline, around the long-term downward trending intrinsic, true, or fair value line.

The exploring-compensating condition is more fully explained in chapter 4. Mr. Market is part of the exploring-compensating condition in the stock market which is explained next.

Graph 2 - 1: Irregular Short-Term And Intermediate-
Term Movements Along A Long-Term Trending
Intrinsic, True, Or Fair Value Line

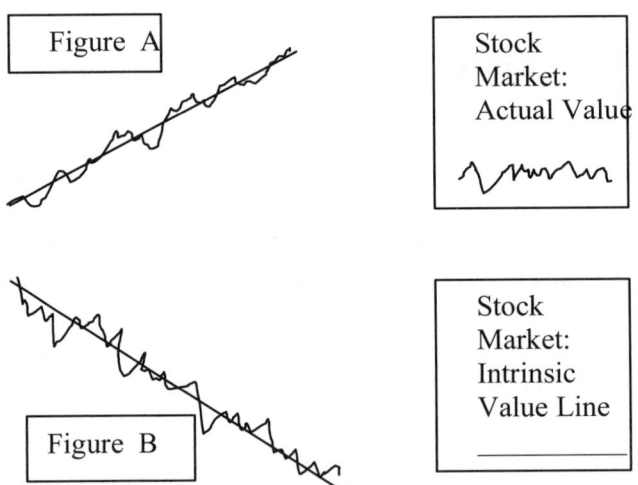

Mr. Market

Benjamin Graham, a long time practitioner in the stock market, wrote a classic book on investing while a professor at Columbia University. He noticed that the stock market is intermittently miss-priced and offered the following amusing fable about Mr. Market to graphically illustrate this recurring phenomenon.

The following tale of Mr. Market is presented for investors to understand how stock price movements may sometimes seem the product of overly emotional investors. As a result, stock prices may become completely disconnected from intrinsic, true, or fair value. The fable goes like this.

You and Mr. Market are in business together. Mr. Market is the most accommodating partner possible. He is full of opinions, which he readily shares with you, about the worth of the company that you jointly own. His pockets are deep and every day he either offers to buy as much of the business that you care to sell, or if you like, he will sell you more stock in the business.

Sometimes you agree with Mr. Market's opinion on the value of the business. Company operations and business prospects are being similarly evaluated by you both at this time. Sometimes, however, Mr. Market's emotions get the better of him and his manic depressive fears and jubilant greedy passions takes his daily offers for sale or purchase of the company to ridiculously high or low price levels.

In this tale, you pride yourself on being an intelligent investor and a shrewd businessperson. Financial and operating reports from the company are studied and prospects for the company are assessed. You determine on your own the intrinsic, true, or fair value (please see chapter 6 for a proper calculation) of the company. Mr. Market may be used to your advantage in the following ways.

The value of Mr. Market is not his knowledge and insights, for his price judgments may often be wrong. It is Mr. Market's exceedingly large bankroll that is of value. When Mr. Market arrives at the door spouting outrageous sayings and making foolish stock price offers, he may either be safely disregarded or taken advantage of; but, coming under the spell of Mr. Market and following his lead will be ruinous. One should never let the daily ravings of Mr. Market influence one's judgment about the value of the company's stock, as it is counter productive.

The only sensible option is to be aware of Mr. Market's offers and agree with him or not agree with him. The best approach is to let Mr. Market have the stock shares when he quotes an absurdly excessive price, and be as delighted to purchase his stock at exceedingly depressed prices. In other instances, Mr. Market may be safely ignored since his feelings are never hurt regardless of the action that you take. Mr. Market comes back day after day with recurring offers and never gets tired of the process.

Owning listed common stock is analogous to the presented Mr. Market fable. Based on an investor's beliefs, daily stock market fluctuations are there to be taken advantage of or to be disregarded. Important stock market price movements are to be noticed so that they may be compared to intrinsic, true, or fair value. To be successful in the stock market, business and stock market judgment are paramount along with the ability to protect oneself from the folly of Mr. Market in the marketplace.

Warren Buffett, a value investor and protégé of Benjamin Graham, keeps the Mr. Market story in mind to shield himself from the devastating emotional calamities that Mr. Market often causes. For value investors, daily price variability is important only in so far as it allows an opportunity for purchases when prices fall too much and sales when prices spurt too high. At all other times, it is better to take no notice of the stock market and instead concentrate on analyzing companies and their prospects.

Benjamin Graham noticed that the stock market is intermittently miss-priced; but, neglects to tell us when this occurs, how much the market is miss-priced, and the best time to take advantage of the absurd Mr. Market – he is not yet put into context for the best use of this phenomenon. Mr. Market will be put into context in chapter 12 so that we can recognize him when he shows up at our door, and as astute investors we can take advantage of his emotional ravings. Knowing the timing of Mr. Market's arrival in the overall market is the essence of using him properly.

The Efficient Capital Market Theory is a core conceptual foundation in finance. The Efficient Capital Market Theory is supported by the Random Walk Theory (RWT). A discussion of the Efficient Capital Market Theory follows.

The Efficient Capital Market Theory

The Efficient Capital Market Theory to describe the overall stock market relies on the Random Walk Theory (RWT) and the random walk process as a way to represent seemingly random daily movements of individual stock prices based on random breaking news. The Random Walk Theory assumes that stock prices are set based on fast-breaking relevant news which can not be predicted. Because relevant information comes into the market randomly – it is expected that stock prices respond randomly to this random breaking news.

The Efficient Capital Market Theory maintains that current market prices incorporate all existing information and that prices move immediately as new random information becomes available. The equilibrium stock market price that reflects all obtainable information at any point in time is by definition considered an efficient capital market. The Efficient Capital Market Theory states that the stock market is by definition always at an intrinsic, true, or fair valuation and is therefore always efficient.

The stock market, says the efficient capital market theorists, is efficient because so many skilled participants who posses a collection of all relevant information are setting prices. Because the participants as a whole know all the relevant information then the market is competitive, and that intrinsic, true, and fair values will always prevail. The stock market is efficient because of the numerous professionals participating in the stock market, they are doing an excellent job of performing analysis and correctly responding to random information as it comes becomes known.

Given that prices in the marketplace respond quickly to freely available information, and that information arrives in a random manner, stock prices are a random walk process say the efficient capital market theorists. Therefore, since information and prices are unpredictable, any series of stock price movements have to be random. This leads to the theory that stock prices always reflect intrinsic, true, or fair value and are never wrong.

Stock Market Prices Are Never Wrong

If corporate stock prices at all times mirror all pertinent available information, then prices will only adjust as new information becomes accessible; but, since new information is not predictable, but random, then changes in stock prices are random. In essence, the Efficient Capital Market Theory is saying that corporate stock prices always indicate intrinsic, true, or fair value and are never wrong. Certainly in the following regard this is absolutely true.

A stock is only worth what an investor can get for it in the marketplace. So by definition the stock price is never wrong. *The Astute Investor* also believes that the stock market is never wrong, but not because the overall stock market is always efficient. The stock market is never wrong because a common stock is only worth what it may be sold for.

The Efficient Capital Market Theory is not universally accepted, with many practitioners questioning its accuracy, therefore it has splintered into three different versions depending on the availability and quality of the information assumed to be quickly incorporated into stock prices. The three versions of the Efficient Capital Market Theory are presented next.

Three Versions Of The Efficient Capital Market Theory

The Efficient Capital Market Theory is based on the Random Walk Theory, and is described as having the following three versions:

1) *The weak form of efficiency* – corporate stock prices follow a random walk process in which prices mirror all of the information present in the past performance of prices. Therefore predicting future corporate stock prices based on prior stock prices is impossible, and making the use of any technical analysis is ineffective when trying to make money on a particular stock.

2) *The semi-strong form of efficiency* – this is the next higher level of efficiency. Corporate stock prices now encompass not simply all past prices but all published information. Corporate prices respond quickly to any publicly known information as it becomes available, as a result keeping up with the news is now a useless effort to make money on a particular stock.

3) *The strong form of efficiency* – this is the highest level of efficiency. Corporate stock prices are now comprised of all past prices, all published information, and all of the information available to anyone anywhere. Everything that is possible to be known about a corporate stock is now included in its price, making even fundamental analysis a wasted effort when trying to make money on a particular stock.

The Efficient Capital Market (ECM) Theory has the following three assumptions:

1) Market participants are rational and always act rationally.

2) News travels immediately to all market participants, and investors respond correctly to all new information.

3) Pricing is fair and corporate stocks always sell at their intrinsic, true, or fair value price. The purchase or sale of any corporate stock at any time in the market will be a zero net-present-value transaction.

Questions about the Efficient Capital Market (ECM) Theory revolve around the assumptions necessary to support its proper functioning. These astute investor concerns are included in the critique of the Efficient Capital Market Theory which follows next.

Critique Of The Efficient Capital Market Theory

A critique of the Efficient Capital Market (ECM) Theory begins with a discussion of its assumptions.

Critique Of The ECM Theory Assumptions

The first assumption represents investors as always being rational and acting rationally. Human nature and the human mind always has the potential to subvert, undermine, and impede an investor's rational thinking, intelligent recognition of the truth, and in taking appropriate action.

Because the human emotions of fear and greed are more compelling than reason, the investing public may not act rationally. Mob psychology of boom-bubble buying or panic selling sometimes takes over and becomes a dominating factor for stock market movements (please see chapter 5 for an in-depth discussion of trading psychology).

Simply ignoring human nature will not make it any less real. This is a serious deficiency to the ECM Theory. Consequently, the assumption that the investing public always acts rationally is not realistic and should never be assumed by astute investors.

The second assumption is how market participants respond to the news. It is reported that professionals from mutual fund companies, insurance companies, bank trust departments, and other financial management institutions make up over ninety percent, as this is written, of the share volume being traded on the New York Stock Exchange (NYSE). These professionals may be expected to act properly based on breaking news.

Assuming that mutual fund company professionals make up a large percentage of the share volume being traded on the NYSE and other exchanges, and make good tactical decisions based on breaking news, it is still the investing public that makes the strategic decisions. The investing public determines when to invest new money or to pull out existing money invested in mutual funds based on the news. The investing public may act contrary to what is appropriate concerning the news (please see chapter 8 for problems in how the investing public treats the news). Consequently, mutual fund managers should not be held accountable for the actions of Mr. Market.

The last assumption that corporate stock prices always sell at intrinsic, true, or fair value should be more of a question. A zero net-present-value transaction in the market means that neither the buyer nor the seller has an advantage over one another. ECM theorists say that pricing in the marketplace for stocks should always be trusted, so why bother to know more about a company than its stock price? When it comes to the stock market, is stock market pricing a true assessment of the true, fair, or intrinsic, true, or fair value and how is intrinsic, true, or fair value determined? This vitally important question which is addressed and answered in chapter 6.

Trying to ascertain future corporate stock prices can never be exactly determined beforehand. And certainly, not everyone who invests in the stock market knows how to correctly calculate intrinsic, true, or fair value. Perhaps it would be better here to say that the stock market is never wrong rather than to say that corporate prices are always efficient and always represent intrinsic, true, or fair value. The likely timing of the breakdowns of the ECM Theory assumptions are discussed next.

Efficient Capital Market Theory Breakdowns

The Efficient Capital Market (ECM) Theory assumptions are expected to break down at long-term stock market peaks and long-term stock market bottoms. The Efficient Capital Market Theory assumptions are not expected to hold up during peak and trough situations in the long-term cycle of the stock market.

It has already been discussed that the random walk process and the predictive qualities of stock prices as a Leading Economic Indicator should be mutually exclusive. A possible explanation is that the assumptions of the Efficient Capital Market Theory may not be practical over the entire long-term cycle experienced by the stock market.

Toward market tops, there is boom-bubble buying by the investing public which brings prices above intrinsic, true, or fair value. At market bottoms, there is panic selling that brings prices below intrinsic, true, or fair value. These two conditions create long-term buying and selling opportunities (please see chapters 5 and 12). The ECM Theory is based on the Random Walk Theory (RWT), consequently the RWT is critiqued next.

The Random Walk Theory Critique

The Random Walk Theory (RWT) presumes that stock prices are straightforwardly set based on relevant fast-breaking news which can not be predicted. Because it is believed that all news information comes into the market randomly – it is fully expected that stock prices respond randomly to the latest breaking news.

The random news premise for the RWT is incomplete, too straightforward, and not sophisticated enough to adequately describe what is actually happening in the stock market (the explanation supporting this statement is fully presented in chapter 8). It will be shown that the reasoning behind the random walk process to sustain the Random Walk Theory (RWT) is too simplistic to adequately describe what professional stock market participants are doing in practice. The stock market is much more complex, refined, and sophisticated to respond in a so straightforward a way to the news as described by the Random Walk Theory (RWT).

The stock market is made up in large part by professional stock traders who make their living in the stock market. Consequently, the stock market is as sophisticated and worldly as those participating in it. The paradoxes identified in *The Astute Investor* need to be resolved by the financial community which are more fully explained in chapter 12. A way to organize how the stock market is viewed or discussed is presented next in a stock market taxonomy.

Stock Market Taxonomy

Intellectual problems come down to the twin challenges of deciding on appropriate nomenclature and the classification of the area under study into categories. The first mentioned challenge is a system of names, and the second is to arrange the area under study according to like attributes to facilitate communication.

An overall structure or classification of capital markets will help investors visualize the major divisions that are in place in the overall stock market. The categories offered help in presenting the information necessary for astute investors. Another name for this structure or classification is a taxonomy which is a division of all aspects of the stock market into categories or subdivisions.

A taxonomy is an structured model whose major groupings reveal inherent associations among categories or subdivisions that may be later combined to represent an overall system. The stock market is a enormous field that may be talked about at cross purposes. This is why the Stock Market Taxonomy is so important.

A Stock Market Taxonomy model offers a firm foundation of what is being discussed, and will help in the analysis that is so important when learning about the stock market. Please see Table 2 - 1 that structures the overall stock market along two dimensions: 1) an S&P 500 Index and individual stock dimension; and 2) along a time dimension. A taxonomy of the stock market is presented next.

There are eight major categories or subdivisions in the Stock Market Taxonomy along X and Y axes. The first dimension or axis separates what can be said about the stock market as a whole, using the Standard & Poor's (S&P) 500 Index as the proper proxy, and what can be said about an individual corporate stock.

X Axis: S&P 500 Index Vs. Individual Stocks

The first axis in the X direction in Table 2 - 1: Stock Market Taxonomy is by S&P 500 Index and then by an individual company stock. What can be said about the S&P 500 Index can not necessarily be said about an individual corporate stock. Due to unsystematic company stock risk and systematic S&P 500 Index risk, their prices often act differently.

Differences in the S&P 500 Index and individual stock price behavior should be kept in mind as various issues are discussed throughout this book. What works for the S&P 500 Index may not work when analyzing individual stocks, and methods should not be assumed to work in both major categories along the X axis. As already mentioned, the limited technical analysis techniques recommended here are only for the S&P 500 Index and are not to be used on individual stocks or for any other stock averages of any type (e.g., the DJIA, the semiconductor index (SOX), etc.).

Table 2 - 1: Stock Market Taxonomy

S&P 500 Index	Individual Company Stock	Time Dimension
1 (Chapter 11)	2	Super Long-Term: 20 Years or More – Use Yearly Data
3 (Chapters 3 – 5 and 7 – 10)	4 (Chapters 6 and 10)	Long-Term: 1,2,3,4,5 Years or More – Use Monthly Data
5	6	Intermediate-Term: 1,2,3,4,5 Months or More – Use Weekly Data
7	8	Short-Term: 1,2,3,4,5 Days or More – Use Daily or Hourly Data

Chapters 1, 2, and 12 are general and cover all categories.

Y Axis: Time

The second axis in the Y direction is the time dimension on Table 2 - 1. The S&P 500 Index and individual company stocks have associated characteristics along the time dimension.

The super long-term in the stock market is any time period that lasts at least two decades or more. Yearly data use is the most appropriate over the super-long-term.

A long-term period of time lasts one, two, three, four, five or more years in the stock market. The use of monthly data will give the best perspective or view over the long-term.

The intermediate-term in the stock market is defined as lasting one, two, three, four, five or more months and the use of weekly data would be most appropriate.

The short-term may last one, two, three, four, five or more days and daily and/or hourly data gives the best perspective or viewpoint into daily price movements.

Do not confuse what is possible with the S&P 500 Index using monthly data with that same index using daily data. Similarly, do not confuse what is possible using the S&P 500 Index with what is possible for an individual corporate stock. Proper analysis and discussion on the stock market, as represented by the S&P 500 Index and by individual corporate stocks over differing planning horizons, along with the organization of this book are now presented using the Stock Market Taxonomy.

Using The Taxonomy For Proper Analysis

For proper analysis, the stock market should not be thought of as one entity. The Stock Market Taxonomy stipulates that for proper analysis there are really eight separate subdivisions or categories of the stock market that need to be studied and understood.

The shaded areas in Table 2 - 1: Stock Market Taxonomy covering categories 1, 3, and 4, indicates the subject matter presented in this book and are delineated below:

Chapters	Shaded Areas
Chapters 3 - 5 and 7 - 10:	Category 3
Chapters 6 and 10:	Category 4
Chapter 11:	Category 1

Chapters 1, 2, and 12 are general in nature and cover all segments in the Stock Market Taxonomy. Comments about one segment or subdivision of the stock market taxonomy will not necessarily hold true about the other seven categories included in the taxonomy. The time dimension within the stock market profoundly effects S&P 500 Index and individual stock analysis, perspective, and strategies.

The Stock Market Taxonomy makes discussing what is appropriate for fundamental analysis and limited technical analysis in each category specific. The taxonomy reduces the confusion associated with these different subdivisions. Without the taxonomy, subjects within investing may all be talked about at cross purposes. The Stock Market Taxonomy greatly helps when discussing what approaches work or do not work for the S&P 500 Index and for individual corporations.

Summary

Life and matter in motion requires the four dimensions of space-time for description. A person' selfhood is their beliefs and values which is the source for their actions. Socrates said to know thyself, while Aristotle said to plan. Time and dates, called scheduling, have been added to the planning process as essential to its success. Time and timing are crucial to life, to money, and to the stock market.

Time is life. Time is money within contractual obligations. In the sophisticated and worldly stock market however, timing is money. Since an investor has no control over daily stock price movements in the market, he or she has to take advantage of the opportunities that the stock market presents as they occur.

Mr. Market is a famous fable that which graphically illustrates the emotional nature of how the investing public on occasion participates in the stock market. Mr. Market is presented for investors to understand how stock prices may sometimes become disconnected from intrinsic, true, or fair value in the marketplace.

Stock prices in the Random Walk Theory are described as moving either up-or-down in a random pattern due to random news releases. As a result, daily stock prices can not be predicted. Because the stock market is compared to a true random walk process, such as American Roulette, belief in the Random Walk Theory allows luck to be a rational strategy for success in the stock market.

It is shown that the stock market differs from the symbolic stand alone American roulette game because the symbolic stock market is tied to political-economic conditions which are not random but cyclical in nature. After reading *The Astute Investor,* it is expected that investors will believe that luck is not a rational strategy for successful investing. Simply being fortunate while investing is not enough. Having the correct investing knowledge and beliefs are paramount.

It is a paradox that individual corporate prices, from day-to-day, seem to follow a random walk process while the overall stock market, as represented by the S&P 500 Index, shows positive drift over the super-long-term and is a positively correlated time series. The paradox is expected to also be in evidence during the long-term positive drift upward trend, and during the long-term negative drift downward trend in the overall stock market as represented by the S&P 500 Index. The use of 500 common stock prices as a Leading Economic Indicator is an example of another paradox requiring a resolution by the financial economic community.

The Efficient Capital Market Theory has three versions: weak, semi-strong, and strong. Assumptions of the Efficient Capital Market Theory are explained. The Efficient Capital Market Theory maintains that corporate stock prices incorporate all available information, and prices move immediately as new information becomes available.

The Efficient Capital Market Theory relies on the random walk process and the Random Walk Theory as conceptual foundations. Day to day news events may seemingly move daily company stock prices randomly. This is too simplistic an explanation for incredibly sophisticated stock market participants.

A descriptive Stock Market Taxonomy model is presented to offer a firm foundation of what is being discussed and will help in the analysis that is so important when learning about the stock market. Knowing when the overall stock market, as represented by the S&P500 Index, is expectedly either overvalued or undervalued is presented next in chapter 3.

3

Equity And Bond Fundamentals

Introduction

BOND AND STOCK FINANCIAL analysis fundamentals are reviewed. Corporate management's financial responsibilities are specified. The price to earnings (P/E) ratio is thoroughly discussed and a sample calculation is presented to identify its limitations. The stock market is described as a discounting mechanism. Due to stock market discounting, which is the ability to look ahead to what will happen in the future, the P/E ratio is deceptive. The forward P/E ratio for use is emphasized.

A summary review of the Standard & Poor's (S&P) organization is offered. Why the estimated future reported earnings of the S&P 500 companies are essential to astute investors is explained. How to find on Websites the estimated future reported earnings of the S&P 500 companies and current interest rates to properly calculate the S&P 500 Index Expected Fair Valuation Model are presented.

Bond Fundamentals

Securities may consist of both stocks and bonds. An understanding of bond fundamentals is especially valuable for all investors. When purchasing bonds, a legal document explicitly stipulates – through what is called an indenture – what the obligations and duties of the borrower of the funds are towards the lender of the money. The legal document is binding on the parties in the transaction and specifies exactly the loan's provisions.

One especially important proviso is the coupon yield which is the rate of interest the borrower agrees to pay the lender. Bonds are usually sold in the primary market, when initially issued, in increments of one thousand dollars each – called the principle or face value.

Bonds are bought or sold on the secondary market between traders after the initial issue and are listed by dropping the last zero, for a face value of 100. On the secondary market, bonds may be listed for sale at 103 which means that it is trading at a premium; or bonds may be listed at 96 which means that the bond trades at a discount to its face value price of 100.

Unlike common stocks, corporate bond bids and offers are not available at a centralized corporate bond exchange; because there is no centralized corporate bond exchange. The internet seems to be able to easily rectified this oversight however, by setting up a corporate bond market based on the NASDAQ model. The buying or selling of corporate bonds on the secondary corporate bond market is currently one for bond brokers who execute corporate bond trades in the over-the-counter secondary corporate bond market.

Bond prices fluctuate on the secondary market. One key component causing the change in investment grade bond prices on the secondary market is a change in the prevailing interest rates. It is assumed that the bond, when initially sold, has a coupon yield that matches the prevailing interest rates in the market at that time.

As economic situations change, interest rates will vary through time which changes the price of investment grade bonds – and ultimately its current yield which takes into account the original coupon yield and current bond price. The current yield may be different than the coupon yield. The current yields on bonds trading in the secondary market are often quoted by bond brokers.

Bond Prices And Current Interest Rates

As Marilyn Cohen explains, a seesaw is an excellent way to visualize what the relationship is between bond prices and current interest rates. Graph 3 - 1 shows two relationships. The first is of a 30-Year U.S. Treasury Bond with a face value of $1,000 dollars and a coupon yield at issue of 8.5 percent which pays $85 dollars per year in interest, shown in Graph 3 - 1 as Figure A.

Graph 3 - 1: Bond Prices Vs. Prevailing Interest Rates

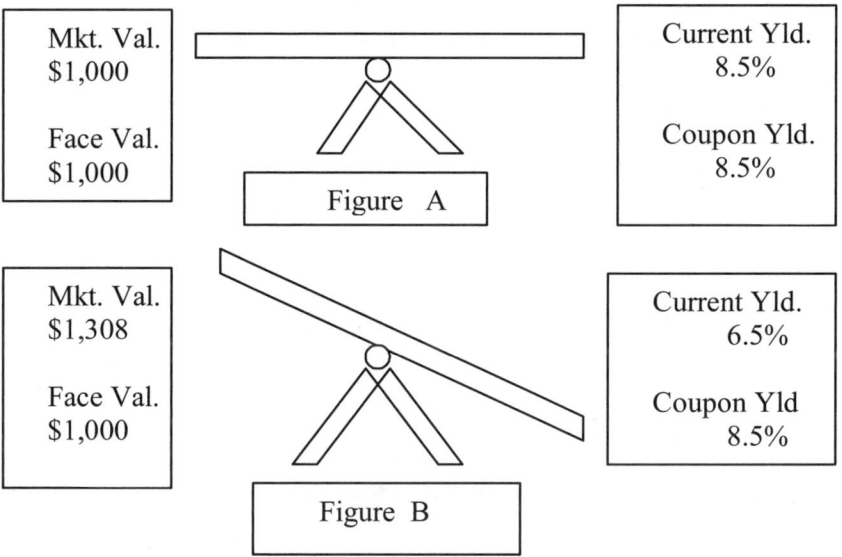

The second relationship shows that after two years the political-economic conditions have slowed and consequently long-term interest rates have declined – lets say by two percent to 6.5 percent – which is called interest rate risk. In this case, events transpired that are positive for the purchaser of the bond; but, economic conditions could have improved and inflation could have gone up, thereby lowering the bond's market value, which now may be easier to see why it is called interest rate risk.

Lower prevailing interest rates will increase the price of the 30-Year Treasury Bond on the secondary market to approximately $1,308 dollars, shown in Graph 3 - 1 as Figure B. The same interest of $85 dollars is paid each year for the next 28 years; but, the investor will have to pay $1,308 to get that $85 dollars of interest, thereby bringing the current yield on the bond down to 6.5 percent.

When investing in bonds, the total return from bonds is the highest when the economy is near a long-term top and interest rates and inflation for the long-term cycle are relatively high. As the economy peaks and begins a slowdown, inflation and interest rates should decline as the Federal Reserve becomes more accommodative (please see more on this in chapter 7). Thus, long-term U.S. treasury bonds purchased during Stage 4: Market Top - Distribution (please see chapter 4) are expected to have superior returns from both high interest earned on the bonds and increased capital appreciation.

Once interest rates and inflation have bottomed, at the beginning of a market upturn, the prospects for the total return from long-term bonds is poor relative to stocks. Consequently, long-term U.S. treasuries should be sold during Stage 2: Market Bottom – Accumulation (please see more on this in chapter 4).

Corporate Bond Prices And Credit Risk

Corporate bonds, in addition to interest rate risk faced by investors in government bonds, also have credit risk which means that the lender of the money may not receive interest payments or return of the principle in full and or in a timely manner from the borrower. If this occurs, the corporate borrower would be in default on the loan's provisions and the lender would have legal recourse – perhaps going so far as forcing the borrowing corporation into bankruptcy.

If a corporation does go into bankruptcy there is an order of what obligations are paid off first. They are in order:

1) Bank Loans
2) Senior Bonds
3) Senior Subordinated Debt
4) Preferred Stock
5) Common Stock holders

To asses credit risk on corporate bonds, prior to purchase on the primary market, bonds are rated by the following bond rating agencies.

Bond Rating Agencies

Credit risk determinations on corporate bond issues are important to the interest rates that may be expected on bonds when first sold in the primary market. The following are the four principle corporate bond rating agencies:

1) Standard & Poor's
2) Moody's Investors Service
3) Fitch Incorporated
4) Dominion Bond Rating Service Limited

The rating agencies will look at the capacity or ability of the borrowing corporation to repay interest and principle in a timely manner by reviewing the interest expense on the corporation's income statement.

A margin-of-safety multiple of perhaps five times, depending on the corporate bond's investment grade – of earnings before interest and taxes (called EBIT or operating earnings) – should be available to pay all interest expense obligations. This is crucial for corporate solvency and a focal responsibility for the corporation's financial management.

Additional factors associated with grading corporate bonds include the reputation of the company, the collateral available on the bonds or on the balance sheet if anything should go wrong, and the covenants in the legal document specifying the loan's provisions.

Corporate bonds may be divided into investment grades and are ranked from BBB- up to AAA: as determined by Standard & Poor's, or Baa3 up to Aaa: as determined by Moody's. Non-investment grade corporate bonds, also called high yield or junk bonds, are ranked from BB+ down to D: as determined by Standard & Poor's, or from Ba1 down to D: as determined by Moody's.

Corporate Bond Redemption Provisions

Corporate bonds are taxed by federal, state, and local governments. And almost without exception, corporate bonds may be called-in or redeemed by the issuing corporation if interest rates decline after a set time during the bond's maturity period. This allows corporations to issue new bonds at a lower interest rate. The newly raised capital will cover the effected corporate bonds being redeemed early.

Redemption provisions are important because if investors plan to make money on increased bond prices, as interest rates fall, it is advisable to purchase U.S. treasuries. For corporate bonds, the yield to worst call is one way to objectively compare corporate bonds that may be redeemed during the maturity period. This is another reason why using an expert bond broker is advisable when purchasing or selling corporate bonds on the secondary market.

Equity fundamentals are analyzed based on essential financial factors, especially corporate earnings. Other important factors include management capability, industry competition, and stock share prices which are all discussed next.

Equity Fundamentals

Equity fundamental analysis relies primarily on the corporation's financial facts and statistics when considering whether to purchase stock. Financial, management, industry, and economic statistics are used to value a corporation or an entire industry. A determination of under-or-over valuations and comparisons of intrinsic, true, or fair value to the current market value may identify market discrepancies.

Purchasing or selling stock based on the these financial determinations may secure an advantage to the investor. Research into the corporation's market facts and financial data help investors maintain discipline when adverse market moves tests their investing convictions.

Financial Analysis

As John A. Tracy explains, investors using fundamental analysis typically want answers to the following important financially based questions to help determine whether a stock should be either purchased or sold:

1. What are the corporate earnings?
2. What is the corporate capitalization (debt vs. equity)?
3. What is the return on equity?

4. What is the return on assets?
5. Is the corporation solvent?
6. What dividends are being paid?
7. What are the earnings per share?
8. What is the corporate cash flow?

Answers to the above important questions may be found by using financial analysis and studying the corporation's financial reports which include the following:

1) Balance Sheet
2) Income Statement
3) Cash Flow Statement
4) Footnotes
5) Management Narrative

The balance sheet is a point-in-time listing of the corporation's assets (including: current assets, plant & equipment, and other assets) on the left side, and the corporation's liabilities (including: current liabilities, long-term liabilities, and owner's equity) on the right side of the balance sheet.

The income statement summarizes cumulative sales revenue and all corporate expenses, typically over a quarter or a year's time period, to arrive at a net income or loss for the period. The calculation of net income (also called the bottom line, profit, or earnings) on the income statement relies on accounting based decisions made by management to arrive at this highly scrutinized number. A discussion of accounting decisions and management actions on the bottom line follows.

Accounting Decisions And Management Actions

When calculating net income, two especially important expenses are within the purview of management and accounting decisions. The first is how to account for the cost of goods sold. Accounting inventory methods include: 1) average cost method; 2) last in first out (LIFO); and 3) first in first out (FIFO). Depending on which of these three inventory methods are selected will have a profound effect on reported earnings for many goods producing companies.

The second accounting decision is how to account for depreciation of plant and equipment. Depreciation may be accounted for by using several different methods: 1) the straight line approach; and 2) the Modified Accelerated Cost Recovery System (MACRS). Which ever depreciation method is selected will normally have a major influence on reported earnings on the income statement.

Inventory and depreciation accounting methods may have a profound impact on total corporate costs, and consequently the corporate earnings shown on the income statement. The timing of these inventory and depreciation expenses, in an accrual based accounting system, may have a major impact on reported earnings. A full understanding of how management or accounting choices effect corporate net income is paramount for all investors.

Choices in the accrual based accounting system revolve around when to record sales revenue and corresponding corporate expenses. The actual cash flows, in accrual based accounting systems used for financial reporting, may occur either after or before the revenue or expense period assigned by accountants when calculating net income for the income statement.

When attempting to increase net income, sales revenue may be booked as soon as feasible and related expenses may be deferred as much as possible. While all the accounting standards selected may be approved by the Financial Accounting Standards Board (FASB), which helps institute regulations for financial reporting, they may still be open to interpretation. This is why corporate cash flow analysis, discussed next, is so important to investors.

The Importance Of Cash Flow Analysis

It may be naïve to assume that all accounting derived numbers are absolutely credible and not open to interpretation. It is because net income may be so variable, depending on the accounting standards selected by management, that many investors prefer to look at actual cash flow as a check on reported corporate earnings.

Corporate cash flow is identified in the cash flow statement (CFS). The cash flow statement (CFS) gives investors an important glimpse into the company's sources and uses of money over the time period in question. The importance of cash flow is that these numbers – regardless of the management and accounting choices made to determine net income – are precisely what they seem and are impossible to adjust. For corporate cash flow, either the money is on hand or it's not on hand.

Managers and accountants establish net income based on many accounting methods and standards such as for inventory, depreciation, and when to book sales and expenses. However, both managers and accountants are powerless in the face of cash flow analysis and this is the leading reason for its use by investors. When the growth of reported net income can be corroborated by similar increases in corporate cash flow, then investors may feel especially confident concerning the excellence of the reported earnings in the income statement.

Investors, when doing financial analysis, should feel that it is as important to look at corporate cash flow as well as the net income on the bottom line. More on corporate cash flow analysis in chapter 6. Management capability is also an important component in fundamental analysis and is discussed next.

Management Assessment

As Peter Lynch explains, in addition to financial analysis, equity fundamental analysis also necessitates evaluating management competence, customer demand, and the analysis of both service and/or product quality. Headquarters' personnel may be contacted about capital expansion efforts or new marketing plans. New product introductions or new more efficient plants coming on-line may be an indication of increased corporate competitiveness. Finding out about these plans may be accomplished by calling the corporation's investor relations people to ask specific questions about product lines or prospective clients.

Visiting the companies' stores, especially if they are a franchised retail chain or a franchised restaurant to inspect the store locations, merchandise, or to sample the food may be field work that will have a major pay off. Calling a company's competitors to ask about who their best competition is may put the investor onto promising leads.

It should be remembered that studying current fundamental facts, ratios, and financial analysis of a company is not the same thing as discounting political-economic conditions. The symbolic discounted stock price is different than the current state of the entity that it represents. More on this essential distinction in chapter 6.

Fundamental analysis of the internal facts of the corporation, and the external statistics and evaluation of industries, competitors, and the economy is in direct contrast to technical analysis which concentrates on actual price graphs, trends, and confirming technical indicators to form opinions about the condition of the overall stock market. Limited technical analysis of the S&P 500 Index is presented in the next chapter. The best time to invest in stocks is briefly discussed next and then more thoroughly presented in chapter 4.

Best Time To Be In The Stock Market

The best circumstances for investing in stocks is when the political-economic conditions have bottomed after a slowdown, and when the increasing rate of economic growth and political conditions are positive and inflationary expectations and interest rates are low. This occurs during Stage 2: Market Bottom - Accumulation which is explained in chapter 4. The next best situation is when positive political-economic conditions are accompanied by rising inflationary expectations and rising interest rates. This occurs most often during Stage 3: Mark-Up - Uptrend.

An unfortunate state of affairs for stocks is slowing economic growth, troubled political conditions, all coupled with disinflationary expectations and falling interest rates. An exceedingly detrimental situation for stocks is slowing economic growth, troubled political conditions, all coupled with rising inflationary expectations and rising interest rates. This condition is called stagflation which is normally disastrous for stock prices.

Both of the above two political-economic conditions will force the stock market into Stage 1: Mark-Down - Downtrend, the only difference being the resulting severity of the stock market decline. How to identify these different stages in the marketplace is fully explained in chapter 4. Managers have the following three primary financial responsibilities.

Corporate Management's Financial Responsibilities

The three chief financial responsibilities that corporate managers assume include:

1) Maximizing net income, called the bottom line.

2) Managing the companies assets and liabilities.

3) Staying solvent and insuring against cash outs.

One way to review how proficient management is in each of the above areas is to perform ratio analysis. Ratio analysis is a study of financial variables that may be compared among like firms or similar industries to determine likely strong corporate candidates for stock purchase.

Financial ratios, such as: debt-to-equity ratio; times interest earned ratio; return-on-sales ratio; return-on-equity ratio; return-on-assets ratio; and the price-to-earnings ratio all rely on accounting facts and figures that are fundamental to the company's condition and an excellent indication of management competence. Perhaps no other financial ratio is both more scrutinized by the investing public or more miss understood than the price-to-earnings (P/E) ratio.

The P/E ratio is often keyed on by the investing public to indicate whether a stock or the stock market is a good investment. In its favor, the P/E ratio compares the current price per share to the prior twelve month's earnings per share to arrive at a positive number, assuming the earnings are positive, that may be easily compared to other stocks undergoing similar analysis.

The P/E ratio may be thought of as the market's assessment of how well a corporation or the overall market will grow in the future. The P/E ratio is much preferred as an estimate of a stock's value, rather than only inspecting the current market price by itself. A link between earnings and stock price is the principal benefit of the P/E ratio.

While it is not recommended to decide to purchase or sell a stock based solely on its P/E value, the P/E ratio is often sought after by investors and a discussion is helpful to understand its strengths as well as its four fundamental inadequacies.

Price-To-Earnings Ratio

What makes a stock valuable? In general, the answer is corporate earnings. Corporate earnings per share in relation to the current market price per share links the company's bottom line financial performance with now the market is valuing the corporation. Investors concentrate on the P/E ratio because it is one frequently used measure for judging fairly priced stocks and stock markets, all linked with the ability of the corporation to make money.

Investors in cyclical companies, such as basic materials and manufacturing, find that P/E ratios used for investing are turned on their head. When cyclical stocks have especially high earnings, as at its market top, its P/E ratio is very low but the investment potential is poor. It is an investing paradox that a cyclical company's stock is often best purchased at high P/E value and sold at low P/E value.

Therefore, evaluating price-to-earnings ratio valuations are not so simple or straight forward as many investors would like to think. This is the first inadequacy of the P/E ratio – it can not be realistically compared across all companies, or among different industries.

The P/E ratio evaluation is not straight forward because it depends on investing style as well as the type of industries being investigated. Investors may be told that the lower the P/E ratio the better, and value investors may decide to only purchase low price-to-earnings stocks. Growth investors, on the other hand, may consider higher P/E ratio stocks; but, at the same time demand a commensurate high growth rate in earnings. This is the second inadequacy of the corporate P/E ratio – it has no universality – investors with growth or value investing styles look at the P/E ratio in different ways.

P/E standard values are often discussed and put forward for investors to use to judge stocks and the stock market. The question is, how good are P/E standards and should investors focus on them to make investment decisions? A discussion follows.

Price-To-Earnings Standards

Earnings fluctuate and share prices fluctuate through time, resulting in changing corporate P/E ratios over time. Investors are told to always know what the P/E ratios are because they are told to shun stocks with P/E ratios that are too high.

"How high is high," they ask? Well, they may be told, avoid stocks with a P/E ratio that is high relative to competing corporations in the same industry. Or avoid stocks with a P/E ratio that is higher than the corporation's earnings growth rate, and especially those twice as high as their earning's growth rate. Bargain stocks may be described as those with a P/E ratio only half the corporate earning's growth rate.

A stock P/E ratio standard may be looked for and analyzed by investors. Investors may feel that if they have a P/E standard they will have a way to judge companies. Corporate P/E ratios higher than the earning's growth rate may now be the P/E standard by which investors gauge corporate stocks.

Investors may now feel confident because they have all in one number a universal P/E gauge, that may be compared among all corporations, which represents a standard benchmark. Unfortunately, this is often a false confidence.

Are these P/E standards all that are needed to know? And how useful are these standards, and if they are followed will they convince investors to take incorrect action? That is, to stay out of the market or a corporate stock when they should actually be investing in that stock or stock market because it will make investors money. Lets now concentrate on the overall stock market P/E standard.

Historical P/E Standards

What about a P/E standard for the overall stock market, investors may ask. Historical standards are offered. For example, over the period of 1871 to 1970, the stock market's average P/E ratio is reported to have averaged 14.26. From 1982 to 1987 the market's P/E is reported to have ranged between 8 to 16.

Or investors are told, in 1971, the market's P/E reached a reported climax of twenty which was clearly way too high because the P/E came crashing down during the 1973-1974 market correction.

A static, or fixed standard P/E value of twenty may now be thought of and used by investors as a benchmark for the overall valuation of the stock market. But how useful is a fixed P/E standard of twenty as a gage for the overall stock market? Changing interest rates complicate the evaluation of a P/E standard and are discussed next.

Interest Rates And P/E Standards

It is interesting to note that for the past six months, as this is written, the S&P 500 Index P/E ratio has been between thirty and thirty-five. Now, investors trained to think that a stock market P/E ratio of over twenty is excessive would judge that the stock market is way overvalued and wait before investing. But is this judgment wise?

As this is written, the S&P500 Index over the last six months has increased in value by almost fifteen percent. Investors with a S&P 500 Index P/E ratio standard of twenty missed out on this market's advance, but why? Interest rates are often mentioned as a cause for changing P/E standards. Investors may be told that interest rates have a significant influence on whether a P/E ratio standard is either overvalued or undervalued.

An explanation of the fluctuations of stock market P/E values is offered which explains that they are strongly influenced by the rate of inflation and the corresponding interest rates prevailing in the economy. In general, P/E ratios are higher when inflation and interest rates in the economy are low and vice versa when inflation and interest rates are high. Investors may well bid up stock prices when interest rates are falling, thereby causing P/E ratio values to increase.

When interest rates increase, bonds compete for investment dollars – meaning fewer dollars get invested in the stock market and stock prices come down, thereby lowering the P/E ratio value. This seems to be good advice, so interest rates are investigated over the time period under review.

Interest rates for the 30-Year U.S. Treasury Bonds (T-Bonds) actually increased from approximately 4.95 percent to 5.25 percent during the time period under discussion. Because interest rates are rising during this period, investors should expect stock prices to be falling; but, instead the S&P 500 Index actually increased by nearly fifteen percent. Again, what is happening?

P/E Standards Are Incomplete

The S&P 500 Index P/E ratio by itself is incomplete when trying to judge whether the stock market is appropriate for investing. The idea being that static stock market P/E ratio standards, such as an S&P 500 Index P/E ratio of over twenty should always be considered excessive, should be dropped from an astute investor's thinking. This is the third inadequacy, P/E standards for the S&P 500 Index change through time – there are no static standard ratio figures that can be relied upon. Obviously, more is going on then has been made clear so far by simply reviewing P/E ratios.

What is needed is an appropriate model that investors may employ whenever they desire to get a good estimation on whether the overall stock market is either overvalued or undervalued. To adequately address this topic it is necessary to review how P/E ratios are actually calculated. The S&P 500 Index price-to-earnings (P/E) ratio calculation is considered next.

Price-To-Earnings Ratio Calculation

The price-to-earnings (P/E) ratio actually has many names. It may also be called the P/E multiple, market multiple, times earnings, the actual P/E ratio, or the current P/E ratio. To calculate the S&P 500 Index price-to-earnings ratio, the price of the S&P 500 Index is divided by the actual reported per share earnings for the last twelve months of all 500 companies in the S&P Index.

The price of the S&P 500 Index, as this is written during October, 2003, is at 1,050. The actual as reported per share earnings, as this is written, for the last twelve months for companies in the S&P 500 Index are $34.55 per share. The P/E ratio is approximately 30.4 (1,050 divided by $34.55).

The S&P 500 Index and individual company P/E ratios are reported on by the media and are used as a measure to evaluate how expensive a stock or the stock market is for investment. The question is, "how useful is this the P/E ratio?" The answer, because the investing public is so attached to P/E values may be shocking – is not at all. This is the fourth and the most egregious of the inadequacies of the P/E ratio – the P/E ratio should never be used for investing purposes because it is a backward looking ratio.

The S&P 500 Index P/E ratio, or the P/E ratio for an individual company, is often deceptive because the stock market is a discounting mechanism. Discounting is the reason the P/E ratio is immaterial for investing purposes which is discussed next.

Discounting

A P/E ratio of approximately 30.4 for the S&P 500 Index may be considered extreme by the investing public. Many investors would like to see the S&P 500 Index P/E ratio closer to twenty and therefore decide to wait before investing. However what the investing public may fail to realize is that the stock market never looks back, only forward.

The stock market is a discounting mechanism. As Richard D. Wyckoff explains, the stock market looks ahead to what will happen in the future, called discounting – at a long-term market top possibly as much as the next six to twelve months – and reacts based on those expectations (please also see chapter 4).

Stock market price action discounts political-economic conditions because collectively the millions and millions of investors see more clearly into the future than any one person possibly can. All investors express themselves through the purchase and sale of securities. Therefore, studying the tendency of overall stock market prices corresponds to the study of the collective investors' minds.

Discounting: Market Peak

At a long-term market peak, the ability of the market to discount the future is an acknowledgment that astute investors will sell if they anticipate looming political-economic difficulties. When the dilemma finally presents itself and the danger is self- evident, the preponderance of the foresighted selling has by now taken place.

Because the market is made up of millions and millions of minds making their judgments known through the purchase or sale of stock, a study of the general bias of stock market movements is instrumental in deciphering the composite opinion of all investors in the market to detect a long-term market top – when the investing public is at their most optimistic. A long-term stock market peak is reached when all investors' expectations reach their collective height which precedes the actual summit of business and economic conditions (see also chapter 7).

The discounting at the long-term market top is beneficial because a vast quantity of stock selling happens when political-economic conditions are good and therefore does not compete with the forced selling later on by unaware investors which would drive stock prices even lower at a long-term market bottom. In effect, by studying the market's long-term discounted trend at the market peak the investor is in a position to manage their own opinions and actions based on the actions and opinions of many millions of other investors.

Discounting: Market Bottom

At a long-term market bottom, due to panic selling, the look ahead feature of the stock market is severely diminished and it may actually be reduced to nearly zero. This is to be expected since panic selling has nothing to do with looking ahead and everything to do with actions based on the investing public's heightened emotion of fear.

Coming off a long-term market bottom, buying by the investing public reactivates slowly and improving political-economic conditions normally have to be proved before investors begin to actively purchase stocks. Waiting for the stock market to establish itself with an upward trend and with improved reported earnings and improved political conditions, rather then trying to guess at a long-term market bottom, is often the correct strategy for novice investors.

Discounting And Foresight

Anticipating the future is the stock market's function, and that is what investors with foresight and vision are striving to predict and estimate. Foresight and vision for investors requires them to imagine what will happen in the future, based on all the information available to them, and then to adequately prepare and properly position themselves for the expected consequences.

The stock market continually looks ahead. The P/E ratio, as it is calculated, is a backward looking ratio and should have no place in an investor's evaluation of whether the stock market is either undervalued or overvalued. Making investment decisions based on past earnings is a novice investor's mistake.

Proper investing requires foresight by investors to look ahead and discount the future. It is an investor's foresight concerning expected market conditions that should be relied upon. Understanding that the stock market is a discounting mechanism is the premise which supports the expected news discounting process and in turn the Discounted News Theory which are both discussed in chapter 8. The Discounted News Theory supports the Discounted Capital Market Theory which is fully presented in chapter 12.

The P/E ratio is the antithesis of foresight and is therefore inadequate when used for investing purposes. In order to effectively assess and discount the future, only future estimated earnings should be considered. The way to do that is to use forward estimated corporate earnings to calculate a Forward P/E ratio.

Forward Price-To-Earnings Ratio

Stocks are only promising to purchase when astute investors can discount future corporate prosperity and good political conditions. The prior twelve month corporate earnings for the S&P 500 companies, or for individual companies, have already been fully discounted in the stock market and have absolutely no influence on the future direction of the S&P 500 Index price. This means that the S&P 500 Index P/E ratio is useless at best and severely misleading at worst, and therefore should be completely ignored by astute investors.

What makes a stock valuable today and more valuable tomorrow? In general, the answer is corporate earnings and then higher corporate earnings – all relative to prevailing interest rates. There are many other considerations used to determine an individual company's stock price; but, in the aggregate, total future earnings for all S&P 500 companies relative to prevailing interest rates are a good general basis for determining the expected valuation of the overall U.S. stock market.

A method to calculate the expected fair valuation of the overall U.S. stock market uses the S&P 500 Index as a proxy. The forward-looking estimated as reported earnings are imperative for correct valuations in the stock market. The reason that the S&P 500 Index is a good proxy for the overall stock market is explained next.

Standard & Poor's

Standard & Poor's is a global source to the credit markets, investment services markets, and to the internet of stock quote data, investment information, and fundamental security analysis. Standard & Poor's (S&P) originally developed and currently maintains the S&P 500 Index. The S&P 500 Index includes 500 of the major corporations from ten major U.S. industries, including: Energy, Materials, Industrials, Consumer Discretionary, Consumer Staples, Health Care, Financials, Information Technology, Telecommunications, and Utilities.

The companies included in the S&P 500 Index are usually the leading companies in their industries and often represent the largest capitalized corporations in the United States (U.S.). The S&P Index Committee maintains the S&P 500 Index by periodically adding or deleting companies from the index based on mergers, changing rules, or significant adjustments to corporate financials. In this way the S&P 500 Index is continually kept up to date with current financial conditions.

The Standard & Poor's (S&P) 500 Index represents, as this is written, about eighty percent of the overall U.S. common stock market capitalization of all equities on the New York Stock Exchange (NYSE), the National Association of Securities Dealers Automated Quotation (NASDAQ) system, and the American Stock Exchange (AMEX).

The S&P 500 Index has long been used as a benchmark with which to compare the total returns of competing investments, and it is an excellent proxy of the overall U.S. stock market. As this is written, nearly one trillion dollars are in stock fund accounts indexed to the S&P 500 Index. Because the S&P 500 Index is such a good proxy of the stock market, it is used in the valuation model presented in this chapter.

Fundamental analysis is often used to determine the best investment securities and is the cornerstone of Standard & Poor's investing approach. A step-by-step method to calculate the expected fair valuation of the overall U.S. stock market is presented here, starting with the estimated future reported earnings for the S&P 500 Index companies.

S&P 500 Estimated Future Reported Earnings

Standard & Poor's (S&P), as this is written, is reported to employ approximately 1,250 analysts who perform fundamental analysis. Standard & Poor's employees regularly use their expertise to estimate future corporate earnings of those companies included in the S&P 500 Index. The S&P 500 Index is an excellent benchmark and proxy for the overall stock market. Investors may use estimates of future corporate earnings to gauge whether the overall stock market is either undervalued or overvalued.

Estimated future reported earnings for S&P 500 companies may be found at the Standard & Poor's Website. Go to the following address and use the information provided to locate actual and estimated earnings, as this is written, in the Earnings and Estimate Report for the S&P 500 Index:

Logon: http://www2.standardandpoors.com

Where: On the main heading along the top of the computer screen find Indices
Click: Indices
Where: On the left side column of the computer screen find **Browse By Index**
Where: Under **Browse By Index** find S&P 500
Click: S&P 500

Where: In the upper middle of the computer screen find Choose Data
Where: Next to Choose Data is a box labeled Index Data
Click: The blue down arrow on the right side of the Index Data box
Where: In the resulting drop-down list find Earnings.
Click: Earnings

(Caution – if page marking for ease of future reference use, do it at this point. Then simply follow through from here to get the frequently updated information in the S&P 500 Earnings and Estimate Report.)

Where: In the middle of the computer screen under S&P 500 Earnings and Estimate Report find click here.
Click: click here
Where: A box named File Download should appear on the screen.
Click: Open

When it comes time to logoff after the analysis is made, it is best to elect "no" and not to save any changes.

The resulting computer screen should list the pertinent S&P Quantitative Services' report entitled "S&P 500 EARNINGS AND ESTIMATE REPORT," which is partially reproduced in Table 3 - 1. A discussion of this report follows.

In Table 3 - 1, the first column lists the quarter ending dates. The second column chronicles the actual S&P 500 Index closing prices for each quarter for which historical information is available (as this is written, up to 6/30/2003). Please notice that actual historical figures are reported for all columns for 12/31/2001 to 6/30/2003 and estimated figures are presented from 6/

30/2003 to 12/31/2005. The third column is a listing of the Operating Earnings Per Share.

Table 3 - 1: S&P 500 EARNINGS AND ESTIMATE REPORT

Quarter End	Price	Operating Earnings Per Share	As Reported Earnings Per Share
ESTIMATES			
12/31/2005			12.90
09/30/2005			15.10
06/30/2005			15.80
03/31/2005			16.50
12/31/2004		16.66	14.00
09/30/2004		15.73	14.70
06/30/2004		15.12	13.80
03/31/2004		14.03	13.10
12/31/2003		14.47	10.10
09/30/2003		14.30	11.75
ACTUALS			
06/30/2003	974.50	12.92	11.10
03/31/2003	848.18	12.48	11.92
12/31/2002	879.82	11.94	3.00
09/30/2002	815.28	11.61	8.53
06/30/2002	989.81	11.64	6.87
03/31/2002	1147.39	10.85	9.19
12/31/2001	1148.08	9.94	5.45

Copyright © 2003 The McGraw-Hill Companies, Inc. Standard & Poor's including its subsidiary corporations ("S&P") is a division of The McGraw-Hill Companies, Inc. Reproduction of this Article in any form is prohibited without S&P's prior written permission.

The data necessary to run the S&P 500 Index Expected Fair Valuation Model are presented in the fourth column marked: "As Reported Earns Per Share (estimates are top down)." As this is written, the first four columns of the "S&P 500 EARNINGS AND ESTIMATE REPORT" presents the information shown in Table 3 – 1.

From Table 3 - 1, the next twelve month (presented by quarters) estimates for as reported earnings (9/30/2003 to 6/30/2004) for the S&P 500 Index total $48.75 per share (11.75 + 10.10 + 13.10 + 13.80). The estimated as reported earnings per share for the next twelve months are about 41 percent higher ($48.75 verses $34.55) than the actual reported earning of the prior twelve months (8.53 + 3.00 + 11.92 + 11.10 = $34.55).

Calculating the Forward P/E ratio, based on future estimated as reported per share earnings, results in a much different solution than the P/E of approximately thirty. The Forward P/E ratio is calculated by dividing the S&P 500 Index price by the future twelve months estimated reported earnings per share: 1,050 divided by $48.75 equals a Forward P/E of approximately 21.5.

The Forward P/E ratio of 21.5 is much closer to what the investing public would likely say is a more realistic P/E value then a P/E ratio of 30.4, and beginning investors might feel more comfortable in investing during October, 2003 when the forward earning estimates are used.

Looking further into the future, the estimated as reported earnings for the year 2004: which equals $55.60 (13.10 + 13.80 + 14.70 + 14.00) per share, and for 2005: which equals $60.30 (16.50 + 15.80 + 15.10 + 12.90) per share – may designate an expected upward market trend. A fourteen percent improvement ($48.75 verses $55.60) in estimated as reported earning in 2004 over the forecast of the next twelve months, and a twenty-four percent improvement ($48.75 verses $60.30) for 2005 would be expected.

It is imperative to fully comprehend that forward earnings are merely estimates and may be revised at any time; nevertheless, they may indicate that the overall U.S. market's long-term trend should be in an investor's favor at least until the end of 2005, or until the reported earning's estimates or interest rates change.

It is advantageous to calculate the Forward P/E ratios for 2004 (1,050 divided by $55.60 equals approximately 18.9); and for 2005 (1,050 divided by $60.30 equals approximately 17.4). The S&P 500 Index Expected Fair Valuation Model results change through time and are dependent upon both estimated as reported earnings and prevailing interest rates which are discussed next.

Prevailing Interest Rates

Estimated reported earnings are important but are only part of the information necessary to calculate the S&P 500 Index Expected Fair Valuation Model. Prevailing interest rates are a second component. Corporate earnings, when interest rates are high, are not worth as much as when interest rate are low; because, the present worth value of future earnings discounted at a higher interest rate is less than the present worth value of future earnings discounted at a lower interest rate.

Astute investors should demand the highest present worth value today, and with all other factors being equal they get it with lower interest rates. The widely reported 10-Year U.S. Treasury Note (T-Note) interest rate is used in calculating the S&P 500 Index Expected Fair Valuation Model and the current yield may be found, as this is written, on the CNBC - MSN Money Website at:

> **Logon:** http://moneycentral.msn.com/investor/home.asp
>
> **Where:** On the left hand column under Markets find Market Report, Breaking
> **Click:** Market Report, Breaking
>
> **Where:** On the left hand column under Market Statistics find Lists and Trends
> **Click:** Lists and Trends
> **Where:** Under Market Snapshot and Today's Market find Major Indexes
> **Click:** Major Indexes

The resulting Leading Indexes computer screen lists at the top, under U.S. Indexes, the current daily prices for the major U.S. stock indexes. Scroll down to the U.S. Treasury Indexes Table which lists the current daily yields for 3-month and 6-month U.S. Treasury Bills (T-Bills), 1-year through 10-year U.S. Treasury Notes (T-Notes) and for the 30-Year U.S. Treasury Bond

(T-Bond). The 30-Year T-Bond interest rate yield found here is used in Chapters 5 & 6. Find the 10-Year U.S. Treasury Note (T-Note) yield which, as this is typed, is 4.40%.

The current S&P 500 price, the estimated twelve month earnings, and the 10-Year T-Note yield are used in a model to value the overall stock market as represented by the S&P 500 Index. The Standard & Poor's 500 Index Expected Fair Valuation Model calculation is presented next.

S&P 500 Index Expected Fair Valuation Model

The fundamental approach to this S&P 500 Index model is reported to be developed at the U.S. Federal Reserve. For the model calculation, the next twelve month estimated as reported earnings ($48.75) are divided by the S&P 500 Index price (1,050) resulting in a "S&P 500 Estimated Reported Earnings Yield" of 4.64 percent. The 10-Year T-Note interest rate (4.40%) is divided by the S&P 500 Estimated Reported Earnings Yield (4.64%), resulting in a S&P 500 Value Factor (in our example: 4.40 percent divided by 4.64 percent = .95).

The S&P 500 Value Factor of .95 is less than 1.00 signifying that the S&P 500 Index may be currently undervalued by approximately five percent. An expected fair valuation for the S&P 500 Index is calculated by dividing the S&P 500 Index price by the S&P 500 Value Factor (in our example: 1,050 divided by .95 = 1,105). The S&P 500 Index Expected Fair Valuation Model is indicating that the S&P 500 Index is undervalued and the expected fair valuation is approximately 1,105 – or approximately a five percent increase above the actual, as this is written, S&P 500 Index price of 1,050.

A table may be prepared using a spread sheet program that will calculate the Actual P/E ratio, the Forward P/E ratio, the S&P 500 Value Factor, and S&P Index 500 Expected Fair Valuation (EFV) Model. Once the required data are input (i.e., the S&P 500 Index price, the 10-Year T-Note yield, the actual reported twelve-month earnings, and the future estimated reported twelve-month earnings – all information available on Websites already identified – the spread sheet will automatically make the necessary calculations. The table may be updated as regularly as thought necessary, however in most circumstances once a month would be sufficient.

Assuming that earnings estimates do not change and 10-Year T-Note interest rates remain stable, S&P 500 Index EFV Model valuations may be calculated for January, 2004 (4.40 percent divided by 5.30 percent = .830 which is divided into 1,050 equaling 1,265) and for January, 2005 (4.40 percent divided by 5.74 percent = .767 which is divided into 1,050 equaling 1,369). The example information is filled in and is presented in Table 3 - 2:

Table 3 - 2: S&P 500 Actual & Forward P/E Ratios & Expected Fair Valuation Model

D A T E	S&P 500 Index Price	10-Yr T-Note Yield	Actual 12-Mo. Earn.	Actual P/E	Est. 12-Mo. Earn.	For-ward P/E	S&P 500 Val. Fac-tor	S&P 500 EFV Mod
Oct '03	1050	4.40	$34.55	30.4	$48.75	21.5	.95	1105
Jan '04	1050	4.40			$55.60	18.9	.832	1265
Jan '05	1050	4.40			$60.30	17.4	.767	1369

The S&P 500 Index EFV Model values, shown below for October of 2003 to January of 2005, indicates the S&P 500 Index is expected to be in an uptrend which may further give confidence to beginning investors:

October, 2003 - S&P 500 Index EFV Model of 1,105
January, 2004 - S&P 500 Index EFV Model of 1,265
January, 2005 - S&P 500 Index EFV Model of 1,369

The S&P 500 Index Expected Fair Valuation (EFV) Model results can be volatile over a two or three month time period and the S&P 500 Index can remain undervalued or overvalued for an extended time period. Earning estimate revisions and especially 10-Year T-Note interest rate fluctuations may significantly effect S&P 500 Index EFV Model values.

Summary

Bond fundamentals are discussed. Equity fundamental analysis relies on corporate financial analysis, management, and competitor evaluations to determine whether a company's stock should be bought or sold. The Standard & Poor's (S&P) 500 Index is a closely followed benchmark and an excellent proxy for the overall stock market.

The P/E ratio is a backward looking statistic and the information has already been fully discounted in the marketplace. The P/E ratio has many inadequacies and may actually convince investors to take the wrong action when investing in the stock market. The stock market is a discounting mechanism that requires investors with foresight to look ahead to be successful.

Forward P/E ratios rely on forward estimated as reported earnings to correctly valuate the stock market. Forward P/E ratio information combined with prevailing 10-Year U.S. Treasury Note interest rates are used to calculate the S&P 500 Index Expected Fair Valuation Model.

A step-by-step method for calculating the S&P 500 Index Expected Fair Valuation (EFV) Model is presented, and while it is not precise it will give the astute investor approximate correct forward-looking valuations for the S&P 500 Index. This model gives a good estimation on whether the stock market is currently overvalued or undervalued and perhaps as importantly, the expected future price direction of the overall stock market.

Astute investors may now keep abreast of future estimated reported earnings, current interest rates, and whether the overall U.S. stock market is at present under-or-over valued based on the expected fair valuation of the S&P 500 Index.

Some technical analysis techniques may be used, but only with the S&P 500 Index. These techniques are recommended to help identify the four long-term stages in the stock market and are presented next in chapter 4.

4

Stock Market Technical Analysis

Introduction

THE GOAL OF THE ASTUTE INVESTOR of being able to recognize either distribution or accumulation in the stock market is made clear. The exploring-compensating condition of stock market traders to determine intrinsic, true, or fair value is further discussed. What happens when the overriding of the exploring-compensating condition leads to inefficient capital markets is explained. Why market signals should be heeded are also described.

A belief in stock market cycles over the long term is stressed. Perspective into the long-term nature of the stock market using monthly data is discussed. How share volume changes depending on stock market cycles is investigated.

Four long-term stock market stages are defined: 1) Mark-Down - Downtrend; 2) Accumulation - Bottoming; 3) Mark-Up - Uptrend; and 4) Distribution - Topping. The significance of the S&P 500 Index Nine Month Moving Average (MA) Trend Line is explained. Important S&P 500 Index technical analysis techniques are presented.

Japanese candlestick graphing techniques using a charting Website are specified using actual historical data to depict each of the four log-term market cycle stages. The confirming indicators to the S&P 500 Index Nine Month MA Trend Line examples are expressly identified to help astute investors when performing their own analysis. S&P 500 Index Nine Month MA Trend Line methodology back-tested results are presented.

Goal Of The Astute Investor

Investors in the stock market, at any point in time, hold all of the common stock outstanding in the market. The only question in general is, are astute investors holding the common stock or are unaware investors holding the common stock? At long-term market tops, astute investors may sell common stocks to investors who are unaware of market valuations or market direction which is called market distribution.

Distribution of stock at a long-term market top is a process of marketing the good news in the stock market with supplying an allotment of stock over time to the investing public. The investing public still clamors to purchase more stock at this time because most people say and most people agree, called the conventional wisdom, that the political-economic conditions are exceptional and may well remain so. Also, at this time employment is high and many investors have the money to purchase additional common stocks.

At long-term market bottoms, astute investors buy back stock from unaware investors in a process called market accumulation. Accumulation at a long-term stock market bottom is the process of gathering or amassing common stock over time on the bad news from those unaware investors who are fearful or have to sell due to their own financial necessity.

The goal of *The Astute Investor* is to transform unaware investors into astute investors. Being able to recognize either distribution or accumulation is a chief objective in *The Astute Investor*. Astute investors should not begin new investments while the stock market is in a long-term downward trend.

Pricing of stock in the market is an issue that is constantly reported on in the media. Determining whether stock pricing is justified is often a central question for investors which is included in the following review.

Pricing In The Stock Market

A stock is only worth what an investor can get for it, therefore the stock market can never be wrong. Normally the overall stock market price swings over the short-term and intermediate-term around intrinsic, true, or fair value making the overall stock market exceptionally efficient.

Stock markets daily crisscross back and forth probing for a correct market price that conforms to political-economic conditions. Intermediate term swings bring stock market pricing further away from intrinsic, true, or fair value than short-term swings; but, it is still an irregular swing around intrinsic, true, or fair value. Short-term and intermediate-term irregular swings combine to created chaotic day to day price movements, but are all predicated on a stock market at intrinsic, true, or fair value.

Investors use the exploring-compensating condition by inquiring, studying, experimenting, and examining the best fit between current market pricing and expected political-economic conditions. Millions and millions of stock market participants diligently search for and intensively pursue the market direction that conforms correctly to political-economic conditions.

As the current stock market and expected political-economic conditions get out of alignment, the exploring-compensating technique used by traders will correctly realign the stock market. Individual stock prices, due to specific expected problems or exceptional prospects associated only with that company called unsystematic factors, can rise above or fall below intrinsic, true, or fair value at any time.

The process is not perfect, pricing may often fall below or exceed fair value and the market direction may over adjust causing temporary market bulges or dips. These bulges or dips may take place over a many days or months and result in the short-term or intermediate-term swings that are so evident in the stock market.

For most of the time however, the overall stock market pricing closely approximates intrinsic, true, or fair value and is exceptionally efficient. Like individual stocks, the overall stock market can markedly move away from intrinsic, true, or fair value and may be described as inefficient.

Inefficient Capital Markets

The exploring-compensating condition is healthy for the stock market and ensures that in aggregate that the stock market, during this time period, is extremely efficient in pricing securities. Keeping stock prices on track with the underlying aggregate expected political and economic conditions is best accomplished when conditions seem uncertain to the investing public.

If the investing public's exploring-compensating condition is temporarily suspended, as when things seem the most rosy at long-term stock market peaks or the most frightening at long-term stock market bottoms, then the stock market intrinsic, true, or fair value may be temporarily suspended for a period of time. When conventional wisdom is all in one direction at long-term market peaks or long-term bottoms, inefficient capital markets may prevail.

When the stock market has been advancing for an extended period of time and the market pundits and investing gurus are now giving an all clear to invest, typically the investing public only now becomes interested in putting money to work in the stock market. When the conventional wisdom in the stock market is either all-up or all-down and the exploring-compensating condition is temporarily suspended then the stock market may become inefficient and grossly overshoot intrinsic, true, or fair value both on the way-up and on the way-down.

Inefficient capital markets and suspension of the exploring-compensating condition typically occurs at long-term stock market peaks or troughs. The overall stock market may significantly overshoot on the way up at a long-term market top during boom-bubble buying or on the way down at a long-term market bottom during panic selling. For more on this please see chapter 5. The stock market, at these long-term turning points, has a tendency to reach unexpected high and low price levels. The following are noteworthy long-term signals that every astute investor should heed.

Market Signals To Be Heeded

In the long-term, once the overall stock market turns down off its peak prices or up from its market low prices, regardless how good or bad the news is (please see chapter 8) or what certain stock market pundits, investing gurus, or experts say, this event is of surpassing significance and the astute investor heeds this cogent indicator.

It is interesting to note that the news is often the best at long-term market tops and the most terrible at long-term market bottoms. But if investors think about it this is the way it is expected to be to get the unaware investing public to either buy the most stock at long-term market tops or sell the most stock at long-term market bottoms. While the actual news may be fantastic, the discounting of expected news could indicate changed market conditions.

Having the market pundits or experts agreeing with the conventional wisdom at long-term turning points is also to be expected since free advice often merely matches the investing public's sentiments and does not lead them. The following discussion should help astute investors spotlight long-term market turns, which are based on market cycles that are common in the real economy and as a result also prevalent in the stock market.

Premise Of Stock Market Cycles

Long-term cycles in the U.S. stock market are irregular and may take one, two, three, four, five years or more. These alternating oscillations vacillate to and fro and waver as if hampered by differing predictions, expectations, and investors' foresight. The stock market over the long-term moves in cycles – down, bottom, up, top – and a belief in the premise of stock market cycles is important for success in long-term investing.

That stock market long-term cycles have formerly occurred is irrefutable. The proposition is that long-term cycles in the stock market are as certain as the four seasons, but with erratic timing. The stock market in the past has experienced long-term cycles and the premise is that it always will.

Business Cycles

Business cycles are a main determinant to stock market cycles. The National Bureau of Economic Research reports that going back to 1854 that their have been thirty-two business cycles. A main determinate of stock market cycles are changing business cycles, resulting from changing corporate earnings and interest rates. In addition, changes in political, natural, and world conditions will impact the stock market cycle.

Whenever the real economy is in a down-turn and reported profits decline it is only logical to anticipate that common stock prices, which are loosely tied to corporate earnings, will also decline.

Market Pundits

The news and market pundits also contribute to stock market cycles because they add momentum at long-term highs and lows. Many times the opinion makers will remain pessimistic for up to a year about the future outlook of the stock market, even though the real economy has clearly turned the corner and corporate profits are noticeably getting better.

Similarly, after the stock market has turned down off its long-term peak – the opinion makers may be telling the investing public for up to a year that conditions still look good even though the stock market has clearly turned down.

The Stock Market Shock Absorber

The stock market may be thought of as a shock absorber for the real political-economy. If the real political-economy runs into a recessionary pot hole in the road, the stock market absorbs the brunt of the shock wave. In effect, the stock market is the shock absorber cushion on which the real political-economy rests.

Often the political-economic problems need only be a minor non-recessionary indentation on a road of extremely good conditions for the stock market to respond abruptly and badly. The real economy need not fall into nor be in recession for the stock market to react negatively. Other factors, such as politics, nature, and world events also play a major role in overall stock prices.

No matter how stable the Federal Reserve tries to keep the real economy, the stock market will feel any aberrations, possibly multiplied manyfold (please see chapter 7 for more on the Federal Reserve), and because of this the stock market is cyclical and by definition – volatile. In order to see now conditions play out over the long-term, a proper vantage point is required which is best accomplished using investor perspective.

Investor Perspective

The stock market, over the long-term, often moves much more slowly than the investing public thinks, and typically both goes much higher and much lower in price than most investors think possible. Major political-economic changes in the United States take a long period of time to accomplish, and the stock market cycles merely reflect these slow changes.

Long-term moves in the stock market may take many years to play out. Typically a complete business cycle, from downturn-bottom-upturn-top, may take a little over 4.5 years. However, the longest complete business cycle to date has taken a little over 10.5 years and the shortest 2.5 years.

In order to adequately view how slowly the stock market actually moves over the long-term, investors need perspective. This is where the discussion of the adage "not being able to see the forest for the trees" comes in. What is required is an ability to objectively evaluate long-term stock market price movements with a full or unimpeded panoramic view of how real actions are playing out in the symbolic stock market.

Perspective facilitates an investor's understanding of the long-term rhythm of the U.S. stock market. The rhythm of the stock market is a never-ending flow of seesawing fundamentals, behaviors, and factors characterized by the irregular repetition of commonplace conditions.

Daily or even weekly stock market data does not give the investor the best point of view that adequately relates the relative significance of the parts to the whole. Consequently, it is paramount to study monthly stock market price data to perceive the relative position of market stages evident over stock market long-term trends of one, two, three, four, five or more years. The perspective of monthly data helps facilitate an investor's appreciation of long-term moves in the stock market.

Monthly Data And Moving Averages

Monthly data are instrumental in dampening out the random short-term volatility of day-to-day price movements in the stock market. The long-term trend is easier to recognize when the daily and weekly price movements are smoothed out by using longer term time units The time frame for which stock market price movements will be reported on are collected in monthly units only. This will allow investors to get a required panoramic view of an extremely long-term time dimension on the chart being studied.

Often daily price action represent only frantic short-term movements that are difficult for investors to but into the long-term perspective so important to long-term investing. Once the perspective of the monthly data are viewed, it is often easy to see the effect of the normally slow moving political, economic, natural, and world forces that are being played out on stock market prices.

Using last month's stock price to forecast next month's stock price does not allow for a long-term trend development. A moving average of many prior months smooths out variations in stock market price movements and in addition takes the long-term trend into consideration. In effect, the stock market is being viewed with a time frame that matches its long-term characteristics.

The monthly moving average is determined by averaging together the monthly average closing prices and connecting a trend line. The direction of this trend line is the indicator to the long-term direction of the stock market. The fewer months of data that are included in the moving average calculation the faster the response of the trend line to the underlying conditions in the marketplace. In addition, share volume data may give astute investors a window into confirming what current stock market stage is present in the marketplace.

Share Volume

Usually when the stock market is in a long-term uptrend, daily share volume increases on rallies and decreasing share volume occurs on dips. Encouraging share volume action during up-trends occurs when volume increases over the last rally with commensurate price advances, and the next correction is on low volume.

As long as the share volumes increase from rally to rally, the long-term market uptrend should be expected to remain intact. While this is normal when markets are coming off of market bottoms, this is not always the case at the end of an uptrend situation.

Share Volume At Market Peaks

Huge volume increases with disproportionately small price advances often occurs at long-term market tops. Thus, market churning of high volume on little market price headway is a definite sign of forecasted trouble ahead.

Long-term market peaks happen when shares are being distributed from astute investors to unaware investors. Thus the market turning down prior to the real economic conditions turning down is a positive display of the market's predictive ability. The recognition of the transition of a long-term uptrend to a long-term downtrend is often a change in how volume figures are evaluated.

Investors with foresight have already sold, so dips on low volume should now be of vital concern. Low volume dips occur because the investing public is still optimistic and there is no unease on their part and there are few sellers in the stock market making bids for sale. Prices decline, then they may improve but only on low volume, and then decline once more.

After a market has rolled over and started a long-term downward trend, if the market rallies back to the resistance level of a long-term trend line on light trading volume, this is an overt indication that this is a short-term bulge and the stock market will quickly be continuing its long-term downward direction.

When even the optimists are aware of problems and the long-term trend is down, share volumes become high on down-days and any rallies are now on modest volume. This is a tell-tail signal of a market transition from a long-term upward to a long-term downward stock market based on an evaluation of share volume alone.

Share Volume At Market Lows

Long-term stock market lows happen when the majority of everyone who wants to sell has already sold. Low share volume corrections are expected during the beginning of a long-term stock market upturn because there are fewer sellers left to sell.

Long-term upward markets indicate both higher-highs and higher-lows on the monthly graphs. As the S&P 500 Index dips to the now new support line on lower volume and then rallies to new highs for this long-term move on increased volume – this is an excellent indication that the long-term direction of the market is now up. Stock market averages will advance through resistance levels which will then become support levels.

In this way, a succession of higher-highs and higher-lows progress with the requisite volume confirmation figures to support the judgment that a new long-term upward move has begun and remains ongoing.

Upside And Downside Share Volume

Volume may also be separated into upside share volume and downside share volume. Upside and downside volume are reported for the NYSE, NASDAQ, and AMEX stock exchanges. If the market averages make new highs on huge share volume; but, the upside volume does not surpass prior rally peak values, then this is a divergence from what is expected and should be a warning of a possible long-term market top.

Tracking upside and downside share volume in the major markets will be beneficial for investors. If the stock market averages are still going up but upside and downside volume figures are deteriorating with much more down volume revealed, this will add credence to a market roll over. Four distinct stages of a complete stock market cycle may be identified and are discussed next.

Four Stock Market Stages

The stock market will go through long-term cycles that in general precede, at market tops up to twelve months and at market bottoms hardly at all, with what is occurring in the political-economy. When these stock market cycles take place is the most important question to answer.

The second most important question concerns the magnitude of the peaks and troughs. Having the foresight to know how high "high is" and when it occurs, and how low "low is" and when it occurs is all that investors need to know to become fabulously wealthy in the stock market. However, no investor will ever know this while it is occurring with complete certainty; therefore, being close enough is the goal to be considered an astute investor.

The stock market's long-term cycle is a process or a phase in development in which a market stage will occur that will last a period of time. Cyclical pattern magnitudes change and the periods of time that each of the stages lasts are variable and normally never exactly repeated. The market stages are named next for ease of discussion.

Market Stages Named

As Richard W. Schabacker explains, there are four main stages in a long-term stock market cycle. In practical terms, the most important question is correctly determining what stage the stock market is in currently.

For astute investors especially, this is the foundation for correctly identifying the proper action to be taken to take advantage of the long-term swings in the stock market. Investors need to have confidence in their determination of the current stock market stage so that the follow-on stage may be anticipated with assurance. There are four main stages in a long-term stock market cycle which are:

Stage 1: Mark-Down - Downtrend
Stage 2: Accumulation - Bottoming
Stage 3: Mark-Up - Uptrend
Stage 4: Distribution - Topping or Rounding Over

Graph 4 - 1 shows these typical four stages of a long-term stock market cycle:

Graph 4 - 1: Four Stock Market Stages

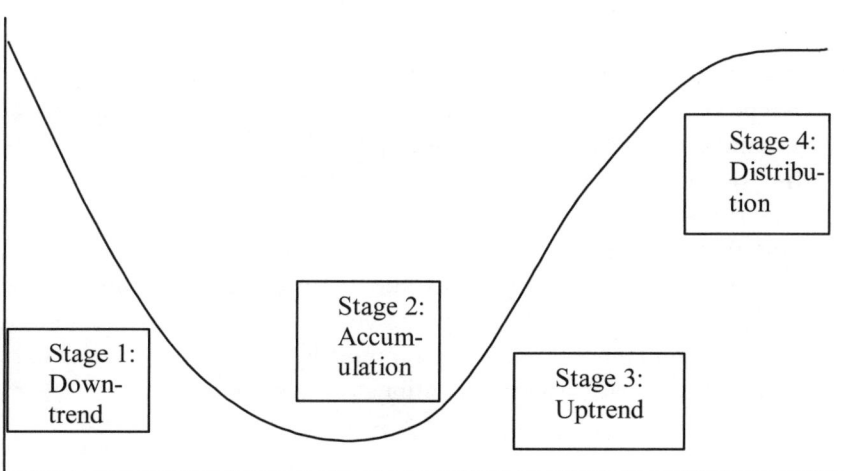

Market Stages' Boundary Lines

It is important to realize that there are no hard and fast boundary lines between the four long-term stock market stages. Even though names are given to each of the four stages they tend to blend into one another and boundaries are hard to recognize when stages are changing, especially when studying real time information.

There are no precise systems that determine the exact timing and magnitude of each market stage. Stages may combine with and turn into one another exceedingly slowly, almost imperceptibly. It is comforting to know however that one stock market stage always follows another in the exact same order, time after time.

Since market stages never jump around, investors can know with confidence that Stage 1: Mark-Down - Downtrend will always trail Stage 4: Distribution - Topping, and Stage 3: Mark-Up - Uptrend will always follow Stage 2: Accumulation - Bottoming. A discussion of each of the four stock market stages are presented next.

Stage 1

Stage 1 is the markdown of the stock market which results in a long-term downtrend in the stock market averages. Since the stock market discounts the future, at market tops as much as the next six to twelve months, the market will turn down even though the news and market pundits are saying things still look splendid in the real economy.

The market will be predicting a preponderance of poor political-economic news in the future even though the real economy may still be improving. The downturn in the stock market averages may be rationalized by the market pundits as a plain consequence from over eagerness on the investing public's part that has now been removed from the marketplace, and by all rights the averages should now go higher – but they in fact never do during this time period.

Corporate earnings may continue to improve for a short time, employment may continue to grow, the corporate news may be nothing short of stellar, and market pundits and investing gurus will continue to be optimistic – but the stock market continues to decline. Why?

Economic and Stock Market Dichotomy

The dichotomy here between the real economy and the symbolic stock market is often the most difficult for new investors to reconcile. The investing public's rational thinking when the economy is fantastic, implores them to continue buying stock; but, the pain of losing money as the stock market moves lower is challenging for these investors to stomach.

Often these new investors will convince themselves that the stock market is wrong and they are right and it is only a matter of time before the market correctly responds to their thinking (please see chapter 9 on being contrarian for more discussion on incorrectly thinking that the market is wrong).

Besides, unaware investors may rationalize, look at all the magnificent "price bargains" that can be picked up as prices descend off the their price highs. It is important to remember at these times that the overall stock market is never wrong – a stock is only worth what an investor can get for it.

When the S&P 500 Index monthly average is far below its long-term trend line, and then begins an intermediate-term rally back to its downward sloping long-term trend line and hits resistance at that point – investors may be assured that this advance will again fail and the downward movement of the S&P 500 Index will continue.

S&P 500 Index V Shaped Bottom Failures

A bounce off of a new low in the move that forms a V shaped bottom on the monthly S&P 500 Index graph will always fail with a retest of that low price to follow. The downward movement on the monthly graph will continue to show lower-highs and lower-lows until support in the form of a double bottom or head and shoulders bottom pattern is formed (much more on these technical patterns later in this chapter). This can be easily seen in Graph 4 - 2: S&P 500 Index V Shaped Bottom Failures.

A new initial low occurred during March 2001 and an intermediate rally lasting approximately three months back to resistance of the downward sloping long-term trend line may be seen. This rally failed with a lower-low happening during September 2001 and again a three month rally back to the resistance of the long-term trend line beginning in 2002 occurred.

Graph 4 - 2: S&P 500 Index V Shaped Bottom Failures

Lower-highs and lower-lows are continuing and are plainly evident in Graph 4 - 2 during Stage 1. Again failure happened with a new low for the move occurring during July 2002. At this point investors should expect any intermediate rally to the long-term trend line to also fail and have the lows that occurred during July 2002 to at least be tested at the support level that occurred during this July 2002 downward move.

Recession Announcements

It is interesting to note that long-term stock market bottoms occur almost invariably only after a recession has been officially announced by authorities. If the market is in a long-term downtrend, it is imperative not too begin investing too early solely because stock prices have come way down from their highs and seem like good bargains at current prices.

Buying good stocks at even lower prices later on is highly likely which is after all one of the objectives of *The Astute Investor*. The other is selling at the right time. This is an effort to minimize investing risk. Go with the probabilities and remain patient, the opportunity to buy good stocks will present itself and should not be simply guessed at – relying solely on hope or luck in the stock market is not a wise strategy.

Stage 1 Volume

The end of Stage 1, when market prices are fairly low and begin to lose negative price momentum – after it has been in progress for a usual interval which is half the time of the prior advance during Stage 3 – is typically highlighted by a drying up of the volume of shares trading over an interval of weeks or months.

It is during Stage 1 that the stock market is most efficient and correctly discounts the future slowdown and poor expected political-economy conditions. All investors should treat Stage 1, and what it is telling investors, as trustworthy. In general, if investors see the overall market is in Stage 1: Mark-Down - Downtrend it is wise to wait to invest.

Stage 2

Stage 2 is the long-term stock market bottoming and accumulation of stock from frightened investors dumping their stock or selling out due to fear of the market going even lower, or the requirement to sell stock to get money to live on in poor economic times.

Stock prices during this stage are usually reduced to irrationally depressed levels during panic selling when stocks are thrown on the market to fetch whatever is grudgingly offered. Stock prices are driven down below their sensibly defensible intrinsic, true, or fair values in a maelstrom of public investor emotions.

Market Low Turning Points

The defining moment of the reversal of the long-term trend from downward to upward is often difficult to spot. There are three typical scenarios that may describe a stock market turn off the bottom and are:

1) A sluggish, exhausted, lethargic, low share volume market with many pathetic rallies that are followed by quick dips in price; but, with the saving grace that the low is in place and that future dips hold above old low prices. Many investors are now selling because they are tired of the long drawn-out low market or need the money for personal use.

The price range is limited but low enough so that eventually these low prices appeal to enough buyers to have stock demand surpass supply. Many astute investors may now recognize strength of buying on the dips, and when a breakout of price to the upside confirms the condition – a new long-term upward trend may now be begun.

2) A dramatic, furious, shattering catharsis of selling, over approximately three to five days, in which all stocks seem to crash together which engenders universal concern and stimulates more and more stock liquidation and panic selling. Market hysteria is at a peak here with mob psychology prompting many novice investors to dump stocks for whatever price they can obtain.

At this point novice investors may feel ill used by the market and by cashing in their stock they do not have to be confronted by the fact that they were wrong about their previous investment decisions. Astute investors should recognize this for what it is, a buying opportunity that perhaps happens only a few times in their investing lifetime.

3) A blend of 1) and 2) above where both the sluggish and crashing market may be in force at the same time.

It is at Stage 2 that the stock market is the most inefficient and most out of sync with intrinsic, true, or fair value. On the positive side, this is the correct time to be contrarian (please see chapter 9). It is the astute investors who are purchasing common stock at the market bottom from those who are unaware of what stock market stage is being played out.

Stage 2 Volume

During Stage 2, the number of shares being traded in the overall market falls to extremely low levels because the investing public becomes fed-up and prefers to not even think about the stock market let alone invest in it. Shunning the market by the investing public at its long-term lows is the norm. This is ironic since it is the exact time that the most interest in the market should be engendered to be successful when investing.

At the end of Stage 2, the number of shares trading hands each day is revived from the extremely low levels prevalent at the end of Stage 1. Real improvement in the political-economic conditions have encouraged investors to take an interest in the stock market again.

The important question at the end of Stage 2 is: if one were impervious to the news, the market pundits, and all rumors – what is the market itself telling investors? Look for solid fundamental and technical indications that the market is indeed turning around and shun everyone else's opinions, especially those of the market pundits.

Market Bottoms Should Not Be Guessed At

Trying to guess or relying on what the market pundits are saying should be happening next in the economy is detrimental to one's financial health. In general, when investors determine that the overall market is in Stage 2: Accumulation - Bottoming and being contrarian is the appropriate course of action – it is at this stage that confidence in one's ability to identify the stage correctly and the actual courage to make the investment is paramount, even when all around you are bemoaning their losses and the conventional wisdom is seemingly against investors.

The stock market is a symbolic representation of not only the real corporate economy but also everything that impacts on the real economy. For example, political action by the federal, sate, and local governments and agencies that include: the decision to go to war; the policies on fiscal deficits and taxes; currency values; trade laws; decision on the Fed Funds rate; immigration; natural disasters; world conditions; etc.

The U.S. Gross Domestic Product in the real economy may start expanding again after a long decline, but the stock market may continue to decline for an extended period of time. Being vigilant to all the factors represented in the stock market is paramount.

The stock markets upturn from the often long drawn out process occurring during Stage 2: Accumulation - Bottoming is frequently dramatic and is based on solid political-economic improvement. Waiting for the political-economic improvement is fundamental to sound investing.

Stage 3

Stage 3 is the markup of stock prices and an easily identified uptrend in the general market which has actually been in place for a period of time. The investing public is still uncertain about the correct direction of the market, since they have been fooled by false rallies during the Stage 1: Mark-Down - Downtrend period.

Upward Trend

The stock market progresses in a long-term upward direction as business corporations consistently report higher aggregate earnings and any political, natural, or world issues are not overpowering the now positive economic factors.

It is interesting to note that the stock market is expected to forecast the real political-economic conditions. While this is clearly in evidence at long-term stock market peaks, at long-term stock market bottoms the look ahead feature of the stock market is severely reduced.

Because it takes considerable buying power to put the stock market prices up again, even the most intrepid investors have difficulty investing until they actually see the stock market begin to rise. Investors typically wait until all conditions, including corporate, political, economic, and natural are once again in their favor.

The Investing Public Is Usually Late

The investing public is usually late to the markup stage and only get fully on board after they get the all-clear from the market pundits which is close to another market top. Astute investors try to be on time to Stage 3, not too early and not too late.

Although the stock market advance customarily goes through many fits and starts during Stage 3, the underlying trend in the overall stock market is clearly up. When investors notice that the overall market has bottomed out and is in Stage 3: Mark-Up - Uptrend, then that would be the time to invest and stay invested in the market. Stock market prices begin to react to improving corporate earnings and continue to improve as the political- economic conditions strengthen.

Stage 4

Stage 4 is the distribution, topping, or rounding over phase in the stock market. At the top of a major long-term cycle during Stage 4, this vital span at the market peak may extend over a number of weeks. Near the conclusion of this critical span of weeks, if one particular day has share volume trading of gigantic proportions while at the same time the overall stock market shows no price advancement; but, actually losses ground, that could indicate the key defining moment that signals the start of a long-term downward trend.

Market Highs And The Discounting Horizon

Economic, natural, and world conditions are all exceedingly favorable at this time; but market traders begin to see expected problems ahead – most notably in the actions by the Federal Reserve (more on this in chapter 7) – and begin to unload their stock and sell them to the investing public who are still clamoring for more stock.

Boom-bubble buying is now in full swing by the investing public and at this stage the over enthusiasm for purchasing stock drives prices much higher than any rational intrinsic, true or fair value. Since prices are advancing more than they should at this stage, value investors and market traders are taking profits and allowing the investing public to carry common stock shares throughout the coming expected Stage 1: Mark-Down - Downtrend in the stock market.

Market Churning

When prices increase beyond the high values of previous market peaks to exceedingly lofty ranges, and the upward price progress starts to lose momentum and churn about on extremely high share volume – without making any appreciable price progress – this is the definition of Stage 4: Distribution - Topping or Rounding Over.

Even though fundamental conditions in the real economy may continue to improve – other factors, most notably political, are changing. The symbolic stock market during Stage 4 is telling investors to beware of the coming decline. High volume of stock shares traded, after a relatively long and significant stock market price advance, with now price churning, foreshadows a reversal of trend.

Stock Market Long-Term Trends

Stock market prices, over the long-term, tend to move along trend lines. The stock market proceeds in the line of least resistance. Unbalanced supply and demand for stocks creates the least resistance line and market trends. The stock market long-term trend is the overall tendency of price movements as they fluctuate over the intermediate-term and the short-term.

Once a price trend is identified over a long-term time frame there is a higher probability that overall stock market prices will continue along this trend line, along with the usual intermediate-term swings and short-term bulges and dips, then reverse course. When the stock market is making a long-term move, either upward or downward, higher profits are to be expected from investing in the stock market by following the trend line of least resistance then by fighting and attempting to invest against this trend line. Why the long-term trend line may be called the line of least resistance is discussed next.

Line Of Least Resistance

The line of least resistance may be best understood by imagining that the entire stock market is under the command of one fictitious investor called Mr. Big. He has complete sway in the stock market and every price change is either the direct consequence of his buying or selling, or is directly influenced by him. Now Mr. Big wants to know what is happening in the stock market so he tries to force all stock prices upward with exploratory purchases.

Some stock's prices move up quickly while others hardly budge at all. The responsive stocks are reviewed and now the decision is made by Mr. Big to continue buying the responsive stocks and discontinue buying the stocks that hardly moved in price. Notice that Mr. Big is following those stocks with continued purchases that demonstrate the line of least resistance to his initial purchase of stock.

The stocks that are effortless to force up in price with the least buying power would be those stocks showing the line of least resistance. This could be as easily demonstrated for the overall market. The overall stock market may demonstrate the line of least resistance as it trends upward. Buying has the tendency to easily force overall stock prices higher.

The line of least resistance continues until it meets at first a hardly noticeable opposing force that begins to stop the market's upward or downward long-term trend. The problem for investors of course is how to determine, in real time while it is happening, what is occurring to the stock market's long-term trend.

Recognizing A Trend Reversal

Identifying the reversal of the long-term trend line in a timely manner to allow the investor to cash out of one ending trend and climb aboard and stay aboard the new trend to allow him or her to make money is also a key issue. It is at these changes in the long-term trend, if caught correctly, that the outsized stock market profits are realized.

The recognition of the timing of reversals in market long-term trends hinges on the fundamental political, economic, natural, and world factors that normally move the stock market incredibly slowly. Once stock market price momentum is flowing in a long-term direction, it takes time to reverse course.

The investor, by relying on the stock market's long-term trend line, is accepting the judgment of the marketplace as to the composite direction of the real factors that move the symbolic stock market. Plausible market theories offered by market pundits, that do not match the stock market's long-term trend, may now be looked on with skepticism. It is best to remember that the market is never wrong.

Over the long term (1-5 years or more), the U.S. stock market tends to move along an uptrend or downtrend line. Also, the long-term up-or-down trend, once apparent, is most likely to continue in that same up-or-down direction until conclusively changed.

Long-term trends in the stock market are shaped by an unbalanced supply or demand for common stocks that correspond with long-term market cycles that are identified by the four market stages. Monthly charts using moving average trend lines are important to identify long-term trend lines and are explained next.

Monthly Moving Average (MA) Trend Lines

The Standard & Poor's (S&P) 500 Index produces superb long-term trend lines that may be relied upon during both upward and downward long-term trending stock markets. The duration or the number of prior monthly averages to include in the trend line calculation is as a rule 200 stock market trading days.

Converting 200 trading days into months is approximately nine months. Nine prior months of data are averaged together to determine the value used to draw the trend line. The moving average requires the oldest month's data to be dropped from the calculation whenever a new month's data is included. In addition to the nine months of data, a 50 trading day stock market moving average trend line is often used to help confirm the longer term moving average. The 50 day moving average trend line is approximately two months of data.

To determine the long-term trend in the U.S. stock market the Nine Month Moving Average (MA) Trend Line of the S&P 500 Index is followed which smooths out the volatility of shorter-term price movements and gives perspective to the rhythm of the U.S. stock market. A Two Month Moving Average (MA) Trend Line of the S&P 500 Index is also helpful when analyzing the long-term trend.

As will be seen, the S&P 500 Index Nine Month Moving Average (MA) Trend Line is easy to calculate by computer and it is easy to visualize what is happening in the stock market by looking at its long-term trend direction. In addition to the S&P 500 Index Nine Month MA Trend Line, the S&P 500 Index Moving Average Convergence Divergence (MACD) also helps to visualize the long-term stock market stages.

Moving Average Convergence Divergence (MACD)

The Moving Average Convergence Divergence (MACD) is developed by Gerald Appel in 1979 as a market timing system. The monthly MACD also helps see the big picture in the stock market. MACD can indicate a stock market's momentum as well as indicating its trend. Momentum in the market refers to the acceleration of price movements in either the upward or downward direction.

When prices accelerate in either direction the momentum is high, and the probability is high that stock market prices will continue in that direction. As long as stock market price trend is increasing in momentum, the MACD will persist in making either higher-highs or lower-lows. As stock market prices begin to decelerate and momentum slows down, it becomes more likely that a reversal in trend is evident.

As prices trend, either up or down, they are also experiencing either an increase or a lessening of momentum. As momentum is being lost during an upward or a downward movement, and stock market prices are either going up or going down at a diminished speed – this is a cautionary indicator often forewarning that the trend could soon be changing. The combined trend and momentum capability of the monthly MACD make it a particularly good long-term stock market indicator of market trend reversals.

The MACD derives two lines from three exponentially weighted moving averages. The exponential moving averages (EMA) confer more weight to the most recent results, thus making the averages more responsive to the latest data. The MACD (12,26) is considered the first line and is highlighted in blue on BigCharts.com & CBS MarketWatch.com (discussed later in this chapter). The MACD (12,26) line is the dissimilarity between a 12-period EMA in relation to a 26-period EMA. The second line, identified as the EMA (9) and drawn in red on BigCharts.com & CBS MarketWatch.com, is referred to as the signal line and is the 9-period exponential moving average of the MACD (12,26) line.

When the monthly MACD (12,26) line and the EMA (9) line crosses, this is an indication of a change or reversal in the long-term stock market trend and momentum. The trading rule in the MACD system is to purchase stocks when the MACD (12,26) blue line crosses over and is shown above the EMA (9) signal red line.

Conversely, selling of stocks would be indicated when the MACD (12,26) blue line crosses underneath the EMA (9) signal red line. Divergence of the MACD (12,26) blue line above the EMA (9) red line may be indicated as a positive histogram, and a negative histogram when the EMA (9) is on top of the MACD (12,26) line during a market downturn.

The monthly MACD is often effective as a long-term confirming indicator of the S&P 500 Index Nine Month MA Trend Line for each stage in the stock market cycle. Another confirming indicator for each stage, the S&P 500 Index Two Month MA Trend Line, is also helpful and will be discussed more fully later in this chapter. Japanese candlestick graphing techniques are suggested for use and are discussed next.

Japanese Candlestick Graphing Techniques

Visually pleasing graphs to interpret are those developed by the Japanese. Japanese candlestick graphs are reported to be introduced to the United States by Steve Nison in 1989. Candlesticks are figurative, more visually appealing, and make stock graph illustrations attractive and, in one glance, easy to use. It is apparent whether the trend is upward or downward, depending on the candlestick colors on the graph.

The same information is required to draw candlestick graphs as the standard bar charts; however, candlestick graphs include candlestick bodies that may be left open (hollow) or filled in (solid), depending on whether the close is above or below the opening price. The open and close indications depicted on the real bodies are of crucial importance and are the very core of the candlestick graphing technique.

Reading Candlestick Graphs

Hollow or white candlesticks identify a closing price that is higher than the opening price and represents buying force (shown as Figure A in Graph 4 - 3). Solid, either black or red in color, candlesticks signify that the closing price is less than its opening price and depicts selling force (shown as Figure C in Graph 4 - 3). See the example candlestick formations in the following graph.

The open, high, low, and closing values are used to form the candlestick. The rectangular portion of the candlestick is named the real body. Real bodies signify the extent of the change linking the period's open and closing prices. Solid candlestick bodies signify a close lower than the open. White candlestick bodies indicate a close higher than the open.

The length of the real body has significance. The longer the real body the more momentum is evident in the stock market, either upward or downward. Also, the higher the volume of stock traded the more power that goes into the extensive price move. A large price move on relatively low volume is suspect. As the bodies get smaller, this may be an indication that momentum is slowing and consolidation is occurring.

Graph 4 - 3: Candlestick Formations

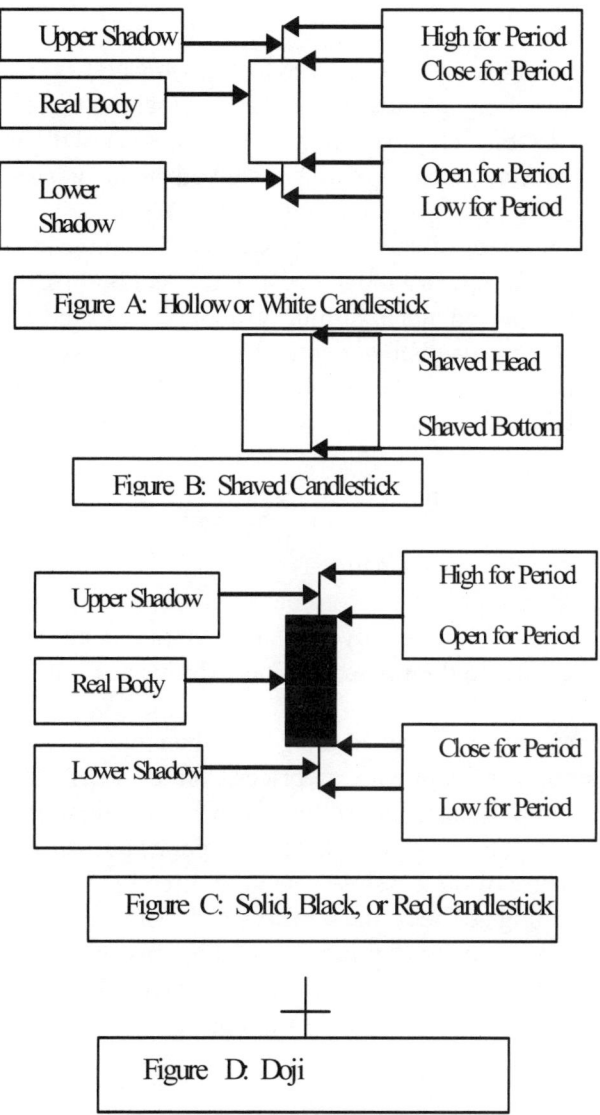

Figure A: Hollow or White Candlestick

Figure B: Shaved Candlestick

Figure C: Solid, Black, or Red Candlestick

Figure D: Doji

The thin lines above and below the candlestick real bodies are called upper shadows and lower shadows, and designate the high-and-low price range. Solid candlesticks showing a lengthy upper shadow and a minuscule lower shadow designates a trading period where buyers initially held the upper hand and bid up stocks only to have them come down again later in the period.

White candlesticks with lengthy lower shadow and a minuscule upper shadow point to sellers initially dominating, but with buyers later exerting themselves to drive stock prices higher. A candlestick with no upper-and-lower shadows may be designated a shaved head or shaved bottom, respectively (shown as Figure B in Graph 4 - 3).

A long white candlestick with both a shaved bottom and a shaved head signifies a powerful upward move because the real body signifies the real meaning of any price advance. Similarly, a long solid candlestick with the open and high for the day being identical and the low and close for the day being identical for a shaved head and bottom is demonstrating convincing momentum to the downside.

Doji Formations

An important candlestick formation is called a Doji. A Doji is formed when opening and closing prices are very nearly identical and upper and lower shadows are equal in length, buyers and sellers are deadlocked in a face-off with neither able to dominate the other (shown as Figure D in Graph 4 - 3).

Doji are possible trend reversal signals when they come at the end of a trend of either upward or downward prices. At the end of a trend decline in the market, a doji indicates that selling force has begun to subside and the supply and demand for stock has started to balance out with neither buyers or sellers now sure of the possible changing direction of stock prices.

After a trending advance, the doji serves the same purpose and may be signaling a market top for that move. The benefits of candlestick graphs includes being easy to read as well as understand. Technical indicators, useful to investors, may be important to confirm trends or the possibility of a trend reversal.

Technical Analysis

As Robert D. Edwards and John Magee instruct, the rational behind using technical analysis is that the stock market continually replicates graph patterns time after time. Repeated common patterns in the stock market prices are at first difficult to accept by most novice investors.

How could unique events in history cause similar patterns in stock prices, over and over again? But they do, and it is up to astute investors to know what these patterns are. Patterns repeat themselves because individuals react to different events in similar ways (for much more on this please see chapter 5).

The pattern replications may not be exact and there may be exceptions, however common movements repeat often enough to be included in every investor's knowledge base. Two following signals identify either a continued long-term market upturn or a downturn, and are useful technical indicators for the S&P 500 Index using monthly data.

Lower-Highs And Lower-Lows

An indication that the market will continue in its downtrend is for lower-highs and lower-lows to be prevalent on the S&P 500 Index monthly graphs. The general trend of the market fluctuates in a downward direction.

Swings in the market may bring prices, after a period of time, close to a prior monthly intermediate peak but the upturn will fail below the intermediate peak price and prices will once again continue on their downward path. The next swing down will bring prices below the last market low resulting in a monthly S&P 500 Index lower-highs and lower-lows graph pattern. The second signal occurs during a market upturn.

Higher-Highs And Higher-Lows

As the market fluctuates in an upward long-term trend, S&P 500 Index monthly higher-highs and higher-lows become evident. Coming off a long-term market bottom an intermediate move may reach a high price and then a dip will bring prices down, but not as low as the bottom price reached at the end of the long-term trend.

The next swing up will send stock market monthly prices above the prior intermediate monthly price high and any reduction in price will hold above the first dip's low price. Thus S&P 500 Index higher-highs and higher-lows become clearly visible on the monthly graphs. The following reversal patterns are important when identifying a change in the market's long-term trend.

Double Top Or Double Bottom Reversal Pattern

An S&P 500 Index double top, evident in Stage 4, is a primary reversal pattern which looks like an upside down W or a letter M on a graph. The market advances on high share volume to a top price and then retreats on light volume. The second peak point tests resistance but then retreats on high share volume forming the letter M.

The S&P 500 Index double bottom, evident in Stage 2, is a primary reversal pattern which looks like a letter W on a graph. The two bottom troughs, or price declines, stop at approximately the same intraday price levels. The second bottom point on the W pattern tests support and the share volume during this time is normally extraordinarily light.

Head and Shoulders Reversal Pattern

A variation of the double top or double bottom is the head and shoulders reversal pattern. At S&P 500 Index market highs the person's head and shoulders outline forms the pattern on a graph and at market lows the person's outline is viewed upside down.

At an S&P 500 Index long-term stock market top, three peaks are in evidence with the middle peak the highest price value. The two shoulder price values reach approximately the same intraday price level.

The volume during the head peak may be less than the volume during the first shoulder formation. A neckline may be drawn connecting the two downward swings off the first or left shoulder and the head. The swing down from the right shoulder should break through the neckline to confirm a head and shoulders top.

During a S&P 500 Index head and shoulders bottom there are three intraday trough lows – the first or left shoulder trough roughly matches the right shoulder trough in intraday price with the head intraday price the lowest value of the three. The rally up from the second bottom point should be rapid with higher volume.

Outside Reversal Day

The outside reversal day (ORD) may be used in conjunction with the double bottom or double top formation or the head and shoulders reversal formation to confirm a trend reversal and more importantly, may identify the exact day the reversal occurs. The outside reversal day (ORD) for a double bottom should happen on the second trough and the S&P 500 Index will make a new intraday low for the current move and then close above the intraday high of the previous day on exceptionally high share trading volume.

For a double top, the S&P 500 Index makes a new intraday high for the current move and then breaks sharply and closes below the intraday low of the previous day on especially high share trading volume. For a head and shoulders formation the outside reversal day (ORD) should occur on the head or the right shoulder. Graphs are important to identifying these patterns and may be constructed by using computer generated graphs.

Computer Graphs

Computer graphs may be developed using the BigCharts.com & CBS MarketWatch.com research and investment Website. The Quotes Tab when clicked brings investors to a computer screen that allows for stock symbols to be saved so that selected price quotes may be retrieved whenever requested. The News Tab is a link to CBS MarketWatch.com for all the latest investment news.

The Industries Tab brings investors to lists of the ten-best and ten-worst Dow Jones industries. The Historical Quotes Tab is useful when a stock's prior volume and pricing information are required for previous dates. The Big Reports Tab identifies stocks with the greatest price or volume percentage gain or loss and those hitting 52 week high or low prices.

For the purpose of *The Astute Investor*, the Home Tab is required and automatically accessed when the investor logs on to the internet Website for BigCharts.com & CBS MarketWatch.com at http:// bigcharts.marketwatch.com. To create the S&P 500 Index Nine and Two Month MA Trend Lines and the monthly MACD with Japanese candlestick graphs, logon to the BigCharts.com Website to retrieve current market data that are vital for investors to run investment models for themselves.

Website individual commands, as this is written, necessary to find BigCharts.com & CBS MarketWatch.com current data and information are identified – first, where to look on the screen is given, then either what to click on or what to type in will be specified. First, look to the right-hand column to get started – and after the sample chart is pulled up on the screen – all of the information is found in the left-hand column to properly setup the BigCharts.com & CBS MarketWatch.com computer site.

Logon: http://bigcharts.marketwatch.com

Where: Right Column – find My Favorite Charts
Click: The Red Sample Icon
Where: In the left column find the white box labeled
Enter Symbol or Keyword
Type: SP500

Click: The dark blue "time frame" box (if not already opened)
Where: The white box labeled Time
Click: The blue down arrow at the right side of the Time box or the box itself
Where: In the resulting drop-down list find 4 Years
Click: 4 Years

Where: In the white box labeled Frequency
Click: The blue down arrow at the right side of the Frequency box or the box itself
Where: In the resulting drop-down list find Monthly
Click: Monthly

Click: The dark blue "compare to" box
Where: In the white box labeled Index
Click: The blue down Arrow at the right side of the Index box or the box itself
Where: In the resulting drop-down list find <None>
Click: <None>

Where: The white box labeled <u>Symbols</u> is left empty

Click: The dark blue "indicators" box
Where: The white box labeled <u>Moving Averages</u>
Click: The blue down arrow at the right side of the <u>Moving Averages</u> box or the box itself
Where: In the resulting drop-down list find SMA (2-Line)
Click: SMA (2-Line)

Where: Just to the right of the above <u>Moving Averages</u> box (may have to move slide to the right at the bottom of the column to see this box) there is a separate small white box that is not labeled
Click: The mouse cursor in this small white box to allow the typing of:
Type: 2,9 (Only these two numbers, separated by a coma, should now be in this small white box – remove any other numbers if listed)

Where: The white box labeled <u>Upper Indicators</u>
Click: The blue down arrow at the right side of the Upper Indicators box or the box itself
Where: In the resulting drop-down list find <None>
Click: <None>

Where: The white box labeled <u>Lower Indicator 1</u>
Click: The blue down arrow at the right side of the <u>Lower Indicator 1</u> box (may have to move slide to the right at the bottom of the column or the slide down along the side of the column to see this box) or the box itself
Where: In the resulting pop-up list find MACD near the top of this list
Click: MACD

Where: If <u>Lower Indicator 2</u> and <u>Lower Indicator 3</u> white boxes already indicate <None> skip to "chart style," if not continue:

Where: The white box labeled <u>Lower Indicator 2</u>
Click: The blue down arrow at the right side of the Lower Indicator 2 box or the box itself
Where: In the resulting pop-up list find <None>
Click: <None>

Where: The white box labeled <u>Lower Indicator 3</u>
Click: The blue down arrow at the right side of the Lower Indicator 3 box or the box itself
Where: In the resulting pop-up list find <None>
Click: <None>

Click: The dark blue "chart style" box
Where: The white box labeled <u>Price Display</u>
Click: The blue down arrow at the right side of the <u>Price Display</u> box or the box itself
Where: In the resulting drop-down list find Candlestick
Click: Candlestick

Where: the white box labeled <u>Chart Background</u>
Click: The blue arrow at the right side of the Chart Background box or the box itself
Where: In the resulting drop-down list find Default
Click: Default

Where: The white box labeled <u>Chart Size</u>
Click: The blue down arrow at the side of the <u>Chart Size</u> box or the box itself
Click: Large, or Medium, or Big (i.e., the largest size that best fits your monitor)

To Draw the S&P 500 Index Chart:

Where: Go back up to the top of the column (may have to move the slide at the side of the column up)
Click: In the big red box labeled "Draw Chart"

Once setup, investors should save on http://bigcharts.marketwatch.com, the above settings so the S&P 500 Index graph may be easily redrawn with new or current data whenever requested. To save the newly created S&P 500 Index graph for future updating and use:

Where: Along the top of the S&P 500 Chart highlighted in blue find add to favorites
Click: add to favorites

Where: An Add Favorite box appears and in the white box
Type: Astute Inv
Click: OK
Where: My Favorite Charts box appears
Click: OK

To check if the chart is properly saved:

Where: Along the top of the S&P 500 Chart highlighted in blue find list favorites
Click: list favorites
Where: My Favorite Charts computer screen appears
Click: The Red Icon in the Astute Inv box.

On the resulting computer screen, a monthly graph of the S&P 500 Index with the Nine Month MA Trend Line shown with a blue line and the Two Month MA Trend Line shown in orange should now be visible. In addition, the computer drawn graph on the investor's computer should now show the S&P 500 Index MACD as the Lower Indicator with the MACD (12,26) line in blue and the MACD EMA (9) line in red.

The resulting computer graph should represent data using the figurative Japanese candlestick charting technique. There are times when custom S&P 500 Index graphs may be useful. How to easily produce these historical graphs is discussed next.

Custom Graphs

BigCharts.com & CBS MarketWatch.com, although appealed to by the author, does not as a rule grant permission to reproduce graphs from their Website for use in other publications. Consequently, the S&P 500 Index graphs presented in *The Astute Investor* uses Microsoft Excel to produce the Japanese candlestick graphs and then transfers them to Microsoft Word. Once the data are inputted, the resulting graphs are superb – easy to read and understand. The MACD portion of the graphs are illustrated using the draw feature of Microsoft Word which produces satisfactory results and are trouble-free to interpret.

For those who would like to view the BigCharts.com & CBS MarketWatch.com S&P 500 Index charts directly however, the custom feature of their Website is versatile and simple to use. Once the BigCharts.com & CBS MarketWatch.com Website setup is completed, so that the S&P 500 Index graphs may be reproduced at any time, use the following commands to reproduce graphs over the time period specified.

Logon: http://bigcharts.marketwatch.com

Where: The time frame in the dark blue box, left hand column
Click: time frame (if not already opened)
Where: The white box labeled Time
Click: The blue down arrow at the right side of the Time box

Where: In the resulting pop down list go to the bottom and find Custom
Click: Custom

This causes the Custom Time Frame: From: and To: boxes to open.

Where: In the From: box (may have to delete what is currently in the box)
Type: The month, day, and year that you want the chart to start (e.g., 12/1/2000)
Where: In the To: box (mat have to delete what is currently in the box)

Type: The month, day, and year that you want your custom chart to end (e.g., 3/31/2003)

Where: The red Draw Chart button
Click: Draw Chart

The resulting graph produced using dates from 12/1/2000 to 3/31/2003 is Graph 4 – 4: Stage 1: S&P 500 Index Market Mark-Down – Downtrend which is discussed in the next section. Historical S&P 500 Index graphs presented in this book may now be quickly recreated on the BigCharts.com & CBS MarketWatch.com Website.

Before investing, check the S&P 500 Index Nine Month Moving Average Trend Line to identify its long-term trend line. Astute investors should examine this S&P 500 Index chart at least monthly to help correctly identify current stock market stages. Practical examples using historical data are presented next to fully explain how to identify the four main market stages over the long-term.

Stage 1: Mark-Down - Downtrend

The S&P 500 Index, Graph 4 - 4, from December 1, 2000 to March 31, 2003, a twenty-eight month time frame, indicates the S&P 500 Index Nine Month MA Trend Line (the smooth downward sloping trend line on the Graph 4 - 4 just above the majority of the monthly candlesticks) pointed downward which correctly predicted the direction of the overall U.S. stock market. Over these twenty-eight months, shown in Graph 4 - 4, the S&P 500 Index declined thirty-five percent, from approximately 1,310 to 850.

Keying on the direction of the S&P 500 Index Nine Month MA Trend Line is paramount, however other confirming indicators are also helpful in recognizing long-term stock market stages.

Stage 1: Confirming Indicators

The following Stage 1 confirming indicators are not all required to conform market direction, but should be checked to help convince investors that the stock market is in Stage 1.

Graph 4 - 4: Stage 1: S&P 500 Index Market Mark-Down - Downtrend

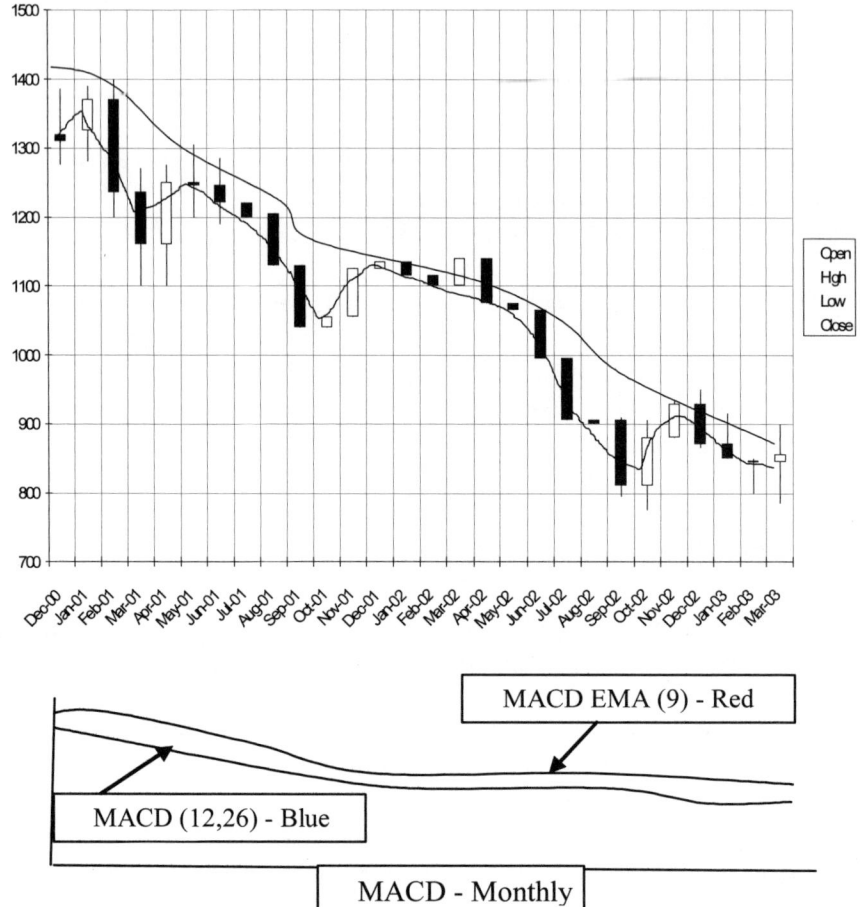

1) The MACD is the first confirming indicator. As shown on BigCharts.com & CBS MarketWatch.com, Graph 4 - 4, the monthly MACD displays two moving averages – the MACD (12,26) blue line and the MACD EMA (9) red line.

When the MACD EMA (9) red line crosses over the MACD (12,26) blue line on the monthly graph, that is the blue line is below the red line, and the Divergence (black histogram) on the monthly graph indicates negative values – this confirms that the long term trend direction in the stock market is now downward. (Divergence is shown on the BigCharts.com & CBS MarketWatch.com charts but does not appear on any of the drawn MACD graphs included here.)

2) The second confirming indicator is that the S&P 500 Index chart, on Graph 4 - 4, shows lower-highs and lower-lows for the S&P 500 Index monthly prices.

3) The third confirming indicator on Graph 4 - 4, the more active and fast responding S&P 500 Index Two Month MA Trend Line (the jagged sudden moving line connecting the monthly candlesticks on Graph 4 - 4) is beneath the smooth downward sloping S&P 500 Index Nine Month MA Trend Line over the entire twenty-eight months.

4) A fourth confirming indicator is the Dow Jones Utilities Average (DJUA). The DJUA is normally in sync with the long-term trend in the overall stock market and its nine month moving average trend line is also pointing downward.

To produce the Dow Jones Utilities Average (DJUA) graph at BigCharts.com & CBS MarketWatch.com, DJUA should be typed into the "Enter Symbol or Keyword" box on the saved S&P 500 Index stock graph and then saved using the procedure presented above.

The DJUA stock graph may now be retrieved wherever requested The DJUA Nine Month MA Trend Line should be further confirmation of the direction of the overall market.

5) The fifth confirming indicator, during a market downtrend, typically the overall S&P 500 Index price may be up in the morning and then down in the afternoon.

In general, avoid purchasing stock as the overall stock market declines. For investors, the power to refuse an investment is his or her most cherished stock market advantage. Lower-and-lower stock prices, relative to stock prices at a market top, may seem a compelling value; but, investing during the markdown stage should be curtailed.

Stage 2: Market Bottom - Accumulation

Once established, the downward trend of the stock market will continue until clearly defined reversal indicators develop. Beginning investors should not try to guess at a bottom, but wait for the S&P 500 Index Nine Month

MA Trend Line to unmistakably point upward which is evidence that a base has formed and a stock market upturn has begun.

The stock market usually takes a long time to change direction based on real political and economic conditions. Once the majority of investors have a set belief in their minds, it takes a prolonged period of time for these same investors to change their opinions and begin investing again.

Improving conditions, after a long market decline, normally have to be demonstrated with significantly increased reported earnings in order to get the investing public re-interested in stocks. Given that human nature is so consistent (see chapter 5), reversal graph patterns have developed that have been continually repeated in the stock market.

To confirm a change in the S&P 500 Index MA Trend Line direction, watch for three possible reversal patterns to form on the monthly charts: 1) a double bottom; or 2) a head and shoulders bottom, in conjunction with 3) an outside reversal day (ORD) on the second trough of a double bottom or the head or right shoulder of a head and shoulders bottom. Graph 4 - 5 shows the Stage 2: S&P 500 Index Market Bottom - Accumulation for November 1, 2001 until June 30, 2003.

Beginning Investors should be looking for the S&P 500 Index Nine Month MA Trend Line to clearly point upward to indicate that a bottom has occurred which is visibly evident in Graph 4 - 5 during May 2003.

The S&P 500 Index Nine Month MA Trend Line, at the end of May, 2003, with the S&P 500 Index at approximately 960, is clearly signaling a bottom for this cycle in the stock market and a new upward long-term trend.

Stage 2: Confirming Indicators

The following Stage 2 confirming indicators are likely, but not necessary, in confirming the changed direction of the S&P 500 Index Nine Month MA Trend Line and should be checked:

1) The first confirming indicator in Graph 4 - 5, is that of a double bottom reversal pattern that occurred on July 24, 2002 with an intraday S&P 500 Index low of 776, and on October 10, 2002 with an intraday S&P 500 Index low of 769.

2) The second confirming indicator in Graph 4 - 5, happened on October 10, 2002 the S&P 500 Index experienced an outside reversal day (ORD) on the second trough – the S&P 500 Index made a new intraday low for the

current move and then closed above the intraday high of the previous day on exceptionally high share trading volume (approximately 2,048,650,000 shares were traded on the NYSE, or 1.5 times the NYSE average daily volume).

Graph 4 - 5: Stage 2: S&P 500 Index Market Bottom - Accumulation

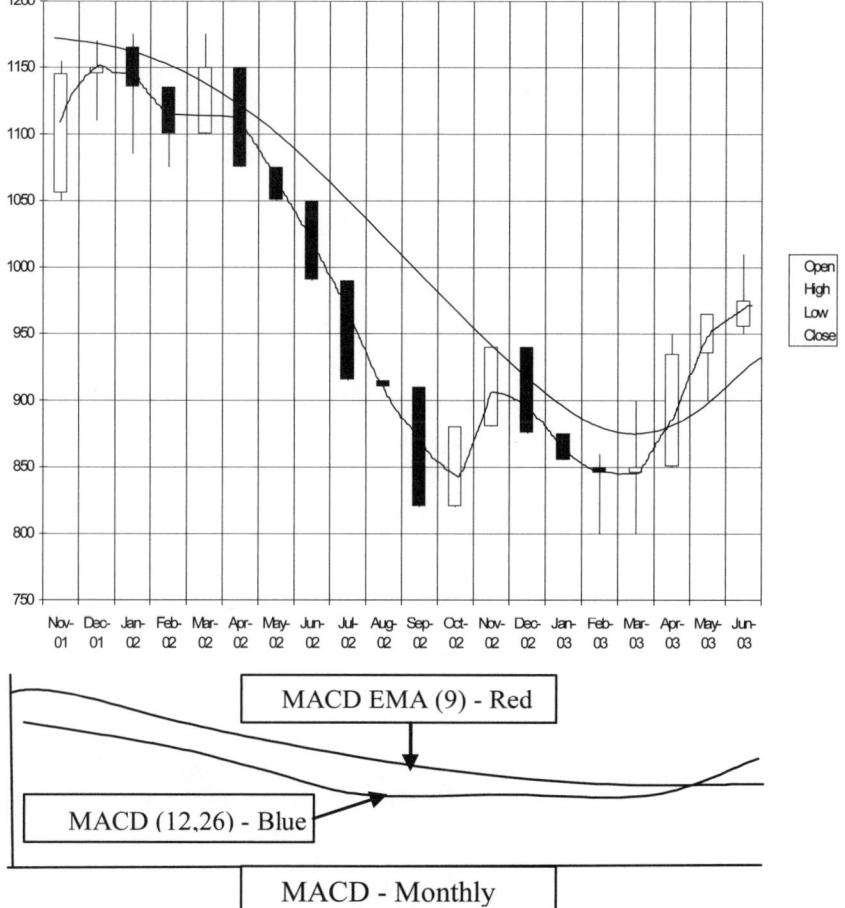

The October 2002 double bottom, and outside reversal day on the second trough persuaded aware and astute investors that this was in fact the market bottom for this long-term market cycle.

3) Third confirming indicator: On March 12, 2003 the S&P 500 Index reached an intraday low of 789 which held above the double bottom lows on Graph 4 - 5.

This could also be interpreted as a head and shoulders bottom reversal pattern (at market lows the person's outline pattern is upside down) with three intraday trough lows — the first trough occurring on July 24, 2002 at 776 (the left shoulder, at about the same price as the right shoulder), the second trough on October 10, 2002 at 769 (the head and lowest price), and the third trough on March 12, 2003 at 789 (the right shoulder, at about the same price as the left shoulder).

4) Fourth confirming indicator: On Graph 4 - 5, during May 2003, the S&P 500 Index monthly MACD (12,26) blue line has crossed and is above the MACD EMA (9) red line; additionally, the Divergence is positive.

5) The fifth confirming indicator in Graph 4 - 5, the S&P 500 Index Two Month MA Trend Line is both above the Nine Month MA Trend Line and in an upward trend in May 2003.

6) A sixth confirming indicator is the Dow Jones Utilities Average (DJUA) Nine Month MA Trend Line, normally in sync with the overall market, is also now pointing upward.

It is during market accumulation during Stage 3 that the astute investor aspires to separate himself from the crowds' behavior (please see chapter 5) and begin purchasing stocks at the appropriate time regardless how bad the news is (see chapter 8) and what select market pundits and experts are saying (see chapter 9).

Stage 3: Mark-Up - Uptrend

An upward long-term trend in the overall U.S. stock market, as represented by the S&P 500 Index, lasted from approximately January 1, 1995 to October 31, 2000 (see Graph 4 - 6) and is represented in the upward sloping S&P 500 Index Nine Month MA Trend Line. At no time during the seventy months did the S&P 500 Index Nine Month MA Trend Line plainly point downward, thus signaling a continued upward trend. The S&P 500 Index increased approximately 960 points, a total of 210%, or 36% per year.

Graph 4 - 6: Stage 3: S&P 500 Index Market Mark-Up - Uptrend

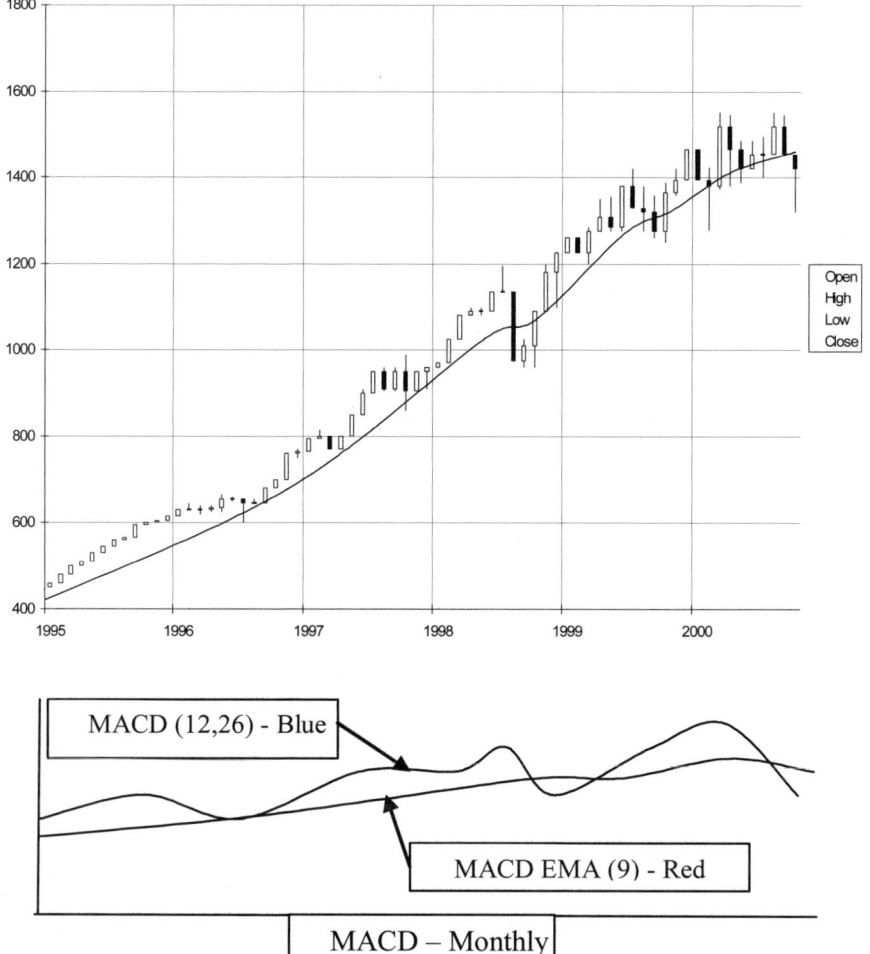

By relying on the S&P 500 Index Nine Month MA Trend Line, investors are able to stay in the market during extraordinary advances and are able to make considerable gains. It is exactly during this uptrend, during Stage 3, that an investor eagerly wants to be investing along with the crowd (see chapter 9).

Stage 3: Confirming Indicators

The following Stage 3 confirming indicators are likely, but not necessary, in confirming the changed direction of the S&P 500 Index Nine Month MA Trend Line and should be checked:

1) The first confirming indicator in Chart 4 – 6, also displays S&P 500 Index higher-highs and higher-lows.

2) A second confirming indicator, during a market uptrend, typically the S&P 500 Index price may be down in the morning and then up in the afternoon.

3) After Stage 3 has been ongoing for approximately twelve months, the issuing of highly promoted initial public offering (IPO) stock, that does well on the day that it is issued, is regularly an indication of a market clearly in a markup uptrend.

In general, the overall stock market takes about half the time to make a long-term downtrend as it does to make its prior long-term uptrend. For this example cycle, the uptrend lasted approximately seventy months throughout Stage 3 and the downtrend lasted approximately twenty-eight months during Stage 1.

Stage 4: Market Top - Distribution

Calling a top or rounding over of the S&P 500 Index is again demonstrated by the S&P 500 Index Nine Month MA Trend Line noticeably turning down. Graph 4 - 7 shows S&P 500 Index price data from January 1, 1999 to January 31, 2001.

Unmistakably in Graph 4 - 7, the S&P 500 Index Nine Month MA Trend Line began pointing downward as of November 30, 2000 with the S&P 500 Index at approximately 1,310. It is at this moment that contrarian investors (please see chapter 9) commence to separate themselves from the crowds' behavior (see chapter 5).

Stage 4: Confirming Indicators

The following Stage 4 confirming indicators are likely, but not necessary, in confirming the changed direction of the S&P 500 Index Nine Month MA Trend Line and should also be checked.

Graph 4 - 7: Stage 4: S&P 500 Index Market Top - Distribution

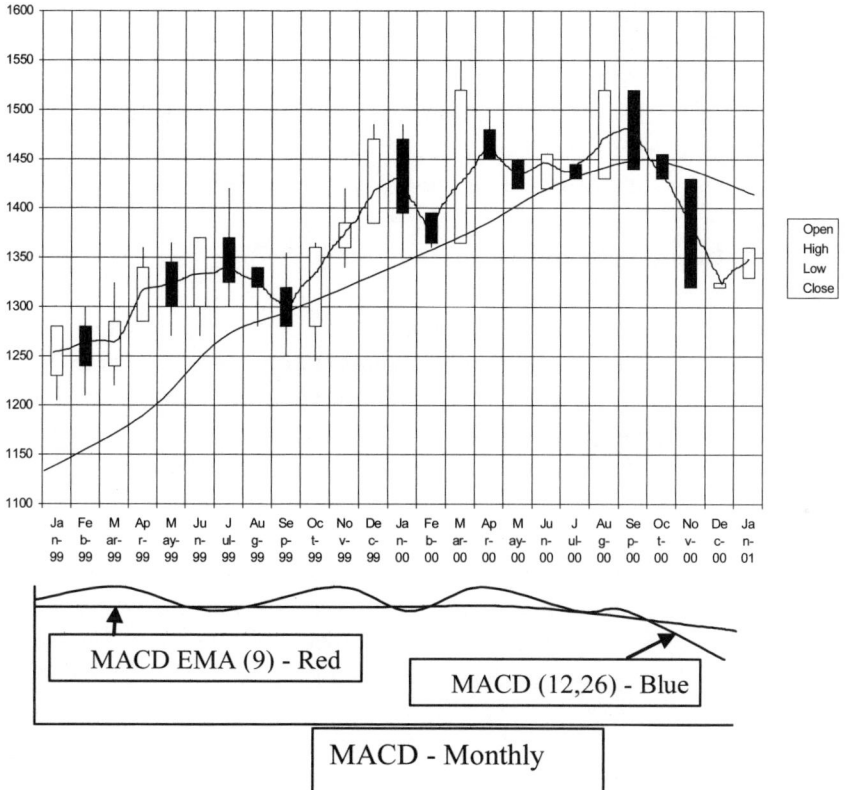

1) The first confirming indicator in Graph 4 - 7 is the S&P 500 Index double top reversal pattern, looks like an upside down W or a letter M, developed with its two intraday peaks in March and September of 2000. The first peak occurred on March 24, 2000 with the S&P 500 Index reaching an intraday high of 1,552. The second peak occurred on September 1, 2000, the S&P 500 Index reached an intraday high of 1,530.

2) A second confirming indicator of the downturn in Graph 4 - 7, the S&P 500 Index Two Month MA Trend Line is below the S&P 500 Index Nine Month MA Trend Line.

3) The third confirming indicator shown in Graph 4 - 7 is the S&P 500 Index monthly MACD (12,26) blue line is below the MACD EMA (9) red line, and the Divergence is negative.

4) The failure of a highly promoted initial public offering (IPO) to hold above the share price at which it is offered, on the day that it is issued, is regularly an indication of a market peak and should be heeded. If something noteworthy happens in the stock market that ought not to, this is an excellent indicator of a changing long-term trend.

Actual Cycle Indicator

The rolling over of the S&P 500 Index usually precedes a downturn in the real economic conditions at a long-term market top of between six to twelve months. The Business Cycle Dating Committee of the National Bureau of Economic Research (NBER), which officially gauges U.S. recessions, determined that U.S. business activity peaked and that a recession started in March of 2001 (see www.nber.org).

The S&P 500 Index peaked for the second time on September 1, 2000, or approximately seven months prior to the NBER declared beginning of the U.S. recession in March of 2001. This falls within the six to twelve month range and is an excellent example confirming the overall stock market accurately predicting a long-term downtrend for this long-term cycle. The S&P 500 Index Nine Month MA Trend Line methodology is expected to work well when back testing historical data which is presented next.

Back Testing

The S&P 500 Index Nine Month Moving Average Trend Line methodology has been back tested over the past thirty-three years to 1970 with good results. Other S&P 500 Index technical indicators, such as double tops, double bottoms, or outside reversal days, have been ignored here even though they probably would have improved these back testing results.

Eight long-term cycles over the tested thirty-three years were evident with the following approximate returns: +15%, +2%, -8%, -5%, -7%, -6%, -2%, +27%. Using the S&P 500 Index Nine Month Moving Average Trend Line methodology to determine when to buy and sell, five cycles would have resulted in negative returns while three cycles would have resulted in positive returns.

Assuming a twenty percent federal and state long-term capital gains tax rate and a 0.5% transaction charge for moving funds to a money market account if the S&P 500 Index Fund is held less than six months, the astute investor would be ahead over these thirty-three years (1970 to 2003) by approximately eight percent, with all other factors being held constant.

Over the thirty-three year time period from 1970 to 2003, the S&P 500 Index Nine Month Moving Average Trend Line methodology is shown to have been an exploitable opportunity.

Summary

The goal of *The Astute Investor* is to transform all investors into astute investors. The exploring-compensating condition normally keeps the stock market pricing extremely efficient during uncertain times; but, at long-term stock market peaks or bottoms, when the conventional wisdom is either all-up or all-down, boom-bubble buying or panic selling can take stock prices high above or well below intrinsic, true, or fair value.

Perspective is crucial when interpreting market signals during the slow moving long-term cycles, so monthly data should be used for the best view of what is happening in the stock market. Share volume characteristics should be studied to help determine the stage of the market and whether the market may be transiting from one stage to another.

The S&P 500 Index Nine Month MA Trend direction indicator helps astute investors determine whether the stock market is in a long-term upward trend or long-term downward trend. The value of interpreting and heeding market signals over the long-term stock market cycle is explained.

Four stages of a stock market cycle over the long-term are identified; Stage 1: Mark-Down - Downtrend; Stage 2: Accumulation - Bottoming; Stage 3: Mark-Up - Uptrend; and Stage 4: Distribution - Topping or Rounding Over, and are indicated by following the S&P 500 Index Nine Month MA Trend Line. The BigCharts.com and CBS MarketWatch.com Website is used to construct the necessary graphs using Japanese candlestick graphing techniques.

Additional technical indicators for the S&P 500 Index act only as confirming indicators such as the: Two Month MA Trend Line; monthly

MACD; double top or double bottom; head and shoulders top or bottom; outside reversal day (ORD) on the second trough of a double top or bottom; monthly lower-highs and lower-lows; monthly higher-highs and higher-lows etc. The confirming indicators all help in giving support to the S&P 500 Index Nine Month MA Trend direction indicator. Not all of the confirming indicators are necessary, but are likely in validating the direction of the S&P 500 Index Nine Month MA Trend Line.

Knowing how to accurately judge and interpret stock market action, as represented on monthly S&P 500 Index stock graphs, and acting promptly are essential to long-term investing success. The astute investor would be ahead over thirty-three years, from 1970 to 2003, by approximately eight percent when taking into account taxes and transaction costs with all other factors held constant. Therefore, the S&P 500 Index Nine Month MA Trend Line methodology is shown to have been an exploitable opportunity. Trading psychology has a marked influence on the stock market which is explored in chapter 5.

5

Trading Psychology

Introduction

BASIC HUMAN NATURE is reviewed. How symbols are used to represent the things themselves are evaluated. The three foremost stumbling blocks to successful investing: 1) vanity; 2) greed; and 3) the will to believe are investigated in detail. Investors are described as being either impulsive or lethargic, each having a unique trading style.

Fifteen desired character traits for the astute investor are listed and described. Rational actions by investors that raise anxiety or self-doubt are explored. Non-rational emotions, such as greed which contributes to boom-bubble buying at long-term market tops and fear which is a factor in panic selling at long-term stock market bottoms are fully discussed. Irrational influences that investors may not be fully aware of in themselves are explained so that investors may guard against these self-destructive powers.

Basic Human Nature

Basic human nature and the human mind are unchanging. Basic human nature may be described as the qualities and character traits held in common with other human beings. Humans may be described as proud, sensitive, vain, fearful, having a need for recognition, and often ambitions, hopeful, and greedy.

Psychology, the study of the mind, concerns peoples' mental processes and their actions or behavior. A person's objective understanding of the facts along with their subjective beliefs – which are prioritized values, be they right or wrong – and a person's needs, wants, hopes, and desires, along with their decisions determine their actions and reactions to life's events. This is the basis for the Life and Happiness Model which is presented in chapter 12. Investors exhibit the following common behavior through time in the stock market.

Common Investing Behavior

Company specifics and economic conditions may change, the investing public may change through time, but actions and reactions in the stock market to comparable circumstances are timeless. Beginning investors continually come into the stock market and make similar mistakes, over and over again.

Many investors find the stock market confusing because they get an idea that they hold onto, and then believe what they want to believe. Although conditions change and no two markets are identical, different stock markets do have essential movements in common.

Although millions of minds are engaged in the stock market, unchanging basic human behavior produces chart movements that continue to routinely repeat themselves as demonstrated in chapter 4. The stock challenge is timeworn, but new and experienced risk-takers alike are persistently pursuing their fortunes – acting and reacting through time with familiar tendencies. The use of symbols are imperative in the stock market and are discussed next.

Symbols

As John Magee emphasizes, society has agreed on arbitrary symbols (i.e., written, spoken, and signed language; mathematics, maps, etc.) to represent the things themselves in order for humanity to effectively communicate. Symbols are indispensable for communication among ourselves, and all of man's achievements make use of symbols. Students learn in an academic setting through the use of symbols, but a person's true understanding only comes through actual experience with the things which the symbols represent (more on this later in the chapter).

Symbols and the substantive things being symbolized can be detached from one another – another way of saying this is the symbols are not the things themselves. A stock price is a symbol and represents, in one number, what is actually occurring within the publicly listed corporation, in the U.S. economy, in politics, in the courts, within the context of natural events (e.g., earthquakes, hurricanes, a pandemic disease, etc.), and in world affairs.

Listed stock prices only symbolize what is actually occurring and represented in political-economic conditions. The expected value for stocks – not its current stock price – exists in the minds of those investors who are participating in the stock market by buying and selling stock based on price symbols. This is covered more fully in chapter 12.

Often, individuals believe the symbol to be a true representation of the thing itself whenever they hope the symbol to be true. However, in the stock market it is best to hope only when factual reasons and the thing itself supports that hope. Therefore, investor beliefs are crucial to success in the stock market.

Investor Beliefs

In the short and intermediate term, overall stock market prices normally cycle through and around intrinsic, true, or fair value and are determined solely by the investing public's beliefs, right or wrong – regardless of the political-economic conditions. Over the long-term however, the overall stock market will anticipate political-economic conditions and investor beliefs should match reality for success in the stock market.

An astute investor's beliefs should not be delusional, but instead closely conform to the underlying actual occurrences of the truth or the things themselves that ultimately determines the long-term direction of the overall

U.S. stock market and individual stock prices. The astute investor should be resolved to recognize the truth of the things themselves and only then to take appropriate action. Clinging to illusions are extremely detrimental for investors as presented next.

Investor Illusions

An illusion is a mistaken concept or a false belief about the truth and or reality. Fred C. Kelly explains how the frailties, flaws and limitations of human beings set up mental obstacles to being successful when investing. In general, people love illusions – especially when these illusions personally involve themselves.

Many individuals are gullible, trusting, and susceptible to plausible reasons for circumstances even when the supporting rationale is specious or not substantiated. Individuals tend to desperately wish to believe in illusions to cover-up for their own real or imagined inadequacies. Investor inadequacies are often a lack of knowledge or incorrect knowledge about the stock market, or possessing the wrong character traits necessary for trading stocks.

The symbolic stock market is linked to political-economic conditions which are real. The symbolic stock market may seem an illusionary challenge but is better thought of as a representation of the truth. The investor's task is to be always looking for and recognizing what the truth is as represented by the stock market. This book is written to help investors confront their illusions and thereby become astute investors. Humans are by nature emotional which is a weakness when investing in the stock market.

Human Weaknesses

Individuals often demonstrate their emotional weaknesses when participating in the stock market. Being emotional in the stock market is an intense natural mental state that may be illusory and not rational. Emotions can create strong feelings that may agitate and militate against the intellect.

Studying typical investor behavior may be instrumental in understanding an individual's emotional weaknesses. The stock market could be considered a human laboratory which gives one the possibility to gain knowledge of the habits and idiosyncrasies of individuals engaged in this voluntary, normally stressful, and exciting investing enterprise.

Many mental perils await unwary investors. Psychological hazards may compel investors to lose money in spite of themselves. For example, why do many investors watch their losing stocks go lower and lower in price without ever selling? Or why do most novice investors sell their winning stocks and keep their losing stocks? The answers to these questions are based on common human weaknesses.

Often vanity, greed, and the will to believe are basic human weaknesses and conditions within the investor's mind that gets in the way of making money in the stock market. These three psychological factors play emotional games with investor's minds and need to be fully understood and closely monitored by individuals to counteract their negative effect on actions taken while investing. Vanity, discussed next, is the first major stumbling block to successful investing.

Vanity

The number one impediment and most inflexible obstacle to investing success is personal vanity. Vanity is tremendous pride in one's self or actions and a sense of exalted self-worth. A vain person's conceit is in evidence even if the resulting action is worthless, futile, fruitless, or does not produce the preferred outcome. By necessity, any resulting poor outcome is overlooked by the vain person.

Not wanting to face one's failures is a common human shortcoming. If an investment is not working out as planned, one's own pride gets in the way of fully recognizing this fact because it would mean admitting failure – especially to oneself. To accept a loss on a stock is an admission that one's initial judgment is emphatically mistaken, and that self-confession is often exceedingly painful to accept. Going to all lengths to avoid facing this upsetting self-confessions is a very human activity.

Small Profits - Large Losses

It is vanity that compels investors to quickly sell winning stocks for small gains, but to hold on to poor stocks and sell them eventually for large losses when the pain of holding them becomes too much to endure. Investors, due to vanity, doing the exact opposite of what should be done is played out time-after-time in the stock market.

A small stock profit when taken is acceptable because that means the investor has triumphed over the stock and this feeling of mastery is a pacifier to one's vanity. A small loss on a stock however may do grievous damage to one's pride. Better, it is thought, to wait out the expected minor dip in price and get out even.

But the small stock loss may turn into a larger loss and again the stock is not offered for sale because a loss of dignity would be involved. Perish the thought that one's stock broker should know that the investor has misgivings and that he or she is now a casualty or a victim of the stock market. Vanity causes investors to resist selling losing stocks against their will because they do not want to feel forced or obliged to comply by the stock market.

Selling the good stocks with small profits saves face while keeping the losers with the hope that they will come back becomes the tactic of choice for novice investors. Even though it is far more likely that the good stocks will come back when the political-economic conditions pickup, due to vanity it is the good stocks which are sold first.

Stock broker's books typically show more completed transactions with gains than losses, however the total losses outstrip total gains because most losses are substantial while most gains on the sale of stock are insignificant. Vanity is blamed for investors selling profitable stocks and retaining losing stocks when the pressure is on. Astute investors should realize that it is far better to sell the losers for small losses, and keep the winners for large gains.

Averaging Down

Worse yet, investors may try to unconsciously hide the fact of this losing stock from themselves. This is often when the idea of averaging down takes shape in the investing public's mind. Averaging down is a strategy of buying more stock, as its price declines, with the idea that the investor can get out even once the stock price eventually comes back up by even a little.

The vast majority of these averaging down investors will buy more stock, in an unrecognized downward trending market, in a stock that already shows them a loss. The investing public may be waiting to get out without a loss even as the stock price continues to decline, until finally it is too financially and psychologically painful to hold on and the sale is made and then quickly forgotten. This is investor's vanity at work in the stock market.

Averaging Up

Rather than averaging down, which is a poor strategy, it is a much better strategy to average up. Astute investors ought to purchase more stock in the same company only when the original acquisition is already showing a profit.

The strategy of averaging up is beneficial because current profits are used, rather than one's own money, to purchase additional stock in the company. Also, do not be vain enough to kick oneself for not purchasing the company's stock at the exact bottom price. It is far better to be happy with the profit that is resulting from correctly selecting the right stock that is in an upward trend.

Margin Buying

Buying stock on margin may also be attributed to vanity. Margin is partial payment for securities where the securities act as collateral for a loan. Margin carries a relatively high interest rate from the brokerage company for the money lent on the remainder of the stock's purchase price.

Pride may be the likely reason why investors feel more important purchasing 500 shares of stock on margin when they only have funds enough for 400. The first objection to buying stock on margin is the investor must not only choose the right stock, but also one that will not have even a temporary dip that will force them out of their position by the margin clerk.

The second objection to purchasing stock on margin is psychological. Always being in the financial control of an outside force during a stressful act like trading stocks will only add to any anxiety that the investor experiences. In a margin position, the investor is under the power of the brokerage firm acting as a creditor and this is not a pleasant expectation or position to be in. With this added pressure, investors are more likely to sell out too early when the stock is advancing because patience is by necessity in short supply.

As the stock price changes, the margin account may fall below a set minimum requirement which then necessitates a margin call for additional funds or the stock will be sold by the margin clerk. The cardinal rule, if a stock is purchased on margin, is never to met a margin call and always let the brokerage clerk sell the position. In this way the investor is forced out of the losing stock, normally at the beginning of a downward trend. In short, astute investors do not buy stocks on margin. Greed is the second leading obstacle to investing success.

Greed

The next enemy of and the way to undermine, after vanity, sound investing judgment is greed. Greed is an disproportionate or insatiable longing to obtain a vast quantity of material wealth. More never seems to be enough. What is wanted is more, always more, with no limits in sight.

Greed gets in the way of astute investing. Attempting to be a hog and craving outsized gains in the stock market is usually deadly to one's financial health. The best policy is to only maintain a position in stocks if the prospective rewards greatly outweigh the possible losses. Greed and optimism often go hand in hand.

Optimism

Optimism plays a role here. Individuals investing in the stock market usually expect the future market to be better than the present market, so they find it hard to sell. Optimism in the stock market is often welcome since it would be difficult to practice investing without it. However, while optimism is embraced, it is best not to become a dupe to optimism. The market optimist constantly imagines that stock prices will continually move higher which may well turn into greed.

Few stock market investors can wait to purchase stocks at bargain prices because optimism and greed gets in the way. Greed is an opponent and works against investors having patience in the market. Investors' greed may also force stock prices higher than intrinsic, true, or fair value during boom-bubble buying at a long-term market peak. A method to counteract greed is offered next.

Counteracting Greed

Voluntarily placing oneself in the position that will take one out of the possibility of making even more money is disheartening for optimistic investors. If the stock continues to advance after the sale and the investor takes this occurrence personally, this becomes a crushing blow to one's ego. This needs to be guarded against.

Because of basic human nature and greed in the stock market, buying is always easier than making up one's mind to sell. The rationale is that investors purchase stocks with the hope and expectation of making money while when they sell stock, investors forsake all hope of additional monetary increases.

The following approach to counteract greed, if followed, will save investors untold grief. At the time of purchase, decide what is a realistic return on the investment and then feel thankful that the stock has now reached that price, and then sell. The third major obstacle to investing success is the investor's will to believe.

Will To Believe

The third psychological hurdle to investing success, after vanity and greed, is the will to believe. Hope is a powerful force in investing, especially among optimistic investors which may describe almost every investor in the market at any time. To wish, anticipate, or have trust that something will fulfill one's expectations in the stock market is the cornerstone of hope.

Hope

Unfortunately, it is too easy to flip this optimistic outlook on its head and have the hope become an end unto itself. Therefore, the investor now believes to be true whatsoever they simply hope to be true. The will-to-believe illusion now substitutes for the reality of political-economic conditions giving this illusionary investing process a surreal characteristic.

The investor may decide they need quick money and may hope that the stock market is going to go up simply because they need the funds to pay medical bills, have a night on the town, or to go on a long vacation.

These somehow confident yet self-delusional investors may convincingly declare that the stock market will advance and make money for them, but in reality they are only wishing or dreaming that the stock market will advance. The stock can not be willed or cheered on to make gains, instead the stock market adamantly refuses to pay simply for one's wishes or dreams for wealth. The will to believe in investors often wins out – with disastrous consequences.

Market Gurus

Those investors who refuse to do their own studying of the stock market, but instead insist on relying on market gurus or stock tips are again trusting to strangers for good advice and engaging in the will to believe. Often this free outside advice is designed to be what the unwary investor most wants to hear or may describe past events perfectly.

The novice investor may wish they had caught the last move in the stock market mentioned by the market guru because it would have made him or her rich, and consequently convince themselves that it is not too late. Discounting is disregarded and investing based on past events becomes the will to believe – again with the expected disastrous results.

Holding On

Another condition of the will to believe is that once investors have achieved a certain success in the stock market they hate to give up even a small percentage of their gains. They have a will to believe and decide to simply hold on for the stock to regain prior gains before selling.

Lets say the investor has made a sizeable sum of money recently in the stock market, e.g., $165,000 dollars, and the market then begins a decline and the portfolio slips back in price and is now worth only $130,000. The will-to-believe investor may not be able to tolerate this setback. Even though the $130,000 extra money from the stock market would be greatly welcome, the investor has already spent in his or her own mind the entire $165,000 dollars and does not appreciate this reduction in funds by $35,000.

So believing the dip to be temporary, the investor averages down and purchases more stock at the lowered price with the expectation that on the next upturn all the stock will be sold at a $165,000 dollar profit. Unfortunately, the upturn may never come and eventually the entire $130,000 profit may now be lost simply because the investor had a will to believe. Investors may be separated into the following two classifications for analysis.

Types Of Investors

In general there are two classes of minds or basic types of investors in the stock market at any one time, each with vastly different approaches to buying and selling stock. The first is the impulsive investor.

Impulsive Investor

The impulsive investor decides to make purchases or sales all at once. Purchases may be made even as the stock advances. The entire line of stock is accumulated all at one time and may be based on valuation calculations, financial analysis, or technical factors.

When the impulsive investor determines that conditions have changed for the worse, he or she will sellout at a moments notice. The small investor is normally characterized as an impulsive investor. The second type of investor is called lethargic.

Lethargic Investor

The lethargic investor rarely ever buys stock during its price advance. This investor may rightly believe that short-term and intermediate-term price swings move some price points away from intrinsic, true, or fair value. The lethargic investor strives to catch these minor price variations from intrinsic, true, or fair value and therefore decides to wait to purchase advancing stocks.

Expecting a stock dip and not being clairvoyant, the lethargic investor may decide the safest approach is to purchase the stock at every half point down for two points. On the other side, as the stock advances in price, the lethargic investor may now expect after a price point is reached that a short-term bulge will develop and therefore leaves orders with a broker to scale-out of the position at half point intervals up to two points.

Large institutional investors such as mutual funds, retirement funds, or NYSE stock specialists may normally be characterized as lethargic investors. Large institutional investors and specialists will not normally buy or sell all at one price. They usually use the scale-in-or-out average price approach for buying and selling. This frequently results in a more erratic stock price movement. These investors prefer averaging in or out of a position rather then trying to move large blocks of stocks all at one time or price.

Large institutional funds or specialists usually have sizeable amounts of capital and can easily set up scale-in buy and scale-out sell orders with their brokers. A normal stock market is usually honeycombed with these scale-in buy orders or scale-out sell orders and an understanding as to how these scale orders are being absorbed by the marketplace is instrumental in judging the market's tendency and technical nature.

Investing At Cross Purposes

Impulsive and lethargic investors take actions that work at cross purposes to one another. The impulsive buying and selling of small investors has the effect of pushing prices either upward or downward. The effect of the scaling-in or of the scaling-out done by the lethargic large institutional investor has the tendency to be in opposition to any stock market movements.

Recognizing when either large or the many small players in the market has the upper hand is beneficial to analyzing the state of the stock market. The following is a discussion of the essential personal character qualities necessary to be a success when investing.

Investing Character Traits

Personal characteristics distinguish one person from another. Character traits describe one's disposition, temperament, moral, and ethical qualities – the sum total of which helps determine one's overall personality.

Sometimes investors have the right personality to trade stocks in the stock market, other times these crucial character traits have to be learned and practiced for an individual to reach their full investing potential. Suitable character traits and investing virtues are as necessary as correct knowledge to be a successful investor. Disposition and temperament are two character traits important to investors.

Disposition is best thought of as a person's usual mental condition or spirit when going into those often challenging life situations. As an example, to have a patronizing disposition is to always be condescending to others and to consider oneself superior at all times. A patronizing disposition should never be adopted when dealing in the stock market.

Temperament is the totality of objective, emotional, and intellectual identity that shapes a person's actions as well as all reactions to life's travails. As an example, to be considered overly temperamental a person may be thought of as being highly strung and ready to fly off the handle at any provocation. Overly temperamental people should find the stock market to be vexing and not to their liking.

Fifteen Desired Character Traits

Many individuals may find that not all of the following character traits presently fit their personalities. Consequently, some investors may be required to build on and practice the proper character traits to be successful in the stock market. Desired character traits and trading actions necessary for successful investing include the following:

1) *Perspective* – Investors need an appropriate point of view on the symbolic stock market. This helps in the ability to perceive interlocking relationships of one aspect to another to form a systematic whole. Perspective facilitates understanding when learning the rhythm of the U.S. stock market. Being too detail oriented is a detriment for investors, learn to pull back to see the big picture.

For the overall U.S. stock market, long-term trends that may take one, two, three, four, five years or more – use monthly technical data for best effect. For super-long-term trends lasting two decades or more, use yearly technical data.

2) *Analysis* – A division of the sum total into component parts for study is paramount in all investing situations. Fundamental, financial, and technical analysis should always be performed prior to investing. Think, observe, concentrate, know what is important to look for, gather relevant facts, build appropriate models, and detect the correct signals.

Investing without doing suitable analysis is pure gambling which is not recommended to be considered an astute investor. Separate the reality and the facts from only superficial hopes or simply the will to believe.

3) *Compliance* – Once investors have developed an investing approach, it is imperative that they adhere to that method during the normal course of investing. Be willing to abide by the methodology that has been developed. Do not decide that the investing approach is all of a sudden not appropriate

without reviewing the reasons why. Astute investors should follow the integrative and practical ten-step method for investing success presented in chapters 1 through 10.

4) *Self-Confidence* – Be self-reliant and do one's own studying. Do not listen to any stock tips from reputed insiders, market pundits, or investing gurus on what the stock price will do in coming months, or the opinions of any so-called experts on the overall U.S. stock market direction or valuation – without checking the facts. Perform the practical ten-step method for investing success and once the facts are checked and one's mind is made up, be confident in one's resulting determination.

5) *Flexibility* – Patterns repeat themselves but never in the exactly same way. Ask yourself, "have things changed?" – be ready to change also. To be foolishly consistent in the stock market is to be obstinate. Obstinacy is not a character trait to embrace in the stock market.

The stock market is deadly for a person who has deep-seated convictions about political-economic conditions that once arrived at are impossible to change. The typical business person from a main stream business may find that a compelling resolve and strong beliefs are character traits that work well for them when accomplishing an important business task. However, on Wall Street that same compelling resolve to see things through is unimportant.

In the stock market it is better to act like a weather vane and be ready to change depending on how the market is performing. The typical business person is often in control of the situation and regularly relies on his or her energy and determination to direct events and carry the day. Neither of these main stream business virtues are useful when investing in the stock market.

In the stock market, only true beliefs, examination, understanding, and proper action are virtues that are valuable. Investors should be adaptable and pliable, and when the many conditions out of one's control necessitates change – investors are required to change in a timely manner with them.

6) *Judgment* – Bring everything together to form a judgment. Always ask yourself, "does my conclusion make sense?" Evaluate, perform due diligence, if you have any concerns by all means go back to the beginning of the analysis. Relying solely on mathematical models to supply the required judgment is not the answer.

Mathematical models may well supply accurate answers given a predetermined and defined premise. A premise is a thesis or a proposition that relies on logic that is put forth for agreement by the group upon which a debate is conducted or a deduction is made. In the practical sphere of investing, the whole problem of success concerns deciding on correct premises. Mathematics does not determine correct premises, it relies on correct premises.

Mathematics may be used effectively only when the premises or assumptions have been finally decided upon by those with extensive professional practical experience and a thorough understanding of the pertinent theories and concepts. Mathematics is an abstract tool, noting more. The point here is that mathematical solutions are only beneficial insofar as the investor has a complete understanding of the questions being asked and the scope of the problem requiring resolution (more on this in chapters 8 and 12).

Relying simply on mathematical models to supply required judgment is poor policy. Mathematics often relies on mathematical certainty and answers the question why, and has a cause and effect relationship. Albert Einstein (1879-1955) is reported to have commented that mathematical laws pertaining to reality are uncertain, and if mathematical laws are in fact certain then these laws do not pertain to reality. Kurt Gödel's (1906-1978) Incompleteness Theorem, that states that mathematics use of formal logic produces paradoxes where particular true statements are not provable within the mathematical system, further cautions against how mathematics is used.

Using a strictly mathematical approach to reducing the stock market to a series of set rules that guarantees success in all market situations should be rejected. Instead, the astute investor should cultivate sound investing judgment to analyze all of the expected state of affairs and then act appropriately.

7) *Conviction* – Upon a thorough consideration of all the information, develop a fixed or certain belief that allays self-doubt and establishes an educated and assured opinion. Recognize that the answer is familiar, feel good about it, and trust one's judgment – be confident in the assessment of the situation.

The type of monetary successes in the stock market which bolsters conviction are those that are the result of one's own experience and endeavors. This is were having the confidence to go against conventional wisdom, at long-term stock market tops and bottoms, requires bucking the crowd and personal conviction.

8) *Be Decisive and Act* – After performing due diligence and a reaching a judgment – act! Both be willing to make the decision and take timely action – have the nerve to act promptly. Timing is most important in the stock market.

The crucial reason that investors decide not to purchase stocks when prices are at a long-term low or sell stocks at a long-term high is that they lack the nerve, initiative, or strength of mind to act on that knowledge – even when they know that they should. Have the right disposition or frame of mind to purchase stocks at long-term stock market lows. At market lows it is helpful to keep fear at bay and have faith in the U.S. Of America, her people, laws, and institutions.

9) *Patience* – Wisdom requires patience. The means to making money on stocks is nothing extraordinary. Yes, knowledge is exceptionally valuable; but, as valuable is having patience. Once one knows they are correct in an upward market advance, allow the long-term political-economic changes to become fully reflected in prices on the scale which is the stock market.

Once having purchased stock, it requires the utmost patience to hold the stock without selling too soon. Timing in the stock market is a crucial factor – long-term planning horizons necessitates extended patience. During a long-term market decline, being able to sit idly by with money only earning meager interest in a bank or money market account is also often demanding.

To wait and only invest when the time is the most auspicious requires self-control and the readiness or capacity to endure often long delay. Leading up to a long-term bottom, the patience to wait until the time is right to invest should ultimately benefit the investor. Have confidence in and trust one's action to work out over the allotted time frame. Greed challenges patience, do not give in to it.

10) *Temperament* – Investing is frequently stressful, consequently do not be high strung. Keep one's mind clear and try to practice poise and composure under pressure and have confidence in the outcome. Enthusiasm, which is enormously beneficial in business or when coaching, is totally useless when investing.

Getting emotional, attempting to give the stock a pep talk, or cheering it on from the sidelines is meaningless. All passionate emotions, be they anger, fear, greed, anxiety, hope etc., will only render the intellect less trustworthy. Remain composed, tranquil, and serene especially when it seems that things are going against one's stock position.

The successful investor learns to take his or her character traits into consideration and permit more latitude for usual faults. If normally too hurried when coming to a decision – he or she will concentrate on reflection and delaying judgment until all the factors are in place.

11) *Humility* – Develop a modest attitude and have respect for the stock market. Remember, the stock market is never wrong, many investors on the other hand are time and again wrong – sometimes tragically so.

The need for personal perfection and high self-regard often prevents investing success. Separate the person from one's own investing position. Do not possess a patronizing disposition, be overconfident, or have an arrogant attitude when investing in the stock market.

12) *Experience* – In the practical and technical sphere of investing, once one has the knowledge and appropriate character traits, there is no substitute for the actual experience of investing real money. In order to fully understand investing, one has to take responsibility for one's actions and commit one's own money on an investment – in order to test one's investing emotions. Be wary of the mental and emotional obstacles of vanity, greed, and the will to believe.

13) *Keep Records* – Write down the reasons, both pro and con, for buying or selling a stock. Review investing results with the idea that right or wrong this new knowledge may be incorporated into revising future investing approaches and decisions.

14) *Maintain Private Counsel* – Keep one's investing successes and failures to oneself. Do not be boastful about big gains or complaining about losses to others – keep one's own counsel. Try to control the need to feel important and guard against the addictive nature that may be associated with stock market trading.

15) *Persistence* – Steady perseverance to become a successful investor requires holding fast to a course of action regardless of the complexity or obstacles that may be in the way. Learning about and practicing successful investing is not effortless but very doable, keep at it. Persist in reading, studying, and improving one's investing technique.

Obviously, some of the above investing virtues may seem to run at cross purposes, such as being both decisive and having patience. However what is recommended is the investor have a steadiness when balancing seemingly conflicting character traits. For example, once the decision is made and action is taken – have patience for the stock position to work out.

Investors are assumed to be rational and to reach completely rational decisions in the Efficient Capital Market Theory. This is not realistic. Investors are not always rational when it comes to decisions and actions in the stock market. The investing public's conduct may be rational, non-rational, and irrational – any of which can interfere with his or her ability to recognize the truth of the thing itself and to act appropriately. It is shown next that even rational investors under stress have to deal with self-doubt and anxiety which may cloud a totally intellectual and reasoned approach to investing.

Rational Action

A completely rational investor wants only logic and reason to prevail in controlling their investing actions. Therefore, he or she would like to know absolutely everything about a company and its stock before making a purchase. However, it is impossible for anyone to know categorically everything about a company and its stock with verifiable certainty.

First of all, the company (i.e., its management, employees, products, markets, clients, suppliers, etc.) keeps changing, and secondly, its future circumstances can not be known with any exactitude. If the overall future economic, political, regulatory, etc. impact on the company are also included, it is hopeless for any investor to know positively everything that will determine a stock's future price.

The closest that the completely logical investor can come, on a practical level, is "necessary and sufficient information" on which to make a decision on buying or selling stock. But, in the back of the completely rational investor's mind is always doubt or a lack of certainty about whether he or she actually knows enough to make a buy or sell decision.

A company's stock price is unable to be determined in advance, without doubt, prior to its outcome. This creates stress and consequently self-doubt in the mind of any investor. This feeling of self-doubt, while facing the fear of losing money on investments, is an awfully uncomfortable position to be in – consequently, this may make even entirely rational investors anxious, apprehensive, or uneasy about their uncertain investments.

Investor Anxiety

Anxiety is based on past painful experiences, and is a natural and rational emotion based on a person's human instinct for self-preservation. Anxiety, which may produce mental-pressure or stress in investors, can subvert an investor's correct judgment. Anxiety and stress can develop in investors during the investigation, buy, hold, and sell cycle of making a stock decision.

During the investigation stage the investor finds, as this is written, that there are approximately 7,500 different common stocks traded on the New York, NASDAQ, and American stock exchanges each day. These stocks are included in a myriad of sectors, including: energy, consumer staples, utilities, consumer cyclicals, transportation, services, financials, capital goods, basic materials, and technology. In addition, companies are growing at different rates, have unique investment needs, and have vastly different prospects.

The investor looks at the market whirl around him or her and feels tentative on which stock would be best to buy. The rational investor may feel stressed or anxious at this point since he or she is not invested and therefore missing out on the action and the possibility of making money. Many investors feel, incorrectly, the need to be fully invested at all times. Consequently, the rational investor may decide to purchase his or her favorite stock.

Once the stock is purchased the stock market does not stop. The stock market goes on and on which beckons to the investor to make more and then more decisions – this results in greater stress, anxiety and unease. Self-doubt, anxiety, and stress are the rational deterrents to intelligent investing. Investors also have to deal with their non-rational emotions.

Non-Rational Emotions

The fundamental examination of companies requires financial analysis, accounting, and mathematical capabilities; but, responding to the way the market ebbs and flows demands that investors be in command of their emotions. The rational head and the emotional heart are habitually in conflict in the stock market. Fear and greed, particularly, are two passionate human emotions that need controlling.

Fear And Greed

Fear and greed are non-rational human emotions that often overwhelms the investing public's ability to think logically or to act rationally. Consequently, stock prices repeatedly move both higher or lower than intrinsic, true, or fair value for a company.

Frequently when investors are either frightened or greedy they will purchase or sell stocks at ridiculous prices, conducting themselves in ways that later appears silly. Investor's feelings often have a more prominent effect on stock prices than a rational understanding of company fundamentals.

After an investor purchases a stock – the stock price may either advance, decline, or fluctuate through the purchase price. The recent investor will experience a range of emotional feelings, some of them passionate, as he or she watches the purchased stock price dance to unforeseen forces. Investors' emotions may overpower their reason and move stock prices beyond intrinsic, true, or fair value.

Range Of Investor Emotions

The following range of investor emotions and actions are characteristic:

Table 5 - 1: Investor Emotions

Boom-Bubble Buying	(purchase at any price)
Greed	(stock way up – holding on)
Optimism	(stock up slightly)
Hope	(purchase stock)
Worry	(stock down slightly)
Fear	(stock way down – holding on)
Panic Selling	(sell at any price)

A new investor may hope or wish that once purchased the stock price will increase, ultimately leading to his or her desired prosperity. Assume that the stock price, instead, goes down a little and the investor begins to worry somewhat; but, experience in an upward market has taught him or her that it is best to hold on to their position.

The new investor may nervously check the stock price daily and experience concern if it continues to decline. Assuming that an upward market prevails, and the stock turns around and rises above the purchase price, now the investor is confronted with an always constant decision – should I sell?

Ironically, investors can feel more emotional when stocks are showing profits then when stocks are in the loss column. Because the investing public tends to sit on losing stocks, the public does not now worry about having to sell. All impending decision requirements disappear and the investing public may rest comfortably.

Emotional Roller Coaster

The stock price may quickly decline through an investor's purchase price, but the new investor convinces himself or herself that this is a short term setback and decides that he or she is a long-term investor anyway. The investing public is often most at ease when sitting with moderate stock losses.

Being down, often the public will hold through the entire downward cycle and only sell once the stock returns to their original purchase price and they can get out even. During this time no decisions are necessary, so the general investing public can wait calmly. If the stock price goes down and stays down and then begins to crash in a general market decline, the beginning investor's emotions may escalate to passionate fear and cause him or her to sell the stock in a fit of panic selling.

Once stocks show a profit however, many investors fear finalizing the trade by selling. Investors may become timid and sell too soon and then watch in horror as the stock now zooms upward. Or, after a long price increase, the investor may experience the passionate emotion of greed, the feeling of wanting more and more, and not sell at all.

The stock price may then turn around and the investor may ride the stock all the way down below their own purchase price. By not selling the investor never feels he or she has to face reality and that tomorrow will be better in the markets than today. The dramatic emotions of fear and greed may trigger the investor to make impulsive, solely non-rational emotional decisions.

Investing Public Craves Certainty

The public craves certainty in there lives and consequently demands the reassurance and security of being instructed in the best course of action. Having been so instructed, the public feels at ease moving in a crowd based on their need for companionship and to feel the safety of other human's company.

The novice investor having been told that everything now looks good for investing, and seeing how far the market has already come, may now feel comfortable buying late in the upward market cycle. The beginning investor finds it almost impossible to resist the general mood of public and mass market viewpoints. The upward or downward movement of the market starts to build on itself as countless new investors now become mesmerized by the stock market's rapid advance or decline and naively see no end in sight.

The passions of greed or fear may impulsively take command of these investor's actions. The stock market now becomes a manifestation of mass psychology and crowd behavior. This causes the overall stock market to overshoot both on the way up and also on the way down.

The Madness Of Crowds

Boom-bubble buying at long-term peaks or panic selling at long-term bottoms occurs when investors act with a herd mentality. Throughout history it is well documented that when people delude themselves and start acting with the madness of crowds that market bubbles are the result. Mass psychology and crowd behavior may determine stock market prices at long-term tops or bottoms by vastly overshooting intrinsic, true, or fair market value.

Charles Mackay documents this mass hysteria during the money crazed obsession of the Mississippi Scheme of 1719, the South Sea Bubble of 1720, and the Tulip Mania that occurred in Holland in 1636. Investor's behavior has not changed in over 300 years. When the entire community becomes fixated on a market scheme, they may take it to ridiculous heights before it all comes crashing down. Human collective movements are measured at their inception, but often they end in a monumental hysterical climax. The recognition of this mass thinking on economic outcomes, especially as it relates to the stock market, should be explicitly accounted for.

As the stock market and stock prices advance, the investing public begins to take notice. Paradoxically, when stock prices surge upward faster and faster the more the investing public wants to acquire these same stocks at higher and higher prices. This forward price momentum may finally result in boom-bubble buying at market tops.

Similar crowd psychology occurs at market bottoms. As G. C. Selden explains – as increased selling sets in, more public selling is engendered leading to general liquidation. As prices crash, the less the public wants to purchase these same stocks at now lower and lower prices. Stock markets have a way of staying down for an exceedingly long time, causing further selling due to the necessity of funds for living or for emergencies.

It is the herd mentality of human nature demonstrating its overwhelming need to follow the crowd. Individuals seem to act crazed when getting worked up by a crowd and only restore their levelheadedness afterward, one person at a time. In addition to anxiety, stress, and non-rational human emotions, investors may have to deal with the following three irrational influences which may also get in the way of successful investing.

Irrational Influences

Investors may also conduct themselves in irrational ways. Irrational influences have the ability to effect investors, often without these same investors being fully aware of their existence and power that they have over them. Most individuals need to feel within themselves that they are superior in some way, any way, somehow distinct, unique and special. These investors may have a need for appreciation and high self-regard.

Need For Appreciation And High Self-Regard

Humans have a need for recognition and appreciation. Being appreciated by others and the need to save face and not look foolish are fundamental human traits. It may be argued that a person's most important possession, and what numerous investors try jealously to safeguard, is his or her own high self-regard or self-esteem.

A person's need for appreciation, high self-regard, self-respect, and pride in oneself may overcome all else, even money. An inordinately high self-regard investor would rather lose money in the stock market than admit to themselves or have others know that their opinion was wrong and thus lower, in their eyes, their own self-esteem. Inordinately high self-regard investors can not bring themselves to exit a clearly losing position because this would be conceding defeat. Investors conceding that they are wrong to themselves or to others, have a feeling of self-inflicted wounding of their own pride and loss of face.

Another high self-regard manifestation is that many individuals love the big payoffs associated with exceedingly risky stock investments or by playing lottery games – although the odds are extremely low relative to the payout, making them poor investments. Needing to dream of the big payoff, bragging to family and friends, being in the newspapers or on television if they win the really big one, becomes the principal motivation. The big payout equating to the need for appreciation and high self-regard, regardless of the odds, is another example of this irrational influence overcoming the practical concern of money.

To help guard against irrational high self-regard, do not take what happens in the stock market personally. The stock market neither knows nor cares who is, or who is not, invested. Thinking of the stock market as an adversary is mistaken, the stock market is utterly aloof and impersonal. The next irrational influence over investors is the need for perfection.

Need For Perfection

The second irrational influence is the high value that U.S. society puts on constantly being right and always winning. The sanctioned need by U.S. society to continuously strive for perfection is often carried over to the field of investing. However, investing is an imperfect arena. Striving for perfection and trying not to look silly in the imperfect investing realm, so that every move in the stock market proves oneself infallible, is self-defeating and therefore irrational.

If a need-for-perfection investor thinks that a stock is going up and instead it goes down, even a fraction, it hurts his or her pride and they do not want to get out then because to take a loss would be to painfully admit to themselves that their original opinion was wrong. This investor may say, "I will wait until I get out at the original purchase price," even as the stock continues to decline. The need-for-perfection investor wants to put off admitting failure as long as possible. After all, the investor may incorrectly reason, "if I do not sell the losing stock it is only a paper loss and not a real loss."

The need-for-perfection investor may look at their portfolio of stocks and decide to sell those stocks with a slight gain because as small as the gain is they can say to themselves, "I have won on this stock" and that soothes their pride. The rational thing to do of course is to sell the losers and keep the winners, but personal vanity often leads investors to do the exact opposite of what should be done.

Even profits are painful if investors hold themselves to a standard of perfection. If an investor identifies with a stock that has been purchased and is performing favorably, it may be hard to sell if they would severely punish themselves for selling too early if the stock continues to advance once exited.

The irrational need for perfection is especially costly for investors. No investor to date has ever made a perfect stock trade. Buying an active stock at the exact bottom and selling at the exact top, over an extended time period, is a mathematical improbability; but, even if the investor did accomplish this miraculous feat, they would be berating themselves for not having purchased a larger number of shares.

If perfection is the standard, one's pride can not suffer the smallest reversal in fortune because the humiliation of looking foolish, especially to oneself, would be intolerable. Consequently, trying to be error free in every action, in an imperfect stock market, and the need to be always proved right is irrational.

The much better course of action is to decide to lose one's mind-set rather than to lose one's money. If investors are to be proud of anything, hold oneself in high self-regard for being capable to identify and act in a timely manner to correct one's own mistakes.

Stock Trading Addiction

The third irrational influence concerns stock trading addiction. The investor may discover that they are compulsive about stock trading and find it habit-forming. As Frank Norris explains, certain individuals get addicted to the fun, thrill and excitement that the constantly beckoning stock market can provide.

Stock trading can become as addictive as alcohol or take on the fascination of gambling. It becomes not a question of the money; but, the fun and excitement of proving themselves correct, having others know that they are triumphantly right, and the need to feel important.

The addictive investor may start to get boastful after successful trades and start basking in the glory of the admiration from others. In order to magnify the highs, the addictive investor may feel the need to risk more and more money on each successive trade. Eventually, the addicted investor may feel that the fun only comes from risking much more money than they can ever afford to lose.

This type of irrational conduct may lead to an investing catastrophe and ultimately to possible financial ruin. For some investors, irrational trading addiction needs to be closely monitored and guarded against. Self-discipline is required to not fall into this irrational addictive trap. Maintaining private counsel may be one way to help protect against addictive stock trading behavior.

Summary

Basic human nature and the human mind are unchanging. Objective understanding of the facts and subjective beliefs – which are prioritized values, be they right or wrong – along with a person's needs, wants, hopes and desires leading to decisions determine their actions. Vanity, greed, and the will to believe are all human frailties that get in the way of investors making money in the stock market. Studying people's emotional weaknesses when participating in the stock market are instrumental in supplying the insight necessary for astute investors not to fall into these same traps.

A stock price is a symbol and represents, in one number, what is actually occurring as a result of political-economic conditions. The symbolic stock market may seem an illusionary challenge but is better thought of as a representation of the truth. The investor's task is to be always looking for and recognizing what the truth is as represented by the stock market.

In general there are two classes of minds or basic types of investors in the stock market at any one time, the impulsive and the lethargic, often taking actions that work at cross purposes. The impulsive individual investor will buy or sell stock all at once which has the predisposition to push prices either higher or lower while the lethargic institutional investor will average in buy and sell orders which has the tendency to oppose the movement of market prices.

Investors should recognize and practice the following fifteen important character traits and actions which are desirable for success in the stock market: perspective; analysis; compliance; self-confidence; flexibility; judgment; conviction; be decisive and act; patience; temperament; humility; experience; keep records; maintain private counsel; and persistence. It is important for investors to have an even temperament, not to take things personally, to practice self-discipline, have poise, and to keep their mind orderly and judgment focused and untroubled during the customarily stressful act of investing.

Human nature and the human mind always has the potential to subvert, undermine, and impede an investor's rational thinking, intelligent recognition of the truth, and taking appropriate action. Investors experience anxiety and stress based on the necessity of using incomplete information, become emotional at times with non-rational hope, fear or greed, and may display the irrational influences of need for appreciation and inordinate high self-regard, need for perfection, and stock market addiction. Irrational influences may take precedent over the investor's concern for money.

Mass psychology and crowd behavior may determine stock market prices at long-term tops or bottoms by vastly overshooting intrinsic, true, or fair market value. Learning about the margin-of-safety investing style and a step-by-step methodology to calculate corporate intrinsic, true, or fair value is offered next in chapter 6.

6

Intrinsic, Market, And Bargain Values

Introduction

MARGIN-OF-SAFETY, THE CORNERSTONE of the Graham-Dodd-Buffett value investing style, is explained for both bonds and for stocks. The margin-of-safety tenet is fully applied and defined when calculating the intrinsic, true, or fair value for a corporation's stock. The investing methodology of Philip Fisher adds immeasurably to the margin-of-safety approach to investing. A prosperous and gifted company or a prosperous because they are gifted company may now be selected which has the best margin-of-safety multiple and excellent growth prospects.

The margin-of-safety investing methodology, based on Warren Buffett's value investing style, is presented in five steps by calculating: 1) intrinsic, true, or fair value; 2) market value capitalization; 3) bargain value; 4) margin-of-safety multiple; and 4) additional crucial factors. Intrinsic, true, or fair value being at least twice the market value capitalization signifies a company meeting the minimum margin-of-safety requirement for stocks.

High margin-of-safety multiples may be rank ordered along with bargain values to determine by comparison the best companies' stock of the group to make an investment. Ten additional crucial factors are specified to be investigated prior to making any stock investment and at least once a year after the investment is made.

Graham-Dodd's Margin-of-Safety

Benjamin Graham and David L. Dodd developed a margin-of-safety tenet that summed up their investing style. Margin-of-safety shapes their investing policies, strategies, and tactics and explicitly ties together the Graham-Dodd approach to value investing.

Graham-Dodd have long been associated with the value investing approach which specifies that corporate value should be revealed through quantitative factors. Their convictions about selecting securities are predicated on the following two assumptions:

1) Securities are often priced incorrectly in the marketplace because of the human emotions of fear and greed. When the investing public's optimism is supreme, investor's greed pushes prices above their intrinsic, true, or fair value which produces an overpriced market. During other times, investor's fearful nature causes securities to decline below their intrinsic, true, or fair value which establishes an undervalued market.

2) Security averages will eventually return to their mean values. The conclusion is drawn that when the market displays inefficiencies by straying high above or below intrinsic, true, or fair value that investors may take advantage of this condition. Profits can be made by assuming that corrective forces will be at work during an inefficient market and the overall market will eventually return to its intrinsic, true, or fair value.

The margin-of-safety theory incorporates how all securities, be they stocks or bonds, should be analyzed to determine their suitability for investing based on a factual value calculation. The approach to a margin-of-safety bond evaluation is presented next.

Margin-of-Safety For Bonds

The margin-of-safety value investing methodology is especially useful when applied to bonds. If fundamental analysis determines that over the last ten years that a company on averaged earned five times its fixed debt obligation charges, then the company's bonds may be purchased with assurance that the bonds comply with the margin-of-safety principle.

Quantitative Analysis

Graham-Dodd rely on quantitative analysis to determine the suitability of bonds for investment. Decisions based solely on short-term data are to be rejected as not significant enough and too momentary to be of any real consequence when judging the suitability of bond investments. Thus, short-term concerns are considered unimportant when compared to the long-term considerations of investors.

For bonds, the ability of a company in prior periods to produce a significant margin-of-safety surplus over any interest requirements is factual proof and may be relied on to shelter the investor from any possible decline in company revenue and profits.

The margin-of-safety concept may be viewed in another way. It may be interpreted as the mathematical factor that identifies how much revenue or net income may deteriorate prior to putting interest payments or repayment of the bonds into jeopardy.

Forecasting Future Earnings Are Not Necessary

The margin-of-safety approach for bonds requires no assurance that future earnings will match prior earnings, therefore no future corporate earnings need be forecasted. If forecasted future profits were incorporated into the bond methodology then the margin-of-safety might be considerably reduced. The bond investor may simply assume that projected earnings will be comparable to prior earnings.

Consequently, projected earnings are not the issue for bond analysis as the entire determination is based solely on historical earnings. Therefore, forecasting future earnings is unnecessary since the margin-of-safety supplies a sufficient cushion for fixed income investors against the vicissitudes of changing future corporate earnings.

If the margin-of-safety is substantial, in this case five times, it may be assumed with equanimity that future revenues and profits will be more than adequate to cover all fixed income interest obligations. The margin-of-safety, relating net income and fixed interest charges, is an adequate amount to safeguard the investor from any unforeseen deterioration of the company's profit.

The margin-of-safety methodology to evaluating the appropriateness of bond investments is relatively straight forward. Using the same basic methodology to evaluating stocks as bonds is Graham-Dodd's distinguished breakthrough and a unifying force in their value investing methodology.

Margin-of-Safety For Stocks

The Graham-Dodd margin-of-safety tenet is also applied to the area of common stocks. There may be times when a company has no debt on its books and the stock is selling for a lesser amount than fixed income securities could reasonably be issued against the company's assets and earnings capability. In this instance, the company's common stock may be evaluated like a bond which follows.

Earnings Yield Higher Than Bond Yield

For corporations with no debt, common stocks purchased for investment may have a corporate earnings yield higher than comparable bond interest rates. Lets assume that a corporation has a historical earnings yield over the last ten years of ten percent a year. Earnings yield may be determined by turning over the P/E ratio. A company with a P/E of 10 has an earnings yield of ten percent.

If investment grade long-term bonds are returning five percent, then the stockholder will enjoy a standard yearly margin-of-safety of five percent (10% - 5%) in the stockholder's favor on earnings returns of the P/E = 10 stocks over bonds. The excess returns may be paid directly to the stockholder in the form of increased dividends, stock repurchases, or reinvested in the business to increase future income.

The surplus earnings power of stocks verses bonds of fifty percent over ten years (5% x 10 years) may supply the necessary margin-of-safety for P/E = 10 stocks and help avert any possible losses on the stocks. Using this methodology does not require accurate forecasts of projected growth rates for companies to give assurance that a company's stock does posses a margin-of-safety.

If a suitably large two-to-one earnings yield to comparable bond interest rates margin-of-safety is calculated, as in this instance, then the common stock may be as sound as an equivalent bond investment. In addition to the margin-of-safety of the equivalent bond investment, the common stock investor enjoys the prospects of increased earnings and stock appreciation.

The only downside is that the investor does not benefit from the legal safeguards that interest be paid on the stock investment. This loss of legal protection may be considered a small price to pay for the expected outsized advantage of the possible common stock's price appreciation.

Margin-of-Safety And Value Investing

The margin-of-safety theory is the cornerstone for a prudent value stock investing style. Common stocks should only be purchased when the stock price is significantly beneath its intrinsic, true, or fair value.

Relying on corporate facts is the appropriate method for determining the stock's intrinsic, true, or fair value. The single decisive issue when calculating intrinsic, true, or fair value is the estimation of future earnings growth relative to capital expenditure needs. The value of an investment in stocks should not be determined based only on what the company will earn next month or the month thereafter, but what the investment is projected to return over the life of the investment.

Stock prices include both investment features and speculation features. Investment features are covered by intrinsic, true, or fair value calculations. For speculative features, Graham-Dodd thought that stock market fluctuations are only the result of fear and greed moving stock prices above or below intrinsic, true, or fair value. Consequently, a dichotomy in stock prices verses intrinsic, true, or fair value may be present.

Conceptually, a company's intrinsic, true, or fair value is found by estimating the growth of owner earnings and then discounting these future owner earnings by an appropriate discount rate. Owner earnings, however, are not the same thing as net income as determined by accounting standards. Owner earnings may be directly equated to free cash flow which is used for our calculations.

The economic value of a corporation should be determined based on a free cash flow calculation that is defined as operating income less total capital expenditures. Free cash flow is then discounted to find the present worth of the corporation. This is presented in a step-by-step approach later in this chapter. For the margin-of-safety strategy to work in practice, it needs to be uniformly applied in a systematic manner with a standardized technique that will help identify undervalued stocks which is presented next.

Margin-of-Safety And Intrinsic, True, Or Fair Value

The Graham-Dodd margin-of-safety tenet is fully applied when determining that common stocks are undervalued or bargained priced based on an intrinsic, true, or fair value calculation. An advantageous disparity between the market price of the stock verses the intrinsic, true, or fair value of the corporation may be determined. A company's stock whose intrinsic, true, or fair value is at least twice its market value capitalization is a deserving candidate for purchase based on the margin-of-safety concept.

The two-to-one advantage is the safety margin that supplies the stock its cushion for any forecasting miscalculations or unexpected market circumstances. The purchaser of undervalued stock, based on intrinsic, true, or fair value, is emphasizing the need to have assurance against the possibility of undesirable future political-economic conditions. It is expected that stocks purchased based on a large margin-of-safety multiple, even if there is a possible reduction in profits, will help ensure that the investment achieves acceptable returns.

Graham-Dodd Limitations

Graham-Dodd concentrate on identifying cheap or inexpensive stocks in which to make investments. Warren Buffett's approach, as explained later in this chapter, moves away from this solely cheap stock strategy.

Graham-Dodd limit their investigation to financial analysis and corporate reports. They give little thought to the type or prospects of the business or to management capabilities. Philip Fisher's approach, as presented presently in this chapter, adds many qualitative factors that should be investigated prior to making a stock investment.

Graham-Dodd advises broad stock market diversification, therefore it is expected to be a mathematical probability that money will be made with an extensive portfolio consisting of many stocks. Concentration, by investing in a limited number of stocks, is not an option for a strict Graham-Dodd investing style. Fisher adds the capability of using stock concentration when building a stock portfolio which is successfully implemented by Warren Buffett.

Margin-of-Safety Conclusions

Intrinsic, true, or fair value may be thought of as the cornerstone of the margin-of-safety policy. The margin-of-safety is instrumental in understanding the investment feature, while investor's emotions of fear and greed help explain the speculative features.

The intrinsic, true, or fair value calculation for bonds relies on historical data only. Intrinsic, true, or fair value is the value of the company's stock that is calculated based on fundamental factors such as revenue, assets, net income, and free cash flow.

Readily Applicable In Three Main Areas

Intrinsic, true, or fair value is a valuable concept because it is theoretically appealing, systematic in application, relies on fundamental facts, and is distinct from quoted market prices. The margin-of-safety intrinsic, true, or fair value approach is readily applicable in the following three areas:

1) The margin-of-safety method works very well with steady interest paying securities such as bonds or preferred stocks.

2) For stocks, the forecasting ability of analysts will be mitigated if the margin-of-safety is significant between its market value capitalization and intrinsic, true, or fair value.

3) The intrinsic, true, or fair value approach is systematic and may be applied consistently to all companies which makes it valuable in stock comparative analysis to rank order investment possibilities.

A stock's intrinsic, true, or fair value may never be precisely determined with the Graham-Dodd approach because security analysis is not an exact science. Many quantitative figures located on the balance sheet, income statement, or cash flow statement may be analyzed mathematically. However, there are still many qualitative issues, such as management expertise and company prospects, which are not straightforwardly measured or evaluated.

Consequently, the Graham-Dodd approach de-emphasizes the importance of qualitative aspects. Quantitative factors are considered the most important that may be easily measured and calculated to arrive at an intrinsic, true, or fair value calculation which is highly dependent on the investor's ability to predict a company's future growth prospects.

Growth Projections Should Be Realistic

Intrinsic, true, or fair value calculations depend upon historically measurable facts such as revenue, net income, free cash flow, and total capital expenditure requirements. The margin-of-safety approach relies on realistic growth projections. The margin-of-safety concept is materially weakened if overly optimistic growth projections are used without a strong logical tie to historical company facts.

The margin-of-safety concept helps mitigate the need for exact future estimates of corporate performance. If the positive spread between the company's intrinsic, true, or fair value price and its share price is considerable then the margin-of-safety approach is useful when choosing sound value investments.

For fixed-income securities, the margin-of-safety approach necessitates that a company earn abundantly more, perhaps five times more, than its fixed interest obligations. For common stock securities, Graham-Dodd demands that the stock's intrinsic, true, or fair value be at least twice its market value capitalization to be considered a deserving candidate for purchase. The Graham-Dodd style of investing is quantitative which leaves room for the following important qualitative issues put forth by Fisher.

Fisher's Investing Style

Philip Fisher takes a qualitative approach to investing. His strategy is that excellent profits may be secured by investing in high potential growth companies that have supremely able management. High potential companies are defined as leading first-rate companies in first-class industries that may be expected to greatly increase their intrinsic, true, or fair value over a long-term planning horizon.

Fisher And Intrinsic, True, Or Fair Value

The way to increased intrinsic, true, or fair value is dependent on growing sales and profits at superior rates when compared to other companies in the same industry and to other industries. Fisher identifies the means-to-the-end of considerable growth to be the qualities of the company's products or services.

Companies who possess excellent products or services that dominate the competition based on low prices, superior features, excellent availability, and the highest quality may be expected to experience outsized growth of both revenue and profits for an extended period of years. Fisher may be characterized as a growth investor looking for leading companies in their industries.

Fisher believes that the business cycle, which is outside the corporation's control, may effect in the short-term revenue and sales results. Rather than taking a short-term approach to investing, he recommends taking a long-term look at historical and prospect company conditions.

High Potential Companies: Two Types

For Fisher, two types of companies may be classified as having high potential and therefore attain above-average growth. The first type are those companies that are both prosperous and gifted, and the second type are those companies that are prosperous because they are gifted.

A company may be considered prosperous and gifted when corporate management posses the vision to identify products, services, or processes that are instrumental in supplying markets that – due to political-economic conditions out of the control of corporate management – are in favor and are rapidly expanding. Thus the prosperous and gifted leading company in the rapidly expanding industry may grow at a phenomenal rate and dominate the competition.

The second type of company may be classified as high potential and attain above-average growth and be prosperous because they are gifted. Gifted companies are those who specifically use their talent or aptitude to bestow on themselves a valuable endowment or legacy of their own making. These gifted companies are diligently working to make their own inheritance.

As an example, gifted companies may use an extensive research and development budget to produce new products or new operation's processes to supply an existing market. The company being prosperous is a direct consequence of their gift to themselves in making their products and services superior to the competition. Market share is taken away from competitors to allow these companies to prosper because they are gifted and consequently are able to grow at above industry rates.

Fisher feels that a significant research and development budget should be part of every high potential company's strategy, for both product or service design and as well for new operations process development.

Sales Organization Importance

The sales organization is examined because increased sales growth is essential when evaluating and considering a corporation to be high potential. Exceptional products and services are only part of the equation necessary for a successful business model, the ability to generate increased revenue is also imperative.

Outstanding marketing, sales, and distribution are necessary to deliver the right products and services to the right customers at the right time. Properly trained sales personnel are necessary to help customers be aware of how the corporation's products and services will benefit them. Sales is the company's contact and face to customers. The sales force may observe how the customer does business and be able to identify new needs or products or services that could be offered in the future.

The link between the marketplace and with corporate research and development may be enacted only with an enormously capable marketing and sales organization. Only at the point of the sales transaction will superior products and services be translated into needed increased revenues for the corporation. Extraordinary products, services, and sales force are by themselves still only part of the equation for evaluating a corporation for possible stock purchase. Superior operations management is the next requirement.

Operations Management Importance

Product, service, and market power taken together are still inadequate. Rapidly rising sales revenue growth by itself is only half the input necessary to determine whether a company is a good candidate for investment. If the company' operations are managed so poorly that the resulting profits generated for the stockholders do not match sales growth or do no better than industry averages then the company would not be considered first rate and would not be an appropriate investment.

Examining a corporation's operations management and operating profit margins are also necessary. Operating profits should keep pace with revenue growth which are paramount for potential stockholders to evaluate.

Invest Only In Leading Companies

Fisher believes that exceptional investments are only attained by investing in leading companies in their industry and never achieved from second tier or marginal companies. Marginal companies may perform adequately or even admirably during economic boom times, but may often experience rapidly shrinking profits during the economic down times that are sure to come.

Fisher wants to invest only in leading companies that are dedicated to maintaining their product, service, quality, and cost leadership in the industry. Second tier companies are not considered appropriate for investing purposes. The most prosperous and gifted companies are in the best position to dominate the competition and increase their own market share.

Increasing profits also give companies the flexibility to easily deal with changing markets, increased competition, or expansion plans, all without the need for new equity financing. A company limited to growing only by issuing more shares of stock in its company will increase the number of shares outstanding which will then dilute earnings per share, and thereby check the benefit to stockholders from any business growth.

High operating profit margin companies with significant earning's growth, on the other hand, will generate significant funds within the company. Internally generated corporate funds may easily be put to work by management to support growth without the need for issuing more shares of stock and thus resulting in a less valuable corporation in the eyes of astute investors.

Invest Only With Superior Top Managements

Top management competence at the company should be evaluated and judged to be of the highest quality. Three character traits are determined to be of utmost importance – integrity, intelligence, and vitality. It should be self-evident that a good investment deal can never be made with unscrupulous managers who can not be trusted. Stay with corporate managers who are well-liked, one has faith in, and are brilliant.

Corporate leaders should consider themselves trustees for the owners of the company, the stockholders, and not simply be concerned with issues that will make these managers seem more important. If corporate management's first concern is how to use new funds for their own self-aggrandizement and increased compensation, by pursuing questionable acquisitions or by mindlessly following what the competition is doing, this is behavior that directly opposes stockholder welfare.

Corporate management's intentions should be scrutinized by what they say and how they say it in quarterly and annual reports. Good communication between management and the stockholders is determined by how open and frank management is in describing what is occurring in both good times and more importantly in bad times. Trying to hide a problem or skirting an issue is an indication that a company does not have an upfront management, consequently these corporate managers should not hold the confidence of the stockholders.

Management leaders should present themselves as embracing a gifted policy. Management should strongly support research and development so that new products, services, and processes may be available for introduction over ten or fifteen year period. This may reduce shorter-term corporate profits, but is important to investors who are frequently in an investment for the long term.

Good working relations need to be maintained with all employees of the company, especially the workers who should be treated with courtesy and respect. The company's policy and actions should demonstrate that merit determines promotions rather than nepotism or cronyism.

Top management is expected to assemble a talented group of functional managers, delegate authority for a smooth running of the business, and have a clear management succession plan in place for the chief executive's position. Top management is judged on its ability to develop, implement, and communicate good policies, and strategies as well as effectively and efficiently run its day-to-day operations.

Interviewing Technique

Fisher also utilized an interviewing technique to help identify leading companies. By interviewing how employees at other companies in the same industry view their competition may be instrumental in gaining an understanding of corporate performance. Often simply asking a manager who their best competitor is will point investors toward investigating a promising new company for possible investment purposes.

In addition, customers, vendors, and subcontractors may be interviewed for clues about company merits. Also, former employees, consultants, government employees, university scientists, and trade-association members may all have useful inputs. The interviewing process may be time consuming, but it is judged worthwhile to gather many qualitative insights necessary for successful investing.

Portfolio Concentration

Fisher's investment style relies on portfolio concentration with an entire portfolio that may consist of fewer than ten stocks. Sometimes only three or four stocks may represent over seventy-five percent of total stock market investments for Fisher.

Therefore, knowing as much as possible about a handful companies is deemed the best investment methodology and is readily worth the amount of time and effort necessary to gather this information. Fisher believes that investors only have to stay within their area of competence, in industries they know well, and do the above straightforward qualitative analysis to be successful when investing. Relying on both the Fisher and Graham-Dodd approaches, Warren Buffett brings together their investing methods with enormous success.

Warren Buffett's Investing Style

Warren Buffett , the director of Berkshire Hathaway, is enormously experienced and perhaps the most highly recognized and respected investor today. Warren Buffett is a extraordinarily successful investor, having increased Berkshire Hathaway's shareholder returns by a compound annual rate over approximately thirty years of over twenty-three percent per year which easily beats the S&P 500 Index benchmark.

Warren Buffett relies on the quantitative application of the margin-of-safety theory and intrinsic, true, or fair value, which is the investing style championed by his teacher Benjamin Graham at Columbia University. Buffett's investment style is a synthesis between the quantitative value approach offered by Graham-Dodd and the qualitative growth principles as presented by Fisher.

Buffett takes the Graham-Dodd and Fisher doctrines to heart and produces his uniquely successful investing strategy. The goal here is to clearly present Buffett's methodology so that astute investors may learn from and adapt it into their own approach to investing.

Buffett Fully Embraces Margin-of-Safety

Warren Buffett fully embraces the Graham-Dodd margin-of-safety methodology to selecting undervalued stocks and implements value investing, in his area of competence, with excellent success.

The strength of intrinsic, true, or fair value investing is that an exciting stock may be recognized using a systematic valuation methodology rather than merely an investor's wishful hopes and desires. The key to the value investing approach may be likened to comparison shopping – looking for, recognizing, and striving to pay the proverbial "50 cents on the dollar" for splendid stock bargains.

Anxiety, non-rational emotions, and irrational conduct may take stock prices to unrealistically low prices; but, a value investor's confidence may be maintained in their investments if undervalued stocks are purchased in good companies at a significant discount to intrinsic, true, or fair value. It is expected that value investing will triumph over any shorter-term setbacks in the stock market, and the stock price will eventually bounce back to affirm a good company's true worth.

Buffett agrees with Graham-Dodd that an investor should shield himself or herself from the emotional torments of most traders in order to take advantage of their often non-rational or irrational stock market behavior. In addition, Warren Buffett includes in his investment strategy the importance of qualitative factors associated with the company and its management as professed by Philip Fisher.

Buffett Incorporates Qualitative Factors

Warren Buffett, like Fisher, highlights those aspects that over the long term are expected to enhance the intrinsic, true, or fair value of the company. Future corporate prosperity and management integrity, intelligence, and vitality are as important as looking only for inexpensive stocks as proposed by Graham-Dodd.

Buying only cheap stocks, as Graham-Dodd seems to champion, is determined not to be the best overall investing strategy. Warren Buffett, as a value investor, may well shun a company with poor prospects regardless of its stock price. Inexpensive stocks are normally cheap because either the industry is under pressure from factors above and beyond management's control or the company itself is mediocre.

The fundamental business may be in such distress that any pickup in business will result in a higher stock price, but the cheap stock strategy can only work consistently if another investor is willing to play the company liquidator role. If company assets may be purchased cheaply enough, at a discount to the stock price, then money may be made upon liquidation of the company if circumstances sour; but, only if the assets can be disposed of quickly. If a long time is required for asset liquidation then the return on this investment is probably less than originally expected or required.

Experience in cheap stocks in weak industries, such as his prior investments in U.S. textile manufacturing, convinces Buffett to retain margin-of-safety as a key concept; but, to move beyond simply buying cheap stocks to include Fisher's growth approach when making investing decisions. Time is the ally of a terrific business, but time is the enemy to a poor or weak company.

Good Companies At Reasonable Prices

The margin-of-safety concept has at its heart the search for a divergence between the underlying intrinsic, true, or fair value of a business and the way the market is presently evaluating the corporation.

Buffett searches for good businesses but is only willing to pay a reasonable price for them. Sound judgment is demonstrated in paying an appropriate price for a business with good prospects. The idea is that buying the securities of good companies at reasonable prices will ensure that the investor receives fair value for their investment dollar.

Buffett learned from Fisher the value of the type of business and its industry, management factors, interviewing efforts, and the strategy of concentration on investing in only a relatively few stocks rather than broad diversification. Like Fisher, thoroughly knowing and understanding the few companies that are being invested in, rather than taking a less knowledgeable diversification approach, is the Buffett investing style of choice.

The synthesized Warren Buffett style of stock selection, that relies extensively on the proper calculation for a corporation's intrinsic, true, or fair value, is presented here. An investigation into additional crucial factors that go into making the investment decision are also explained.

The following example goes through a step-by-step methodology for calculating corporate intrinsic, true, or fair value, market value capitalization, bargain value, and the margin-of-safety multiple. High margin-of-safety multiples and bargain values for different companies may be rank ordered and compared to help determine the best stocks of the group to make investments.

Step 1: Calculating Intrinsic, True, Or Fair Value

Intrinsic, true, or fair value of a corporation is that value solely contained within the corporation and is best determined by a sound calculation methodology conducted by an investor after reviewing all relevant facts, and making appropriate estimates of future conditions.

Fundamental analysis is relied on to determine intrinsic, true, or fair value which is then compared to corporate value as denoted by the marketplace. It is expected that the marketplace price will move toward the corporation's intrinsic, true, or fair value over a period of time. That is the market will eventually recognize the corporations true, fair, or intrinsic, true, or fair value and respond appropriately.

Cash Flow Statement

The method for calculating intrinsic, true, or fair value for a corporation begins with the Cash Flow Statement (CFS). A cash flow statement for each U.S. public corporation is filed with the Securities and Exchange Commission and the information may be found in the corporation's annual report, on the corporation's Website, on financial Websites, or available on-line from most stock brokers.

The Cash Flow Statement (CFS) is where the company reports on where it receives its cash and what it does with its cash over a fixed period of time. The CFS has the following three sections:

1) Cash from Operating Activities
2) Cash from Investing Activities
3) Cash from Financing Activities

The last section, Cash from Financing Activities, is not needed for our use and is therefore not presented or discussed.

The intrinsic, true, or fair value calculation uses the cash from operating activities section's bottom line figure (in bold numbers in Table 6 - 1). From the cash from investing activities section, the figure from property and equipment costs, the acquisition costs of other company's subsidiaries, plus any proceeds from the sale of assets are summed. The following example cash flow statement (CFS) is presented in Table 6 - 1 for the fictitious XYZ Corporation.

To indicate required information, only the data necessary for our use have been included in Table 6 - 1. The Purchase of Investments, and Maturities and Sales of Investment accounts are not needed for our purposes and consequently have been left blank. The figures in parentheses – e.g., the (239) in year 2003 – in the capital expenditures row indicates a negative number (i.e., an increase in the use of funds). All monetary figures are shown in millions of dollars.

Total Capital Expenditures

When total capital expenditures are supplied out of the company's cash from operating activities, then corporate management will not be required to secure additional money from sources outside the company.

Purchasing property and equipment, the acquisition/disposition costs of purchasing or selling subsidiaries, plus any proceeds from the sale of other assets are defined here as total capital expenditure costs. To determine total capital expenditures, simply add the three account rows together for each time period.

Often times a capital expenditures account is substituted on a summary cash flow statement available on many independent Websites offering financial report information. This capital expenditure account typically includes only property and equipment costs and is therefore incomplete for our use.

171

Table 6 - 1: XYZ Corporation - Cash Flow Statement
(in millions of dollars)

Year	1999	2000	2001	2002	2003
Net Income					
(Etc.)					
Cash from Operating Activities	**62**	**85**	**111**	**123**	**319**
Purchase Of Property And Equip.	(24)	(44)	(66)	(69)	(44)
Purchase of Investments					
Maturities and Sales of Investments*					
Proceeds from Sale of Assets			10	12	
Acquisitions, net of cash acquired					(195)
Cash from Investing Activities					

*Accounts not pertinent for the calculation of free cash flow.

Astute investors should ensure that they find the complete breakout of the cash from the investing activities section. The complete breakout may be usually located on the specific corporation's Website. It is important to include the purchase of acquisitions since acquisitions will typically increase the cash flow from operating activities when the subsidiary company operations are incorporated.

The disposition of subsidiaries will reduce total capital expenditures and should also reduce corporate operating cash flows associated with the subsidiary sold. Since the definition of free cash flow (FCF) is not standardized by the accounting profession, astute investors should also question a FCF figure when listed alone on many financial Websites. Astute investors should make sure of all accounts going into a FCF calculation.

Total capital expenditures should be determined by subtracting the purchase of property and equipment, the acquisition/disposition costs or gains from the purchase or sale of subsidiaries, plus the addition of any proceeds from the sale of other assets. Free cash flow may now be calculated which is the basis for determining a corporation's intrinsic, true, or fair value.

Free Cash Flow Calculation

Free cash flow (FCF) is calculated by adding the normally negative total capital expenditures derived from the cash from investing activities section of the cash flow statement (CFS) for the year to the hopefully positive cash from operating activities for the year.

Astute investors are searching for companies that have the strongest positive FCF growth. Positive FCF is considered a benefit because management then has the option of increasing dividends, buying back their own stock, developing promising new products/markets, or meeting competitive challenges all without the need to raise additional funds from outside sources.

The free cash flow (FCF), for XYZ Corporation in our example, is calculated by adding together the positive cash from operating activities and the negative (shown in parentheses) property and equipment, and the acquisition costs of purchasing subsidiaries, plus any proceeds from the sale of other assets.

Some financial Websites may call the three accounts of interest: 1) Property and Equipment; 2) Acquisitions/Disposition of Subsidiaries; and

3) Other Investing Activities – which should all be added together to get Total Capital Expenditures for the period. For a good example as this is written, see the Zacks Website at www.zacks.com for a breakout of these three accounts for each company's financial cash flow statement under study.

The resulting free cash flow, in millions of dollars, for XYZ corporation is presented in Table 6 - 2:

Table 6 - 2: XYZ Corporation - Free Cash Flow
(in millions of dollars)

Year	1999	2000	2001	2002	2003
Cash from Operating Activities	62	85	111	123	319
*Total Capital Expenditures	(24)	(44)	(56)	(57)	(239)
Free Cash Flow (FCF)	**38**	**41**	**55**	**66**	**80**

Total capital expenditures are determined by subtracting the purchase of property and equipment (sometimes called capital expenditures), the acquisition/disposition costs or gains from the purchase or sale of subsidiaries, plus the addition of any proceeds from the sale of assets.

From Table 6 - 2, free cash flow (FCF) has been growing by approximately twenty percent a year from 1999 to 2003 ($38 x 1.2 x 1.2 x 1.2 x 1.2 = $79). The annual report also indicates that the five year growth rate for XYZ Corporation's sales revenue and net income are growing by approximately twenty percent per year.

With sales, profits and FCF all increasing by approximately twenty percent per year, astute investors may feel confident in using a twenty percent growth rate figure over a specified time period to make expected future calculations for the XYZ Corporation.

Discounting Free Cash Flow

Because a dollar in the future is worth less than a dollar today, the astute investor will discount future free cash flow by a risk-free discount rate. The 30-Year U.S. Treasury Bond (T-Bond) interest rate is used for discounting the risk-free rate of return.

The current 30-Year T-Bond interest rate may be located on the CNBC - MSN Money Website at http://moneycentral.msn.com/investor/home.asp as presented in chapter 3. As this is typed, the 30-Year T-Bond interest rate is 5.45 percent after having made a rapid advance over the prior two months. Therefore, a five percent risk-free discount rate may be considered appropriate.

When discounting future free cash flow by the risk-free discount rate, the single payment present worth factor is utilized. The present worth factor (P/F) means that given future worth values these P/F's are used to bring the future values back in time to present worth values.

Present Worth Factors

Present worth factors (P/F) may be easily calculated using the formula: 1 divided by (1 + i) raised to the power of n (where i = interest rate, and n is the number of years in the future). Normally, compound interest tables are employed which are found in many finance textbooks, in virtually all engineering economy texts, and on many quantitative factor Websites. A Website address is offered next as an easily accessible source of present worth factors.

The present worth factors (P/F) for a five percent discount rate are now necessary for our calculations and may be found, as this is written, at www.outfo.org which is the Open Information Project Website. The different interest rates are represented by i and the years into the future are represented by n. To use this Website to find P/F's for 5%:

Logon: www.outfo.org

Where: Top of page find Science

175

Click: Science
Where: Middle of page under Science find Economics
Click: Economics

Where: Middle of page under Economics find Discount Factors
Click: Discount Factors
Where: Middle of page under Discount Factors find Tables
Click: Tables
Where: Middle of page under Discount Factors - Tables: find the Table for i = 5.00%
Click: Table for i = 5.00%

The present worth factors necessary for the intrinsic, true, or fair value calculation are located in the P/F column. The single payment present worth factors (P/F) for 5.00 percent are shown in Table 6 - 3: Discount Present Worth Factors (P/F). Only those present worth factors (P/F) that are needed for our calculations are included in Table 6 - 3 for years one through eleven.

Table 6 - 3: Discount Present
Worth Factors (P/F)

5.00%	Single Payment
n (years)	Present Worth Factor **P/F**
1	0.9524
2	0.9070
3	0.8638
4	0.8227
5	0.7835
6	0.7462
7	0.7107
8	0.6768
9	0.6446
10	0.6139
11	0.5847

Intrinsic, True, Or Fair Value: First Stage

Future worth free cash flow values at different points in time may now be brought back to a present worth value and summed to represent the corporation's intrinsic, true, or fair value. The corporate present worth calculation of intrinsic, true, or fair value is then compared to the market value capitalization to calculate bargain values.

As Robert G. Hagstrom, Jr. explains, when a corporation's free cash flow (FCF) increases faster than the risk-free discount rate a two-stage valuation model may be prepared. The astute investor may assume that the XYZ Corporation's twenty percent growth rate may only continue for the next ten years, followed by a slower growth rate thereafter.

Table 6 - 4 shows the expected future twenty percent a year increase of XYZ Corporation's free cash flow (FCF) (in the third row), over the next ten years. The present worth factors (PWF) (which have been rounded off) from Table 6 - 3 are used to discount the future FCF figures back to today's prices (called present worth of FCF) which are located in the last row in Table 6 - 4:

The intrinsic, true, or fair value of XYZ Corporation for the first stage is the sum of the future ten years of the present worth of the discounted free cash flow values, residing in the last row of Table 6 - 4, and is: ($91 + $105 + etc... + $302) which equals $1,789 million dollars.

Intrinsic, True, Or Fair Value: Second Stage

The second stage assumes that XYZ Corporation will grow at a slower rate after year ten, let's assume five percent, and that the risk-free discount rate of interest will increase to eight percent. The Capitalization Rate is calculated by subtracting the expected second stage growth rate of five percent from the expected risk-free discount rate of eight percent which is (8% - 5%) equals a three percent capitalization rate.

A two percent capitalization rate would assume a higher corporate growth rate (e.g., eight percent discount rate less a six percent growth rate equals two percent) and may be considered an aggressive valuation. A four percent capitalization rate would assume a lower corporate growth rate (e.g., eight percent discount rate less a four percent growth rate equals four percent) and may be considered a conservative valuation.

Table 6 - 4: XYZ Corp. - Stage 1: Expected Discounted FCF to Today's Prices

Future Years	1	2	3	4	5	6	7	8	9	10
Prior Yr's FCF	80*	96	115	138	166	199	239	287	344	413
Growth/Yr	20%	20%	20%	20%	20%	20%	20%	20%	20%	20%
Free Cash Flow	96**	115	138	166	199	239	287	344	413	495
Pres. Wth. Factors	0.95	0.91	0.86	0.82	0.78	0.75	0.71	0.68	0.64	0.61
Present Worth of FCF	91#	105	119	136	155	179	204	234	264	302

* Actual Free Cash Flow (FCF) of XYZ Corporation in Year 2003

** Multiply $80 million dollars x 1.2 = $96 million dollars

\# Multiply $96 million dollars x 0.95 = $91 (rounded off) million dollars

The free cash flow (FCF) value in year eleven would increase from $495 million dollars, the FCF in year ten from Table 6 - 4 (third row), by five percent to 1.05 x $495 = $520 million dollars.

To calculate the present worth from year eleven of a uniform series of all future FCF values, divide the $520 million dollars by the capitalization rate of three percent which equals $17,333 million dollars. Bring the $17,333 million dollars to today's prices by multiplying by the present worth factor (PWF) of 0.58 (from Table 6 - 3: Discount Present Worth Factors (P/F) for year eleven). The second stage intrinsic, true, or fair value equals $17,333 times 0.58 totaling $10,053 million dollars.

XYZ Intrinsic, True, Or Fair Value

The intrinsic, true, or fair value for both stages are then added together to equal the intrinsic, true, or fair value for XYZ Corporation. XYZ intrinsic, true, or fair value for stages 1 + 2 equals $1,789 plus $10,053 or $11,842 million dollars. The next step is to calculate the market value capitalization of the XYZ Corporation.

Step 2: Calculating Market Value Capitalization

Calculating the market value capitalization of a corporation is imperative to determine how investors are currently valuing the corporation. From XYZ Corporation's annual report, the company's Website, or on-line stock brokers the total diluted number of shares that are outstanding (including common and preferred stock, options, warrants, and convertible bonds) and the current stock price are identified.

XYZ Corporation's market value capitalization is the total diluted number of shares outstanding (let's assume 190 million diluted shares here) multiplied by current stock price (let's assume $30 dollars per share). The market value capitalization, which is also in today's dollars, for XYZ Corporation is: XYZ market value capitalization equals 190 million diluted shares times $30/share totaling $5,700 million dollars.

A bargain value may now be calculated based on a comparison of XYZ Corporation's intrinsic, true, or fair value and market value capitalization.

Step 3: Calculating Bargain Value

Bargain values may now be calculated for all of the companies under consideration for purchase. A positive bargain value would signify an undervalued company and a negative bargain value would signify an overvalued company.

XYZ Bargain Value

The intrinsic, true, or fair value for XYZ Corporation is now compared to the market value capitalization of XYZ Corporation. If the intrinsic, true, or fair value for XYZ Corporation is superior to its market value capitalization, then the corporation is undervalued. The bargain value calculation for XYZ is the $11,842 million dollars of intrinsic, true, or fair value less the $5,700 million dollars of market value capitalization to equal $6,142 million dollars. XYZ Corporation is undervalued by $6,142 million dollars.

Step 4: Calculating Margin-of-Safety Multiple

Determining if the intrinsic, true, or fair value is at least twice the market value capitalization is the cornerstone of the margin-of-safety value investing style. This is determined by calculating the margin-of-safety multiple.

Margin-of-Safety Multiple

The margin-of-safety multiple is calculated by dividing XYZ's intrinsic, true, or fair value of $11,842 million dollars by its market value capitalization of $5,700, equaling 2.08.

Because the intrinsic, true, or fair value is slightly over twice the market value capitalization, this prospective purchase will qualify as being within Graham-Dodd-Buffett's margin-of-safety for stocks and be considered an acceptable buy.

Rank Ordering Margin-of-Safety Multiples

The margin-of-safety multiple for each corporation investigated may then be rank ordered, highest to lowest multiple, along with their bargain value to help determine by comparison the best companies' stock of the group to make an investment.

A presentation of the synthesized Warren Buffett style of stock selection is shown to rely extensively on the proper calculation for a corporation's intrinsic, true, or fair value. Once the intrinsic, true, or fair value, market value capitalization, bargain value, and a margin-of-safety multiple calculations are made; an investigation into the following additional crucial factors are performed. Ten additional crucial factors necessary for study are presented next in Step 5.

Step 5: Additional Crucial Factors

In addition to calculating corporate intrinsic, true, or fair value, market value capitalization, bargain value, and a margin-of-safety multiple – it is necessary to augment these calculations to get a more complete analysis of the prospective corporation being considered for investment.

Initial And Yearly Calculations

Prior to investing in a company using rank ordering of margin-of-safety multiples and bargain values, and at least once a year after investing in that company, it is always prudent to test for solvency, corporate capitalization, return on equity, operating profit margin, and the many qualitative factors championed by Philip Fisher.

Solvency is the capability of corporate management to pay all liabilities in a timely manner. Corporate capitalization is the amounts and types of debt and equity financing used by corporations. Timely debt payment allows management to stay away from legal proceedings which may result when there is a default on corporate debt.

Problems in debt payment may force a company into bankruptcy. Bankruptcy may force a company out of business, or severely disrupt operations if the company goes through a court ordered reorganization, either of which would be decidedly detrimental to the share price and to stockholder's value. A review of all of the above issues may be made by investigating the ten additional crucial factors in points one through ten that follow.

Ten Additional Crucial Factors

The ten additional crucial quantitative and qualitative factors follow beginning with the current ratio calculation.

1) Calculate the current ratio – total current assets divided by total current liabilities –

which is located in the most up to date balance sheet. The current ratio tests the short-term liability-paying capability of the corporation. In general, the current ratio should be greater than two to one.

Creditors prefer a cushion of twice the assets to liabilities as a safeguard for the reimbursement of their short-term liabilities. It is fully expected that a company should stay solvent and pay back its liabilities in a timely manner. Short-term providers of credit, since they are not owners and do not receive a portion of the profits, seek to minimize as much as possible their risk on such loans.

2) Determine the debt-to-equity ratio – total liabilities divided by total stockholders equity. Some debt may be appropriate, but substantial debt is clearly dangerous to stockholder and corporate viability if and when political-economic conditions change for the worst. If a corporation is overextended with debt it is important that it be identified.

All liabilities, whether long or short and interest or non-interest bearing, are included along with all owner's equity. Leverage refers to the quantity of debt a corporation has on its balance sheet. Many industries have an effective maximum limit of a one-to-one debt to equity ratio – and such companies may be considered highly leveraged.

Other industries, such as utilities and financial corporations may normally experience higher debt to equity ratios. Existing debt requirements for leading companies are expected to be low and getting lower every year as the cash flow from operations are expected to be ample to pay down any debt.

3) Calculate return-on-equity (ROE) – annual net income, less dividends on preferred capital stock from the income statement, divided by stockholders' equity from the balance sheet. Profit is compared to the amount

of equity that the owners have put into the corporation. The ROE should be a high percentage, over twenty percent may normally be considered good, and may be compared with industry averages.

The opportunity cost of capital concept is useful here. If equity funds could be invested in other ways to earn more than the invested company's ROE, then the opportunity cost of capital of the alternative investment would be forfeited. Therefore, the alternative investment may well be the better investment of the two.

4) Identify operating earnings, from the income statement, which are the earnings before interest and tax (EBIT) payments. Calculate the operating profit margin (OPM) by dividing the EBIT operating earnings by net sales. OPM reveals how effective and efficient the corporation's operations are and should be closely monitored. Ideally, the OPM should be a high percentage of perhaps fifty percent or higher. The OPM percentage should not be materially worsening over time.

5) Basic net earnings per share (EPS) and diluted net earnings per share (DEPS) (the denominator now includes common and preferred stock, options, warrants, and convertible bonds) figures should be appropriate and improving in line with the corporation's revenue growth.

6) The long term prospects, based on the investor's area of competence, for the company and the company's industry must be judged and be considered either prosperous and gifted or prosperous because they are gifted.

7) Top management's integrity, intelligence, and vitality should be investigated to insure that they are of the highest quality. Issues such as looking out for stockholder welfare, effective communication skills, endorsing research and development, good employee relations, and a talented management team with a clear succession plan in place are all important factors for study.

Corporate management is judged on its ability to develop, implement, and communicate good policies, and strategies as well as effectively and efficiently run the day-to-day operations of the company.

8) An outstanding marketing/sales/distribution organization should be in place to grow sales revenue. Sales personnel are the company's contact and face to customers. The link between the marketplace and with corporate research and development may be enacted only with an exceptionally capable marketing and sales organization.

9) Invest in leading first-line companies with excellent operations management that can translate increasing sales revenue into correspondingly increasing profits. Research and development into effective and efficient operations' processes should be ongoing.

10) Interviewing customers, vendors, subcontractors, government, university scientists and employees at other companies may give insight into the nature of the corporation or leads to alternative investment ideas.

By investigating the above ten crucial factors and making intrinsic, true, or fair value, market value capitalization, bargain value, and margin-of-safety multiple calculations – the necessary due diligence is performed to make appropriate value investing decisions.

Summary

Benjamin Graham offers the conviction that stocks are often incorrectly priced and that they will eventually return to their mean values. He along with David L. Dodd develop a margin-of-safety principle that relies on quantitative data to analyze both stocks and bonds using a common research methodology.

While Graham-Dodd concentrate on identifying cheap stocks in which to make investments, Philip Fisher champions a qualitative investing style with the idea that high potential growth companies make the best investments. The company under study should be considered either prosperous and gifted or prosperous because they are gifted, have outstanding marketing/sales/distribution to grow revenue, and have excellent operations management to increase corporate profits.

Warren Buffett embraces the Graham-Dodd margin-of-safety concept, but has moved away from simply buying cheap stocks to incorporating Fisher's ideas which results in a strategy of paying reasonable prices for good companies. Value investing relies as much as possible on corporate facts and sound methodology rather than minimally using current stock prices and hopeful thinking.

Warren Buffett style stock selection relies extensively on the proper step-by-step calculation for a corporation's intrinsic, true, or fair value, market value capitalization, bargain value, and margin-of-safety multiple to help determine appropriate stock investments. Additional crucial factors, such as solvency, corporate capitalization, return on equity, corporate/

industry prospects, and management's integrity, intelligence, and vitality should be reviewed and judged suitable prior to investing and at least once a year thereafter. Margin-of-safety multiples and bargain values, when rank ordered, should help in making comparisons and identifying the best common stocks for investment. A concentrated stock portfolio may now be assembled.

Identifying undervalued stocks using Warren Buffett's methodology has many strengths. Perhaps the most important is that it presents a model that is appropriate and consistent in its methodology so that different companies' results may be uniformly compared. Consequently, selected stocks with high margin-of-safety multiples, high bargain values, and excellent additional crucial factors are expected to triumph over any anticipated setbacks in the marketplace.

7

Interest Rate Principles

Introduction

INTEREST IS DEFINED. Why interest rates adjust through time is reviewed. Fiscal and monetary policies, controlled by the U.S. federal government, help achieve political and economic goals which are discussed in detail.

It is explained how the Federal Reserve, the U.S. central bank, manages the money supply through reserve requirements, the discount rate, and open market operations which are controlled by the Federal Open Market Committee (FOMC). An example of FOMC meeting minutes explaining the modification to the federal funds rate is presented. How to locate additional meeting minutes on their Website is specified.

How a yield curve is constructed using federal funds and government security interest rates is presented. The following four types of yield curves: 1) normal; 2) steep; 3) inverted; and 4) flat or humped are explained. How to interpret these yield curves and what they may represent in relation to the political-economic condition are discussed.

A dynamic yield curve Website is offered so that yield curves may be easily drawn for most historical dates. Why the interest rate spread is a good leading political-economic indicator is specified. And perhaps most importantly, it is explained why monitoring the federal funds and 30-Year T-Bond interest rate spread will help identify an expected long-term stock market peak.

Interest Defined

Interest is the price demanded by a lender on money provided to a borrower for the use of their funds. Interest is the rate charged, normally specified as an annual percentage rate, for the privilege of using someone else's savings over a period of time. Interest rates compute the requisite fee required for having access when borrowing other people's money.

Credit History

Money may be borrowed by many individuals for numerous sorts of uses. Interest rates charged are dependent on three fundamental issues: who borrows the funds; for what purpose; and from which institution. Each adult has a different financial background, credit history, and expected use for the borrowed funds.

Consumers possessing good credit history have the ability to secure a loan at a competitive interest rate so that they may purchase goods and services today with only the obligation of repayment of the funds plus interest at a later date. Examples of different credit histories may include someone coming out of personal bankruptcy verses another person who has never missed a credit payment in over thirty years.

Use of Funds And Lending Institutions

The use of the loan may be as diverse as using the money for a home mortgage, where the home itself is used as collateral, verses using the money for an around the world trip. Therefore, different interest rates are in force for different types of monetary use even for the same individual.

Interest rates indicate the borrower's credit history, where higher risk borrowers are expected to pay a higher interest rate. In addition, varying lending institutions such as mortgage lenders or credit card lenders may be expected to vary their interest rates based on their particular circumstances and field of lending.

Consequently, individual consumers are advised to shop around and compare lending rates from competing sources of funds. Interest rates move over time based on the aggregate supply and demand for money which is described next.

Why Interest Rates Adjust Through Time

Interest rates vary through time based generally on the aggregate supply of funds obtainable for all loans from all lenders verses the aggregate demand for funds from all borrowers.

When the economy is expanding rapidly, the aggregate demand for funds is expected to be pronounced which will consequently push up all interest rates. Similarly when the economy is weak or in a recession, the overall demand for funds is lower and interest rates are expected to decline.

Political-Economic Conditions

While the aggregate demand for money may be attributed to the real economy, the supply of money in the United States, in the main, is controlled by the U.S. government. Half of the monetary supply and demand equation that determines interest rates in the shorter-term for the U.S. economy is controlled by the U.S. political process.

Interest rates are a vital indicator for the political-economic condition and consequently the stock market, and are dependent upon the demand strength in the real economy and the monetary and credit supply controlled by the U.S. government. These two real economic and political factors expressly indicate why conditions in the money market should be described as both political and economic.

Since changing interest rates are tied to both the strength of the real economy and changing politics, interest rates should be monitored as an indicator to political-economic change. Stock movements in relation to the outlook for cheap or dear money are deserving of study and are fundamental to investors' interests.

Watching Interest Rate Trends

For the condition of the overall stock market, next to identifying the stage and long-term trend in the stock market (chapter 4), and knowing the forward aggregate earnings for the S&P 500 Index Expected Fair Valuation Model to determine whether the market is undervalued or overvalued (chapter 3) – having a clear understanding of the expected circumstances of the money market and interest rates will give investors the third best insight into expected stock market conditions.

Watching the trends in the money and bond markets are fundamental statistics that combine both political and economic factors. It would be considered extraordinary for the stock market to progress separately from the money supply and credit conditions in the money market. How the U.S. government controls the money and credit supply are crucial to understanding the money market and ultimately the resulting stock market movements.

The U.S. Government And Money Supply

As the aggregate amount of money in the economy increases, the supply of funds available for loans also increases which normally has the overall effect of reducing shorter-term interest rates. Declining shorter-term interest rates encourages corporations to borrow to make business investments and consumers to purchase more goods and services due to easier credit conditions.

Higher consumer sales and investment spending has the effect of growing total economic demand which usually leads to an improved economy, increasing employment, and enhanced pricing – at least in the short run. Productivity helps determine how effective the monetary policy is.

Money Supply And Productivity

The federal government can not rapidly increase the money supply at will without rather dire consequences. The penalty is that a money supply increase that is too expansive for the overall economy to properly assimilate through either excess slack in the economy or increased productivity may cause general price inflation.

The effect of rapidly expanding money supply may simply be to push prices up without a corresponding increase in production effectiveness or efficiency. If the products or services being requested for purchase are simply not available, or their quantities do not increase along with the money supply, then prices and consequently inflation escalates. Therefore, the U.S. government needs to balance competing demands when deciding on the rate of money supply increases.

One way to moderate price increases is to ensure that productivity, the ability to produce more with less, is increasing sufficiently over time to keep inflation in check as the money supply is expanded. Investors are looking for a way to invest money today to safeguard and hopefully augment their purchasing power in the future, unfortunately inflation complicates this undertaking.

Inflation robs investors of their purchasing power. If inflation is increasing with the expectation that it will continue to increase, investors will demand and ultimately receive higher interest rates prior to lending their money. Fiscal and monetary policies, presented next, help control inflation and the economy.

Fiscal And Monetary Policies

The U.S. government decides on two policies to achieve national political and economic goals. The first is called fiscal policy. This is the guiding principle for government expenditures, used to accomplish government program objectives, as well as the method that the government will use to supply the money for these expenditures.

Two methods are open to the federal government to supply the necessary financing for fiscal policy: the first is taxation; the second is borrowing. The U.S. government is required to borrow money if and when they pay out more money for federal programs than is being taken in through taxes. Deficit financing is the term used to describe governments whose programs cost more than the taxes collected to pay for them.

The second guiding policy open to the federal government to achieve national political and economic goals is called monetary policy which may be used to help shape the overall economy. The U.S. government has the authority to control the aggregate supply of money and credit in the economy, and by so doing endeavors to influence economic achievements to be consistent with the government's political aims.

The stated political aims of the federal government normally are economic steadiness which includes economic growth, low unemployment, a sound currency, and low inflation. The Federal Reserve is the U.S. government agency charged by the federal government to manage U.S. monetary policy.

The Federal Reserve

The Federal Reserve Act of 1913 stipulates the Federal Reserve's responsibilities to manage money and credit availability for the U.S. economy. The Federal Reserve is the central bank of the United States whose goal is attaining U.S. economic stability through adjusting the amount of currency in circulation, the accessibility and charge for credit in the financial system, and the makeup of how the U.S. national debt is financed.

The Federal Reserve may purchase or sell government securities on the open market which effects money volume, credit, and interest rates in the banking system. Reserves are created when government securities are purchased, and selling government securities withdraws reserves in exchange for government securities. The Federal Reserve is directed by a monetary policy.

Current Monetary Policy

The Federal Reserve manages the following, as this is written, U.S. monetary policy:

> To promote effectively the goals of maximum employment, stable prices, and moderate long-term interest rates.

The theory is that by determining the monetary policy and setting the money supply parameters that economic growth, unemployment, inflation, and interest rates may be monitored and controlled. A steadily expanding economy is desired that will result from a balanced financial condition in which secure savings and additional investments will spur continued economic development.

The Federal Reserve has a difficult balancing act. The Fed wants to make available adequate reserves to promote the growth of money and credit, however this has to be tempered with maintaining price stability while economic expansion is sustained.

The Federal Reserve has categories for where and what instruments that money is being held to better control money supply. The money supply consists of M1 which is the basic measure of what may normally thought of as money (i.e., paper currency, coins, and demand deposits such as checking accounts).

In addition to M1, the Federal Reserve includes money market deposit accounts and mutual funds, savings accounts, and overnight repurchase agreements in the M2 account. The M3 account contains M1 plus M2, and institutional money market funds and time deposits, term repurchase agreements, and term Eurodollars. With so many categories and factors making up the money supply, controlling it requires an extensive knowledge and understanding of the money market which is discussed next.

Means For Controlling Monetary Policy

The Federal Reserve has the following three means available to effectively put into practice the U.S. government's monetary policy:

1) Reserve Requirements
2) The Discount Rate
3) Open Market Operations

Reserve requirements are under the authority of the Board of Governors who determine the percentage of funds that commercial banks and additional depository organizations must maintain as reserves at the Federal Reserve as stipulated by banking regulations. A change in the banking reserve requirement percentage is rarely ever made, but would have a momentous effect on both credit and money supply in the U.S. economy.

When the reserve requirement percentage rate becomes larger, this has the effect of dropping the money supply because a larger percentage of commercial banking funds would be required to be at the Federal Reserve.

As the money supply drops, interest rates are expected to increase as a smaller amount of currency is in circulation and accessible to borrowers.

The discount rate is the second means to controlling the money market. The discount rate window at the Federal Reserve lends monetary reserves at the discount rate to depository institutions who are in need of short-term funds. The Board of Governors has rules for lending and controls the discount rate. By making loans to commercial banks, the money supply is maintained at member banks who are temporarily in need of a short-term loan. The Federal Open Market Committee (FOMC) controls the third means to implementing monetary policy, as described next.

Federal Open Market Committee (FOMC)

Open market operations include the sale and purchase of U.S. treasury bills, notes, bonds, and federal agency securities by the Federal Reserve in the open market. The Federal Open Market Committee (FOMC) controls this process by agreeing on the short-term interest rate objective or targeted quantity of reserves.

When the FOMC purchases U.S. fixed-income securities in the open market, the intended effect is to increase the money supply which should reduce short-term interest rates. When fixed-income securities are sold, money is withdrawn from the economy which reduces the money supply and short-term interest rates should rise.

Creating or withdrawing reserves by the FOMC influences the supply and demand of Federal Reserve Bank balances which adjusts the federal funds interest rate.

Federal Funds Rate

The federal funds rate is the interest rate charged among depository institutions, usually overnight, on loans of excess reserves held by depository institutions at the Federal Reserve. The FOMC only sets a target for the federal funds (fed funds) rate which may vary slightly as money market conditions adjust. Any change in the fed funds rate also changes the benchmark prime rate for short-term lending to business and consumer borrowing.

The prime rate is a benchmark lending rate that may be offered by commercial banks to their most credit worthy businesses, and is normally set three percentage points above the existing fed funds interest rate. Longer maturity U.S. debt interest rates are influenced by the Federal Reserve, but are freely established by competitive bidding in the open market for U.S. treasuries.

Using the three means open to the Federal Reserve to implement monetary policy, the balances of money at depository institutions may be managed which helps determine the federal funds rate. The FOMC is an important committee at the Federal Reserve and has the most direct influence when implementing U.S. monetary policy. Consequently, the FOMC is described in more length in the following section.

FOMC Organization And Procedures

The Federal Open Market Committee (FOMC) is comprised of twelve members – consisting of the seven Federal Reserve Board of Governors, the Federal Reserve Bank of New York President, and four other Reserve Bank Presidents. Eleven Reserve Bank Presidents are available to serve on the FOMC, four are selected yearly on a rotating basis.

The FOMC controls the federal funds (fed funds) rate which is an overnight lending rate between depository institutions on the balance of funds held at the Federal Reserve. Changes to the fed funds rate has a direct effect on short-term interest rates such as the prime lending rate, the value of the U.S. dollar internationally, the quantity of currency, and credit which all have a fundamental influence on the U.S. political-economic condition.

The Federal Open Market Committee (FOMC), of the Federal Reserve, regularly meets eight times a year. During each meeting the FOMC members appraise the economic and financial situation, decide on the recommended monetary response to current conditions, and make an assessment on the risks of future price stability and economic progress. At the end of each FOMC meeting, a statement is produced explaining their reasoning and any actions taken.

FOMC Meeting Statement

A new economic growth and price stability assessment may result in a revised target for the fed funds rate. The FOMC issues a meeting statement, normally occurring around 2:15 P.M. eastern time, explaining any change to the fed funds interest rate.

The FOMC meeting statement should be closely monitored and may be located on the Federal Reserve's Website at: www.federalreserve.gov/ FOMC/. To find the Federal Reserve meeting statement, as this is written, for June 24/25, 2003:

> **Logon:** www.federalreserve.gov/FOMC/
>
> **Where:** Fourth line down from top of page find Meeting calendar, statements, and minutes
> **Click:** Meeting calendar, statements, and minutes
>
> **Where:** The line at the top of the page lists the years in a row, beginning with the current year – find 2003
> **Click:** 2003
> **Where:** For June 24/25, find Statement
> **Click:** Statement

The Federal Reserve meeting statement for June 24/25, 2003 described an economy that was weak, with price increases restrained, and consequently issued a new target for the fed funds rate. The June 24/25, 2003 FOMC statement reads in part:

> The economy, nonetheless, has yet to exhibit sustainable growth. With inflationary expectations subdued, the Committee judged that a slightly more expansive monetary policy would add further support for an economy which it expects to improve over time. The FOMC decided today to lower its target for the federal funds rate by 25 basis points to 1 percent.

FOMC meeting statements may be reviewed by clicking on the appropriate year (located just above the calendar), and then clicking the Statement on the date of interest. A discussion of an important common misconception about the Federal Reserve and the FOMC follows.

Federal Reserve Misconception

A widespread misconception is that the Federal Reserve, through the FOMC, has control over all interest rates in the economy. In reality, the Federal Reserve has direct power over and helps control only the fed funds interest rate. The marketplace freely sets interest rates on all other securities.

However, other shorter-term interest rates, such as 3-Month T-Bills through 2-Year T-Notes, normally respond in kind to lower or higher expected fed fund's interest rates. Longer-term interest rates however may not respond as directly, especially the 30-Year T-Bond. How fed funds and all treasury interest rates respond in the political economy may be shown on a yield curve which is discussed next.

Yield Curve

The yield curve is a visual illustration of interest rates or yields in graphical form depicted over a range of scheduled lending terms or maturity lengths.

The yield curve is an expectation of how bond investors judge the direction of interest rates and what may happen in the future to political-economic conditions. The yield curve is dynamic and may change daily as news and expectations change in the bond market and the overall political economy.

Interest Rate Term Structure

The term structure or configuration of interest rates is the association among bonds of varying lengths of maturities through time. The concern here will be for U.S. treasury bills, notes, and bonds.

For example, the treasury yield curve may begin with the interest rate for federal funds, followed by 3-Month Treasury Bill (T-Bill), next the 6-Month and 1-Year T-Bills, then the 2, 5, and 10-Year Treasury Notes (T-Notes), and finally the 20 and 30-Year Treasury Bonds T-Bonds). The interest rates for the fed funds, T-Bills, T-Notes, and T-Bonds may now be plotted on a graph resulting in a yield curve. Monitoring the interest rate spread between different securities is also of concern to investors.

Interest Rate Spread

The yield curve may also describe the difference or spread between the 3-Month T-Bill and the 30-Year Treasury Bond (T-Bond). The appearance or profile of the treasury yield curve takes into account the interest rate risk between shorter-term and longer-term maturities as well as bond investors' expectations on political-economic conditions, including inflation.

Normally, shorter-term interest rates are lower than longer-term interest rates. Bond investors often demand a higher rate on longer-term maturities due to the possibility of economic uncertainty or future inflation increases.

All interest rates do not move in lock step however. Interest rates on T-Bills, T-Notes, and T-Bonds change completely independently from one another. In fact, treasury interest rates on different duration bills, notes, and bonds may shift simultaneously, either plus or minus, and by different magnitudes.

Yield Curves And Political-Economic Conditions

What is often the most important consideration to understanding the money market is not the absolute magnitude of interest rates, but the relative configuration of interest rates taken as a whole.

What the yield curve is saying about the future of the political-economic condition is vitally important to investors if they know how to read this key data. The yield curve gives insight into the future expectations of the real economy, the bond market, the stock market, and political conduct.

It is mandatory for investors to analyze the treasury yield curve as normal practice in their stock market decision-making process. Typically, short-term T-Bills have lower yields than longer-term T-Bonds because the investor's T-Bills carry less economic risk.

The longer money is tied up in a bond investment the more things can go unexpectedly wrong; therefore ordinarily, higher rates are demanded and received by these longer-term bond investors. Consequently, a normal yield curve may slope moderately upward as length of maturities grow longer and the corresponding bills, notes and bond interest rates increase.

A prediction of political-economic conditions by using the four main yield curve shapes should help all investors when deciding to invest. When the yield curve changes into another form, it is normally time to be flexible and change one's belief about the political-economic condition and the coming prospects for the stock market.

The yield curve is dynamic and can be transformed into four distinct forms at various stages relating to political-economic conditions. Four typical yield curve shapes, starting with the normal yield curve, are presented here along with how best to interpret them.

Normal Yield Curve

Expected normal economic growth, where the economic risks due to future growth, inflation, or changing money supply and credit are low, may produce a moderately upward sloping yield curve. The normal yield curve is usually in evidence during the middle to the end of the long-term uptrend of the stock market political-economic cycle (see Stage 3 in chapter 4).

Graph 7 - 1 depicts a normal yield curve. The vertical axis is the yield percentage rate while the horizontal axis lists in the following order: federal funds rate; 3-Month T-Bill; 2, 5, and 10-Year T-Notes; and the 30-Year T-Bond.

Graph 7 - 1: Normal Yield Curve

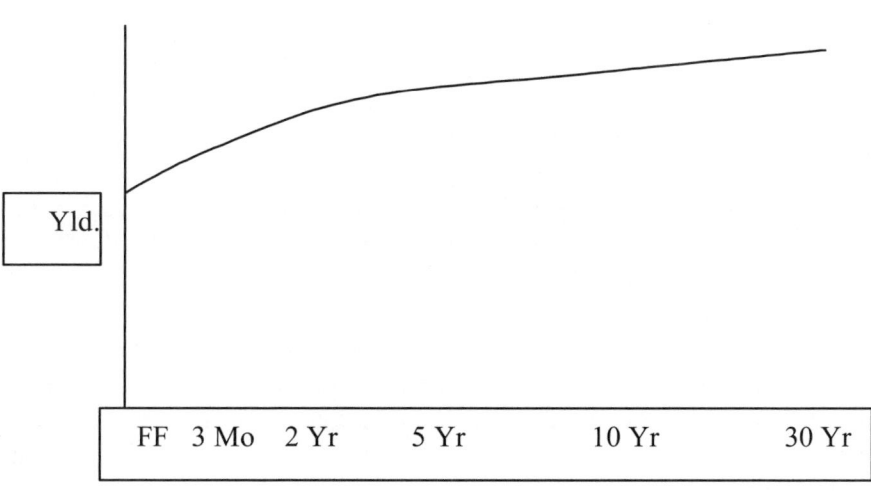

Fixed-income investors during this time frame, who commit their money over longer and longer periods of time, expect and receive increased interest rate rewards. With a lack of economic or political disturbances, longer-term investors should receive higher rewards for their fixed-income investments than shorter-term investors. Therefore as term maturities lengthen, yields increase gradually and the resulting yield curve slopes gently upward.

A normal sloping yield curve is usually a plus for the stock market as it depicts a customarily positive political-economic condition. With positive political-economic conditions affirmed by a normal yield curve, the overall economy may be expected to grow at between two and five percent per year without any significant adjustments to inflation rates. This is the reason it is called a normal yield curve. A steep yield curve however predicts a different reality for political-economic conditions.

Steep Yield Curve

When the yield curve interest rate spread between the 3-Month T-Bill and the 30-Year T-Bond exceeds three percentage points, the yield curve is considered to be steep. Greater than a three percentage yield curve interest rate spread, where the slope of the yield curve angles steeply upward to the right, signals that long-term bond investors expect the economic prospects to rapidly improve. Graph 7 - 2 shows a steep yield curve.

Political-economic influences may have pushed 3-Month T-Bill rates significantly lower than 30-Year T-Bond rates. A steep yield curve is typically in evidence after an economic recession, near the end of a stock market long-term downward trend, at a stock market bottom, and into the beginning of a long-term uptrend in the stock market (see Stages 1, 2 and 3 in chapter 4).

The steep yield curve indicates political financial support for the economy because a larger money supply and better credit terms will reduce corporate prime rates and allow companies to more easily borrow to support their required business investments.

A steep yield curve is a result of a relaxed monetary policy by the Federal Reserve that injects the economy with increases in both money and credit. The reduced short term rates also reflect a reduction in inflationary expectations that often occurs after an economic recession, at a market bottom, and at the beginning of a long-term political-economic upturn.

Graph 7 - 2: Steep Yield Curve

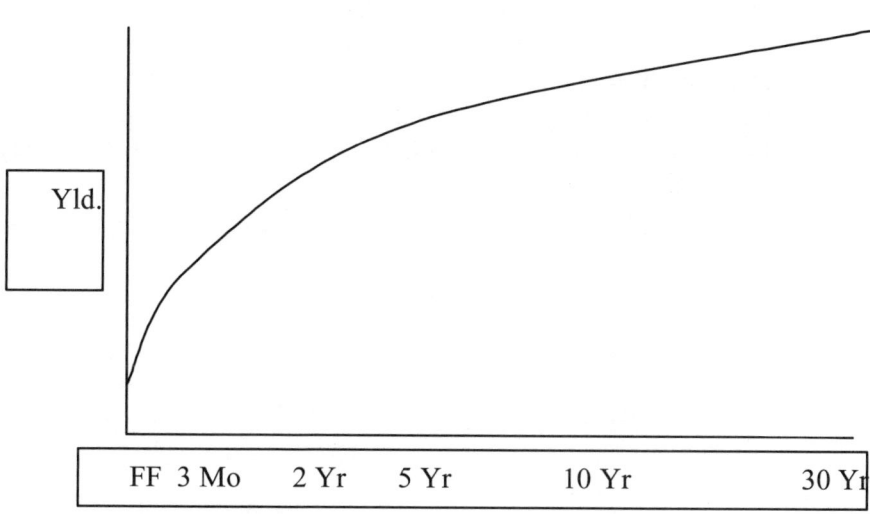

The Federal Reserve is expected to have reduced the fed funds rate and consequently short-term interest rates after a recession; but, as the political economic conditions begins to pick up and the circumstances are supportive, demand for long-term capital and an expected eventual increase in inflation will push long-term bond rates upward faster than 3-Month T-Bill rates which will contribute to a steeper yield curve. Therefore, long-term rates are now rising faster than 3-Month T-Bill interest rates.

Long-term bond investors have expectations of higher rates ahead and are concerned about being trapped with low long-term interest rates in an improving political-economic environment. Therefore, long-term T-Bond holders demand and receive a higher increase in interest rates over 3-Month T-Bill investors because they face greater interest rate risk.

Short-term holders of T-Bills may redeem their positions when they come due, in a matter of months, and now have many options open to them for the use of their money. Equity investors who witness steep yield curves may feel confident that the economy will eventually bounce back from the last political-economic downturn.

Inverted Yield Curve

An inverted yield curve on fed funds, T-Bills, T-Notes and T-Bonds is in evidence when interest rates on shorter duration maturities are higher than longer duration maturities. The inverted yield curve normally occurs late in the long-term uptrend of the political-economic cycle at a stock market top (see Stage 4 in chapter 4). On Graph 7 - 3, an inverted yield curve would slope down from left to right.

Graph 7 - 3: Inverted Yield Curve

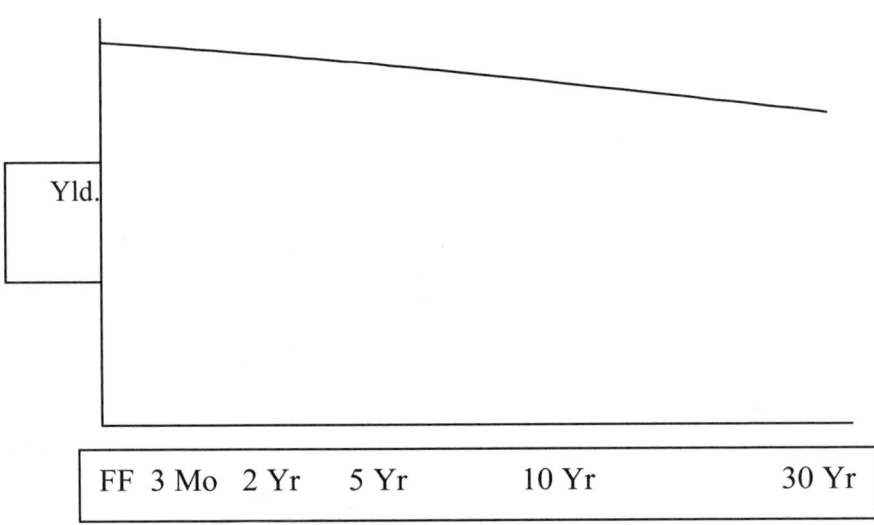

A restrictive monetary policy by the Federal Reserve will raise short-term rates over the 30-Year T-Bond rate. Money and credit supply are tight which consequently forces up short-term rates when demand in the economy is still exceptionally strong. Long-term investors may use their foresight to anticipate an eventual slowing of the economy, a reduction of interest rate expectations, and ultimately a relaxation of the tight monetary policy by the Federal Reserve once a slowing economy is realized.

Inverted yield curves commonly arise when both money and credit are tight and are being restricted by the Federal Reserve which has the intended result of increasing the fed funds rate. The inverted yield curve always foreshadows an economic slowdown at the very least and normally, at worst, a full blown economic recession – so be ready to change expected investment outlooks.

Inverted yield curves occur infrequently, but when they do they should never be ignored. It is reported that inverted yield curves have preceded five successive recessions in the United States. The inverted yield curve on Fed Funds, T-Bills, T-Notes and T-Bonds has been shown to be a good indicator of U.S. economic downturns which are in turn detrimental to overall stock market prices.

The inverted yield curve is a bond investing paradox. Why would long-term bond investors prefer a lower interest rate on longer term securities when seemingly they hold much greater economic and political risks? Why not hold only the short-term T-Bills, which after all pay higher interest rates, with investors having the flexibility to use this money after a few months as conditions change? The answers to these questions are best answered through the use of an example which is presented next.

Inverted Yield Curve: An Example

When the yield curve is inverted, long-term bond investors now expect the economy to slow in the future which will reduce long-term interest rates even more. Consequently, long-term bond investors now have the opportunity to invest in long-term bonds prior to the slow down in the economy becoming obvious to most investors which will then result in a sharp reduction in long-term interest rates.

As seen in the bond fundamentals section in chapter 3 (see Graph 3 - 1), the example is for a 30-Year T-Bond purchased with a coupon yield of 8.5 percent. Lets assume that the short-term yield on the 3-Month T-Bill is at 9.5 percent. If the bond investor purchases the long-term T-Bond with the market and face value of $1,000 dollars and the coupon and current yield of 8.5 percent, at a time when the yield curve is inverted, it may be expected to result in an improved return to putting money in the short-term 3-Month T-Bill at 9.5 percent for two years.

The long-term bond investor may earn in two years, when current yields decline to 6.5 percent, $85 dollars per year in interest for two years plus the capital appreciation of $308 dollars on the $1,000 dollar bond. That works out to over a twenty percent return per year for the long-term T-Bond investor which handily beats the 9.5 percent per year which is the maximum expected earnings on 3-Month T-Bills.

Flat Or Humped Yield Curve

On the way to being inverted, the yield curve will normally spend a period of time when rates on the 30-Year T-Bonds are exceedingly close to the yields on the 3-Month T-Bills. This flat or more often with a slight upward bulge or hump in the middle of the yield curve is usually, but not always, an indication of slower economic growth resulting in an economic downturn, or may even signal that a recession may be expected.

Graph 7 - 4: Flat or Humped Yield Curve

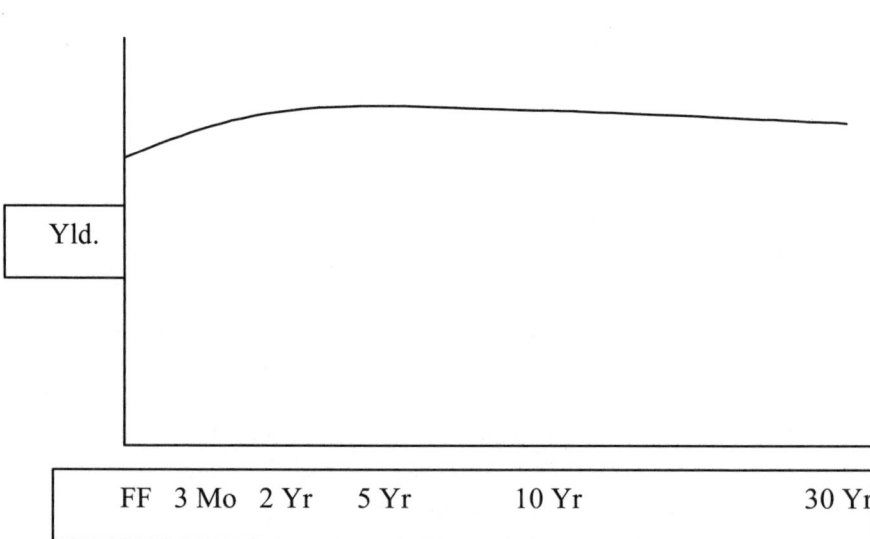

This minor variation in long verses short treasury interest rates normally happens late in the upward trend of the political-economic stock market cycle (see Stage 3 in chapter 4). Inflation expectations might be increasing along with a concurrent tight money and credit policy being implemented by the Federal Reserve. Increased short-term rates result from less money available for circulation.

While the fear that a recession may be on the way when a flat or humped yield curve becomes noticeable, it can not always be relied upon. Otherwise, riches would be guaranteed to all simply by purchasing 30-Year T-Bonds the moment 3-Month T-Bills and 30-Year T-Bonds yields matched. Flat or humped yield curves usually indicate slower economic growth ahead, but it could be that the flat or humped yield curve is a result of bond investors' positive future prospects or a simple matter of a reduction in the supply or quantity of long-term bonds available for purchase.

Yield curves may be easily constructed and reviewed by going on-line and using the internet address presented next to depict daily graphical yield curves. These daily yield curve graphical displays may be termed dynamic.

Dynamic Yield Curves

The relationship of interest rates on Federal Reserve federal funds, U.S. Treasury Bills (T-Bills: 13, 26 and 52 weeks in duration), U.S. Treasury Notes (T-Notes: 2, 5, and 10-years in duration), and U.S. Treasury Bonds (T-Bonds: 20 and 30-years in duration) can be drawn on a yield curve. The yield curve is an expectation by bond investors as a result of monetary and fiscal policy effecting existing economic conditions over time.

The current treasury interest rates for differing maturities may be found on http://moneycentral.msn.com/investor/home.asp, the CNBC - MSN Money Website presented in chapter 3.

Yield curves can change daily and examples of these dynamic yield curves are available on-line. For examples of T-Bills, T-Notes and T-Bonds' yield curves at different points in time please, as this is written, see StockCharts.com at: www.stockcharts.com.

Logon: www.stockcharts.com

Where: In the left hand column under Tools & Charts find Dynamic Yield Curve
Click: Dynamic Yield Curve

Where: Find the Dynamic Yield Curve chart with the S&P 500 chart next to it
Click: At any desired point on the S&P 500 chart to produce the Yield Curve existing during that point in time

Click: The Animate box for a slide show of moving Yield Curves through time

A normal yield curve gently slopes upward from left to right, and an example is shown on Graph 7 - 1. While this situation is normal, the yield curve may change over a period of months into an inverted yield curve. As an example, lets look at how the inverted yield curve worked out in practice during the downturn in the stock market that occurred during 2000.

Yield Curves In Practice

The Federal Reserve is, in general, expanding the monetary base as the target for the fed funds rate declines, and tightening the monetary base as the target for the federal funds (fed funds) rate increases.

The loosening or tightening of money by the Federal Reserve is reflected in the overnight cost of money – the fed funds interest rate. The fed funds rate may be used in conjunction with the 30-Year T-Bond interest rate to help predict a stock market top.

Yield Curves Help Identify Market Tops

Monitoring interest rates may help investors identify stock market tops. Closely monitoring the Federal Reserve federal funds interest rate and the 30-Year U.S. T-Bond interest rate may give an early warning to investors when the overall stock market is close to a market peak.

An inverted yield curve is an excellent predictor to economic slowdowns and recessions. An example occurring over November, 1999 to May, 2000 is instructive.

Yield Curve Predicting A Market Peak: An Example

Monitoring the federal funds rate will help to determine whether monetary policy is either accommodative or restrictive. Table 7 - 1 shows the target fed funds rate, the 30-Year T-Bond rate, and S&P 500 Index closing prices for selected dates from November 12, 1999 to May 31, 2000:

Table 7 - 1: Federal Funds & 30-Year T-Bond Rates, and S&P 500 Prices

Date	Federal Funds Rate Target	30 Yr T-Bond Rate	S&P 500 Index Closing Price
11/12/1999	5.25%	6.03%	1396
12/01/1999	5.50%	6.30%	1398
12/16/1999	5.50%	6.38%	1419
01/03/2000	5.50%	6.62%	1455
01/20/2000	5.50%	6.74%#	1446
01/26/2000	5.50%	6.58%	1404
02/02/2000	5.75%	6.31%	1409
02/15/2000	5.75%	6.24%	1402
03/01/2000	5.75%	6.16%	1379
03/10/2000	5.75%	6.18%	1395
03/21/2000*	6.00%*	5.97%*	1494*
03/24/2000	6.00%	5.98%	1527
04/28/2000	6.00%	5.96%	1452
05/31/2000	6.50%	6.01%	1421

Crest in the 30-Year T-Bond interest rate.
* The Fed Funds target rate now exceeds the 30-Year T-Bond interest rate.

On March 21, 2000 (see * row in Table 7 - 1) the Federal Reserve raised the federal funds target interest rate by 25 basis points to six percent

(100 basis points equals 1 percent). The fed funds short term overnight lending rate of six percent was then higher than the 30-Year T-Bond rate of 5.97 percent, producing an unmistakable inverted yield curve. The Federal Reserve was obviously being restrictive with the money supply and credit, and by its actions trying to slow, at that time, an overactive economy.

The S&P 500 Index continued advancing past March 21, 2000; but, it was within 2.3 percent of its closing high price for this long-term move, topping out at 1,527 three days later on March 24, 2000. Even though the overall economy and intrinsic, true, or fair value are expected to continue to grow past March 21, 2000, there is a lag time here, the stock market will be looking ahead, at a market top as much as six to twelve months in advance, and discounting an expected ultimate slowdown in the economy.

The 30-Year T-Bond interest rate peaked at approximately 6.74 percent, long before March 21, 2000, on January 20, 2000. An explanation for this may be that astute investors were withdrawing money from the overall stock market and buying 30-Year T-Bonds, thus bidding up the 30-Year T-Bond price and consequently reducing its interest rate.

Keeping A Log Book On The Federal Funds Rate

Monetary policy and actions by the Federal Reserve on raising the federal funds rate has a fundamental effect on the future expansion of the U.S. economy and in turn, stock market cycles. Thus, keeping a log book dated on the day of the scheduled FOMC meetings – of the federal funds rate in relation to the 30-Year T-Bond interest rate – is an excellent method for keeping an eye on whether the Federal Reserve has an accommodative or restrictive monetary policy.

The federal funds rate does not always surpass the 30-Year T-Bond interest rate prior to a market downturn. However, if the fed funds rate does exceed the 30-Year T-Bond interest rate, this is an important harbinger that the overall stock market may be peaking and will begin to discount an eventual slowdown in the U.S. economy.

A lag between monetary policy actions and changes in the real economy necessitates the stock market to look ahead at a market peak and discount an economic slowdown (please see chapters 4 and 12) even though intrinsic, true, or fair stock market value may continue to grow and the prevailing corporate and economic news may go on being especially positive (see chapter 8). Foresight into market conditions and being contrarian at the correct time (see chapter 9) are imperative at this time. The spread between the fed funds rate and 10-Year U.S. Treasury Note interest rate is currently used as a leading economic indicator and is discussed next.

Business Cycle Indicators

The National Bureau of Economic Research (NBER) www.nber.org, the official authority on U.S. recessions, uses economic indicators to help determine real economic downturns which have a negative effect on the overall stock market.

The Conference Board www.globalindicators.org, a business and research organization founded in 1916, publishes the Leading Economic Indicator Index that is designed to help identify the peak in the business cycle.

Leading Economic Indicator Interest Rate Spread

The Leading Economic Indicator Index, developed by The Conference Board, is comprised of ten leading indicators. As already discussed in chapter 2, one of leading economic indicators is the aggregate prices for 500 common stocks. Another of the leading economic indicators is the interest rate spread which is calculated by subtracting the federal funds rate from the 10-Year U.S. Treasury Note interest rate. A negative value on the interest rate spread is a negative leading economic indicator.

The Leading Economic Indicator Index has traditionally turned prior to the actual turn in the real economy. It is recommended that investors key on the two crucial leading political-economic indicators to stock market cycles: 1) the aggregate prices for 500 common stocks covered in chapter 4; and 2) the interest rate spread discussed in this chapter.

Fed Funds And 30-Year T-Bond Interest Rate Spread

The fed funds and 30-Year T-Bond interest rate spread is recommended for use by *The Astute Investor* because with an inverted yield curve the 10-Year T-Note interest rate is normally higher than the 30-Year T-Bond rate. Therefore the signal using the yield spread comparison of the fed funds verses the 30-Year T-Bond should come earlier than when using the fed funds and 10-Year T-Note interest rate spread.

The fed funds and 30-Year T-Bond interest rate spread is considered an excellent indicator for long-term stock market tops. The inverted yield curve foreshadows a slowing economy and usually warns of a recession. The fed funds rate higher than the 30-Year T-Bond rate in fact did occur on March 21, 2000. The S&P 500 Index topped out three days later at its closing high price of 1,527 for this long-term move. The National Bureau of Economic Research determined that a recession began almost exactly one year later during March, 2001.

Economists at U.S. government agencies recognize that 500 common stock prices and the interest rate spread reliably project future economic prospects, because a multitude of experienced and suitably informed participants form an expert consensus that help accurately forecast long-term political-economic conditions.

Summary

Interest rates determine the requisite fee required for having access when borrowing other people's money. Consumers having good credit have the ability to secure a loan at a competitive interest rate so that they may purchase goods and services today with only the obligation of repayment of the loan plus interest at a later date. Interest rates signal the borrower's credit history where higher risk borrowers are expected to pay a higher interest rate.

Interest rates vary through time based on the aggregate supply of funds obtainable for all loans from all lenders verses the aggregate demand for funds from all borrowers. While the aggregate demand for money may be attributed to the real economy, the supply of short-term money in the United States is controlled by the Federal Reserve.

The U.S. government decides on two policies to achieve national political and economic goals. The first is called fiscal policy and the second monetary policy. The Federal Reserve manages the monetary policy and has the authority to control the aggregate supply of money in the economy, and by so doing endeavors to influence economic achievements to be consistent with political aims. The theory is that by determining the monetary policy and setting the money supply parameters that economic growth, unemployment, inflation, and interest rates may be managed.

The Federal Reserve has the following three means available to put into practice the U.S. government's monetary policy: 1) Reserve Requirements; 2) The Discount Rate Window; and 3) Open Market Operations. Using these three means open to the Federal Reserve to implement monetary policy, the balances of money at depository institutions may be effected thus determining the federal funds rate.

The term structure or configuration of interest rates is the association among bonds of varying lengths of maturity. There are four main forms of treasury yield curves that investors should know and understand: 1) normal; 2) steep; 3) inverted; and 4) flat or humped. When each of the four yield curve shapes first appear it is time to be flexible and perhaps change one's belief about the political-economic condition and the stock market.

In the example presented, the Federal Reserve raised the fed funds rate on March 21, 2000 to six percent which was then higher than the 30-Year Bond rate of 5.97 percent creating an unmistakable inverted yield curve. The S&P 500 Index was within 2.3 percent of its closing high price of 1,527 on March 24, 2000 for this political-economic long-term stock market cycle.

If and when the federal funds rate does exceed the 30-Year U.S. T-Bond interest rate, this is a convincing harbinger that the overall stock market may be peaking and will begin to discount an eventual slowdown in the U.S. economy. It is reported that inverted yield curves have preceded five successive recessions in the United States. The inverted yield curve foreshadows a slowing economy and usually warns of a future recession which is extremely detrimental to the stock market.

8

Interpreting The News

Introduction

DISCOUNTING THE NEWS BASED on investor foresight is fully explained. What happens when expected news, already fully discounted by the stock market, meets trader expectations or does not meet trader expectations is described. The expected news discounting process is presented which is based on Hegel's Dialectic Theory.

How to evaluate unexpected news, only partially discounted in the stock market, is explored. Breaking unexpected news in a weak market or a strong market is described in detail. The Discounted News Theory is presented to explain how the stock market discounts both expected and unexpected news.

Being skeptical of news headlines is recommended. Why investing based on the nightly news is most often a losing proposition is explained. The folly of following stock tips is fully explored. Market newsletters and advice are compared to taking stock tips. Being dubious of all advice, stock tips, and opinions presented in the media and from all non-paid market analysts or advisers is emphasized.

213

Discounting The News

Discounting the news is a prior bidding up or selling down of stock prices, usually over the short or intermediate term, in anticipation of either good or bad news about political change, the economy, or the particular circumstances of a company.

Discounting the news is practiced when anticipating newsworthy pronouncements or resulting likely actions or any other expected occurrence which may effect a company's stock price or the overall stock market. Investing foresight is required to discount the news and is presented next.

Investing Foresight

Foresight into coming events prior to their occurrence is a cornerstone of intelligent investing. Investors often purchase or sell stock when they can look ahead and discount an expected future event, either positive or negative.

The movement of a stock's price prior to an expected news occurrence is referred to as discounting the news. By discounting the news and anticipating an advance or decline, the stock price is run up or run down prior to the disclosure of the expected news. This occurs due to the foresight of investors.

Discounting the news is why the stock price will often decline during the next few days or weeks after good financial corporate news appears, and advance during the next few days or weeks following the disclosure of bad financial corporate news. Advancing on bad financial corporate news or declining on good financial corporate news may look illogical to novice investors, but this is expected once investor foresight and discounting the news are fully appreciated.

Judging Corporate News

One of the best ways to use corporate or economic news is to judge the effect breaking news makes on the corporation's stock price or overall stock market. In a long-term down market, bad news will continue to send the market down while good news will only stem the market's decline for a short while.

At a long-term market bottom, often when corporate and economic news are the worst and investors are dejected, the terrible news will no longer send the market down. In a long-term up market, good news will send the overall market higher and bad news will only stem the market's advance for a short while.

At a long-term market peak, often when the news is unsurpassed and investor expectations are exuberant, the terrific news will no longer send the market upwards. Fantastic news without a stock market advance is often a warning that the upside potential of the market has vanished and the next major long-term move in the market will be down.

Evaluating and judging the effect of corporate or economic news on the stock market is an investing art for astute investors, requiring careful study. Professional investors have already anticipated and fully discounted all political, economic, and corporate news once expected – how this occurs is explained next.

Expected News

All expected news presented at scheduled times has already been fully discounted in the stock market by professional stock traders. Expected scheduled news releases by corporations, such as quarterly earnings reports, or by governmental agencies, such as production or inflation reports, have been fully discounted by professional stock traders using investing foresight. When the anticipated scheduled news becomes actual news, it is a nonevent in the stock market because prices have previously achieved their approximate expected price levels prior to the actual news being released.

The next corporate quarterly earnings release or government employment report has been thoroughly assessed and incorporated into the marketplace prior to the day on which this news is made public. It is anticlimactic when something is reported in the news that concerned professional investors and traders, using their investing foresight, already expect to happen. Expected scheduled news can either meet expectations or not meet expectations which is explored next.

Scheduled News Meeting Expectations

Corporate financial results are expected and scheduled for release quarterly. Government agencies may schedule economic reports to come out monthly, quarterly, or on a set schedule. Expectations by professional stock traders have been set and traded on prior to the release of all scheduled corporate and government reports.

When the actual good corporate earnings or government economic statistics are released which meet expectations, often the already discounted stock or overall stock market is sold off over the short term as any new information is assessed to develop new expectations for the next scheduled report. Thus, the expected scheduled corporate or government news has already been fully discounted by professional investors with foresight. The following example is instructive for political news that when released, meets expectations.

Scheduled News Meeting Expectations: A Tax Cut Example

An example of expected scheduled news already being fully discounted in the market can be seen as the U.S. government works toward a cut in the capital-gains tax rate. Historically, stock share prices are bid up prior to the passage of the tax legislation in anticipation of the enhanced perception for higher future stock prices over the longer term.

In addition, stock prices improve prior to the capital-gains tax cut bill being passed because knowledgeable investors are reluctant to sell and take profits rather than wait for tax rates to be lower in the future which will increase their expected profits. Deferring stock sales may well reduce the tax bite, so why rush.

Once the capital-gains tax cut legislation is passed and is all over the news, knowledgeable stock traders who have both bought early and delayed selling in anticipation of this news will be selling into purchases by the investing public. All this selling by professional interests has the effect of reducing the overall stock averages.

It is reported that the major stock averages have declined by approximately twelve percent points two months after a reduction in the capital-gains tax rate. This supports the Wall Street adage that to make extraordinary returns in the market, "traders should buy on the rumor and sell on the news."

Over the long term, lower capital-gains tax rates will benefit the stock market and expected returns by helping attract more investment funds which will help expand the economy. However, as can be seen over the shorter-term, capital-gains tax cut legislation can cause the stock market to act in a seeming illogical way.

It is best not to be caught up in the excitement after signification capital-gains tax cut legislation is passed. Either purchase stock early on the expectation of passage, or wait a few months after passage and pick stocks at an expected lower price. Not all expectations come to fruition however, what happens when scheduled news does not meet expectations is discussed next.

Scheduled News Not Meeting Expectations

Expected scheduled news not matching expectations when reported now becomes the news. The result is that revised expectations again become established which then becomes the new standard by which the next expected scheduled corporate or government news is judged. It is the latest anticipated news that moves stock prices going forward as the new anticipated expectations become the standard by which the next scheduled news releases will be compared.

It is this continuous process of first anticipating the news, then the reality of the news not meeting expectations, resulting in a new anticipation by experienced stock traders that defines this ongoing course of investors' reaction to the news. This is the foundation of the expected news discounting process which is based on Hegel's Dialectic Theory.

Hegel's Dialectic Theory

The expected news discounting process follows the Dialectic Theory presented by the brilliant German philosopher G.W.F. Hegel (1770-1831). In Hegel's system there is a thesis put forth for discussion, then an opposing statement called an antithesis is made, and finally a synthesis is developed that resolves both the thesis and antithesis and settles the conflict.

The genius of Hegel's system is that the resulting synthesis now becomes the new thesis in the next cycle. This new thesis now has a new antithesis resulting in a new synthesis. Thus, the Hegelian process may be repeated indefinitely. Hegel's Dialectic explains how progress is made as conditions change through time. This is the exact process that the scheduled news makes in the marketplace when the results do not meet trader expectations.

Investors should assume that all expected scheduled breaking corporate and government news has previously been discounted in the stock market. When the actual news does not match expectations then that in itself becomes news. The result is that revised expectations again become established which then become the new standard by which the next scheduled corporate or government news is judged.

Thus the repeated Hegelian process of news anticipation, then reality of the news, leading to a revised anticipation. This revised anticipation of the news then becomes the next news anticipation which begins the process anew for the next cycle of scheduled news. The Hegelian process fully explains for all expected scheduled news, whether meeting expectations or not meeting expectations, how new expectations are formed through time. This course of action is the foundation of the expected news discounting process which is fully explained next.

Expected News Discounting Process

The expected news discounting process explains how professional investors in the stock market constantly look ahead to predict coming political-economic conditions. Expected news is scheduled news that either meets expectations or does not meet expectations. It is the professional investors' foresight which is instrumental to the look ahead capability of the stock market.

The expected scheduled ongoing process of news anticipation, news reality, updated news anticipation is based on Hegel's Dialectic which supports the expected news discounting process. This process explains how the stock market operates as a discounting mechanism. Expected scheduled news does not startle the stock market or professional stock traders because it has previously been discounted.

When expected scheduled corporate or government economic news meets expectations, often stock prices react counter intuitively to logical assumptions by the investing public, because this expected news has been previously discounted by professional stock traders.

If expected scheduled news does not match expectations then new anticipatory expectations position the market for the next scheduled news release. This explains how the stock market discounts expected scheduled news that both meets and does not meet expectations. But what about major unexpected news releases that can not be scheduled? A discussion of unexpected news is next.

Unexpected News

Unexpected news may happen at any time. Unexpected news includes natural disasters, political calamities, and good and bad corporate or government news. Unexpected news is nonscheduled news with only the likelihood on what, when, who, or where the event may take place.

Unexpected news may be imagined by investors which they determine may effect the stock market. The imagined what, when, who, and where of unexpected news events causes particular investors to modify both their investing actions or non-actions in the stock market. An example of an imagined unexpected news event would be a major terrorist attack that would effect American interests. As a consequence, investors may decide to invest in terrorist detection technology or to hold off investing entirely.

All breaking unexpected news events have already been at least partially discounted, either by what investors have done or have not done, in the stock market. Anything that is possible for an investor to imagine has in some way influenced his or her actions or non-actions when investing. All breaking unexpected news events have to a limited extent been discounted by certain investors. In this way the stock market is a weighing scale for everything possible or probable.

The probabilities of unexpected news actually occurring and when may determine how much of this particular news event has already been discounted by the marketplace. High probability unexpected news – lets say the possibility of a major disastrous earthquake in the U.S., a corporate merger, or corporate bankruptcy in a poor performing firm – all will be more fully discounted than a low probability unexpected news event such as a major land war breaking out in Europe.

While it is interesting to contemplate high and low probability possibilities for unexpected news events, lets treat unexpected news events only as they happen and assume that only limited discounting has already occurred. How unexpected events may be evaluated as they happen and their effect on the stock market are focused on in the next section.

Evaluating Unexpected News Events

Major breaking unexpected news events often creates a serious problem for the stock market, because it may be assumed that only a small percentage of this unexpected news has already been discounted by the marketplace. The following five questions should be asked to evaluate major breaking unexpected news:

1) What is the character of the unexpected news?
2) Is the unexpected news good?
3) Is the unexpected news bad?
4) What is the likely result of the unexpected news?
5) What is the current state of the stock market?

The character of the breaking unexpected news is the nature, quality, and spirit of the news. For example, news character for the unexpected news may relate to the surprise developments of an individual company, involve a natural disaster, or involve the federal, state, or local governments in some way.

Good or bad breaking unexpected news may seem easy to judge. However, an assessment of whether the unexpected news is either all good or all bad may be more difficult if the new development has several elements of both qualities. Any gray area certainly complicates the evaluation by stock traders.

Making an assessment and knowing the likely result of the unexpected news is not always straight forward as well. This often causes the result of the unexpected news to take time in working its way through stock pricing. This causes many options that need to be assessed and evaluated prior to a stock price finally reaching an equilibrium price after a market shock from major breaking unexpected bad news. The most important question for investors to evaluate however is not the unexpected news, but the current state of the stock market which is discussed next.

Evaluating Unexpected News: The Most Important Point

The first four points above are important when evaluating major breaking unexpected news. However, it should be comforting to know that the single overriding concern for investors, when evaluating the major breaking unexpected news, is not the news itself; but, the type of stock market that the unexpected news is breaking into.

Determining and knowing the current stage of the long-term stock market is all that the astute investor need concern himself or herself with when investing for the long-term. The current stock market may be either strong and in a long-term market upturn, or weak and in a long-term market downturn. Lets look at what happens when major unexpected news breaks into a weak long-term market that is in a down trend.

Unexpected News In A Weak Market

Major breaking unexpected good news will normally have only a shorter-term upward effect on a weak long-term stock market in a down trend. The breaking unexpected good news can come from corporate sources or the government. The market will advance for awhile and then most likely continue in its long-term downward course.

What happens however if the unexpected breaking news is clearly terrible? The answer is the long-term downturn in the market will likely continue. The most important issue and of paramount importance for investors to determine is the long-term state of the stock market when evaluating major breaking unexpected news events.

A stock market in a long-term down trend during Stage 1: Mark-Down - Downtrend will incorporate the breaking unexpected bad news by continually forcing the market down much further. The following example may be instructive.

Unexpected News In A Weak Market: An Example

An example of terrible breaking unexpected news that involved both business and government at all levels is the terrorist attack on the two World Trade Center Towers in New York City (NYC) and on the U.S. Pentagon in Arlington, Virginia on September 11, 2001.

Two large U.S. commercial airliners were commandeered and deliberately flow into the World Trade Center Towers by international terrorists causing the towers to eventually collapse with a major loss of thousands of innocent American lives. A third jetliner was crashed into the U.S. Pentagon by the terrorists causing further loss of life. A fourth hijacked airliner crashed prior to reaching its target with several innocent passenger heroes on board credited with saving the lives many others on the ground.

Lets work through each of the five steps from above to evaluate this major breaking unexpected appalling news. The character of the news may be described as an unprovoked, underhanded sneak attack that was frightening, shocking, dispiriting, and further threatening to the American public. Those directly and adversely effected included the innocents on the airlines and those killed on the ground, the people in NYC, the personnel at the Pentagon, airline companies, insurance companies, and government at all levels.

This dreadful news may be expected to result in a reduction in flights as Americans postpone trips, and more stringent rules for airline travel which may further reduce airline travel. Clean up and reconstruction costs to rebuild the World Trade Center for the insurance industry and the Pentagon for government are expected to run in the many billions of dollars. A military response is expected to find and punish those responsible for this terrible crime and to help ensure that it does not happen again.

Undoubtedly, everything up to this point in the analysis is bleak and awfully negative. The most important assessment for investors however is the current long-term state of the stock market just prior to September 11, 2001 terrorist attack which is shown in Graph 8 - 1.

Clearly the state of the market just prior to the terrorist attacks on the World Trade Center Towers and at the Pentagon is that the stock market was in a long-term downturn (Stage 1: Mark-Down - Downtrend). Graph 4 - 5 in chapter 4 also indicates the downward slope to the S&P 500 Index Nine Month Moving Average Trend Line during this time period, and confirming indicators supports the long-term downward trend conclusion.

Consequently, the expected result of this unexpected major dastardly terrorist attack on a weak long-term stock market would be further reductions in the S&P 500 Index price. In fact that is what happened as the S&P 500 Index closed in August of 2001 at approximately 1,130 and did not reach a head and shoulders bottom until March 12, 2003 with an intraday low for the S&P 500 Index of 789. This approximately thirty percent decline of the S&P 500 Index price took about seventeen months after the September 11, 2001 terrorist attacks took place.

Graph 8 - 1: S&P 500 Index - Prior to the Sept. 11th Terrorist Attack

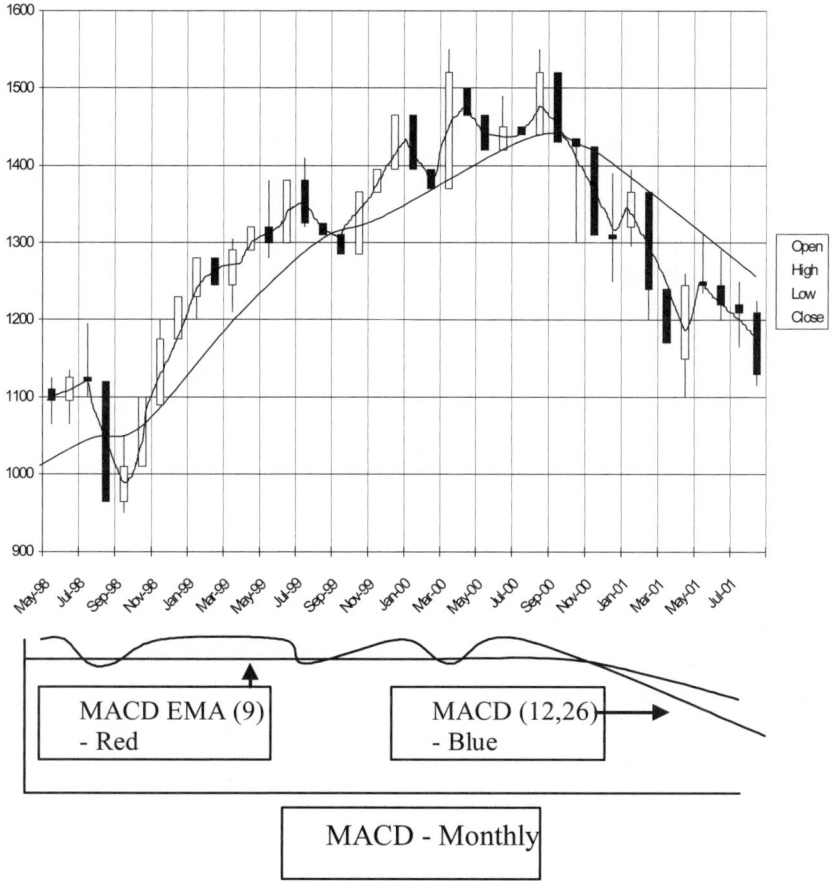

Obviously, this was a weak long-term stock market that could not take the major shock from unexpected terrible news which furthered the stock market's decline. In conclusion, the best way for investors to protect themselves from bad unexpected breaking news is not to be invested when the stock market is in Stage 1: Mark-Down - Downtrend.

What about bad unexpected news breaking in a strong long-term market that is in a Stage 3: Mark-Up - Uptrend? How a strong stock market incorporates unexpected news, whether good or bad, is presented next.

Unexpected News In A Strong Market

Clearly, breaking unexpected good news in a strong long-term upwardly trending stock market will continue to push the stock market higher. This is a case of unexpected good fortune continuing to smile on the aware and unaware investor alike.

What happens if the breaking unexpected news is clearly terrible? The unexpected bad news may come from corporate sources or the government. The most important issue and of paramount importance for investors is the long-term direction of the overall stock market.

Major breaking unexpected bad news in a strong long-term upwardly trending stock market will normally have only a short-to-intermediate term downward effect. The market will decline for awhile and then most likely continue in its upward course. An example, during the 1998 Asian economic downturn, is instructive and is presented next.

Unexpected News In A Strong Market: An Example

Major breaking unexpected bad news occurred during August, 1998. Major Asian economies were found to be financially overextended and heading into recession. How the strong U.S. stock market handled this unexpected Asian economic downturn is described next.

Due to the Asian economic recession, an anticipated money crunch was expected to have a domino effect on the overall global economy. It was feared that with a significant portion of U.S. trading partners' economies falling into recession that they would likely pull the U.S. economy down with them.

The stock market during August, 1998 was then in a long-term upward trend during a Stage 3: Mark-Up - Uptrend as is shown in Graph 4 - 6 which is presented in chapter 4. The S&P 500 Index Nine Month Moving Average Trend Line in Graph 4 - 6 is pointing upward during this time and many confirming indicators also attested to the fact that the U.S. stock market was in a long-term uptrend. This is also in evidence in the monthly Graph 8 - 1 as shown in this chapter.

In response to this major global economic threat, the Federal Reserve began reducing the federal funds interest rate from five and a half percent to five and a quarter percent to be accommodative during this economically difficult period. The statement issued by the Federal Reserve after their September 29, 1998 meeting stated in part:

> The Federal Open Market Committee (FOMC) decided today to ease the stance of monetary policy slightly, expecting the federal funds rate to decline 1/4 percentage point to around 5-1/4 percent. The action was taken to cushion the effects on prospective economic growth in the United States of increasing weakness in foreign economies and of less accommodative financial conditions domestically. The recent changes in the global economy and adjustments in U.S. financial markets mean that a slightly lower federal funds rate should now be consistent with keeping inflation low and sustaining economic growth going forward.

It is interesting to note that the stock market began improving during the beginning of September, 1998. The stock market discounted a fed funds rate cut by the Federal Reserve that actually occurred on September 29, 1998. On October 15, 1998, during the next FOMC meeting, the fed funds rate was again lowered by one quarter of a percent to five percent. Thus the Federal Reserve was being responsibly accommodative during the Asian financial crisis by twice reducing the fed funds rate, each time by a quarter point.

As can be seen in Graph 8 - 1, the S&P 500 Index rebounded after only four months to gain a new S&P 500 Index market high during November, 1998 – after the second Federal Reserve rate cut that occurred on October 15, 1998.

A stock market in a long-term upward trend in Stage 3: Mark-Up - Uptrend will normally take breaking unexpected bad news in stride and soon recover after possibly a few months. Since the planning horizon is over 1, 2, 3, 4, or 5 years or more for the long-term investor, this intermediate-term downturn should not be an overriding concern to the astute long-term investor. It is interesting to note that the news itself does not move the stock market, what really moves the stock market is presented next.

What Really Moves The Markets

Paradoxically, stock market price movements are not determined by breaking news, whether expected or unexpected, but by investors' reactions to the news. Stock prices are determined by how the many millions of investors sense how expected or unexpected breaking news events may effect the stock market.

Making an assessment and knowing the likely result of breaking unexpected news is not always straight forward. It takes a while for this unexpected breaking news to work its way through investors' evaluations of what effect it will have on the political-economic condition. Consequently, waiting for the situation to work its way out in a downward stock market in Stage 1: Mark-Down - Downtrend is clearly the best approach whether the breaking unexpected news seems either good or bad.

Having a market position that is in sync with a strong or weak long-term stock market determination will probably ensure making money in the stock market over the long-term, regardless of breaking unexpected news. This is called being positioned on the right side of the market to take advantage of any breaking unexpected news that investors may react to.

The stock market is ultimately individuals who participate by buying or selling stock. Investors in their own way desperately trying to forecast the future and position their investments to take advantage of their foresight. It is this profoundly human characteristic that produces such dramatic circumstances set against often contradictory assessments of conditions along with all the hopes, fears, greed, and weaknesses of those participating in the stock market.

Bernard M. Baruch, one of the most successful stock traders of his era, passed along the following insight. Baruch explained that in the final analysis his entire education and professional career in the stock market revolved around understanding only one thing – human nature. It should always be remembered that people ultimately move the stock market, and not the news. The Discounted News Theory may now be defined which is presented next.

Discounted News Theory

Discounting the news explains how professional investors in the stock market constantly look ahead to predict the coming political-economic conditions. It is this investor foresight which is instrumental to the look ahead capability of the stock market.

The Hegelian Dialectic supports the expected news discounting process. This process explains how the market operates as a discounting mechanism. All expected scheduled news, whether meeting or not meeting expectations, does not startle the stock market or professional stock traders because the news has all been previously fully discounted.

All unexpected news has already been at least partially discounted in the stock market, either by investors' actions or non-actions. Anything that is possible for an investor to imagine that may effect the stock market has in some way influenced his or her actions or non-actions when investing (this point is more fully developed in chapter 12). All unexpected news has to a limited extent been partially discounted by investors.

There are five questions that may be asked to evaluate major breaking unexpected news – the most important being, "what is the current state of the stock market?" Unexpected breaking bad news in a strong long-term upward trending market will likely have no long term effect – the stock market should continue in its long-term upward trend. Likewise, good breaking unexpected news in a long-term down trending market will likely have no long-term effect – the stock market should continue in its long-term downtrend.

The Discounted News Theory is supported by the expected news discounting process. All expected scheduled news has already been fully discounted by the marketplace. All unexpected news has at least been partially discounted by the stock market by what investors have or have not done. It is investors' reaction to the news which moves the stock market, not the news itself. It is assumed that news travels immediately to all market participants.

The stock market is defined as never being wrong. It is expected that when the stock market is in a long-term upward trend, the market's participants are anticipating that the preponderance of the news over the foreseeable future will be on balance positive. When the stock market is in a long-term downward trend, investors are expecting that the majority of the news over the foreseeable future will be on balance negative.

The Discounted News Theory describes a stock market that is always looking ahead, discounts fully all expected news events, and partially discounts all unexpected news events by incorporating investors' actions and their non-actions. The overall stock market, as represented by the S&P 500 Index, becomes the long-term leading indicator to the political-economic condition (more on this in chapter 12). Investing based on the nightly news is often a losing proposition which is easily explained once the Discounted News Theory is fully understood, which is presented next.

Nightly News Investing: A Losing Proposition

Investing based solely on the nightly business news is often a losing proposition for beginning investors. Naively evaluating the effect of breaking financial corporate news on stock prices is detrimental to novices' pocketbooks.

For beginning investors, the logic of what the nightly corporate news will portend for stock prices will often not match how stock prices actually perform during the following days or weeks. Ironically, to make money in the short term, on breaking financial corporate news, it is often best to do the exact opposite of what the beginning investor thinks is the most logical action to take.

Humphrey B. Neil explains that the stock price doing the exact opposite of what the beginning investor thinks the stock price should do, based on breaking corporate news, is why many beginning investors feel that the stock market is illogical, and incorrectly conclude that the stock market is not for them. Since scheduled news is already fully discounted, this may result in the stock price behaving contrary to what would be logically expected by the novice investor.

Threats More Frightening Then Reality

It is a Wall Street observation that a threat is often more frightening to investors, which results in lower stock prices, than the actual occurrence of the event itself. Stock prices normally first dip lower when a peril or calamity is threatened then when the feared occurrence actually happens. The

228

explanation of the lower stock price preceding or occurring at the same time the incident in reality takes place is because fear of the happening has already driven those to sell stocks who would sell stocks.

Discounting the threat may cause the stock price to actually improve when the news of the actual event is in the media, as those who expect this to be the last such happening move-in to purchase the stock at a bargain price.

When frightening news becomes a reality, it is frequently best to overlook one's logical but hasty response to the news and simply observe the investing crowd's behavior. Remember, individuals move the stock market and not the news. The best way not to panic is to remember that the investing public, who typically relies on the nightly news, often overacts when the nightly news is alarming.

Knee-Jerk Reactions

Putting too high a price on breaking news is in evidence when investors either buy or sell on the news. When keeping up with the political and financial news in the media, do not attempt to translate this breaking news directly into stock trading profits. Realize that a knee-jerk reaction, even if it seems a logical, is more often then not the wrong decision. At least wait for a week or two to reassess the situation prior to taking any action.

Converting breaking financial corporate news into stock market gains is often a short-term losing proposition for beginning investors, who frequently buy stocks on good financial corporate news and conversely sell stocks on bad financial corporate news.

Professional stock traders are aware of the proclivity of the investing public to immediately buy or sell stock depending on the latest breaking corporate news, and therefore learn to do just the opposite of what the novice investor is doing; that is, buying good stocks when the bad news becomes public and selling their good stock into the public's buying on good news.

The financial corporate news is often misleading if beginning investors do not know what to identify as important. When keeping abreast of the financial news in the newspapers, on television, or on the internet, it is best for beginning investors not to buy or sell stock on the latest breaking financial corporate news. Beginning investors should wait until the stock is no longer in the news and is not all over the electronic tape before investing.

Knowing What Is Important

The astute investor learns to become contrarian and not to follow the crowd (see chapter 9) on breaking financial corporate news. One caveat, however, when the market is in Stage 1: Mark-Down - Downtrend, stock prices should continue to decline on bad news as expectations are continually revised downward. Also during a long-term uptrend when the market is in Stage 3: Mark-Up - Uptrend, the market should rally and continue upward on good news as investor's expectations continue to improve.

As a general rule, it is always best to never buy stocks simply on good breaking corporate news because this news can be misleading. Since this breaking news may already be discounted, when the stock opens for trading the next day at a sharply higher price, it is not unusual for stock market professionals to be selling into this morning stock advance.

Prices in the stock market tend to move in advance of fundamental factors, especially at long-term market tops. Have respect for the stock market and plan rather than simply react to situations. Think through the what-ifs if something happens or if nothing happens. Thinking through contingencies is all part of the homework required for investing success. How investors should best use the news reported on by the media is explored next.

The News And The Media

The news media uses many investing reporting sources which are assumed to be authoritative. However, these authoritative investing sources often have conflicting opinions on stocks and the stock market. Consequently, astute investors should be skeptical of the free advice or opinions on which stocks to purchase or the expected direction of the stock market which are daily reported by the media.

Investors Should Be Skeptical Of Free Advice

Skepticism of the intent of those behind the news, that is so freely given in the media, should also always be in the forefront of every investor's mind. To be precise and unambiguous, it is not the reporters or the media companies doing the reporting that are being singled out here, for in general they are doing an excellent job; but, the independent analyst from whom the information is being gathered and reported on whose opinions should be constantly questioned.

There is nothing given free in the investing world without an expected return, and that goes double for investment advice (e.g., opinions about the future trend in the stock market or judgments on which stocks to buy or sell). This free stock market advice is often reported on by the news media and is worth precisely that, frequently nothing.

In very limited instances, the free advice found in the media may be a method to manipulate the investing public to do one thing while the market pundit and his or her accomplices are doing just the opposite. Intelligent and astute investing requires each individual to get their own relevant information, do the proper analysis, evaluate and judge the alternatives, and to arrive at their own sound investing conclusions. Remain skeptical, any trust should be expressly earned.

Reporting On Why The Market Goes Up Or Down

The media reports the financial news and gives possible reasons on why the stock market either goes up or down, because that is what the investing public expects and even demands. It is interesting to note that there is no central clearing house that determines the real reason why stock market prices change. News reporters may publish their own seemingly explanatory reasons based on the available nightly news or may actually interview selected investing gurus for their explanations of why the stock market acted the way it did.

Depending on what is asked and who is answering, the reasons given for the same stock price movement may have different explanations. Since no comprehensive survey is being performed of all those buying or selling with their reasons why explained – the real reasons why stock prices actually move can never be reported with certainty by the media. Therefore, take the reasons for stock price movements reported by the media as interesting

231

but certainly not authoritative. Contradictory news headlines are an often recurring theme in the media which are repeatedly detrimental to investors, an example follows.

Contradictory News Headlines: An Example

The following three sample contradictory news headlines appeared in one media source on June 30, 2003. The names of the three respected market analysts and their institutions are replaced with X, Y, and Z because the names are not germane to the issue that is being raised. The modified news headlines appearing on June 30, 2003 are listed below:

> X**** Turns "Forcefully Negative" On Stocks
> Y****: Stocks Are On Balance A Buying Opportunity
> Z Strategist: Stock Prices Should Drift Sideways

One market analyst presented a case for selling stocks, the next analyst thought it was the right time to buy stocks, and the third thought only that stocks should be held during the coming consolidating trading range. The point is not who is right or wrong, although two of the market analysts evidently were. The sole issue being raised here is that investors should not be swayed in their actions by news headlines.

Contradictory news headlines can cause self-doubt in the mind of an investor and that doubt may produce investor anxiety. Self-doubt and anxiety are rational emotions that interfere with correct investment decisions (please refer back to chapter 5), and often causes the investing public to put off the decision of whether to invest or not. This is an example of self-doubt and anxiety leading to investor non-action which may be detrimental to an investor's pocketbook.

Media headlines are for the lazy investor who does not take the time to see beneath these headlines to get a clear picture of the political-economic realities. Investor delusions may be fed by often contradictory news headlines. What is read in the news is often similar to being on the receiving end of taking a stock tip (more on this later in the chapter). Consequently, relying on news headlines in the media should be avoided when investing.

To help eliminate self-doubt and anxiety, the investor should gather their own information, run their own models, develop their own opinions, form their own judgment, and arrive at their own conclusions on whether to invest. Another problem with news headlines awaits unwary investors when they wait for news headlines to all agree, as explained next.

When News Headlines All Agree It Is Too Late

Investors can be assured that when all the news headlines agree, and the conventional wisdom (see chapter 9) is either all-up or all-down, that it is too late to make much money following the now all agreeing headlines' opinions. In addition, once an investor's position in the market is established, late in a long-term market cycle, that waiting for news headlines' agreement in the opposite direction will only get investors out of the stock market at a loss.

The worst political-economic news normally arrives at a long-term stock market bottom and the best news at a long-term stock market peak. The investing public, caught up in their emotions, as a rule purchases stock on the good news and sells stock on the bad news. Astute investors plan to do the exact opposite from the investing public while either good or bad news is breaking at long-term market tops or bottoms. Supposed inside information is often seductive to novice investors but can certainly be misleading, as explained next.

Inside Information

An investor's reasoning capability seems to become gravely impaired when they believe they have command of inside information or a stock tip. Investors place a high regard on being in a position of importance in knowing what others do not, and strangely whether the information is true or not seems to be irrelevant. Supply the same investor with supposed inside information and they feel they are on an easy street to economic riches.

Sadly, this delusion often quickly fades into the hard reality of stock market losses. Hopefully, investors will only have to learn this lesson once before they begin relying solely on their own detached decision making. Acting on information that is unverifiable with only the most cursory examination of the facts will most probably result in investment losses.

Novice Investors

Often, novice investors who have not read this book will come to a purchase decision on a stock based on a convincing stock analysis by a market pundit, by noticing extraordinary price action on a chart, or by being passed on a stock tip that is assured to be authentic. Unfortunately, the ability of a tyro investor to discern who is or is not a valid source of investing information is almost nil.

It is exceedingly difficult to ascertain who simply has a bogus position to maintain and will prevaricate to support that position. If by some chance the passed on stock information is in fact accurate, the implications of the information and how to put it to work in the stock market are usually totally lost on the novice investor.

Recognizing The Meaning Of Information

Properly recognizing the meaning of information is much the more important factor than simply having the correct facts and figures. It is the capacity to fully comprehend what the data are saying along with the aptitude to act in a timely manner that converts stock information into stock market gains. Investors have to first see and then correctly comprehend what they have seen, for accurate recognition.

There is something seductive about supposedly possessing rumored inside information, in this case a tip, that makes a stock trader image himself or herself invincible and so much more in the know then the uninformed people who are assumed to be outside the loop.

The inside information in question has only the appearance of material or noteworthy intelligence. This inside information feeling may convince even the savviest trader to ignore clearly relevant facts when they do not support the assumed insider position.

Illegal Insider Trading

Illegal insider trading concerns officers of a company buying, selling, or tipping others on their stock based on significant non-public information. It is ironic that even when insiders know what the company is doing they can make grave mistakes in the stock market.

Knowing how to manage a company is not the same thing as knowing the stock market. Insiders have been known to sit on their stocks when it has become clear to almost everybody else that selling would be the wisest course of action.

An investor who knows that he or she should consciously remain outside the loop of supposed inside information will study the political-economic conditions and the practical ten-step method for investing success carefully prior to making a stock market commitment. As discussed next, stock tips, especially, should be avoided.

Stock Market Tips

Capitalistic competition in its purest form is played out in the stock market. Consequently, sometimes stock tips are mentioned in the media or passed on by investing friends, who supposedly heard the information from a good source, which are designed to get the investing public to do one thing while those who think for themselves are doing the opposite.

Stock market tips may not be what they seem to be. The motive behind those initially supplying the tip or passing on the tip can never be known with certainty. The stock market should not be thought of as an overly friendly place where stock traders want one and all to grow rich. With two sides to every stock transaction, just the opposite is true. The veracity of any stock tip should always be on the investor's mind.

Stock Tips Are Not Always Genuine

The plain truth is that on select occasions opinions may be fabricated to fool the often gullible investing public. Since knowing in advance which stock tips are genuine and which are designed to mislead can never be known with certainty, the best course of action is to cast a blind eye and deaf ear toward them all. Be distrustful of supposed inside information and all stock tips. Rely instead on one's own reasoned judgment about the suitability for investing.

By treating one's ears as a liability and not listening to any stock tips, investing takes on the quality of a card game in which one can see what everyone is doing in the market; but, not what they are saying about what they are doing. Therefore the chance of being mislead by simple words, either intended or unintended, is eliminated. By constantly watching and observing one can interpret what others in the stock market are doing without the possibility of being deceived by their words.

Opinions Once Heard Effect Judgment

It is human nature that once an opinion is heard, right or wrong, good or bad, that it will effect one's judgment. Isolating oneself from this emotional turmoil of conflicting opinions has been the method of choice for the best stock traders. All stock rumors, investor opinions, conflicting information, and the wishful thinking of others will now be safely ignored.

A relatively new innovation is the on-line stock chat room that many internet Websites offer. Free stock tips are offered, but the anonymity associated with these chat rooms increases the possibility that information is being offered only to mislead rather than to inform investors. The internet has many wonderful qualities, but by all means stay away from stock chat rooms – they are a seductive trap for the investing public that should be strictly avoided.

Stock Tips Are For The Lazy

Investors who buy or sell stock based on stock tips, gossip, or rumors which may be found in newspapers, on television, on the internet, in brokerage offices, or supplied by friends display the human faults of both indolence and ignorance.

Intellectually lazy investors may desire to get rich quickly by banking on the advice from others or by hoping that the latest stock tip is authentic. In the stock market as in life, one tends to reap the rewards of hard work. Consequently, indolent stock tip takers are more often than not discouraged about their market results and are quickly washed out of the market – never to return.

Legendary stock traders such as Bernard M. Baruch, Nicolas Darvas, Gerald M. Loeb, and Jesse Livermore all forcefully cautioned against taking stock tips. Beginning investors especially are vulnerable to the influential arguments of an exciting market analyst exhibiting cogent reasoning using their scintillating mental brilliance, but astute investors should not be beguiled. This leads to the following caveat for astute investors.

Disregard All Stock Tips

In order to maintain a sound mind, have market poise and composure under pressure, and have confidence in investment decisions – that almost without exception the investor will be solely and financially responsible for anyway – it is imperative to be dubious of all advice, stock tips, and opinions presented in the media and of all non-paid market analysts or advisers.

The information in this book should overcome investing ignorance; but, the investor is still required to think and perform the necessary fact finding, analysis, evaluation, to form a judgment, come to a conclusion, and take proper action. It is unreasonable to expect strangers to perform investment work for free without an ulterior motive. So be skeptical of others' opinions to either buy or sell stock.

By not taking stock tips, investors should save vast amounts of money. *The Astute Investor* gives specific direction on what and where to find pertinent investing facts and information, so decide to take advantage of this knowledge and by all means – please do not take stock tips. Advice from market newsletters should also be questioned, as explained next.

Market Newsletters And Advice

Newsletters give reasons and opinions on what stock prices and the stock market will do in the future. However, a beginning investor would find it beneficial to never see or hear any market advisers' suppositions, rationalizations, and doubts. It would be better for investors to spend his or her time searching for their own market information, once they know what to look for, and drawing their own investing conclusions.

Newsletters And The Internet

Important information and many essential facts are carried by the news media, on the internet, and in newsletter sources. However, comments and opinions on the stock market constantly bombard investors and should not be given too much credibility.

CNBC cable television offers a dedicated stock market channel. The internet supplies many newspaper Websites (e.g., www.nytimes.com and www.investors.com etc.) and financial Websites (e.g., www.thestreet.com, http://money.cnn.com, and www.bloomberg.com etc.). The Hulbert Financial Digest (www.hulbertdigest.com) keeps track of and rates approximately, as this is written, a hundred and twenty market newsletters.

The investing public often finds that copious stock market opinions and conflicting interpretations are perplexing. Internet technology helps investors tremendously, but it also has the potential to confuse beginning investors by producing self-doubt and anxiety as the amount of outside opinions that investors receive increases. The investing essentials are there; but, often beginning investors find the pertinent facts camouflaged or more infuriating yet, hiding right there in plain sight.

Rely On Stock Market Achievement

Rather than simply spending money on newsletters, which may be thought of as just taking stock tips and may cost hundreds of dollars a year, it is far better for astute investors to think for themselves rather than being content being told what to do. The best strategy is for astute investors to commit to stock market achievement, and not to rely solely on market newsletters.

Achievement is successful accomplishment as a result of diligent work that usually requires perseverance. Learn, inspect, practice, and do not give up until gaining the investing knowledge presented in *The Astute Investor,* and the judgment gained becomes second nature.

It is best not to lean on others' opinions on the stock market. Actual investing accomplishments will give those who work hard the satisfaction of monetary gains and the feeling of pleasure over a job well done. Achievement makes one's life extraordinary – it is no longer thought of as work but now as a thrill.

Be skeptical of all investing advice without first making up one's mind to accomplish investing achievement by following the practical ten-step method for investing success. The crucial steps of investing, with examples, in a way that may be practically used by investors on a day-by-day basis are presented in *The Astute Investor*.

Summary

Investors should assume that all expected scheduled breaking corporate and government news has previously been fully discounted in the stock market by professional stock traders. Discounting the news is why the stock price will often decline during the next few days or weeks after good corporate or economic news appears, and advance during the next few days or weeks following the disclosure of bad corporate or economic news.

When the expected scheduled news does not match expectations then that in itself becomes news. The result is that new expectations become established which then become the new standard by which the future scheduled corporate or government news is judged. Thus the continuous Hegelian Dialectic of news anticipation, then reality of the news, leading to a revised news anticipation. This is the basis for the expected news discounting process.

All unexpected news has been partially discounted in the stock market. The stock market will have a sudden and logical reaction after any major breaking unexpected news becomes general public knowledge, however it may take the majority of investors days or even weeks to fully assess the impact of a truly major unexpected event.

Five questions are raised when major breaking unexpected news enters the marketplace. The most important question is the long-term state of the stock market. In a long-term up market, the effect of the unexpected bad news will be relatively short lived and the market should continue to advance. If however the long-term trend in the market is down, unexpected bad news should amplify the market's decent.

Skepticism of news headlines and of the intent of those behind the news should always be in the forefront of every investor's mind. Investing based solely on the nightly business news, by converting breaking financial corporate news into stock market gains, is often a short-term losing proposition for beginning investors.

Market newsletters give reasons and opinions on what the stock market will do in the future. However, a beginning investor would find it beneficial to never see or hear any market advisers' suppositions, rationalizations, and doubts. Treat one's ears as a liability. An investor's reasoning capability seems to become gravely impaired when they believe they have command of inside information or a stock tip. Remain dubious of all advice, stock tips, and opinions presented in the media and of all non-paid market analysts or advisers. Commit instead to stock market achievement.

9

Being Contrarian

Introduction

THE CONTRARIAN PHILOSOPHY is reviewed. Contrarian investing is explained with reference to fundamental analysis, value investing, the Efficient Capital Market Theory, to technical analysis, and to how contrarians view advice from financial experts. A couplet highlighting the sophistication of a market pundit's intent when giving advice is offered.

Contrarian investing and crowd behavior are explored. Implementing the contrarian philosophy, often challenging and disconcerting to execute in practice, is explained. Opposing the market and pride of opinion are defined. Why the self-selected market adviser's strategy is never to be used when attempting to be contrarian is discussed. When to be contrarian in the marketplace is underscored.

The contrarian investing methodology is presented. The fundamental ratios that contrarians use to evaluate corporate stocks for purchase are listed and their use explained. Additional contrarian factors, such as growth at a reasonable price (GARP) or insider purchases, are also discussed. The minimum upside potential that contrarians look for when deciding on a stock to purchase and when to sell are assessed.

Contrarian Philosophy

The philosophy of being contrarian in stock selection while investing is to behave the opposite from the conventional wisdom. Contrarians use and live by the investing motto, "buy low and sell high." Contrarians want to be buying when the investing public is selling, and selling when the investing public is buying. If everyone else is selling, that is the time to recognize value and look for bargains in the stock market.

The cornerstone of contrarian investing is a fervent belief that stock prices are often the result of investors' overwrought emotions which causes either plunging or soaring stock prices that are at a variance from their intrinsic, true, or fair values. Contrarians pride themselves on their discipline, patience, and ability to control their emotions so they do not succumb to these detrimental impulses.

Conventional Wisdom

A contrarian overlooks the current stock market conventional wisdom and opposes what the majority of investors are doing. Contrarians are known to purchase or sell the opposite of what is currently in-favor or currently out-of-favor by the investing public.

Contrarians search out the ignored stocks of fundamentally sound companies that have severely reduced stock prices. The idea being that a good company in a currently unpopular industry may, if purchased near its low, give above average returns if held for the long term. Questioning the prevalent investing assumptions of the day is the correct tactic to use when implementing the contrarian strategy.

It is obvious that if everyone has sold who will sell because they are scarred that the stock price will go lower, the only way for the stock price to go now is higher. Likewise if everyone has purchased a stock that are going to purchase this stock, then the only way for the stock to go now is lower. Thus, optimism is seen to prevail at stock price peaks and pessimism is prevalent at stock price bottoms.

Contrarians Need Discipline

Contrarians need the discipline not to foolishly respond to both the optimism and pessimism that periodically sweeps over investors in the stock market. The contrarian system compels the investor to study and actively search for good companies that are currently way below par in price and neglected by both the investing public and the financial experts.

Being contrarian puts investors in the ostracized out-of-favor stock camp which most investors find unnerving. Being in direct opposition to the popular stock preferences during any point in time requires a display of strong character by contrarians. Going against the crowd requires both the correct knowledge and a strong stomach.

The consequence of investor pessimism is low stock prices. Contrarians invest during pessimistic times not because they love pessimism, but only because they love the resulting bargain prices for stocks. General investor pessimism is to be bought into, not to be sold into.

Contrarian investors have pride in their ability to remain rational during the often emotional act of investing. Realism about the potential of stock gains or losses is foremost in their minds. A buy-and-hold strategy for a single stock is not an option for contrarian traders.

Stock price volatility may seem scary; but, if investors use this market volatility to their advantage to purchase out-of-favor stocks at the right time and then wait for three years for the prices to recover, then investing success should be theirs.

The possibility of at least a one-hundred percent gain should be the minimum objective for a specific stock. The long-term is the planning horizon, and daily stock price movements are ignored as simply the irrational pulse of trading.

Diversification Is Required

Contrarian investors rely on diversification to reduce the risk of purchasing out-of-favor stocks. Some stocks that are low in price deserve to be down because they are headed for bankruptcy, or they may not recover sufficiently in price after a few years.

Depending on the portfolio asset size, investing equally in at least twenty to thirty companies from approximately fifteen different industries will give contrarian investors adequate diversification.

Many beaten-down stocks which do not deserve to be beaten down are prevalent during a long-term stock market bottom. Identifying excellent but out-of-favor stocks with consistent earnings and dividend growth in bad times is the objective. The contrarian philosophy is compared next with other approaches in the investing field to get a better understanding of the contrarian technique.

Comparing The Contrarian Approach

The contrarian approach is founded on the value investing methodology, with certain exceptions, and rejects other important procedures. Comparing and contrasting being contrarian against other important investing approaches and philosophies may be found useful to more fully explain what it means to be a contrarian investor. Lets start by comparing contrarian investing to fundamental analysis and value investing as described by Graham-Dodd.

Contrarians And Value Investing

Graham-Dodd are considered the founders of modern day market or security analysis. With their in-depth look at companies, market or security analysts are considered to be the financial experts employed by brokerage firms to do the basic research and offer investing advice. Security or market analysts use fundamental analysis as a bottom up approach to determining whether a company's stock is either under, over, or fairly valued.

Graham favors a fundamental approach to value investing over a long-term planning horizon which is defensive in nature, thereby protecting investors from the vicissitudes of a volatile stock market. Capital preservation is of utmost concern for value investors.

Contrarian investing is founded upon fundamental analysis and value investing which includes Benjamin Graham as a founding father. Advantage in the stock market should be gained by selecting out-of-favor stocks which are comparative good values. Like value investors, contrarians shun high-flying high-multiple stocks which have prices that reflect highly euphoric sentiments rather than soberly realistic analysis.

Fundamental analysis relies heavily on financial analysis of the balance sheet, the income statement, and the cash flow statement. A fundamentalist presumes that a stock price is able to deviate from its intrinsic, true, or fair value, but that eventually investors will distinguish the difference and move the stock price back toward intrinsic, true, or fair value over time.

While contrarian investing relies on many financial ratios to help determine out-of-favor stocks and concentrates on the low-risk to high-reward analysis of value investing, there is a major strategic difference between the two. Contrarians believe that security analysts and financial experts put too high a value on the expected short or intermediate term prospects for a company which unnecessarily inflates or deflates the corporation's stock price. How contrarians view the Efficient Capital Market Theory is presented next.

Contrarians And The Efficient Capital Market Theory

The Efficient Capital Market Theory (covered in chapter 2), as supported by the Random Walk Theory, is not believed by contrarians. The stock market, says the efficient capital market theorists, is efficient because so many skilled participants who posses a collection of all relevant information are setting prices. Because the participants as a whole know all the relevant information then the market is competitive and intrinsic, true, and fair values will always prevail.

Random walk theorists assume that stock prices are set based on breaking news which can not be predicted. Because unpredictable news information comes into the market randomly – it is fully expected that stock prices respond randomly. Therefore, while abnormalities and inconsistencies prevail in the marketplace there is no way to take advantage of these anomalies. Therefore, over time, doing better than the stock market and getting above average returns is not possible.

Contrarians, on the other hand, assume that the stock market can be mastered by maintaining rationality and keeping emotional feelings under control and by being independent thinkers. Contrarians recognize in themselves the tendency to be caught up in market frenzies and to be overly influenced by the market experts. Contrarians say that investors tend to overreact to the news and to financial experts and that this knowledge and understanding can be traded on to produce above average stock market returns.

Contrarian investors often think of themselves as different from the average investor. Contrarians care little about being popular or fitting in with the crowd. Independence of mind tends to make contrarians appear to be nonconformists, but they believe how one looks is not the issue.

Contrarians prefer to be true to themselves and that is the credo by which contrarians live. Being contrarian requires being knowledgeable about the stock market, understanding human nature and crowd psychology, and being aware of the current political-economic conditions. Contrarians are also doubtful of technical analysis as presented next.

Contrarians And Technical Analysis

Contrarians look askance at technical analysis and stock charting. Technical analysis uses past price movements to help identify stock price trends and as a prediction for future prices. As discussed in chapter 2, if the Efficient Capital Market Theory is true then technical analysis would not be useful in predicting future prices.

If the Efficient Capital Market Theory is false, than technical analysis might work, but correctly projecting a future stock price from studying downward sloping or poor looking price charts for an individual company would contradict the contrarian selection methodology of which out-of-favor stocks to purchase.

Contrarians believe that technical analysis for individual stocks is a purely backward looking technique that should have no bearing on future individual stock prices. Consequently, accurate forecasting using technical analysis of individual stock prices is rejected by contrarians. As previously discussed, contrarians have a disdain for security analysts and so-called financial experts. An in-depth look at this conflicted relationship is discussed next.

Contrarians Evaluate Financial Experts

Contrarians are highly skeptical of the opinions of the market or security analysts and the financial experts employed at brokerage firms. It is felt that the projections offered by market experts are normally incorrect, and if they are correct it is only over the shorter-term. Contrarians think that having financial experts determine short or intermediate-term stock pricing is myopic and not altogether smart.

Contrarians feel that analyzing all the reasons that influence a company's stock price, perhaps thousands and thousands of factors, is too complex and time consuming for anyone to realistically accomplish. The interaction of all these causes make proper interpretation and correct judgment almost a certain impossibility, so why listen?

Market analysts often demand and get more and more information with the idea that more information will allow for better forecasts. Contrarians feel that more data necessitates more judgment and reasoning, not less. Contrarians expect that more information only increases the analyst's confidence in their own opinion, not its quality.

Greater confidence may lead an analyst to make even more optimistic projections which results in forecasting errors once the results are known. Along with their forecasting accuracy, the motives and intent of financial experts are also questioned.

Market Analyst Motives And Intent Are Questioned

The motives of the market or security analysts should stand questioning. During the internet boom of 1999 and early 2000, several stock market analysts were censured for making bogus recommendations even when they were aware that the companies being touted were of suspect quality. Making up fictional assessments of stock worth by stock market analysts or experts is disconcerting and does not instill investor confidence.

Along with questioning motives, the intent of financial expert's statements may be in doubt. Some, but certainly not all, market analysts or financial experts have a clever way of presenting information in such a way as to sway the investing public to take incorrect action.

The most insidious method used by particular market pundits to get investors to take the wrong action may be how the truth is employed. The following couplet, inspired by William Blake (1757-1827) the gifted English romantic poet and painter, captures the spirit of this complex warning:

> *The worst lie that is ever meant*
> *Is the truth told with bad intent.*

This couplet exemplifies how an especially sophisticated strategy may be used to get investors to take the wrong action. Paradoxically, the truth here is engaged as a stalking horse. A lie is misleading and deceitful, but it is straightforward in the sense that it may be disproved. The truth told to deceive or entrap another, so that they unknowingly act in a way harmful to their own welfare, is cold, calculating, malicious, and sinister; but, is also exceedingly effective.

The final insult to the investing public of course is that when unprincipled market pundits tell the truth with sinister intent, nothing illegal can be proved since nothing illegal has been communicated. Due to motive and intent questions, contrarians would like to have financial experts and market analysts prove their worth prior to placing their faith in them.

Disregarding Financial Experts

Because a market analyst or financial expert is making an argument for a position, the investing public may feel overconfident about their resulting stance in the market even in the face of almost complete ignorance about this particular stock or the political-economic condition of the stock market.

The correct way for contrarians to respond to expected poor market analyst forecasts is to invest in depressed stocks with good long-term prospects. The reason that most investors find the contrarian philosophy difficult to implement is that it requires disregarding the financial experts and having patience, since out-of-favor stocks may need three years to turnaround.

Financial experts, it is felt by contrarians, contribute to crowd behavior and market hysteria by pointing investors to the popular stocks of the day, often at market peaks, with overly optimistic forecasts that repeatedly do not pan out in practice. Unpopular and out-of-favor stocks tend to be ignored by the market analysts which contributes to their depressed stock prices. Market analysts and financial experts get media attention which further amplifies their influence.

Financial Experts And Media Attention

Financial experts and market analysts have a way of attracting media attention. Financial experts are used as commentary on the dedicated stock market channel on television. Market analysts are covered on the radio, in the business sections of newspapers, and on weekly Wall Street programs on television. A plethora of financial Websites on the internet are available as an outlet for the opinions of financial experts.

The media focuses on breaking news and analysis by the financial experts because that is what their viewers, readers, and listeners expect. Unfortunately, perhaps unwittingly, the media reinforces shorter-term thinking in the marketplace and contributes to the mass hysteria that this breaking news may engender. Market analysts and financial experts offering conflicting market or stock forecasts in the media may cause self-doubt and anxiety in the investing public, thereby contributing to their non-action in the stock market (see chapter 8).

Contrarian investors try hard to look beyond the shorter-term news and financial opinions by the experts when identifying good value but out-of-favor stocks. Contrarians feel that financial experts, and by association the media, broadcast mainly the hottest and most trendy investment ideas.

As the popular beat for a particular idea gains a following by the investing public, it is most difficult to contradict this Wall Street and media barrage. As a result of these positive broadcasts in the media, the mentioned stocks are going up and political-economic conditions look favorable. Excessive investor optimism now takes over and drives stocks to an overvalued price. It is this investor over optimism that the rational contrarian investor needs to be able to resist.

The psychology of trading in the stock market has been shown in chapter 5 to be rational, non-rational, and irrational. How contrarians deal with the reality of human nature is basic to their investing methodology as described next.

The Psychology Of Contrarian Investing

The investing public eagerly accepts direction from so-called market experts, reassurance, and the approval from others that they are doing the right thing. Humans generally move en mass because they are naturally gregarious and desire the feeling of safety available from belonging to a familiar group.

The Psychology Of Crowd Behavior

Charles Mackay put forth the idea in investing that human nature craves conformity and shuns the hard tasks of forethought, planning, accurate observation, knowing and interpreting the facts, and rational-reasoned-unemotional thinking to arrive at a considered conclusion.

The investing public is swayed by a stock markets that is advancing and going higher. Once an investing crowd is moving in one direction, as discussed in chapter 5, other individuals will naturally follow in that same direction. Investing crowds are eventually wrong at a limit point simply because all crowds will behave alike – like an out-of-control mob. An out-of-control crowd is unthinking, overly emotional, irrational, and maybe even becomes a little bit mad.

An individual is commonly not capable of saying "no" when everyone else in the crowd is saying "yes." However, an investor is neither correct nor incorrect simply because they agree with the investing mob or crowd.

Persons act on their beliefs which may be either true or false. In a crowd mentality, many beliefs are mistaken. Mistaken beliefs plus extreme and non-rational emotions, such as fear or greed, may cause a crowd to act with mass hysteria. In the stock market, mass hysteria takes the form of boom-bubble buying at long-term market tops and panic selling at long-term market bottoms. Investors come by their emotions naturally which is addressed next.

Humans Beings Are By Nature Emotional

The major premise relied on by contrarians is that investors overreact because human beings are by nature emotional. Individuals exaggerate in all levels of society and can be witnessed overreacting in their daily lives over their jobs, spouses, or something as mundane as the morning rush hour. This proclivity for every day overreacting is naturally played out in the stock market.

Fear and greed over money plays itself out in a highly charged and emotional way in the stock market. News, either good or bad, may cause the investing public to overreact. Acting in direct opposition to how all other investors in the crowd are behaving is a highly anxiety producing defiant behavior which few investors can master. Investors naturally cycle between being overly optimistic or overly pessimistic.

Investors have an inclination to overprice the hottest stocks and under price those stocks no longer in favor. In contrast, the cornerstone of the contrarian philosophy compels the contrarian investor to be steadfastly skeptical of the conventional wisdom which requires courage to implement.

Contrarians Require Courage

Contrarian strategy relies on buying out-of-favor stocks or selling stocks that have too much optimism associated with them. The contrarian strategy requires courage on the part of the contrarian investor. Having the stomach to follow one's head is not often easy. Investor emotions frequently get in the way. Investing one's hard earned savings, which represents financial safety, security, and protection against an uncertain future creates self-doubts. Making a decision which results in a loss of capital can be devastating to one's ego.

Since most investors hate to lose money more than they love to win money, a reluctance to buy is a natural impediment to purchasing stocks when in fact they should be purchased. Assuming that prices have now dropped to extraordinarily attractive levels and the stock analysis passes all of the needed tests, everything looks good but the contrarian is still afraid to act. After all, he or she thinks, am I the only one who sees the compelling value in this stock at this time? Where is everyone else? If a purchase is made, one will be fighting the crowd.

Contrarians, like everyone else, feels a twinge of fear buying when everyone else is selling. What if the price continues to decline after the purchase, then investors would regret their decision. Investors detest losing their self-esteem more than appreciate the feeling of winning in the stock market. The following sentiment indicators may be used to bolster contrarian investor courage.

Sentiment Indicators

Sentiment indicators of how optimistic or pessimistic investors are concerning the stock market may be monitored to help gauge investor emotions. The American Association of Individual Investors (AAII), the Consensus Index, or Market Vane may be reviewed to keep abreast of sentiment trends. The idea being that if readings get to historically high or historically low levels, they would be an indicator that investors are getting either overly optimistic or unduly pessimistic.

Extreme sentiment may be an indication that the political-economic conditions that incited the current long-term market move may be close to an end. The extreme of investor sentiment values should be an indication that the investing public is trading on either fear or greed. These powerful emotions may be clouding logical or rational thinking and can cause investors to act foolishly.

When too many investors are optimistic, contrarians want to be pessimistic. When investors are overwhelmingly pessimistic, contrarians want to be optimistic about stock prices. Armed with the information so far presented, the intrepid investor may now feel ready to implement the contrarian philosophy; but, be aware of the following implementation pitfall that needs to be avoided.

Contrarian Implementation

Being contrarian is simple in theory but challenging and disconcerting to implement in practice. The beginning investor may be aware of the contrarian philosophy, finds that he or she agrees with it, and is then eager to put it to good use.

However the following incorrect approach, called the self-selected market adviser's strategy – which is just another form of taking stock tips (as discussed in chapter 8) – is unfortunately frequently misused by the investing public to implement the contrarian strategy.

Self-Selected Market Adviser's Strategy

The novice investor may decide now is the time to be contrarian. He or she will take a long weekend or perhaps many nights after work reading the financial media to review the opinions of many different financial experts or market advisers and get intimately involved in the logic and facts that these market advisers and financial experts present.

The novice investor may learn a profusion of particulars about the U.S. economy, for example: the growth rate of the gross domestic product (GDP); whether the value of the dollar is rising or falling; production output figures; economic capacity availability; the trend in consumer confidence; inflation and interest rate prospects; forecast of the federal government's deficit; the foreign trade gap; and perhaps the tyro investor has time to read up on the housing market.

Of course, these proffered economic indicators and statistics will help support the advisers' predictions on the stock market – which may be that the market is either overvalued or undervalued, ripe for a big fall, or ready for a meteoric rise.

Being successful and well informed in his or her own field of endeavor, novice investors may well say to themselves, "How hard can this be, it looks easy." The investor brings the same capabilities of logical evaluation used in his or her line of business to assessing the stock market and naively selects the adviser's opinion, among those reviewed, with whom the novice investor most closely agrees. This is where the trouble begins.

Believing that the market or an individual stock is now either undervalued or overvalued, based on the financial expert or market adviser's brilliant reasoning, the tyro investor decides now is the time to be contrarian and go against the crowd and takes a contrary position in the market. If, as likely, the market moves against the novice investor, he or she may decide to hold on until the market comes to its senses and begins to correctly reflect the investor's rational opinion.

Predictably, this experiment in being contrarian goes wrong – but why? Two human traits, opposing the market and pride of opinion, need to be particularly guarded against when attempting to be contrarian which are discussed next.

Opposing The Stock Market

Jesse Livermore, perhaps the most accomplished stock market trader, emphasizes the vital importance of being in complete harmony with the stock market and to never oppose either a market's long-term advance or its long-term decline. The novice investor however, not knowing Livermore's sage advice, may mistakenly believe that the market is wrong and that they are right and thus begin to oppose the market. The novice investor now believes his or her now contrarian market position is correct, hopes this to be true, and consequently flatters himself or herself and mistakenly wills it to be true.

Highly intelligent individuals from learned professions especially fall prey to opposing the market. Professors, doctors, lawyers, engineers, and many others may have a deserved self-confidence in their professional opinions; but, they may develop an ego problem when trying to prove, self-importantly, that they are right and the market is wrong. All novice investors should be on guard against foolishly opposing the stock market.

To guard against falling pray to opposing the market, remember that the overall stock market is by definition never wrong. In opposing the market, an immense amount of money has been lost by many beginning investors. Do not count yourself as one who opposes the market based simply upon someone else's opinion that sounds valid but may in fact be specious. Along with opposing the market, pride of opinion often causes investors to hold on to clearly losing positions.

Pride Of Opinion

The overall stock market is never wrong, but beginning investor's opinions and beliefs about the stock market are repeatedly misguided. Conceit and the pride of opinion when attempting to oppose the market should be guarded against.

Numerous novice investors can not stand to admit to himself or herself that they are mistaken as that would be a major blow their own personal vanities (as discussed in chapter 5). The high-ego investor stubbornly holds on even when the stock position is clearly wrong. In effect, the misguided investor is saying, "I would prefer to lose money than admit to myself that I am wrong."

The pride of opinion investor, in order to protect their fragile ego, may rationalize the decision to hold on to the losing position by hoping that he or she can get out even. But that day may not come for several years, and in the interim their money is being lost.

The pride of opinion investor, who is positioned on the wrong side of the market, eventually can no longer take the pain of the market moving against him or her and gets out at a substantial loss. Since vanity, self-esteem, and ego are factors here, typically a scapegoat needs to be found; but who is really to blame? The answer to this question next.

Self-Selected Market Adviser's Strategy Is To Blame

Who is to blame for this money losing fiasco? Not the novice investor of course, because of their own high self-regard, better the market expert or adviser who gave them the idea in the first place. The chagrined tyro investor then decides that the adviser is to blame for their losses, is therefore no good, and vows never to follow that specific market adviser's council again.

The novice investor may now incorrectly believe that they did not go deeply or extensively enough into the economic statistics and vows to do better next time. With literally hundreds of market advisers giving opinions on the stock market, this process can continue unabated over the investor's lifetime producing repeated losing results.

Market advisers do not insure their opinions against an investor's loss, which means that the tyro investor is solely responsible if an adviser's opinions – whether they are right or wrong. Consequently, do not get caught up in this losing circle of: agreed to market advice – loss – new agreed to market advice – loss, etc.

Undoubtedly for novice investors, the self-selected market adviser's strategy to being contrarian, which is just another form of taking stock tips, is incorrect and should never be followed. The best strategy is for the investor to do their own thinking, gather, analyze, and evaluate their own facts, make their own judgments, and arrive at their own investment conclusions. Follow the practical ten-step method for investing success as presented in *The Astute Investor.* The proper timing to being contrarian is presented next.

When To Be Contrarian

Contrarian investing requires the correct knowledge, discipline to follow that knowledge, and the patience to allow the market to right itself and return to a more normal valuation level for out-of-favor stocks. Most investors are optimistic by nature, and by definition the optimism in the market is located in the other industries then would be attractive to contrarians, therefore being contrarian is difficult to implement.

Many investors want to be associated with the hot new industry or company and have dreams of getting rich quickly. Being able to remain contrarian over the long term of three years, where the benefits are to be expected, is frequently difficult to accomplish.

Often, the best time to be contrarian is at the limits of long-term market turning points. All during a long-term stock market upward move the investing public is right, they are only incorrect at the extreme of the long-term move. The investing public earns most of the money on the way up, but they do not get away with the money because the investing public holds on through the long-term downward plunge in the market.

At a long-term stock market low point is when most industries are out of favor. At the extreme of a long-term market bottom, if the astute investor can say to himself or herself that: 1) the awful news is simply a way that panic selling is facilitated; and 2) to be successful investing in the stock market I have to be contrarian to the investing public at the right time and do the opposite of the conventional wisdom. The astute investor, at long-term market lows, should rely on a belief in stock market cycles, the faith and stability of the United States, her institutions, and her customs. Even when one knows what to do, it is often difficult to act on this knowledge.

Action When Correct Is Difficult

Through intelligent stock market observation and controlling the natural urge to mitigate one's own anxiety by remaining with the crowd at the wrong time, astute investors can be contrarian and act correctly at the right times. However, not being able to actually perform and do what one knows should be done is also a common human failing.

Investors, to be successful contrarians, need be able to take action and have the courage of their own convictions. Correct information and market knowledge are essential at market turning points, but many investors still rely on their natural instincts of running with the crowd rather than bravely acting defiantly at the appropriate time. For success in the stock market, timing is crucial – as explained in chapter 2.

The contrarian act is highly anxiety producing, but to be successful it must by necessity contradict with what the general investing public is doing because the majority of investors must be wrong at a long-term market top or bottom.

Contrarian investing necessitates bucking the crowds and their popular viewpoints, controlling emotions and investing against one's gut feel. Standing up to a crowd is impossible without the necessary contrarian theory for support and is why the majority of investors can not bring themselves to act in a contrarian manner. Peer groups and social pressures all reinforce the collective norm. How to think like a contrarian, presented next, may help investors take the correct action.

Contrarian Thinking Is Unconventional Thinking

Contrarian thinking is not typical thinking which has a tendency to make one seem unconventional. Many persons find being unique to be an uncomfortable camp to be in because of a need of support from others. Since positive reinforcement is not there for contrarian thinkers, it is often easier to be co-opted by the prevailing out-of-control investing mob or crowd. But do not be pulled in.

To help themselves, astute investors may perform the practical ten-step method for investing success, to verify the conditions and fortify their courage necessary to buy a stock at long-term market bottoms or sell stock at long-term market tops. Beginning investors should not try to assume or anticipate a long-term market top or bottom but only attempt to react to its signals.

Perfection in trying to catch the exact long-term market peaks or lows is an unreasonable standard – investors should feel good about themselves by being close enough. The following contrarian methodology presents the steps necessary to implement contrarian investing in out-of-favor industries and their stocks.

Contrarian Investing Methodology

As David Dreman explains, when picking specific corporate stocks for purchase the following contrarian methodology may be pursued. The methodology may be applied to all stocks, but to reduce risk only large or possibly medium sized companies are recommended for inclusion for selection. Large companies generally posses extremely competent management and have the financial capability to withstand severe downturns in their industries and not be forced into bankruptcy.

It is imperative that investors investigate and come to the conclusion that the selected corporation's future prospects are excellent and that the current downturn is being addressed by experienced and skilled management.

First Find Out-Of-Favor Industries

The contrarian methodology is systematized and first begins by finding out-of-favor industries in the marketplace. The out-of-favor stocks from each depressed industry that has the best prospects and most value relative to its market price are identified by computing financial ratios.

Solid companies should be selected that are depressed in price and out of investor's favor as determined by the analysis of fundamental financial data. Fundamental ratios that contrarians repeatedly investigate prior to purchasing depressed stocks are the price-to-earnings (P/E) ratio, the price-to-sales (P/S) ratio, the price-to-free cash flow (P/FCF), the price-to-book value (P/B) ratio, and dividend yield ratio. The six steps, using the contrarian methodology to identifying contrarian stocks, are presented next.

Six Steps To Identifying Contrarian Stocks

The fundamental ratios that contrarians use to evaluate corporate stocks for purchase from out-of-favor industries are listed below and their use is explained. The following six steps help identify specific corporate stocks for purchase from the identified out-of-favor industries.

1) Within the depressed industry, find a well managed company with good prospects that has fallen by at least fifty percent in price. Therefore the expected stock price appreciation is at least one-hundred percent, if and when the stock returns to its previous high price.

2) The stock price will be depressed but the earnings should be less so, resulting in a low but respectable P/E ratio. The current earnings or forward earnings may be used when calculating the P/E ratio. Prospective earnings growth should be measured against current price level risk.

Low P/E ratio stocks, in relation to competitors in its industry or to the overall stock market, may be an indication of those companies which are temporarily being ignored by investors. Upon further study, the reason for the depressed stock price may be due to product or management failures, poor industry economics, or a natural disaster which adversely effected earnings.

It may be expected that low P/E stocks will experience added upside earning disclosures than high P/E stocks as they emerge from their recent doldrums. A P/E of twelve or less may be considered advantageous.

3) Having the price-to-sales (P/S) ratio be less than one may qualify the stock as a contrarian buy. The (S) is calculated by dividing the annual sales by the total number of shares outstanding – lets say $750 million dollars in sales divided by 55 million shares equals $13.64 sales/share. If the current share price is $12.00 per share then the (P/S) equals $12.00 divided by $13.64 or 0.88.

4) The price-to-free cash flow (P/FCF) ratio. The free cash flow computation is from the Cash Flow Statement and is determined by subtracting the cash flow required for total capital expenditures from the cash flow from operating activities (see the example in chapter 6). The FCF per share is calculated by dividing the free cash flow by the total number of shares outstanding: lets say $72 million dollars in FCF divided by 55 million shares outstanding equals $1.31 FCF/share. If the current share price is $12.00 per share then the (P/FCF) equals $12.00 divided by $1.31 or 9.16.

A (P/FCF) ratio less than ten would be considered a strong contrarian candidate. It should be recognized that a negative free cash flow company that is in a depressed industry may be headed for bankruptcy. On the other hand, a positive free cash flow (FCF) company can use their positive FCF to continue paying stock dividends, repurchase stock if share prices drop too far, or invest in the business to take advantage of reduced prices for the eventual industry rebound. It is best to invest with the strongest positive FCF companies.

5) The price-to-book value (P/B) of less than one would be a strong contrarian stock candidate for purchase. Book value is calculated from the asset or left side of the Balance Sheet where the Property and Equipment Account at cost has the Accumulated Depreciation to date subtracted. The resulting account is normally named Cost less Depreciation to Date. The total number of shares outstanding are divided into the Book Value. The resulting Book Value per share is divided into the Price per share for the company.

With the (P/B) less than one, fixed assets are being purchased at less than the original purchase cost after depreciation which would be considered a major asset if the industry and corporation have good prospects. This bargain price, at less than cost, would stand the investor in good stead if and when the industry eventually comes back into favor.

6) Looking for high dividend yielding stocks may be another important factor. The stock's dividend yield, calculated by dividing dividends paid

over the last year by the current stock price, should be compared with those in its industry or the stock market overall. A high dividend yield normally signifies a stock which is not currently in favor, but would be welcome income for the contrarian until the company once again returns to prominence.

Dividend yield rate evaluation, unfortunately, is not straight forward. The dividend payout ratio, stock dividends per share divided by stock earnings for each share, when it is above eighty percent may be an indication that the dividends can not be sustained and that a dividend cut is probable. A dividend payout ratio less than sixty percent, depending on the industry, would be preferred. As important as when to buy is having a means to knowing when to sell which is covered next.

Upside Potential And When To Sell

If a stock could be found that meets all of the above six step criteria, this stock would be a strong contrarian selection to increase by one-hundred percent in approximately three years. This would be a compounded rate of return of approximately twenty-six percent per year which would easily beat the average return offered by the S&P 500 Index over the super-long-term.

Contrarians search for undervalued low P/E stocks that are pulled down in an out-of-favor industry. The premise is that the industry will eventually return to favor and restore these fundamentally good companies to their rightfully attractive stock prices. Doing the opposite of what the emotional crowd is doing may pay outsized stock market returns.

Contrarians consider selling their stocks when the P/E for their stocks rises above the average of the S&P 500 Index. Also, if fundamentals change significantly then selling would be an option.

Contrarians what to purchase company's stock at its long-term low point, but at the same time being careful that the stock's low price is not deserved and may actually be going much lower or even leading into bankruptcy. Additional factors may be investigated to further determine the best out-of-favor stocks from neglected industries for selection.

Contrarian Investing Additional Factors

Four additional factors that may further help determine which of the stocks still in the running should be purchased are presented next.

1) An addition factor for study for contrarian investing may include growth in the equation. GARP, which stands for growth at a reasonable price, compares the corporate growth rate to the P/E ratio. For example, a company with a P/E of ten would need to be growing at least by ten percent per year.

Contrarian selected companies growing faster than their P/E ratio may offer investors the low risk of good value along with the possibility of a considerable increase in long-term prospects. Therefore, the purchase of out-of-favor GARP company's stocks may allow investors to reap even greater than one-hundred percent returns for investments over the long term.

2) The debt-to-equity ratio should be low and preferably with no debt on the books. Since the industry is out of favor, the company may experience economic competition. A company with no or low debt has the resources to withstand more than a highly leveraged firm and is expected to withstand any expected economic shocks with equanimity.

In addition, having access to debt when presumably interest rates are low gives management the flexibility to meet the challenges and possibly emerge stronger verses the competition once the upturn begins.

3) Insider purchases should be investigated. Insiders currently purchasing a significant number of shares in their own company should be considered a positive indicator. Company directors or top executives may be buying their company's stock because they see much better future profits around the corner, the possibility of a merger, or simply because their stock is undervalued at the current stock price.

Contrarians what to be investing along with the insiders because the outsiders will never know the reason for a rapid stock advance until after the good news comes out. Insiders may sell their shares for a variety or reasons, but they will only purchase a significant quantity of shares when higher share prices are expected.

4) Technical stocks, in general, are typically avoided by contrarians because they normally have high multiples of over forty times earnings. In addition, the investing public and stock market professionals overly

concentrate on technical stocks which leads to a euphoric outlook. Although, companies considered as tech stocks growing at least as fast as their P/E ratio may possibly be a candidate for a contrarian portfolio.

The contrarian methodology includes identifying out-of-favor industries and using the six step criteria to select contrarian stock candidates. The four additional factors presented in this section help with additional selection criteria for the final selection of contrarian stocks for purchase.

Summary

Buy low and sell high is the contrarians' motto. Contrarians want to be buying when the investing public is selling, and selling when the investing public is buying. Questioning the prevalent conventional wisdom of the day is the correct tactic to use when implementing the contrarian strategy.

Contrarian investors have pride in their ability to remain rational during the often emotional act of investing. Contrarian investors rely on diversification to reduce the risk of purchasing out-of-favor stocks. Contrarian investing is founded on fundamental analysis and value investing with certain modifications.

Contrarians believe that market analysts and financial experts put too high a value on the expected short or intermediate-term prospects for a company which either inflates or deflates a corporation's stock price. The Efficient Capital Market Theory is not believed by contrarians. Likewise, contrarians look askance at technical analysis and stock charting.

Contrarians remain skeptical of the opinions, motives, and intent of market analysts and financial experts. The investing public eagerly accepts direction from the so-called market experts because human nature craves conformity and shuns the hard tasks of forethought, planning, accurate observation, knowing and interpreting the facts.

Being contrarian is simple in theory but challenging and disconcerting to implement. The self-selected market adviser's strategy is incorrect when implementing the contrarian strategy and can lead to the pitfalls of opposing the market and pride of opinion.

The contrarian methodology begins by finding out-of-favor industries in the marketplace. The out-of-favor stock from each neglected industry that has the best prospects and most value relative to its price is identified by computing the following financial ratios: price-to-earnings (P/E) ratio;

the price-to-sales (P/S) ratio; the price-to-free cash flow (P/FCF); the price-to-book value (P/B) ratio; and dividend yield ratio. Additional factors for evaluation for contrarian investing include growth in the equation (GARP), low or no debt on the books, insiders purchasing their own stock, and avoiding technical stocks.

The premise for contrarian investing is that the out-of-favor industry will eventually return to favor and restore these fundamentally good but out-of-favor companies to their rightfully attractive stock price. Contrarians consider selling purchased stocks when the P/E for these stocks rises above the average of the S&P 500 Index. Contrarians expect at least a one-hundred percent return in approximately three years from their investments.

10

The Ten-Step Method For Investing Success

Introduction

THE TENTH STEP, in the practical ten-step method for investing success, is bringing all of the parts together from the previous nine chapters to form an integrated picture of the stock market and of individual stocks for possible investment. As of March, 2004, an example of this ten step process is presented with actual data secured from the Websites already specified in prior chapters. By following this practical example, astute investors will be able to perform their own specific and unique analysis for any future opportunity they desire.

Specific issues presented include: investing goals and strategy; identifying political-economic conditions; calculating the S&P 500 Index Expected Fair Valuation Model; identifying the S&P 500 Index Nine Month MA Trend Line (including confirming indicators); mastering human nature through desired character traits; presenting eBay Inc. intrinsic, true, or fair value, market value capitalization, bargain value, margin-of-safety multiple, and additional crucial factor calculations; yield curve spread analysis; a discussion of the Discounted News Theory; and why it is best to be investing along with the crowd during March, 2004.

The Astute Investor gives a practical ten-step method for investing success that includes what investors most need to know and where to find current data on the internet to run models for themselves, thus empowering investors to form their own reasoned investment opinions without having to rely on possibly dubious outside market advice.

March, 2004: Bringing The Parts Together

This chapter takes the reader through each step of the practical ten-step method for investing success as of March, 2004. Each numbered step corresponds to its chapter number in Part I of *The Astute Investor*. By looking at the entire marketplace picture, the best investment judgments may be determined.

The actual numbers used to calculate the models discussed here are real and are collected from the Websites already fully referenced in the previous nine chapters. In this way, authentic practical examples will help investors do their own investigations and analysis of the S&P 500 Index or individual stocks at a point in time of their choosing.

Step # 1: Investing Goals And Strategy

The goal is to make money by investing in the stock market over the long term. The safety of the principle and making an adequate return are two major concerns. Therefore, a sound investing approach is preferred rather than merely hoping for luck in the stock market. The correct knowledge, calculations, and analysis will allow investors to have confidence in their own decisions.

Perfect solutions to the investing problem are not to be expected, only probabilities will be judged with regard to the best time to be invested in the stock market. Investor foresight and vision of expected future events will be the cornerstone of the investing approach taken here. Investors should not want to invest late in a market upward move that is too near to an expected long-term market top or while the overall stock market is trending downward toward a long-term market bottom.

Strategic diversification is selected because concentration in relatively few stocks is only for investing experts. A diversified low-cost S&P 500 Index stock mutual fund will make up at least ninety percent of the investment portfolio. An individual stock will be selected from the investor's area of expertise to form the additional ten percent of the invested funds by using intrinsic, true, or fair value, market value capitalization, bargain value, margin-of-safety multiple, and additional crucial factor calculations. With the suitable investing goals and strategy decided upon, step two is discussed next.

Step # 2: Political-Economic Conditions

The business cycle only partly controls long-term stock market prices. Over the long-term, the stock market does not move up or down simply based on the business cycle. Political factors also play a major role in determining stock prices. Political factors may include government lawsuits into stock market or corporate practices, major accounting or business legislation, political unrest in the world, shifting national agendas and revisions to fiscal budgets at all level of government, and the Federal Reserve changing the federal funds interest rate. Political-economic conditions over the long-term determine overall long-term stock market prices which are assumed to be irregularly cyclical in nature.

The S&P 500 Index monthly data rather than day-to-day movements for an individual company are studied. Mr. Market is always available to either buy or sell stock. Mr. Market's bankroll is appreciated but as astute investors we endeavor not to fall under his often crazy influence. The overall capital markets are assumed to be efficient much of the time, but not as a result of the random walk process. The symbolic irregularly cyclical stock market is a consequence of political-economic conditions.

Long-term political-economic irregular cycles that influence the stock market are expected. The objective is to properly identify these stock market irregular cycles and invest accordingly which begins in step three next.

Step # 3: S&P 500 Index Expected Fair Valuation Model

Fundamental analysis may be used to answer many important questions about a corporation's finances, such as: return-on-equity; earnings-per-share; and determining corporate cash flows. Cash flows from the Cash Flow Statement (CFS) are particularly useful to investors because they are not under the control of accounting standards or management actions that directly effects the Income Statement.

The price-to-earnings (P/E) ratio is highly scrutinized by the investing public but there are fundamental inadequacies. The P/E ratio can not be compared using the same or set standards over all companies or industries. The gravest failure is that the P/E ratio is backward looking and uses the past twelve months of earnings data for its calculation.

The stock market is a discounting mechanism that looks ahead to what will happen in the future. At a long-term market top, the look ahead feature may be over the next six to twelve months. Astute investors exercise foresight by using the forward P/E ratio to discount future expected corporate earnings. Investor foresight is applied when using the S&P 500 Earnings And Estimate Report as presented next.

S&P 500 Earnings And Estimate Report

The Standard & Poor's (S&P) estimated reported earnings of those companies in the S&P 500 Index are reported on their Website http://www2.standardandpoors.com. The Website commands have been previously presented in chapter 3.

Forward earning estimates for March, 2004 are listed in Table 10 - 1: March, 2004 - S&P 500 EARNINGS AND ESTIMATE REPORT. As of the beginning of March, 2004, the S&P 500 EARNINGS AND ESTIMATE REPORT indicates the reported earnings are preliminary as of 12/31/2003: Standard & Poor's will finalize 12/31/2003 earnings on 4/15/2004. Two months have passed since the end of the 12/31/2003 quarter, during which time actual earnings are being collected. Standard & Poor's designates the 12/31/2003 data with a preliminary indicator as shown on Table 10 - 1; consequently, to facilitate the look ahead capability of this model, 12/31/2003 data are now treated as actual and estimated reported earnings are used beginning with the 3/31/2004 quarter. The next twelve moths of data on Table 10 - 1 are for the 3/31/2004 through 12/31/2004 quarters.

From Table 10 - 1, the next twelve month (presented by quarters) estimates for as reported earnings (3/31/2004 to 12/31/2004) for the S&P 500 Index total $52.30 per share (14.00 + 13.70 + 12.90 + 11.70). The S&P 500 Index in March of 2004 is at 1,155. The forward P/E ratio for 2004 is 1,155 divided by $52.30 or P/E = 22.1. The next twelve month estimates for as reported earnings (3/31/2005 to 12/31/2005) for the S&P 500 Index total $54.20 per share (14.90 + 14.20 + 13.40 + 11.70). The forward P/E ratio for January, 2005 is 1,155 divided by $54.20 or P/E = 21.3.

Table 10 - 1: March, 2004 - S&P 500 EARNINGS AND ESTIMATE REPORT

Quarter End	Price	Operating Earn./ Share	As Reported Earn./Share
ESTIMATES			
12/31/2005			11.70
09/30/2005			13.40
06/30/2005			14.20
03/31/2005			14.90
12/31/2004		16.99	11.70
09/30/2004		16.11	12.90
06/30/2004		15.30	13.70
03/31/2004		14.45	14.00
12/31/2003 Prelim	1111.92	14.93	13.50
ACTUALS			
09/30/2003	995.97	14.41	12.56
06/30/2003	974.50	12.92	11.10
03/31/2003	848.18	12.48	11.92
12/31/2002	879.82	11.94	3.00
09/30/2002	815.28	11.61	8.53
06/30/2002	989.81	11.64	6.87
03/31/2002	1147.39	10.85	9.19
12/31/2001	1148.08	9.94	5.45

Copyright © 2004 The McGraw-Hill Companies, Inc. Standard & Poor's Including its subsidiary corporations ("S&P") is a division of The McGraw-Hill Companies, Inc. Reproduction of this Article in any form is prohibited without S&P's prior written permission.

10-Year U.S. T-Note Interest Rate

The next requirement is to find the prevailing 10-Year U.S. Treasury Note (T-Note) interest rate from Website http://moneycentral.msn.com/investor/home.asp, the necessary Website commands are presented in chapter 3. The 10-Year T-Note interest rate during March, 2004 is at 4.04%.

Using the S&P 500 Earnings and Estimate Report and the 10-Year U.S. Treasury Note (T-Note) interest rate the S&P 500 Index Expected Fair Valuation (EFV) Model is calculated and presented next.

S&P 500 Index EFV Model Calculation

The discounted market valuation using the Standard & Poor's (S&P) 500 Index Expected Fair Valuation (EFV) Model is calculated over the next twelve months.

For the S&P 500 Index EFV Model calculation, the next twelve month estimated as reported earnings ($52.30) are divided by the S&P 500 Index price (1,155) resulting in a S&P 500 Estimated Reported Earnings Yield of 4.53 percent. The 10-Year T-Note interest rate (4.05%) is divided by the S&P 500 Estimated Reported Earnings Yield (4.53%), resulting in a S&P 500 Value Factor (in our example: 4.05 percent divided by 4.53 percent = .894).

The S&P 500 Value Factor of .894 is less than 1.00 signifying that the S&P 500 Index, as of March, 2004, may be undervalued by approximately ten percent. An expected fair valuation for the S&P 500 Index is calculated by dividing the S&P 500 Index price by the S&P 500 Value Factor (in our March, 2004 case: 1,155 divided by .894 = 1,292). The S&P 500 Index Expected Fair Valuation Model for March, 2004 is indicating that the S&P 500 Index is undervalued. The expected fair valuation is approximately 1,292, or approximately a ten percent increase above the March, 2004 S&P 500 Index price of 1,155.

S&P 500 Index EFV Model Valuations

Assuming that S&P 500 Index earnings estimates do not change and the 10-Year T-Note interest rate remains stable, the S&P 500 Index Expected Fair Valuation (EFV) Model valuation is calculated for January, 2005: 4.05

percent is divided by 4.69 ($54.20 divided by 1,155) percent = .864 which is then divided into 1,155 equaling 1,337. These results are presented in Table 10 - 2: March, 2004 - S&P 500 Actual & Forward P/E Ratios & Expected Fair Valuation Model. The S&P 500 Index EFV Model values, shown below for March of 2004 and January of 2005, indicates the S&P 500 Index is expected to be in an uptrend:

March,   2004 - S&P 500 Index EFV Model of 1,292
January, 2005 - S&P 500 Index EFV Model of 1,337

The expected market uptrend identified here in step three is expected to be confirmed in step four which is presented next.

Step # 4: S&P 500 Index Nine Month MA Trend Line

Long-term irregular cycles in the U.S. stock market may take one, two, three, four, five years or more. In the long-term, once the overall stock market turns down off its peak prices or up from its market low prices, regardless how good or bad the news is or what select stock market pundits, investing gurus, or financial experts say, this event is of surpassing significance and the astute investor heeds this cogent indicator.

Perspective And Monthly Data

In order to adequately view how slowly the stock market actually moves over the long-term, investors need perspective; therefore, monthly data are studied. Monthly data are instrumental in dampening out the short-term volatility of day-to-day price chatter in the stock market.

Four Main Stages

There are four main stages in a long-term stock market cycle which are:

Stage 1: Mark-Down - Downtrend
Stage 2: Accumulation - Bottoming
Stage 3: Mark-Up - Uptrend
Stage 4: Distribution - Topping or Rounding Over

Table 10 - 2: March, 2004 - S&P 500 Actual & Forward P/E Ratios & Expected Fair Valuation Model

Date	S&P 500 Index Price	10-Yr T-Note Yield	Actual 12-Mo. Earning	Actual P/E	Estimated 12-Mo. Earning	For-ward P/E	S&P 500 Value Factor	S&P 500 EFV Model
*Mar '04	1155	4.05	$49.08	23.5	$52.30	22.1	.894	1292
Jan '04	1155	4.05			$52.30	22.1	.894	1292
Jan '05	1155	4.05			$54.20	21.3	.864	1337

* In this case many of the actual reporting earnings close for the first quarter of 2004 at the end of March, so there is an overlap with the forward estimated reported earnings.

Check the S&P 500 Index Nine Month Moving Average (MA) Trend Line direction for perspective to reveal market cycle stages. Double tops and bottoms, head and shoulders tops and bottoms, S&P 500 Index Two Month Moving Average (MA) Trend Line, MACD, Outside Reversal Days, and other indicators should be used as confirming indicators as presented in chapter 4. The identification of Stage 3: Mark-Up - Uptrend during March, 2004 is made and presented next.

Stage 3: Mark-Up – Uptrend: March, 2004

The BigCharts.com and CBS MarketWatch.com Website http:// bigcharts.marketwatch.com is used to create Japanese candlestick graphs and the Website commands for setup have been previously presented in chapter 4. The graph for March, 2004 is presented in Graph 10 - 1: March, 2004 - Stage 3: S&P Mark-Up - Uptrend.

The S&P 500 Index Nine Month MA Trend Line is clearly pointing upward. This indicates that the market during March, 2004 is in Stage 3: S&P Mark-Up - Uptrend. For the confirming indicators. The S&P 500 Index Two Month Moving Average Trend Line is pointing upward and above the nine month trend line. The MACD is supporting Stage 3 with the divergence positive and the MACD (12,26) blue line above the MACD EMA (9) signal red line.

No S&P 500 Index double top, head and shoulders top, or outside reversal day (ORD) are in evidence which means the market does not appear to be topping or rolling over. Monthly higher-highs and higher-lows confirms that the market is in a long-term uptrend and in Stage 3. In Stage 3, during a long-term market uptrend, the astute investor should be invested in the market as represented by the S&P 500 Index. Basic human nature and the human mind – including rational, non-rational emotions, and irrational influences – are addressed in step five next.

Step # 5: Human Nature And Desired Character Traits

Basic human nature and the human mind are unchanging. Human frailties, flaws, and limitations set up mental obstacles to being successful when investing in the stock market. In general, humans love illusions – especially when these illusions concern or personally concerns themselves. Trading

Graph 10 - 1: Mar., 2004 - Stage 3: S&P 500 Index Mark-Up - Uptrend

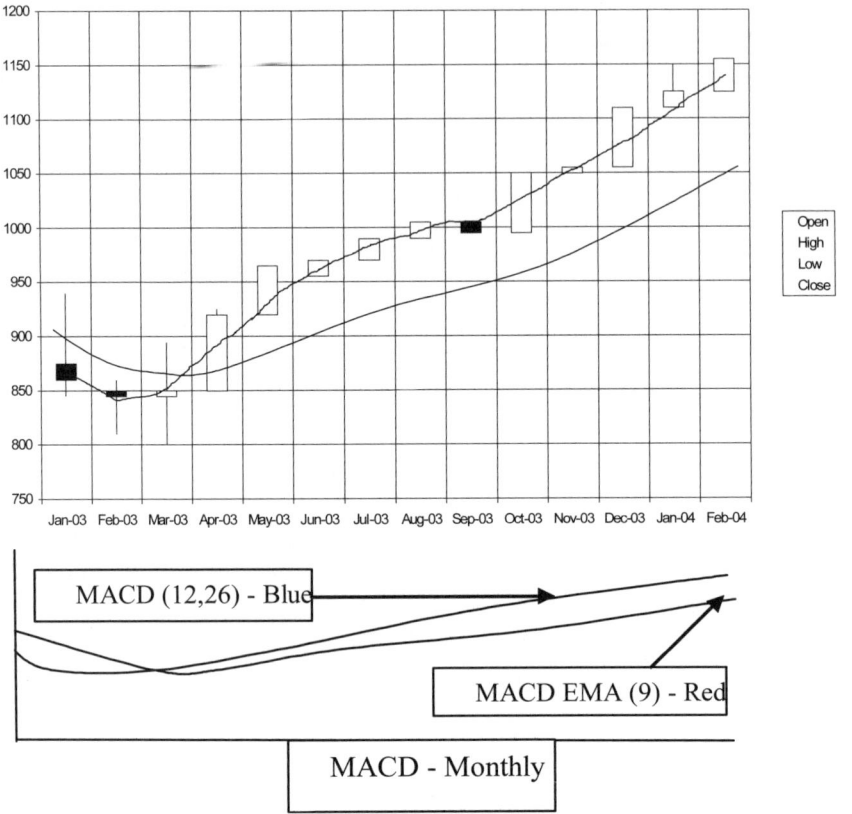

stocks on illusions or mistaken beliefs is often an egregious financial blunder, but is a common occurrence as discussed next.

Vanity, Greed, And The Will To Believe

Investors may demonstrate their emotional weaknesses when participating in the stock market. The number one impediment and most inflexible obstacle to investing success is personal vanity. The next enemy of and the way to undermine, after vanity, sound investing judgment is greed. The third psychological hurdle to investing success, after vanity and greed, is the will to believe.

Rational, Non-Rational, And Irrational Influences

Understanding how rational, non-rational emotions, and irrational influences can undermine intelligent investing is important. Even totally rational investors under stress may display self-doubt and anxiety which are the rational deterrents to intelligent investing. Investors' non-rational emotions of fear or greed may overpower their reason and move stock prices beyond intrinsic, true, or fair value.

Investors may conduct themselves in three irrational ways. The first is an investor's need for appreciation and high self-regard in oneself may overcome all else, even money. The second is striving for perfection and trying not to look silly in the imperfect investing realm, so that every move in the stock market proves oneself infallible, is self-defeating and therefore irrational. The third irrational influence concerns stock trading addiction. Being unaware of these three detrimental irrational influences is necessary when trading in the stock market.

Skilled trading requires investors to control stress that often results in self-doubt and anxiety, their non-rational emotions, and irrational influences that may take precedent over the investor's concern for money. It is important for investors to master investment poise, maintain an even temperament, not to take things personally, to practice self-discipline, and to keep their mind orderly and judgment focused and untroubled during the customarily stressful act of investing.

Desired Character Traits

Investors should recognize and practice the following fifteen desired character traits which support proper actions necessary for success in the stock market: perspective; analysis; compliance; self-confidence; flexibility; judgment; conviction; be decisive and act; patience; temperament; humility; experience; keep records; maintain private counsel; and persistence.

Step six requires performing intrinsic, true, or fair value, market value capitalization, bargain value, margin-of-safety multiple, and additional crucial factor calculations for a specific company's stock to determine its suitability for investment.

Step # 6: Intrinsic, Market, And Bargain Values

The major premise of value investing is that the stock market displays inefficiencies, mainly due to the human non-rational emotions of fear and greed, which causes the market or a particular stock price to be above or below its intrinsic, true, or fair value; however, stock prices should eventually reach or return to their mean intrinsic, true, or fair values. The margin-of-safety tenet is the cornerstone for a prudent value investing style.

Margin-of-Safety

The Graham-Dodd margin-of-safety principle is fully applied when determining whether common stocks are undervalued or bargained priced based on an intrinsic, true, or fair value calculation. An advantageous disparity between the corporation's market value capitalization verses its intrinsic, true, or fair value may be determined. Positive disparity is the safety margin that supplies the stock its cushion for any miscalculations or unexpected market circumstances. The margin-of-safety for stocks should be at least twice intrinsic, true, or fair value over market value capitalization.

As Warren Buffett extols, the strength of intrinsic, true, or fair value investing is that a good stock may be recognized using a systematic valuation methodology which is the value solely contained within the corporation. Intrinsic, true, or fair value is best determined by a sound calculation methodology conducted by an investor after reviewing all relevant facts and making appropriate estimates of future conditions.

Investor foresight and discounting are instrumental when making intrinsic, true, or fair value calculations. The best way to demonstrate this is to take an actual company and show a step-by-step intrinsic, true, or fair value, market value capitalization, bargain value, margin-of-safety multiple, and additional crucial factor calculations as of March, 2004.

eBay Inc. Is Selected

eBay Incorporated is selected because the investor has used their Website to both purchase and sell items of value with pleasing results and feels it is within his or her area of competence. eBay Inc. is listed on the NASDAQ with the stock symbol EBAY and is part of the internet market commerce industry.

Pierre Omidyar is the founder and chairman of the board of eBay Inc. which he created in 1995 to establish an on-line marketplace to buy and sell goods and services using an auction-style format for both individuals and businesses. Prospects for eBay seem excellent because the company is expanding globally and is the dominant company within its category.

The investor knows and appreciates the service provided by eBay and feels that the company has good prospects going forward. The Graham-Dodd-Buffett style of value investing is used to make the required calculations which will determine whether eBay Inc. is a good investment candidate based on the intrinsic, true, or fair value investing methodology.

Step 1: eBay Inc: Intrinsic, True, Or Fair Value Calculation

The intrinsic, true, or fair value calculation for eBay Inc. starts with their Cash Flow Statement (CFS). Go to http://investor.ebay.com for a copy of the eBay Annual Report. As this is written, under the Recent Earnings Releases click on 01/21/04 for the annual 2003 financial results. Data for Table 10 - 3: eBay Inc. - Cash Flow Statement (in millions of dollars) for years 1999 to 2001 are augmented by information from the Zacks Website at www.zacks.com.

Total capital expenditures are determined by subtracting the purchase of property and equipment (sometimes called capital expenditures), the acquisition/disposition costs or gains from the purchase or sale of subsidiaries, plus the addition of any proceeds from the sale of assets.

Total capital expenditures are subtracted from the cash from operating activities bottom line from the cash flow statement, resulting in free cash flow (FCF) for eBay shown in Table 10 - 4: eBay Inc. - Free Cash Flow (in millions of dollars).

Table 10 - 3: eBay Inc. - Cash Flow Statement (in millions of dollars)

Year	1999	2000	2001	2002	2003
Cash From Operating Activities	**67**	**100**	**252**	**480**	**874**
Purchase of Property and Equipment	(93)	(56)	(56)	(139)	(365)
Purchase of Investments*					
Maturities and Sale of Investments*					
Proceeds from Sale of Assets				36	
Acquisitions, net of cash acquired			(112)	(59)	(216)
Cash from Investing Activities*					

*Investment accounts not pertinent for the calculation of Total Capital Expenditures and Free Cash Flow (FCF).

Table 10 - 4: eBay Inc. - Free Cash Flow (FCF) (in millions of dollars)

Year	1999	2000	2001	2002	2003
Cash from Operating Activities	67	100	252	480	874
Total Capital Expenditures	(93)	(56)	(168)	(162)	(581)
Free Cash Flow (FCF)	**(26)**	**44**	**84**	**318**	**293**

eBay's growth rate in free cash flow (FCF) is approximately ninety percent per year ($44 in 2000 x 1.9 x 1.9 x 1.9) equals $302 in 2003. The negative FCF in 1999 is due to a start-up company situation. The growth rate in FCF from 1999 to 2000 is enormously impressive.

The annual report indicates that the five year growth rate for eBay's sales revenue and net income are also especially remarkable and are shown in Table 10 - 5: eBay Inc. Sales Revenue and Net Income (in millions of dollars) are from the income statement.

eBay's sales revenue is growing by approximately seventy-five percent per year from 1999 to 2003 ($225 x 1.75 x 1.75 x 1.75 x 1.75) equals $2,110. The growth in eBay's net income from 1999 to 2003 is approximately 150% per year ($11 x 2.5 x 2.5 x 2.5 x 2.5) equals $430 which is extraordinarily impressive indeed. Profit margins have improved from approximately five percent of sales in 1999 to twenty percent of sales in 2003 which is also laudable.

Top-line sales growth per year of 75%, bottom-line net income growth of 150% per year, and FCF growth per year of 90% signifies a growth company in the early stage of its development. It is expected however that this torrid growth will be restrained by the lowest percentage increase, in this case the 75% growth in sales. To grow for an extended period of time by exceptionally high growth rates is extremely difficult.

Table 10 - 5: eBay Inc. - Sales Revenue & Net Income
(in millions of dollars)

Year	1999	2000	2001	2002	2003
Sales Revenue	225	431	749	1,214	2,165
Net Income	**11**	**48**	**90**	**250**	**442**

Consequently and to be conservative, the projections of free cash flow (FCF) growth rates will be 75% for the next two years, then 50% for the next two years after that, then 25% for two years, and 20% for the remaining four years. Thus, eBay's projected sales revenue will be approximately $48 billion dollars by 2013 which seems feasible as their auction-style internet market becomes more established, they advertise more, and they continue to expand globally.

Because a dollar in the future is worth less than a dollar today, the astute investor will discount future free cash flows by a risk-free discount rate. The 30-Year U.S. Treasury Bond (T-Bond) interest rate is used for discounting the risk-free rate of return.

The current 30-Year T-Bond interest rate is located on the CNBC - MSN Money Website http://moneycentral.msn.com/investor/home.asp presented in chapter 3. For March, 2004, the 30-Year U.S. T-Bond interest rate is 4.90 percent. Therefore, a five percent risk-free discount rate may be considered appropriate.

Present worth factors (P/F) for a five percent discount rate are now necessary for our calculations and are found in Table 6 - 3: Discount Present Worth Factors (P/F). If a different interest rate, say a 6% discount risk free rate were needed, simply go to the www.outfo.org Website discussed in chapter 6 and under Table for i = 6.00% click that risk free discount rate to get present worth factors to match new interest rate conditions.

When a corporation's free cash flow (FCF) increases faster than the risk-free discount rate a two-stage valuation model is prepared. Table 10 - 6: eBay Inc. - Stage 1: Expected Discounted FCF to Today's Prices shows the expected future yearly increases of eBay's free cash flow (FCF) (in the third row), over the next ten years based on the conservative growth rates already estimated earlier.

The present worth factors (PWF) (which have been rounded off) from Table 6 - 3 are used to discount the future FCF figures back to today's prices (called present worth of FCF) which are located in the last row in Table 10 - 6.

The intrinsic, true, or fair value of eBay Inc. for the first stage is the sum of the future ten years of the present worth of the discounted free cash flows, residing in the last row of Table 10 - 6, which is: intrinsic, true, or fair value for the first stage ($487 + $817 + etc... + $3,996) equals $21,731 million dollars.

The second stage assumes that eBay will grow at a slower rate after year ten, let's assume a standard five percent, and that the risk-free discount rate of interest will increase to eight percent. The Capitalization Rate is calculated by subtracting the expected second stage growth rate of five percent from the expected risk-free discount rate of eight percent (8% - 5%) which equals a three percent capitalization rate.

The free cash flow (FCF) value in year eleven would increase from $6,550 million dollars, the FCF in year ten from Table 10 - 6 (third row), by five percent to 1.05 x $6,550 = $6,878 million dollars. To calculate the present worth from year eleven of a uniform series of all future FCF values, divide the $6,878 million dollars by the capitalization rate of three percent which equals $229,267 million dollars.

Bring the $229,267 million dollars to today's prices by multiplying by the present worth factor (PWF) of 0.58 (from Table 6 - 3, the 0.58 is the present worth factor for year eleven). The second stage intrinsic, true, or fair value equals $229,267 times 0.58 equals $132,975 million dollars.

Table 10 - 6: eBay Inc. - Stage 1: Expected Discounted FCF to Today's Prices

Future Yr	1	2	3	4	5	6	7	8	9	10
Prior Yr's FCF	293*	513	898	1347	2021	2526	3158	3790	4548	5458
Growth Rate/Year	75%	75%	50%	50%	25%	25%	20%	20%	20%	20%
Free Cash Flow	513=	898	1347	2021	2526	3158	3790	4548	5458	6550
Present Worth Factors	0.95	0.91	0.86	0.82	0.78	0.75	0.71	0.68	0.64	0.61
Present Worth of FCF	**487#**	**817**	**1158**	**1657**	**1970**	**2369**	**2691**	**3093**	**3493**	**3996**

* Actual Free Cash Flow (FCF) of eBay Inc in Year 2003

= Multiply $293 million dollars x 1.75 = $513 (rounded off) million dollars

Multiply $513 million dollars x 0.95 = $487 million dollars

The intrinsic, true, or fair value in today's dollars for both stages are then added together to equal the intrinsic, true, or fair value for eBay Inc. as of March, 2004: $21,731 + $132,975 equals $154,706 million dollars.

Step 2: eBay Inc: Market Value Capitalization Calculation

Calculating the market value capitalization of a corporation is imperative to determine how investors are currently valuing the corporation. From eBay's 2003 annual report, the total diluted number of shares outstanding are identified.

eBay's market value capitalization is the number of diluted shares outstanding of 657 million shares multiplied by the current March, 2004 stock price of $70 dollars per share, equaling $45,990 million dollars.

Step 3: eBay Inc: Bargain Value Calculation

The intrinsic, true, or fair value for eBay is now compared to its market value capitalization. If the intrinsic, true, or fair value for eBay is higher than its market value capitalization then the corporation is undervalued. The calculation is the $154,706 million dollars of intrinsic, true, or fair value less the $45,990 million dollars of market value capitalization to equal $108,716 million dollars of bargain value.

eBay is clearly undervalued with a towering bargain value. Determining if the intrinsic, true, or fair value is at least twice the market value capitalization is the cornerstone of the margin-of-safety value investing style. This is determined by calculating the margin-of-safety multiple as presented next.

Step 4: eBay Inc: Margin-of-Safety Multiple

The margin-of-safety multiple is calculated by dividing eBay's intrinsic, true, or fair value of $154,706 million dollars by its market value capitalization of $45,990, equaling 3.36.

Because the intrinsic, true, or fair value is 3.36 times the market value capitalization, eBay qualifies as being well over Graham-Dodd-Buffett's margin-of-safety minimum criteria of two for stock selection and would be considered a good buy.

Investors do not have to stop here. Margin-of-safety multiples and bargain values may be calculated for all of the companies under consideration for purchase. The margin-of-safety multiple along with the bargain value for each corporation under study may then be rank ordered, highest to lowest values, to determine by comparison which companies' stock to make investments in.

A presentation of the Warren Buffett value investing style of stock selection is shown to rely extensively on the proper calculation for a corporation's intrinsic, true, or fair value, market value capitalization, bargain value, and margin-of-safety multiple. An investigation into additional crucial factors are also required to complete the review for making a proper investment decision. Those additional crucial factors necessary for study are presented next in step five which includes the points one through ten as listed in chapter 6.

Step 5: eBay Inc: Ten Additional Crucial Factors

Prior to investing in eBay Inc. using margin-of-safety multiples and bargain values, and at least once a year after investing in eBay, it is prudent to test for solvency, corporate capitalization, return-on-equity, operating profit margin, and the qualitative factors championed by Philip Fisher. The following calculations are performed for eBay Inc. during March, 2004 (all values in parentheses are in millions of dollars):

1) Calculate the current ratio from the 12/31/03 eBay annual report balance sheet – total current assets ($2,146) divided by total current liabilities ($647) equals 3.31. The current ratio tests the short-term liability-paying capability of the corporation. In general, the current ratio should be greater than two-to-one which eBay handily surpasses. eBay easily passes the current ratio test.

2) Determine the debt-to-equity ratio from the 12/31/03 annual report balance sheet – total liabilities ($647) divided by total shareholder equity ($4,896) equals 0.13. eBay is using $0.13 of liabilities for every dollar of shareholder equity.

Recently eBay has found it advantageous to include more leverage on its balance sheet with the issuance of an additional $111 million dollars of long-term debt. However, excessive debt is not an issue at eBay since the effective maximum limit of a one-to-one debt-to-equity ratio is not being approached. eBay handily passes the debt-to-equity test.

3) Calculate return-on-equity (ROE) from the 12/31/03 annual report income statement and balance sheet – annual net income ($442), less dividends on preferred capital stock from the income statement ($0), divided by total shareholders' equity from the balance sheet ($4,896) equals nine percent. Profit is compared to the amount of equity that the owners have put into the corporation.

The ROE should be a high percentage and may be compared with industry averages. The opportunity cost of capital concept is useful here. If equity funds could be invested in other ways to earn more than the ROE of the company invested in, then the opportunity cost of capital of the alternative investment would be forfeited. Therefore, the alternative investment may well be the better investment of the two. eBay's ROE of nine percent is acceptable but improvement may be expected.

4) Operating earnings, from the 12/31/03 annual report income statement, are the earnings before interest and tax (EBIT) payments. Calculate the operating profit margin (OPM) by dividing the pretax income of EBIT operating earnings ($662) by net sales ($2,165). The resulting operating profit margin (OPM) is slightly over thirty percent. eBay's OPM is acceptable and is improving over time.

5) eBay's diluted net earnings per share (DEPS) from the 12/31/03 annual report income statement are $0.67 in 2003; $0.43 in 2002; $0.16 in 2001; $0.09 in 2000; and $0.02 in 1999. DEPS has been growing by approximately 140% per year which is in line with net income growth for eBay. The price to earnings P/E ratio calculation is $0.67 per share diluted net earnings divided by the share price of $70 dollars for a P/E (diluted) equaling 104 which may seem high. However, projecting DEPS growth of 75% for 2004 gives a forward DEPS of 1.75 x $0.67 equaling $1.17.

The resulting eBay forward P/E (diluted) ratio is 60. The forward price to earnings to growth (FPEG) ratio is the forward P/E (diluted) ratio of 60, divided by DEPS growth per year of 140% which equals 0.43. An FPEG ratio below 1.00 is good, and below 0.50 is outstanding. eBay's expected DEPS growth rate and FPEG ratio are both exceptionally good.

6) The investor has tried the services offered by eBay and is well satisfied with the results. With the expanded global reach of the company and expected increase in advertising, the long term prospects for eBay are judged to be excellent. In conclusion, based on Philip Fisher's definition, eBay is found to be both prosperous and gifted in the relatively new field of internet market commerce.

7) eBay managements' integrity, intelligence, and vitality are judged to of the highest quality. A talented management team with a clear succession plan is determined to be in place; thereby supporting stockholder welfare, effective communication skills, good employee relations, and endorsing research and development. Management is able to develop, implement, and communicate good policies, and strategies as well as effectively and efficiently run the day-to-day operations of the company.

8) It is felt that eBay Inc. has an outstanding marketing/sales/distribution organization. Sales growth of 75% per year over the last five years has been outstanding.

9) eBay Inc. is the leader in their category with excellent operations management which has demonstrated the ability to translate explosive sales revenue growth into correspondingly excellent increased net income of 150% per year over five years. Research and development into effective and efficient operations' processes are expected to be ongoing.

10) Any interviews of customers, vendors, subcontractors, government, university scientists, and employees at other companies concerning eBay Inc. have all been positive.

Conclusion

With eBay's bargain value equal to $108,716 million dollars, the margin-of-safety multiple of 3.36, and the additional crucial factors being mostly excellent – investors should be encouraged to make a long-term investment into eBay. In addition during March, 2004, eBay has attained an all-time-high price of approximately $70 dollars per share, even in a difficult stock market during 2000 to 2003, which may be interpreted as a good sign.

Step # 7: The Yield Curve

Interest rate spreads are a vital indicator for investors and consequently the stock market. Interest rates vary through time based on the aggregate supply of funds obtainable for all loans from all lenders verses the aggregate demand for funds from all borrowers.

Since interest rate changes are tied to the strength of the real economy and political-economic conditions, interest rates should be monitored as an indicator to political-economic change. Watching the trends in the money market are fundamental statistics that combine both political and economic factors.

Federal Reserve

The Federal Reserve is the central bank of the United States whose goal is attaining U.S. economic stability through adjusting the amount of currency in circulation, the accessibility and charge for credit in the financial system, and the makeup of how the U.S. national debt is financed.

Half of the monetary supply and demand equation that determines interest rates in the short-term for the U.S. economy is controlled by the political process. The latest statement from the Federal Reserve should be checked at www.federalreserve.gov/FOMC/.

The Federal Reserve statement for January 27/28, 2004 states that the federal funds rate is being maintained at one percent. The upside and downside risks in the economy are judged to be in balance and the Federal Open Market Committee (FOMC) believes they can be patient in removing the accommodative monetary policy.

At any point in time, the yield curve is a visual illustration of interest rates or yields in graphical form depicted over a range of scheduled lending terms or bond maturity lengths. The yield curve during March, 2004 is a positively sloped steep yield curve and is presented next.

Steep Yield Curve: March, 2004

The CNBC - MSN Money Website is used to find interest rates for different U.S. government bill, notes, and bond maturities to draw a current yield curve. Go to http://moneycentral.msn.com/investor/home.asp as presented in chapter 3. The yield curve is shown in Graph 10 - 2: March, 2004 - Steep Yield Curve.

During March, 2004 the yield curve spread between the 3-Month T-Bill (0.98%) and the 30-Year T-Bond (4.90%) exceeds three percentage points (4.90% - 0.98% = 3.92%) and is a positively sloped steep yield curve.

Therefore, the steep yield curve during March, 2004 is upwardly sloping and considered to be positive for the stock market based on political-economic conditions. Greater than a three percentage yield curve spread, where the slope of the yield curve angles steeply upward, signals that long-term bond investors expect the political-economic prospects to be fantastically positive. The steep yield curve is an optimistic sign for the overall stock market.

Graph 10 - 2: March, 2004 - Steep Yield Curve

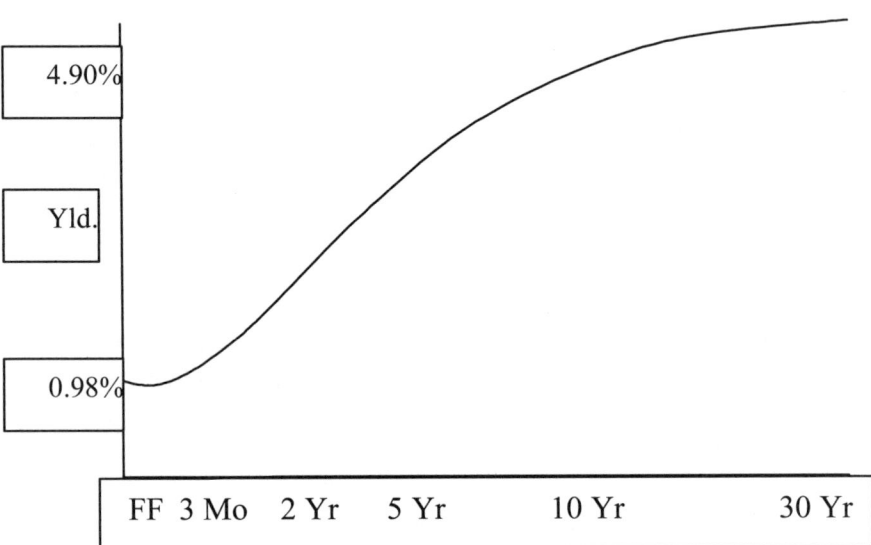

Step # 8: Discounted News Theory

To interpret the news correctly requires understanding that corporate news is often anticipated in advance using investment foresight which is called discounting the news.

Discounting the news is a prior bidding up or selling down of stock prices, usually over the short or intermediate term, in anticipation of either good or bad news from a company or a government agency on the economy.

Prices advancing on bad corporate news and declining on good corporate news may look illogical to novice investors, but is readily expected once discounting the news is fully appreciated.

Expected News

All expected news presented at scheduled times has already been fully discounted in the marketplace by professional stock traders. Scheduled news can either meet expectations or not meet expectations. When actual good corporate earnings are released which meet expectations, often the already discounted stock may be sold off over the short term as all the new information is assessed to develop new expectations for the next quarter. Thus, the expected corporate news has already been fully discounted.

When scheduled actual news does not match expectations then that in itself becomes news. The result is that revised expectations again become established which then become the new standard by which the future scheduled corporate and government news is judged. This is a continuous and ongoing Hegelian Dialectic progression of anticipation, then the reality of the news, leading to a new anticipation by professional stock traders which is the basis for the expected news discounting process.

Unexpected News

Unexpected news is everything that can be imagined by investors which they determine may effect the stock market. Unexpected news is nonscheduled news with only the likelihood of what, who, where, or when the imagined event may take place. Imagined unexpected events causes specific investors to modify both their actions and non-actions in the stock market.

Five questions may be asked to evaluate major breaking unexpected news. The last is, "What is the current state of the stock market?" and is the most important question when evaluating the effect that unexpected news will have on the stock market. Major unexpected good news will normally have only a short-term upward effect on a weak stock market. A weak market will not take unexpected bad news in stride. Unexpected good news in a strong market will push the market higher.

Major breaking unexpected bad news in an up market is expected to be only an intermediate-term obstacle in the marketplace. A market that is trending upward over the long-term is discounting, on balance, positive future breaking news. Likewise, a long-term market trending downward, coming off a market peak, is discounting by as much as the next six to twelve months negative future breaking news.

Discounted News Theory Conclusion

The Discounted News Theory describes a stock market that is always looking ahead, discounts all expected information, and incorporates all investor's actions and non-actions; thereby, the overall market becomes the long-term leading indicator to the political-economic condition.

With the S&P 500 Index Nine Month Moving Average trend line pointing upward and confirming indicators showing the sock market in Stage 3: Mark-Up - Uptrend, the preponderance of all the foreseeable news, expected or unexpected, is projected to be overall positive as of March, 2004.

Step # 9: March, 2004: Invest Along With the Crowd

The philosophy of being contrarian in stock selection while investing is to behave the opposite from the conventional wisdom. Contrarians believe that crowd psychology may cause investors to overreact because people are by nature emotional. The non-rational emotions of fear and greed plays itself out in a highly charged way in the stock market. Contrarians, like everyone else, feel a twinge of fear buying when everyone else is selling and selling when everyone else is buying.

Contrarian investing requires the correct knowledge, discipline to follow that knowledge, and the patience to allow the market to right itself and return to a more normal valuation level for out-of-favor stocks. Solid companies should be selected in out-of-favor industries that are depressed in price, as determined by fundamental analysis of financial data using the contrarian methodology.

Being In Harmony With The Stock Market

Jesse Livermore emphasizes the vital importance of being in complete harmony with the stock market and to never oppose either a market's long-term advance or its long-term decline. The market is never wrong, but beginning investor's opinions about the stock market are repeatedly misguided.

Being contrarian is simple in theory but challenging and disconcerting for investors to implement. Beware of conceit and the pride of opinion when attempting to oppose the market. The question is always, "When is the right time to be contrarian?"

An investigation into which out-of-favor industries are extent during March, 2004 could be undertaken. From the standpoint of the overall market however, now is not the time to be contrarian since the market is currently in Stage 3: Mark-Up - Uptrend. In keeping with our investing goals and strategy initially determined during Step #1, investments should be maintained in the S&P 500 Index and in eBay Inc. It is best to be investing along with the crowd during March, 2004.

Step # 10: March, 2004: Investing Analysis Results

Astute investors should pull together the information gathered during steps 1 through 9 to perform their own due diligence and make their own judgments and arrive at their own investment conclusions. It is the investor's money after all and only the individual investor, almost without exception, will be responsible for gains or losses regardless whose advice is followed – so whether to invest, what to invest in, and when to invest should be based strictly on each individual investor's own considered judgment.

A diversified S&P 500 Index stock mutual fund makes up ninety percent of this example's investment. The eBay Inc. stock is selected from our area of expertise for the additional ten percent of our funds. A summary step-by-step analysis follows.

S&P 500 Index Evaluation

During March, 2004 the forward P/E ratio for the S&P 500 Index is 22.1, and for January, 2005 it is 21.3 which may be considered good because prevailing interest rates remain low. The S&P 500 Index Expected Fair Valuation Model indicates that the stock market is undervalued and points to higher S&P 500 Index prices during 2004 and through 2005 which is extremely positive.

Long-Term Market Trend

The S&P 500 Index Nine Month Moving Average Trend Line is pointing upward during March, 2004, and it has been for the prior ten months. The market is determined to be in Stage 3: Mark-Up - Uptrend. All of the confirming indicators such as the MACD, S&P 500 Index Two Month Moving Average Trend Line, and monthly higher-highs and higher-lows all confirm the Stage 3: Mark-Up - Uptrend determination.

eBay Inc.

eBay Incorporated is selected for intrinsic, true, or fair value, market value capitalization, bargain value, margin-of-safety multiple, and additional crucial factor analysis because the company has good prospects going forward and is judged to be both prosperous and gifted in the new rapidly growing area of internet market commerce. eBay Inc. is determined to be within the investor's area of competence. The bargain value and margin-of-safety multiple calculations are: eBay bargain value equals $154,706 (intrinsic, true, or fair value) less $45,990 (market value capitalization) totaling $108,716 million dollars and is therefore undervalued; eBay margin-of-safety multiple equals $154,706 divided by $45,990 equaling 3.36.

Because the intrinsic, true, or fair value 3.36 times the market value capitalization, eBay Inc. qualifies as being well over Graham-Dodd-Buffett's margin-of-safety multiple minimum criteria of two for stocks and is considered a good buy. The ten additional crucial factors are judged to be mostly excellent.

Yield Curve

The yield curve is positively sloped upward and is considered steep because the spread between the 3-Month T-Bill (0.98%) and the 30-Year T-Bond (4.90%) exceeds three percentage points (4.90% - 0.98% = 3.92%). This is extremely important since the bond market is expecting the future political-economic conditions to remain especially positive for the stock market.

Step # 10: Conclusion

With the stock market being in Stage 3: Mark-Up - Uptrend during March, 2004, the expected and unexpected news should be on balance positive. The S&P 500 Index Expected Fair Valuation Model indicates that the stock market is undervalued and points to higher prices into 2005. eBay has a good margin-of-safety multiple of 3.36 and a bargain value of $108,716 million dollars. The yield curve spread is positive and steeply sloped upward predicting favorable political-economic conditions ahead. Investors should not take a contrarian position with the S&P 500 Index or with eBay investments, but should be investing along with the crowd during March, 2004.

No one can say with certainty what the future holds for the stock market, and past prices are certainly no guarantee for future prices. However, during March, 2004, the practical ten-step method for investing success indicates that this is most probably a good time to be invested long-term in a well diversified portfolio consisting of ninety percent in the S&P 500 Index and ten percent in eBay Inc. which fulfills step number one's stated investing goals and strategy.

PART

II

11

Retirement Planning

Introduction

R ETIREMENT PLANNING USING asset allocation is defined. Goal assessment over a predetermined planning horizon properly begins the planning process. Risk verses return for the broad asset classes of stocks, bonds, real estate, and cash are discussed in relation to the appropriate time when retirement funds will be required.

Risk tolerance, as it is currently used in retirement planning, is explained. The difference between risk verses volatility for a diversified investment, such as the S&P 500 Index, is specified. Why the terms risk and volatility should not be used interchangeably is explicitly discussed.

Volatility tolerance is presented as the more appropriate approach to classifying investors who are saving for retirement using a well diversified portfolio over a selected planning horizon. Volatility verses total return expectations in terms of asset allocation over set periods of time are explored. The compounding of total returns over the super-long-term planning horizon is explained to highlight its crucial significance to investors.

Carrie and Cash, a couple in their thirties, are followed throughout their decisions associated with retirement planning. While they are working, during pre-retirement, two basic strategies are explored – stocks or bonds for their core investment retirement account. Over a thirty-year planning horizon, the results from a stock or bond core investment retirement account are significantly different by a factor of two-to-one.

At or around retirement, Cash and Carrie are expected to rebalance their retirement portfolio to reliably produce income for living expenses. How to best accomplish this rebalancing using fixed-income annuities, a laddered-bond portfolio, social security, and continued equity investments for future long-term growth is fully explained.

Asset Allocation

Asset allocation is the diversification of investments by major asset class and is the equivalent of the adage, "do not put all your eggs in one basket." By dividing funds among broad asset classes, capital may be preserved with lower risk and the liquidity of the funds may be increased. Or simply put, the money will be there when needed. Asset allocation is a technique for creating and managing a different mix of assets that have the highest expected total return that match an investor's needs.

The principle of asset allocation is that money for retirement is split into four different major categories for investment. The asset mix chosen has a substantial bearing on expected total returns and risk levels. Diversification is the cornerstone of asset allocation because it mitigates the consequences of the downturn of one major asset class. The other three asset classes, during the time that one asset class is declining, may very well be improving.

Asset allocation is the allotment of money going into the broad asset classes of stocks, bonds, real estate, and cash. Many subcategories within each broad asset class exists, such as foreign stocks or domestic stocks, real-estate investment trusts (REIT) or owning one's own real property, and corporate bonds or U.S. treasury bonds. The performance and variability of investment portfolios are overwhelmingly, perhaps eighty to ninety percent, tied to the strategic decisions that investors make when determining how their savings are split between these four major asset classes.

Each of the four asset classes have dissimilar rates of return and risk associated with each investment option. For example, cash is not risky but has an expected low return over the super-long-term of less than four percent per year. The S&P 500 Index is expected to return approximately eleven percent per year, over the super-long-term, but is more risky over a few-year-term basis. Bonds and real estate have risks that are somewhere in between these two broad cash and stock categories.

Asset allocation is a systematic strategy for investing funds based on a broad diversification of assets, investment goals (or use for the money), planning horizon (or the time that the money will be invested), and the investor's tolerance for risk. Asset allocation is a technique to balance risk by developing an investment portfolio that matches investor requirements to asset classes. Because each investor has individual needs, no mathematical formula will determine the correct asset allocation mix for all investors.

The correct asset allocation mix determination involves: 1) goal selection; 2) planning horizon; 3) risk verses expected returns; and 4) risk tolerance assessments for each investor. A discussion of each of these four necessary steps follows, beginning with goal selection.

1: Goal Selection

The first step is to determine the reason for investing. Investment goals may include setting aside money for a down payment for a house, saving for college tuition, or retirement savings. Each goal is specific and comes with a different planning horizon.

Planning is important. Every investor should have goals in mind along with a time frame necessary for achieving these goals (please see chapter 2). The plan to achieve selected goals requires adequate funding. All personal goals may be planned for using an appropriate asset allocation mix of investments over an expected planning horizon.

If the planning horizon is over the super-long-term, even conservative investors may find it beneficial to be invested in a well diversified stock fund like the S&P 500 Index. If the goal is to send a daughter to college in five years, an asset mix that includes fixed income securities would be the more prudent investment choice.

If the super-long-term goal is to purchase a condo on the ocean in twenty years, the astute investor should not be at all concerned with the day-to-day or week-to-week fluctuations in the overall stock market. Political-economic conditions that cause downturns to occur in the stock market over the long-term will be more of a concern however. The planning horizon available to investors, described next, is crucial to selecting an appropriate asset allocation mix.

2: Planning Horizon

The planning horizon is the length of time until the money is needed for use. Ten months may be needed for an automobile down payment (intermediate term), five years until college tuition payments (long term), and thirty years until expected retirement (super-long-term). Each goal and different planning horizon has a direct effect on the asset allocation mix decision.

The more time in the planning horizon the more risk in the asset class that is appropriate for an investor's portfolio. As the planning horizon is reduced to less than eight years, the more likely that stock market risk will work against investors by forcing them to exit investment positions at a less then advantageous time thus forcing a losing investment. In such situations, fixed-income bond investments may be a much more prudent choice.

Bond investment durations that match when the money is needed may be the appropriate asset class mix when saving for a goal of less than eight years. U.S. treasury bonds carry interest rate risk while corporate bonds carry credit risk as well; but they are both normally less risky then the stock market and have higher interest rate returns over the long-term than money market options.

Since planning horizons get shorter as one gets older, retirement for a thirty-five year old may be thirty years away while for a fifty-five year old it may only be ten years away. Depending on the investor's stage in life, asset allocation allotments should be modified accordingly. Super-long-term eventually becomes long-term and then intermediate-term, so be ready to change asset mixes as life stages change.

3: Risk Vs. Expected Returns

The major asset groups of stocks, bonds, real estate, and cash typically display different degrees of correlation between expected returns and risk. Since different asset classes behave in a different way to one another, depending on political-economic conditions, they offer broad diversification. When one asset class is decreasing in value another may be increasing while a third may not be increasing in value as much.

It is expected that if the stock market has a bad year that bonds in the portfolio will do well as interest rates are expected to decline which increases the capital appreciation of the bonds. Investors are expected to move money from the stock market to the bond market to earn both interest income and capital appreciation from expected higher future bond prices.

Investors may be losing money on stocks, but at the same time may be gaining money on bonds in their portfolio. A well diversified portfolio spreads the risk and is the appropriate strategy for investors to dampen the results of a stock market downturn. Thus the downside risk is protected at the same time allowing for the essential portfolio growth.

By spreading the risk between major asset classes, the asset allocation investment is highly diversified. Many investors are apprehensive about stock market risks, thus diversification into many asset classes greatly diminishes the risk associated with a specific asset class. The markets for stocks, bonds, real estate, and cash tend not to move together or by the same magnitude. Therefore, a portfolio made up of non-correlated asset types should be less risky while at the same time offering good expected returns. How this works in practice is presented next.

Portfolio Returns In Practice

The relation between risk and expected returns for major asset classes are reported on based on a study over a fourteen-year time period. If all funds are invested solely in the S&P 500 Index, the returns would be approximately eleven percent per year; but, stocks would have declined during seven of those years. If the portfolio is totally invested in bonds during this same time period, the bond investment returned almost nine percent; but, bonds declined during seven of the fourteen years.

If the investor selects a strategic asset allocation of sixty percent in stocks and forty percent in bonds, the overall return would decrease by only half a percent from what was earned solely on stocks and down years would now have only totaled three. By sacrificing a little on the yearly return percentage, the risk of down years in the marketplace may be reduced by assigning some assets to stocks and some to bonds.

If however the asset allocation is split evenly between stocks, bonds, and cash – with approximately thirty-three percent assigned to each major asset class – the total return is reduced by one and a half percent from a total stock portfolio and experiences only two down years. Thus it is seen that a portfolio concentrated in one asset class like stocks is seemingly more risky than one evenly spread among three major investment categories over the selected fourteen-year time period.

Therefore if investors get emotionally upset knowing that their investments are down for the year, the best of the three above strategic asset allocation decisions would be the even split between all three asset classes. This may seem to be the correct decision, but stocks often give the best overall returns as is presented next.

Stocks Offer The Best Return Potential

In general, higher risk investments such as stocks offer the best return potential over the super-long-term. Day-to-day or week-to-week price volatility may be ignored since the cash should not be needed until the stocks have a chance to significantly appreciate in value. Over a less than three-year planning horizon, stocks may be eliminated from a investment portfolio when saving for a down payment on a house lets say.

Over the super-long-term, a well diversified portfolio that includes only the S&P 500 Index is expected to produce superior returns over a conservative portfolio of bonds alone. This will be fully demonstrated later in this chapter in Carrie and Cash's pre-retirement planning example. An investor's tolerance for risk helps determine their asset mix over a specific planning horizon which is normally decided upon using a questionnaire as described next.

4: Risk Tolerance

Depending on the individual investor, he or she may select investing only in a broadly diversified stock portfolio because of the excellent capital appreciation prospects it provides. Or conservative investors may decide that they have no tolerance for risk and elect only to invest in a broadly diversified bond portfolio, thereby completely eliminating the risks associated with a fluctuating stock market.

Many investors, saving for retirement, select a portfolio that includes both stable bond income along with the superior appreciation capabilities associate with stocks. A risk-tolerance assessment questionnaire, described next, may be used to establish whether an individual is in a conservative, moderate, or aggressive classification when it comes to making investments.

Risk-Tolerance Assessment Questionnaire

Each individual investor may have a different tolerance for risk. Often this is arrived at by asking a series of questions to help determine a person's risk-tolerance which may be described as being conservative, moderate, or aggressive. The following questions may be asked:

1) What would be your response if the investment portfolio temporarily plunges fifteen percent in value?
    a) Could not sleep at night.
    b) Would wish that a different asset mix were in place.
    c) Would recognize that growth oriented investments are risky, but future returns will improve.

2) Acceptable losses in the portfolio are:
    a) No downturn in value is acceptable.
    b) A temporary medium sized loss is acceptable.
    c) A temporary enormous loss is acceptable.

An investment adviser would work with the prospective investor, using a more extensive questionnaire, to develop an asset allocation model that best matches their client's tolerance for risk. The questionnaire helps the investment adviser decide if their clients are conservative, moderate, or aggressive investors. Once the investor is classified, the percentage of money going into each asset class may be assigned based on a standard asset allocation model mix as described next.

Standard Asset Allocation Model

Based on the risk-tolerance assessment questionnaire results, asset allocation mix percentages may be determined for each investor by matching their classification for risk against a standard model that gives the percentages that should be invested in for each of the four major asset classes. Of course, investors may modify these recommended percentages to met their particular needs.

Typically if an investor answers "a" for questions 1 and 2 on the risk-tolerance assessment questionnaire above, he or she would be assigned to the conservative tolerance risk class. Conservative investors would rank highly trying to protect the value of their portfolio throughout each step over their planning horizon. The conservative class might have a typical asset allocation model portfolio mix using the following percentages:

1) Money Market -   20 %.
2) Bonds -   60 %
3) Stocks -   15 %
4) Real Estate -   5 %

The moderate class investor would answer "b" for questions 1 and 2 on the risk-tolerance assessment questionnaire. Recognizing that risk of downturn over a few years may cause declines in the asset values, moderate investors will consent to this eventuality with the understanding that it could improve total portfolio returns. The typical asset allocation model mix percentages for moderate investors might be:

1) Money Market -   10 %
2) Bonds -   40 %
3) Stocks -   40 %
4) Real Estate -   10 %

The aggressive class investor would answer "c" to questions 1 and 2 on the risk-tolerance assessment questionnaire. Aggressive investors will ride through a steep downturn in the marketplace with aplomb knowing that a well diversified retirement portfolio should eventually regain its value over a period of time. The typical asset allocation model mix percentages for aggressive investors might be:

1) Money Market -   0 %
2) Bonds -   25 %
3) Stocks -   65 %
4) Real Estate -   10 %

Thus conservative, moderate, and aggressive investors have a standard asset allocation model mix that may be relied on for guidance during the pre-retirement planning stage.

An investor's tolerance for risk has been shown to be a crucial factor when determining their asset allocation mix. Risk is the term used to describe an investor's tolerance for possible loss in the marketplace, but should it be? Risk verses volatility is an important distinction in the area of investing which needs clarification and is explained next.

Risk Vs. Volatility

Risk and volatility are terms which are often used interchangeably in the financial research literature and in retirement planning practice – the question is should they be used interchangeably? Volatility in the marketplace is substituted for risk as an indication of how much better or worse the asset return will be when compared against an average of expected returns.

Volatility is often represented by a standard deviation statistic which is a calculation of dispersion of returns around the mean or average return for that major asset class. The more volatile and the greater the range of returns around the expected return the more risky the investment is defined to be in the financial literature.

Investors may imagine a false sense of fear when discussing the term risk. Also, quantifying risk using volatility and a standard deviation statistic may not be suitable. Warren Buffett has questioned the appropriateness of directly equating risk with volatility in an April 18, 1990 *Outstanding*

Investor Digest article. The following example is useful to help explain the significant difference between risk and volatility.

Risk Vs. Volatility: An Example

Using the methodology explained in chapter 6, the intrinsic, true, or fair value of a company is determined to be $500 million dollars. Because this corporation is currently in an out-of-favor industry and is having management succession difficulties, the market value capitalization is now only $100 million dollars. The bargain value of the company is a positive $400 million dollars ($500 million dollars - $100 million dollars) and is undervalued with a margin-of-safety multiple of five ($500 million dollars ÷ $100 million dollars).

Value investors may realize this out-of-favor corporate stock is worth appreciably more than the current market value capitalization. However, because it will take a long time to work out the problems at the company the stock is recommended to be sold by market analysts and is being sold by the investing public. Thus the low price for the stock.

Recently, prior to the company's difficulties, the stock sold for fifty dollars per share. Currently the stock is selling for ten dollars per share. This would be considered a risky stock because the volatility of the stock price is so extreme, having lately dropped from fifty dollars per share to ten dollars per share.

Based solely on the assessment of price fluctuation, its volatility would signify in the financial literature and by most practitioners that this stock is extremely risky. Compare the financial literature assessment with that of an intrinsic, true, or fair value investor. The intrinsic, true, or fair value investor would not be deterred by the sharp drop in the company's stock. The intrinsic, true, or fair value investor rightly decides, based on a margin-of-safety multiple of five, that now is the correct time and buys ten percent of the company's stock at ten dollars per share – which is possible for Berkshire Hathaway.

The volatility verses risk discrepancy is plainly seen if the stock now continues to decline to five dollars per share. If the intrinsic, true, or fair value investor then decides to purchase another ten percent of the company's stock at this new lower five dollar price per share; he or she would be accused of doing something even more risky, in the financial literature, since the stock at five dollars per share is considered to be still more volatile and therefore risky then at ten dollars per share.

Because the share price is more volatile at five dollars per share then at ten dollars per share, purchasing the second ten percent of the company for significantly less money would be considered riskier in the financial literature than when paying more money for the first ten percent of the same company. This more risky determination for the company at five dollars per share is illogical since the company now has a bargain value of $450 million dollars and a margin-of-safety multiple of ten. Resolving this irrational investing portrayal of risk is the purpose of the following discussion.

Risk And Volatility Differences

Purchasing a positive bargain value company at a now lower price is less risky, not more risky as the financial literature states. High share price volatility does not equate to high risk in this example. The way to resolve this impasse is to investigate the differences between the terms risk and volatility.

A positive bargain value company stock at a set price where the stock price fluctuates and gets even less expensive clearly makes this now cheaper stock less risky – not more risky. This is an important point that has been raised by Warren Buffett in his 1990 article that needs to be seriously addressed and properly resolved.

The risk verses volatility paradox is so severe that it requires a complete rethinking of the use of the terms risk and volatility in the financial literature and in practice. To resolve this dilemma, lets start by looking at the semantics of both words.

Semantics

It will be helpful to investigate the semantics of both risk and volatility to gain an understanding to how best to proceed from here. Semantics examines the meaning of words to individuals, both denotative (actual definition) and connotative (implication suggested by the word), and the influence words have on human behavior. The link between the implied meaning that risk or volatility has on human behavior is investigated.

The following discussion compares the origins, connotations, and denotations for the terms risk and volatility. Substituting one word for the other may not be justified based on how the terms are perceived by investors and how that perception influences their investing behavior.

Risk Semantics

To risk something is to put it in harms way and endanger it by exposing it to the possibility of an injury or a complete loss. The use of the word risk down through the centuries includes using it in the following ways:

1) The King *risked* surrendering his kingdom.
2) The knight *risked* his life at the jousting tournament.
3) He *risked* losing his good reputation forever.
4) In matters of insurance, never *risk* everything in one ship.

It can be seen that risk is used in connection with a terminal circumstance or a complete loss. Thus, to put something at risk may conjure up in an investor's mind the possibility of losing everything. It may be informative to investigate synonyms for risk, or words that may be used in place of the word risk to get a better idea of its purpose for use.

Synonyms to the word risk include: endanger; hazard; jeopardize; and imperil. They may be used in sentences in the following way:

1) Driving while drunk *endangers* innocent lives.
2) Secondhand cigarette smoke is a real *hazard* to one's well-being.
3) Severe competition *jeopardized* the future of the company.
4) No rain *imperiled* the lush vegetation.
5) Speculative stocks are *risky* due to possible bankruptcy.

The common theme of meaning relating each of these synonyms of risk is "to subject something to peril, ruin, or total devastation." A complete loss is at least threatened when using the word risk or its synonyms. Therefore, the connotation of the word risk to investors may be one of complete loss.

Because asset allocation's use of diversification among four different asset classes effectively eliminates complete loss of capital for investors, it would be best not to use the word risk when discussing a well diversified portfolio using asset allocation. Compare the word risk with the word volatility which is presented next.

Volatility Semantics

Volatility is defined as varying frequently and or extensively with different magnitudes. The direction of change and the extent of the change describes something that has volatility and may be used in the following sentences:

1) Corn prices moving quickly describes a *volatile* market.
2) The lover's moods were fleeting and *volatile*.
3) Weather *volatility* caused by local action off he lake is amazing.

It can be seen that volatility is used in the context of variable, oscillating, or fluctuating, but always the assumption is there that whatever it is will come back again. Synonyms to the word volatility include: oscillate; change; fluctuate; and vary. They may be used the following way in sentences:

1) Investors may *oscillate* between fear and greed.
2) The music *changed* for the fourth time.
3) Prices *fluctuated* wildly due to the uncertainty of the weather.
4) Diets *vary* depending on the source.
5) The S&P 500 Index is *volatile* day to day.

The passing of time is a major factor in each of these words as well as specific conditions or actions. The connotation of the word volatility to investors may be one of fluctuation and variability, but not one of complete loss.

Based on the specific meanings and connotations of the words, risk is not the same thing as volatility and these terms should not be used interchangeably; therefore, they should be separated for proper communication when investing.

Separating Risk From Volatility

Using the terms risky and volatile in the same context is incorrect. Something is risky when a complete loss is possible. A speculative company's stock is risky because it may go out of business and the investor may lose their entire investment. An the other hand, a well diversified portfolio like the S&P 500 Index may oscillate irregularly; but, it should always come back in price and is therefore not risky, only volatile.

The well diversified S&P 500 Index is volatile because while prices do vary through time they will always come back based on historical fact. Individual speculative stocks, on the other hand, are risky because they have been known to become worthless. Time is on the side of the volatile diversified S&P 500 Index portfolio because it comes back over time. Since everything may be lost in the speculative stock situation, time is not on the side of the risky or speculative stock that goes bankrupt.

It should no longer be appropriate to simply substitute the term volatility for risk. Also, quantifying risk using the standard deviation statistic for volatility should be considered inappropriate. With the terms risk and volatility no longer used interchangeably, investors may now talk about high volatility investments with low risk and low volatility investments with high risk as presented next.

High Volatility & Low Risk - Low Volatility & High Risk

The terms risk and volatility are now separated. The S&P 500 Index may be described, at a market bottom during Stage 2, with high price volatility but now presenting low risk to investors. A speculative stock, with a massive negative bargain value during Stage 4 at a market top, may be described as displaying low price volatility but now with high risk.

For intrinsic, true, or fair value investors who can calculate the true value of a company, they may be hoping for a highly volatile stock price because that will allow them to purchase these downtrodden undervalued positive bargain value stocks at a lower risk and now lower price and sell them at a higher risk and higher price later on.

Similarly, those astute investors who know the practical ten-step method for investing success may purchase the S&P 500 Index in Stage 2: Market Bottom - Accumulation when the volatility may be high but the risk to investor's funds may now be especially low.

A bond portfolio consisting of triple A investment grade bonds should display both low volatility of prices and have low risk. A single bond issued by a less than investment grade company may have displayed low price volatility, but due to its credit risk still has a higher risk of default than a well diversified investment grade bond portfolio.

If a previously investment grade corporate bond falls below face value due to credit risk and it can be reliably determined that the bond has hit bottom in price, this would be a case of a high volatility bond price with a low risk to investors. The potential for high capital appreciation, as the bond recovers its lost value, would make this out-of-favor bond a good investment. Separating risk from volatility will allow a discussion focusing solely on volatility when making asset allocation decisions as discussed next.

Volatility Tolerance

The asset allocation portfolio with its broad diversification possibilities across bonds, the S&P 500 Index for stocks, real estate, and cash should never be thought of as a risky investment but only as an endeavor that may display volatility. *The Astute Investor* believes that volatility should be the correct term used with individuals to determine their appropriate asset allocation mix.

Instead of asking investors for their risk tolerance, which may create bad visions in investors' minds of completely lost retirement funds, it would be much better to ask investors about their volatility tolerance. In this way investors will realize that given enough time these investments will come back and emphasize that their investment will not be completely lost.

Rather then investment advisers questioning their clients for risk tolerance, it would be much more appropriate to test investors for their volatility tolerance using a volatility-tolerance assessment questionnaire when determining the best asset allocation mix for retirement funds. Investors will still be categorized as conservative, moderate, or aggressive investors as discussed next.

Conservative, Moderate, Or Aggressive Investors

An investor's tolerance for volatility may be described as conservative, moderate, and aggressive. Thus an investor may be classified depending on their tolerance for volatility in their portfolio. The percentages listed for each typical model expresses how much money should be invested in each major asset class.

If volatility is being controlled for in a well diversified asset allocation portfolio, and it were explained clearly to prospective investors that it is not the complete loss of funds that is the issue, rather the timing that is of concern, then inventors might well key on the planning horizon is the most important variable to help determine the best asset allocation mix of stocks, bonds, real estate, and cash. Integrating different volatility tolerances with planning horizons are required to determine the proper asset allocation mix as described next.

Volatility Tolerance And Planning Horizon

The determination of how much to invest by asset allocation mix percentages is dependent on an investor's assessment of how averse to volatility they are. But, the planning horizon is at least as important as an investor's volatility tolerance for determining the proper asset allocation mix. As the planning horizon gets longer for specific investment goals, the model percentages should change for each classification of investor.

As the planning horizon increases, the amount of funds going into a more volatile diversified stock fund should increase. All investor classifications are expected to benefit as the longer planning horizon is expected to smooth over any expected volatility, thus resulting in higher total returns for all investor classifications. An investor's volatility tolerance and planning horizon for specific goals may now be combined in one table to help determine asset allocation mix percentages, as presented next.

Volatility Tolerance, Planning Horizon, & Asset Mix

The Table 11 - 1: Volatility Tolerance, Planning Horizon, & Asset Mix gives the sample relationship between stocks, bonds, and cash over different lengths of time before the money is needed by investors. Real estate investing and cash for emergencies are covered in the next section. For all fixed-income investments including U.S. T-Bills, T-Notes, T-Bonds, and bank certificates of deposits (CD) should be scheduled to come due prior to the need of the money by the investor.

The S&P 500 refers to an index fund of the S&P 500 stocks. T-Bills, T-Notes, and T-Bonds are identified in Table 11 - 1, however higher-return investment-grade corporate bonds may be substituted at the discretion of investors. Real estate investing is often in the form of a personal home. Cash for emergencies may best be separated from other funds which are described next.

Table 11 - 1: Volatility Tolerance, Planning Horizon, & Asset Mix

Planning Horizon	Conservative Vol. Tol.	Moderate Vol. Tol.	Aggressive Vol. Tol.
Less Than 3 Years	Money Market Acct (50%) Bank CD (50%)	Money Market Acct (25%) Bank CD (75%)	Bank CD (30%) Treasury Bills (35%) Treasury Nt. (35%)
3 to 8 Years	Bank CD (50%) Treasury Notes (50%)	Bank CD (25%) Treasury Notes (75%)	Treasury Notes (75%) S&P 500 (25%)
8 to 15 Years	Treasury Notes (75%) S&P 500 (25%)	Treasury Notes (50%) S&P 500 (50%)	Treasury Notes (25%) S&P 500 (75%)
15 to 20 Years	Treasury Bonds (25%) S&P 500 (75%)	S&P 500 (100%)	S&P 500 (100%)
20 Years or Greater	S&P 500 (100%)	S&P 500 (100%)	S&P 500 (100%)

Real Estate And A Separate Cash Account

It should be noted that the S&P 500 Index has real estate stocks included in its index, specifically home building, household furnishing and appliances, and building materials. Also typically included in an investor's real estate portfolio is their personal home. Therefore, the real estate asset class may be considered covered using these two options. However, additional investments into real-estate investment trusts (REIT) may be appropriate depending on investors' needs.

Cash, when saving for retirement over the super-long-term, is not given a percentage of the total amount of money put into the retirement account each month, but will be accounted for separately. In general, the investor's first priority for super-long-term retirement planning should be to set up a cash account for emergencies that will pay all living expenses for two months if anything should go wrong, such as the loss of a job.

This long-term retirement cash should be separate from the retirement planning account and located in a separate money market account so that it may be easily accessed in emergencies. Volatility verses total return assessments help determine correct asset allocation percentages as explained next.

Volatility Vs. Total Return

Expected volatility verses total returns, or having the value of the assets meet expectations at the time the funds are required, is the basis of asset allocation. Without asset volatility the decision would be straight forward. That is, select the assets to invest in that on average gives the highest returns. Everyone, it seems, would want to get rich the fastest.

Unfortunately, simply investing in high average return stocks, regardless of the planning horizon within which the money is needed, is not the answer. An example is instructive to appreciate the volatility inherent in the overall stock market.

Six Years From Peak To Peak: An Example

A well diversified stock portfolio will fluctuate, therefore not having as much money when the scheduled time for the goal arrives is a distinct possibility. The S&P 500 Index reached an intraday high of 1,530 at a double top on September 1, 2000. A long-term down market developed that ended in a head and shoulders intraday market low on March 12, 2003 of 789 (please see chapter 4). The stock market during this time period was in a long-term downtrend for approximately three years.

This almost fifty percent decline in the S&P500 Index is a good example of what can happen when investing in the stock market. Three years is a long time to wait as the market declines, and it may take another three years for the stock market averages to again reach their prior peak price level.

Since 1940, approximately six years – from peak, to return to peak – is reported to be the maximum length of time it takes the S&P 500 Index to once again regain what it has lost during a long-term downturn. This possibility should be recognized by all investors and specifically planned for.

If the money is needed for a particular goal in three years, perhaps the stock market is not the place to be for investors. What distinguishes the greedy return-fixated investor from the prudent investor is the capability to match volatilities with planning horizons for investment assets.

Although aggressive investors should allocate more funds to stocks than conservative investors, investors should not overlook the probabilities associated with stocks returns over a less than eight year planning horizon as discussed next.

The Stock Market And Eight Year Planning Horizons

Investors who can not remain invested, either because they need their funds or they can not stomach the anxiety of a stock market decline, should stay clear of the stock market if the money is needed in a less than eight year planning horizon. The expected fixed-income returns may be lower but more certain for these moderate and conservative investors.

Included in Table 11 - 1: Volatility Tolerance, Planning Horizon, & Asset Mix are factors that will help in making investment determinations. Based on Table 11 - 1, in the long-term of eight years or more, moderate and conservative investors should begin to take on more equity risk when using asset allocation.

Assuming that the stock market situation is favorable and the investor uses the practical ten-step method for investing success, the probabilities should rise appreciably for attractive equity returns over a less than eight year planning horizon. Astute investors knowing which stage the stock market is in while investing should greatly increase their chances of earning eleven percent per year on equity investments over eight years or less.

Compounding of total returns increases exponentially. Why this exponential compounding is vitally important to investors over a twenty-to-thirty year time frame is discussed next.

Retirement Planning: 20 Years Vs. 30 Years

Delaying saving for retirement is a mistake that many individuals make. Time is the friend of those saving for retirement. Having thirty years available until retirement age and delaying the start of saving for retirement by only ten years will require over two and a half times more money out of the investor's pocket merely to arrive at the same amount of retirement funds had they started with thirty years remaining.

Why is saving over thirty years so much better than saving over twenty years? The answer is that compounding of total returns over the thirty-year planning horizon allows for further exponential growth of invested funds as described next.

Compounding Of Total Returns

Compounding of total returns from capital appreciation along with dividends is a powerful force. Compounding of total returns is calculated not only on the amount of money the saver puts into the account, called principle, but also on the interest or capital appreciation plus dividends that are being earned on the investment earnings over time.

In the case of bonds, the principle plus the interest are earning compound interest. In the case of stocks, the total return of capital appreciation plus dividends are earning more capital appreciation and dividends all without additional money from the investor. This may sound like a small point, but is actually incredibly significant over the super-long-term planning horizon.

The power of compounding is that it is an exponential relationship that means that the amount of money earned by compounding in years twenty through thirty vastly exceeds the amount of money earned in years ten through twenty.

The S&P 500 Index may be expected to increase at eleven percent per year for capital appreciation and dividends paid over the super-long-term. One thousand dollars invested over twenty years at eleven percent compounded yearly grows to $8,062 dollars. If the same one thousand dollars were invested over thirty years at eleven percent compounded, it would grow to $22,891 dollars or approximately 2.84 times the growth simply by investing the $1,000 dollars ten years earlier. Compounding of total return is significant over longer-term planning horizons.

Longer-Term Planning Horizons

The longer the planning horizon the greater the percentage of money that can be put into more volatile investments, like the S&P 500 Index. Having a longer-term planning horizon means that the probability that the S&P 500 Index will return eleven percent per year every year approaches one if it is held over the super-long-term of twenty years or more.

Having a super-long-term planning horizon means that expected poor down years in the stock market should be nothing more than an inconvenience when looked at in hindsight. The only concern that investors should make contingencies for is the possibility of starting retirement when the stock market it at a long-term low point.

As much as three years may be necessary for the stock market to return to more normal levels after a long-term downturn. This can be accounted for by using bond savings later in the pre-retirement stage and will be covered in the following pre-retirement planning example. The subsequent example is presented to gain an appreciation of why stocks are so much better than bonds for a core investment over a super-long-term planning horizon.

Pre-Retirement Planning Example

What investors learn here could double their retirement income. The public much prefers certainty to uncertainty and it seems will submit to almost anything to achieve a certain state, even if the uncertain plan predicts superior rewards (please see chapters 5 and 9).

Why this natural human behavior can work against savers when investing for retirement over the super-long-term (two decades or more) is now examined in the following example.

Carrie And Cash Invest For Retirement

Lets follow a fictitious couple as they make decisions about investing for retirement. Carrie and Cash are married and are between 30 and 35 years of age. Either Carrie or Cash plan to be gainfully employed for the next thirty years and the other spouse for a shorter period of time.

Carrie and Cash consult a registered investment adviser and are aware of asset allocation principles. Carrie and Cash have approximately two months of total living expenses in a cash account for emergencies, have purchased a single-family house with the necessary home owners insurance, one working spouse has family health insurance through their company, and an adequate amount of life insurance has been purchased. The following crucial decision awaits them. What should be their core investment strategy over the next thirty years to afford the couple the most prosperous retirement?

Carrie and Cash propose to contribute an unchanging $10,000 dollars each year over the entire thirty years of his or her working life to a retirement account (e.g., 401(k) or a Keogh Plan). Their employer may have a matching funds retirement program which would greatly reduce the out-of-pocket expenses to our couple.

Approximately $833 dollars will be automatically invested each month, called dollar-cost averaging, and our couple will never change their strategy once their retirement plan has been instituted. Carrie and Cash are using a dollar-cost averaging buy-and-hold strategy which is an excellent choice when investing over the super-long-term for retirement.

Two Basic Strategies: Stocks Or Bonds

Two basic strategic options are available to them: 1) fixed-income bonds; or 2) common stocks. As reported in the literature, long-term U.S. Treasury Bond (T-Bond) interest rates, from 1919 through 1998, have averaged approximately 6.43 percent. The noncallable, risk-free U.S. Treasury Bond rate is an fundamental benchmark to measure normally callable, more risky good-quality corporate bonds.

Callable corporate bonds may be redeemed by the issuing corporation whenever interest rates decline, prior to the maturity date. This complicates the investment strategy when investing in corporate bonds Therefore, it is a good policy to find the interest rate (yield) to worst call date for callable bonds prior to investing. Good-quality long-term corporate bonds, suitable for a retirement account, may be expected to yield on average approximately 110 basis points more than the long-term U.S. T-Bond rate (6.43% + 1.1% = 7.53%).

As reported in the literature, over a sixty year period the average total return (including price appreciation and all reinvested dividends) of the S&P 500 Index has been extraordinarily close to eleven percent per year. The difference between average returns for the S&P 500 Index and good-quality long-term corporate bonds is 3.47% (11% - 7.53%).

Returns Of Stocks Over Bonds Average 3.5%

From January, 1969 to March, 2000 the percentage difference between the S&P 500 Index total returns and high-quality 30-year corporate bonds averaged approximately 3.58%, in favor of the S&P 500 Index. Averaging 3.47% and 3.58% gives an approximate 3.5% difference between high-quality corporate bonds, suitable for retirement accounts, and the total return from the S&P 500 Index over the super-long-term.

Any duration of twenty years (i.e., two decades) or more may be considered super-long-term in the stock market. Long-term cycles (i.e., 1, 2, 3, 4, 5, or more years) get averaged out over the super-long-term. Daily, weekly, and monthly S&P 500 price volatility are now immaterial as the super-long-term dampens these shorter term fluctuations and the eleven percent per year return of the S&P 500 Index is expected to be very nearly attained.

The twenty-year period of 1970 through 1989 in the U.S. stock market is presented as representative. The S&P 500 Index yearly prices during 1970 through 1989 are shown in Graph 11 - 1.

Overall stock market returns over the super-long-term (two decades or more) trend upward and are remarkably consistent. The S&P 500 Index price appreciation during the 70's and 80's, shown in Graph 11 - 1, goes from approximately 85 in 1970 to 355 through 1989 which over the twenty years is approximately a 7.4 percent yearly compounded rate-of-return based solely on price appreciation.

The decade of the seventies had sluggish price appreciation with low P/E multiples, but compensated with higher dividend yields that averaged approximately 4.5 percent per year. During the decade of the eighties, price appreciation quickened but dividend yields were lowered to average approximately 2.5 percent per year.

Because additional stock is purchased with the reinvested dividends, especially important during the decade of the 70's, price appreciation plus reinvested dividends from 1970 through 1989 is almost exactly an eleven percent per year rate-of-return which is expected over the super-long-term in the U.S. stock market.

Graph 11 - 1: S&P 500 Index: 1970-1989 Yearly Prices

Stocks Top Bonds Over 30 Years

The question for Carrie and Cash – invest in common stocks or bonds? Notice that the tolerance for volatility is not an issue here, only the length of the planning horizon available to attain the retirement goal (see Table 11 - 1). If 30-year corporate bonds are assumed to yield on average 7.5% per year over thirty years and $10,000 per year is invested, then a corporate bond portfolio would increase to approximately $1,038,690 at retirement.

If however Carrie and Cash are astute and invest their retirement funds over thirty years at eleven percent per year in a low-expense S&P 500 Index account, it will total approximately $1,990,100 at retirement or almost double the return from the corporate bond investment.

Obviously, investing the core of their retirement money over the super-long-term in a low-expense S&P 500 Index account is the way to a more prosperous retirement for Carrie and Cash (for low-expense S&P 500 Index funds, please see www.vanguard.com, or www.fidelity.com).

The same basic relationship holds no matter how much money is invested consistently each year – let's now say $5,000 per year. Over the thirty-year period, the S&P 500 Index account will be expected to return twice the amount of money as that of a good-quality corporate bond investment account.

Carrie and Cash have only invested $300,000 (30 years x $10,000 per year) of their own money from working over the 30-year period into their retirement account. This would even be less if their employer has a matching retirement fund investment policy. Only fifteen percent – of the almost two million dollars that they expect to receive at retirement age from the Core S&P 500 Index retirement account – comes directly from Carrie and Cash. This is the compounding of stock total returns at work. With almost $1.7 million dollars coming from asset appreciation, a Roth IRA may be an appropriate choice which is discussed next.

Roth IRA

Establishing a Roth IRA may be appropriate in this circumstance for Carrie and Cash. Roth IRA's do not permit tax deductions when the money is earned and invested, but do allow the money that is withdrawn at retirement to be tax free.

Approximately eighty-five percent of the money earned over a thirty year period would be tax free. Some income limits apply to the Roth IRA, but it is an astute option to benefit from the enormous compounding of returns in the Core S&P 500 Index retirement account over the super-long-term.

Bonds Are Necessary

Bonds are essential when saving for a goal which has a planning horizon of less than fifteen years for investors (see Table 11 - 1). Since a less than fifteen year time frame is not super-long-term, it is quite possible for common stock returns to fall below U.S. Treasury Note returns.

Let's assume that Carrie and Cash are saving for an around-the-world tour in five years. Plainly, common stocks may not be an appropriate strategy for their objective. Investing in individual U.S. Treasury Notes or Zero-Coupon Treasury Bonds that mature prior to the expected payment for the tour is prudent because payment of both principle and interest are assured and will be paid on schedule.

Zero-Coupon Treasury Bonds (Zeros) are bought at a discount with no interest paid by the U.S. government but are redeemed at par value at maturity. The benefit is that all interest is assumed to be reinvested so that the Zeros may be purchased at a deep discount to par value. There is a disadvantage to Zeros, no interest is paid until maturity; but, the federal government requires taxes to be paid annually, on a pro-rata basis, as if the interest were actually being paid.

Investing in bond mutual funds are less assured because there is no definitive maturity date, i.e. bond mutual funds go on and on, and are vulnerable to interest rate risk. The value of the bond mutual fund will fluctuate, which determines at what price shares may be redeemed, depending on changes in interest rates.

When Carrie and Cash are eight years from retirement, when expected living expenses should be declining, U.S. Treasury Notes or Zeros – that will mature on the day of their retirement – should begin to be acquired. Each year, over the eight year period, bonds should be purchased that will come due on their expected retirement date.

The money going into bonds is over and above the $10,000 each year going into the Core S&P 500 Index retirement account. Each successive year until retirement, Carrie and Cash may purchase U.S. Treasury Notes

(T-Notes) or Zero-Coupon Treasury Bonds that will mature when needed on their retirement date.

Our couple, on the day of their retirement, will have savings from core investments of nearly $2,000,000 dollars in their Core S&P 500 Index retirement account as well as having ready cash from T-Notes or Zeros available for their immediate needs at retirement. This is in case the stock market is at a long-term low point at their retirement date. At retirement or when political-economic conditions permit, a change in asset allocation is necessary to take into account the need for secure income when a regular paycheck is no longer available.

At Retirement: The Example Continued

On or about Carrie or Cash's retirement date, a rebalancing of the portfolio to reliably produce income for living expenses is recommended and a registered investment adviser should be consulted.

One possibility, depending on circumstances, would be to withdraw $1,250,000 from the Core S&P 500 Index retirement account and purchase a fixed-income annuity. Investing legends, Richard D. Wyckoff and Jesse Livermore both stress the importance of buying fixed-income annuities and describe them as the basis for independent financial self-sufficiency.

Fixed-Income Annuity Overview

Annuities have been enormously popular throughout history. Annuities began during Roman times. In the 17th century, European governments issued annuities to individuals. In the 18th century, annuities came to America. Presbyterian ministers contributed to the group fund of a Pennsylvania company that pledged them lifetime benefits.

By 1912 in the United States, annuities could be purchased from private insurance companies by individuals without having to belong to an exclusive group for that purpose. Annuities are currently extremely popular and sales in the United States are reported, at the beginning of the 21st century, to be approximately $200 billion dollars per year.

Insurance Companies Issue Fixed-Income Annuities

Annuities are long-term contracts offered by insurance companies. The same company that safeguards an investor's family with life insurance may also help retirees. A lump-sum payment at retirement in a fixed-income annuity will allow for monthly premium payments to begin immediately at retirement and can be guaranteed to last over the lifetimes of both Carrie and Cash.

Non-qualified (i.e., after-tax) fixed-income annuities are popular because no rollover from a qualified account is necessary, they take little time to set up, money earned is tax-deferred, and taxes are paid only on the interest earned since taxes have already been paid on the principle used to purchase the annuity. Immediate fixed-income annuities have no accumulation phase at all and may begin payments the moment the contract is signed.

Fixed-income annuities are stable and offer owners the predictability of interest earned and credited to one's account. The assurances of fixed-income annuities are unsurpassed. Annuity payments during the payout phase may be specified as monthly, quarterly, or even longer. Payments may be specified over a set number of years, or payments may cover the duration of the investor and spouse's lives. As a general rule, the higher the number of people covered and the longer the payment period – the lower will be monthly payout amount.

Different insurance companies may offer higher initial interest rates or death benefits to attract buyers. Annuities are especially flexible. After-tax non-qualified funds or qualified (401(k) or IRA) money may be transferred to purchase fixed-income annuities. The contentment from knowing that you or your spouse can not outlive fixed annuity benefits becomes an immeasurable solace during retirement age. Retirees have been known to live longer knowing that they can not outlive their retirement savings.

Major Rating Agencies

The insurance company issuing the fixed-income annuity should be of the highest quality. Because these are private insurance corporations, investors should check how the companies are rated to feel comfortable that the money will be there in retirement when needed.

The four major rating agencies for U.S. insurance companies and their Website addresses are: 1) A.M. Best Company www.ambest.com; 2) Fitch Incorporated www.fitchratings.com; 3) Moody's Investors Service www.moodys.com; and 4) Standard & Poor's Insurance Services http:// www2.standardandpoors.com.

The insurance company's financial strength is analyzed by these rating agencies, so collect all four and compare them for each prospective insurance company that you are considering purchasing an annuity. The highest rating from all four agencies would help signify an extraordinarily secure company.

An important restriction on annuities, like IRAs and 401(k) accounts, includes a penalty for withdrawal prior to age 59 ½. However, no contribution limits, unlike IRAs and 401(k) accounts, apply which offers annuities greater flexibility. Lets continue on with the Carrie and Cash example at their retirement date.

Single-Premium Fixed-Income Annuity Purchase

Carrie and Cash decide to take $1,250,000 from the approximately two million dollar Core S&P 500 Index retirement account and purchase a single-premium fixed-income annuity. Assuming that federal and state long-term capital gains taxes are approximately twenty percent and are paid upon withdrawal, the amount available for investment is now $1,000,000 ($1,250,000 x 80% = $1,000,000).

It is assumed that Carrie and Cash are both 65 years old at retirement, and purchase a single-premium fixed-income annuity that begins payments immediately. For our example, a two-life fixed-income annuity, full benefits to the survivor, with a twenty year guaranteed period policy is assumed to be requested.

As this is written, even though interest rates are low, Cash and Carrie would receive a reported $4,600 per month fixed income for the rest of their lives (please check with AIG (American International Group) at www.aig.com or with TIAA-CREF at www.tiaa-cref.com for specifics).

Along with social security income payments, the $4,600 would be the core of their retirement income and give them the peace of mind and serenity in knowing that neither Carrie nor Cash can outlive this fixed monthly income. A portion of the remaining money in the Core S&P 500 Index account may be used to diversify the retirement portfolio for income purposes using a laddered-bond portfolio as presented next.

Laddered-Bond Portfolio

Additionally, another $500,000 may be withdrawn from the Core S&P 500 Index retirement account which equals approximately $400,000 for investment after the twenty percent federal and state long-term capital gains taxes are paid. A laddered-bond portfolio strategy of five years may be appropriate to lower the volatility of interest-rate exposure.

The $400,000 may be separated into five equal amounts of $80,000 each. Initially at retirement, U.S. T-Note maturities of 1,2,3,4, and 5 years are selected which may be thought of as rungs on a ladder. In years 1 through 5 after retirement, a T-Note of $80,000 will mature and may then be rolled over for an additional five years to come due on a free rung on the bond ladder.

In this way a $80,000 T-Note will mature during each year throughout Carrie and Cash's retirement. As this is written, interest rates are low; but, Carrie and Cash would receive in the region of $1,100 a month from U.S. Treasury Note interest income as they begin retirement.

Assuming that the current age for retirement in 2003 of 65 years of age, the maximum social security benefit is $1,721 per month. Total monthly income is now $4,600 + $1,100 + $1,721 = $7, 421 per month or approximately $89,000 per year for the couple. This is comforting to know because this tremendously stable figure of $7,421 per month may be used for budgeting purposes. The additional money remaining in the Core S&P 500 Index retirement account will continue to grow as described next.

Continued Equity Investment

About $240,000 would still remain in the Core S&P 500 Index retirement account to continue growing, untouched for another twenty years (more or less based on life expectancy), to $1,935,000 dollars. The nearly two million dollars is a handsome legacy to pass on to loved ones – all free of income taxes. In addition, $400,000 would remain in the laddered-bond portfolio account.

Carrie and Cash's comfortable retirement comes from just $300,000 of Cash and Carrie's working income going into the Core S&P 500 Index retirement account, the knowledge to invest in a low-expense S&P 500 Index mutual fund, and the capability and determination to stay with the buy-and-hold strategy and dollar-cost averaging through both good and bad times in the stock market. As one can see, it pays to be an astute investor.

Summary

Asset allocation is the allotment of money going into broad asset classes such as stocks, bonds, real estate, and cash. The correct major asset allocation mix determination involves: 1) goal selection; 2) planning horizon; 3) volatility verses return; and 4) volatility tolerance assessments for each investor. The decision of how much to invest in each asset allocation class is dependent upon the investor's assessment of how averse to volatility they are and their planning horizon, or the amount of time that the investment has to work out in the marketplace.

In the Carrie and Cash example, when saving for retirement during their working years, if over thirty years the corporate bonds are assumed to yield on average 7.5 percent per year over thirty years and $10,000 per year is invested – then a corporate bond portfolio would increase to approximately $1,038,690 at retirement. If however investors are astute and invest their retirement funds using a dollar-cost averaging buy and hold strategy over thirty years at eleven percent per year in a low-expense S&P 500 Index account – it will total approximately $1,990,100 at retirement, or almost double the return from the corporate bond investment.

When investors are roughly eight years from retirement, when expected living expenses should be declining, U.S. Treasury Notes or Zeros – that will mature on the day of their retirement – should begin to be acquired. This is money that is over and above the $10,000 each year going into the Core S&P 500 Index retirement account, and is available for use if the stock market is near a low point on the day of their retirement.

On or about retirement, a rebalancing of the portfolio to reliably produce income for living expenses is recommended. Monthly income from a laddered-bond portfolio and social security may be added to a fixed-income annuity that represents a safe, secure, and stable income that may be relied upon for budgeting purposes. Based on the example presented, total monthly income at retirement is now approximately $7, 421 per month or $89,000 per year.

The additional money remaining in the Core S&P 500 Index retirement account will keep on growing untouched for approximately another twenty years to $1,935,000 dollars. The nearly two million dollars is a handsome legacy to pass on to loved ones – all free of income taxes. In addition, $400,000 would remain in the laddered-bond portfolio account. The capability and determination to stay with the buy-and-hold strategy and dollar-cost averaging through both good and bad times in the stock market are amply rewarded.

12

Discounted Capital Market Theory

Introduction

MR. MARKET, FIRST PRESENTED in chapter 2, is put into proper context so that investors know when to look for his arrival. How Mr. Market and stock market intrinsic, true, or fair value interact is explained and presented using a graph. The differences between maps of territories verses actual territories are explained with respect to the stock market.

The What, Who, Where, and When of thought and action are defined as provable by objective truths which are external to an individual. The fundamentally different How and Why of thought and action are defined as subjective truths internal to an individual. The intricacies of changing the How and Why of subjective truths, thoughts, beliefs, and values are explained. Subjective truths are described as either being positive subjective truths or negative subjective truths which relate directly to action and non-action.

The Life And Happiness Model is defined by individuals' objective and subjective truths, thinking and beliefs, plus desires, that supports decisions, leading to actions and non-actions in pursuit of life's happiness. The Life And Happiness Model uses feedback, based on humans' survival instincts, to demonstrate how individuals may determine the best solutions for themselves.

The Life And Happiness Model is used to help explain the Discounted Capital Market Theory in the context of an investor's pursuit of financial happiness in the stock market. The Discounted Capital Market Theory is based on the Discounted News Theory that incorporates the expected news discounting process. The premises of discounting the news and stock market cycles over the long-term as a result of political-economic conditions are emphasized.

Reasons why the random walk theorists may have gone wrong are presented for examination. The Discounted Capital Market Theory is formulated using the strongest form of market effectiveness, and its importance to finance is emphasized. Assumptions for the Discounted Capital Market Theory are presented and appropriate conclusions are drawn.

Mr. Market In Context

Benjamin Graham notices that the stock market is intermittently miss-priced but does not mention when Mr. Market will arrive, the best time to take advantage of the absurd Mr. Market, nor does Graham put Mr. Market into the context of market stages.

Mr. Market is now put into context so that he may be recognized upon arrival, thereby allowing astute investors to take advantage of his emotional ravings and bizarre stock price offers. It is shown how Mr. Market fits into context and how investors should be able to time his arrival during long-term stock market cycles. Presented next is a short summary review of how Mr. Market operates as our business partner.

Mr. Market: A Review

Astute investors know from chapter 2 that Mr. Market is the epitome of both emotional stability and instability. Most of the time Mr. Market, our partner, comes to the astute investor as a sane and rational purveyor of stocks. Mr. Market may be engaged for either purchase or sale of stocks knowing that he is a fair trader. At these times investors can not take advantage of Mr. Market, but must trade along with him for their own benefit. At other times, Mr. Market seems to act crazy and either wants all the stock or none of the stock at absurd prices.

When to trade with Mr. Market, who is acting either sane or crazy, is the question. The quality that separates Mr. Market from almost any partner imaginable is that he has no hurt feelings if disregarded. Mr. Market is always with investors and returns day after day with quotes that one can either take advantage of or ignore. How to recognize Mr. Market's arrival, offered next, is linked to long-term cycles in the stock market.

Mr. Market's Arrival

Mr. Market is now put into context of the long-term cycles in the stock market. As the market lifts off toward a market top in Stage 4, Mr. Market is transformed into a frenzied optimist who can see only the best of times ahead and therefore quotes unrealistically high prices for stocks. At this time, Mr. Market is a flatterer in the stock market and his enthusiasm can not be dampened. Mr. Market is always right, but has now disengaged from the overall market's intrinsic, true, or fair value.

Also, as the market careens downward leading toward a long-term market bottom during Stage 2, Mr. Market is the ultimate pessimist seeing only gloom and doom ahead and quotes the very lowest prices for stocks. At this time, Mr. Market takes on the demeanor of a manic depressive and his fair market judgment is forgotten.

Mr. Market is best taken advantage of when the markets, due to heightened investor emotions of greed at a long-term market top or fear at a long-term market bottom, drive prices either far above or far below stock market intrinsic, true, or fair value.

When the investing public is giddy with greed at long-term market tops as the market reaches unimaginable heights, or scared to death at long-term market bottoms with the fear of losing all their money – it is a given that the investing public will both buy and sell stocks at the wrong time and at correspondingly idiotic prices. The investing public's emotions are far more intense and easily overpower their ability to think or reason at long-term market extremes.

Mr. Market And Intrinsic, True, Or Fair Value

The best way to represent Mr. Market and the stock market is in graph form. Mr. Market is shown on how he fits into the stock market's intrinsic, true, or fair value and boom-bubble buying or panic selling that occurs during long-term stock market cycles.

Graph 12 - 1: Mr. Market & Intrinsic, True, Or Fair Value is a representation of how Mr. Market and the stock market's intrinsic, true, or fair value are close to one and the same during most of the long-term upward or downward trends.

Graph 12 - 1: Mr. Market & Intrinsic, True, Or Fair Value

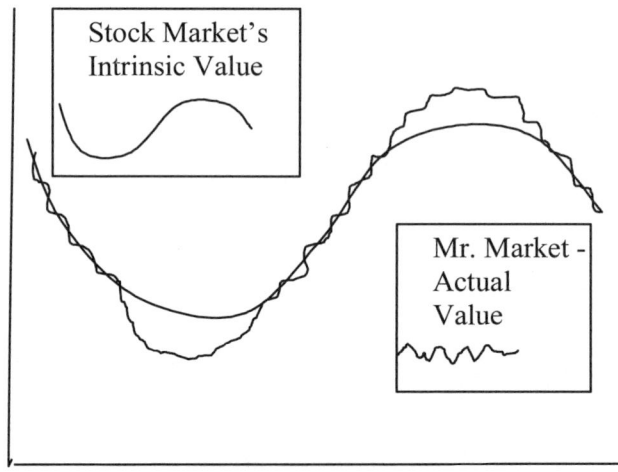

The solid smooth line represents the overall stock market's intrinsic, true, or fair value. Actual market prices, shown as a squiggly line, most of the time closely track the intrinsic, true, or fair value line but move in a short-term irregular pattern as it hunts and retreats in its search for intrinsic, true, or fair value. This is described as the exploring-compensating condition, or the technique that market participants use to asses the stock market's intrinsic, true, or fair value.

Mr. Market At Market Peaks And Troughs

At a market trough during Stage 2, Mr. Market – the actual market prices shown as the squiggly line – significantly detaches himself from stock market's intrinsic, true, or fair value and falls to an unreasonably low price in a fit of gloom and doom over expected future events. Mr. Market can be seen trending upward in Graph 12 - 1 prior to the low of intrinsic, true, or fair value and then again rejoining stock market intrinsic, true, or fair value as the long-term upward trend in the overall market resumes.

Prior to a peak in intrinsic, true, or fair value during Stage 4 in Graph 12 - 1, preceding it by as much as six to twelve months, Mr. Market again significantly separates himself from the stock market's intrinsic, true, or fair value and goes on to a boom-bubble top in a paroxysm of glee about the expected future good fortune for prospects in the political-economic outlook.

Mutual fund managers may do a good tactical job, but it is the investing public that makes the strategic decision of whether to invest new funds or to pull money out of the stock market. Mutual fund managers should not be held accountable however for the actions of Mr. Market, since the investing public is making the strategic investing decisions at long-term stock market peaks or troughs.

The best time to take advantage of Mr. Market is at long-term stock market peaks or troughs. The value of Mr. Market, at stock market peaks or troughs, is not his good judgment at these times but his exceedingly open and rich pocketbook. Mr. Market behaves as an overly emotional partner and wants to act foolishly and to be taken advantage of. It is the astute investor's job to first recognize that Mr. Market is acting foolishly, and then to oblige him by selling stocks at the long-term market peak or buying stocks at the long-term market bottom.

In theory, this sounds easy but it is most difficult in practice. The one thing that astute investors should not do is become the protégé of Mr. Market and fall under his power. Getting caught up in the emotional excesses of Mr. Market, by taking on the characteristics of a flatterer or a manic depressive, and trading along with him at long-term tops or bottoms can be ruinous to an investor's pocketbook. Whether investors are looking at maps of territories or actual territories are critical distinctions when investing, as explained next.

Stock Market Maps And Territories

John Magee explains the differences between maps of territories and actual territories –and how investors, to their own detriment, often get the two confused. The real world, as one experiences it using sight and other the senses, may be described as the actual territory of external reality. Real world experience of the territory may be represented symbolically on a map. However, the map should never be confused with the real world territory as explained next.

Using Maps

The map (abstraction) should conform to the territory (reality) to be considered a legitimate map. Maps require dating because the territory will constantly change through time. All maps need continuous verification to confirm their validity and to retain legitimacy.

Maps are symbolic creations or abstractions that may be detailed in scope (e.g., a city map) or general in scope over a much larger area (e.g., a map of the United States). Since maps have various levels of specificity, the detail on the map should be necessary and sufficient to meet its function and application. When viewing maps, perspective is crucial. Too much detail on a map may disguise the truth by not providing the appropriate perspective, while having a map not detailed enough may not be useful either.

The symbolic representation of reality using either maps, models, words, or numbers are never the things themselves. Maps, models, words, or numbers should never be confused with the actual territory, and are never as comprehensively detailed, as accurate, nor as certain as the territory being represented.

Mapmakers should have direct knowledge of their territory and also decide to make a legitimate map. Unfortunately, the resulting map may fail on both accounts. Charlatan map makers, who have never seen the territory first hand, can come up with all sorts of absurd and illegitimate maps.

If a second mapmaker makes a different map based on the original map, this is making maps-of-maps or an abstraction from an abstraction. Maps-of-maps making is not based on direct knowledge, and in addition may be either legitimate or illegitimate. The lesson here is that it is more important to check the territory and not only the maps or maps-of-maps when forming judgments.

Individuals get use to thinking symbolically about maps, models, words, or numbers and not about the territory itself; but, it should never be forgotten that the abstract symbols that one sees or hears are not reality but only represents the things themselves. This is especially important for investors when dealing with maps of companies as presented next.

Maps Of Companies

The financial statements (the map) of the company (real territory) are relied upon to come to investment decisions. Investors often have little or no direct knowledge of a company. Perhaps at best he or she likes or is aware of the company's products or service. Financial and management statements (maps) are relied upon by investors by necessity. However, investors should be careful when dealing with maps-of-maps in the stock market.

Maps-of-maps creators may include market pundits. Market pundits may arrive at opinions in the form of stock tips (maps-of-maps). Investors can see how easy it is to be lead astray by relying on market pundit stock tips which may be void of any direct knowledge of the territory and in addition, be illegitimate.

On Wall Street, investors are use to dealing with a map of the company's territory, and in many cases maps-of-maps. Anxiety, uncertainty, and self-doubt about whether the abstractions are valid and actually match reality are often in investors' minds. In a real sense, Wall Street exists as symbols in the minds of investors. However, facts should take precedence over symbols and realities should take precedence over abstractions. The necessity of checking the territory is described next.

Checking The Territory

Judgments based on real life experiences are often easy to make. However, cost effective on site review of actual conditions at a company's plant or office is not possible for most investors. For the most part investors rely on financial reports from accountants, written communication from the officers of the company, charts, and opinions from outside experts on the relative merits of a stock.

Since a thorough checking of a company's territory is not possible for almost all investors, self-doubt often causes investor non-action (covered later in this chapter) as he or she tries to make sense of the financial data and other information available on the many maps and maps-of-maps available.

Making a judgment based on a symbolic map or an abstraction of an abstractions (i.e., maps-of-maps) is much more difficult then when using real life experiences. This hesitancy is a learned investor response, by letting proceedings work themselves out prior to taking any action. Investors are striving to see if the reality that is the stock market territory plays out in concert with the map of information they have before them. In this way investors hope to build confidence in the data (maps) and their own judgment.

Wall Street is often a question of who do you trust when inspecting maps and maps-of-maps. Consequently, Wall Street is an abstraction that mostly inhabits the minds of investors as beliefs. How these thoughts and beliefs are turned into proper investor actions are described next using the LifA and Happiness Model as a foundation.

Life And Happiness Model

The Life And Happiness Model consists of one's thoughts and beliefs, plus desires, leading to decisions, that determine one's actions in pursuit of life's happiness. The LifA and Happiness Model uses feedback, based on humans' survival instincts, to demonstrate how individuals may determine the best solutions for themselves. A discussion of the Aife and Happiness Model begins with thought and thinking.

Thought And Thinking

The inspired French philosopher Rene Descartes (1596-1650), considered the father of the scientific approach to problem solving and of modern philosophy, doubts everything. Descartes believes the act of doubting proves the act of thinking. Because Descartes thinks, he believes he exists.

Descartes now makes the immortal statement, "I think, therefore I am." Thus, the Life And Happiness Model begins with thought and thinking.

Thought and thinking produces ideas which are created intellectually using contemplation and reasoning, as opposed to forming ideas simply in response to emotional feelings. Thinking may be separated into the following three distinct levels:

1) What one gets by being there and seeing what is actually occurring and by using one's other senses – which then becomes the basis for ideas.

2) Ideas from actual experience are then used to make judgments.

3) Reasoned inference is giving justification for what is thought by deriving rational conclusions based on premises accepted or known to be true.

The most advanced level of thinking is reasoned inference which is based on one's premises. A premise is a thesis or a proposition that relies on logic that is put forth for agreement upon which a debate is conducted or a deduction is made. A reasoned inference concerns subjects which are not known with certainty, but where logical conclusions may be drawn from premises assumed or known to be true.

Thought, thinking, and knowledge should support beliefs. As Descartes instructs, premises should be systematically examined prior to believing any dependent theories. Only after a thorough review of premises can any reasoned inference that relies on those premises be shown to advance as a theory. The importance of reasoned inference and correct premises runs throughout this chapter, and when discussing the premise of the Random Walk Theory and the premises of the Discounted Capital Market Theory.

Thought or thinking is the fist step in the Life And Happiness Model. Action, the final step, is or should be the result of life's pursuit of life's happiness. Thought and action are discussed next.

Thought And Action

Proper thinking and knowledge supporting one's beliefs, plus desires, leading to decisions, determining one's actions in pursuit of life's happiness defines the Life And Happiness Model which is fully presented later in Graph 12 - 2. Action may be described as a movement, succession of activities, or the style of movement such as being habitual or vigorous. Action is actually doing something, such as a deed, an undertaking, an activity, or performing an act. Happiness is dependent upon our actions.

Action should be the goal of one's thinking, knowledge, and beliefs which is the purpose of life in the pursuit of one's happiness. Thought and action may be defined by the questions of What, Who, When, Where, How, and Why something is thought or is happening.

Based on work of the talented Danish philosopher Soren Kierkegaard (1813-1855), answering the questions of What, Who, When, Where, How, and Why of thought and action can be separated into objective truths and subjective truths.

Thought And Action: Objective Truths

Objective truths are found outside of the individual. Objective truths often concern natural reality that may be able to be conceived and impartially tested in a laboratory. Examples from the physical sciences includes physics, engineering, chemistry, biology, and medicine. Mathematics, history, and the law also encompass objective truths. External criteria may be defined to evaluate these objective truths with a degree of certainty.

Objective truths are external to the individual and answer the questions of What, Who, Where, and When of thought and action. The What, Who, Where, and When of actions are provable facts or truths that are abstracted from the territory or reality that may be tested and found to be true. Since objective beliefs may be tested, individuals may hold these beliefs with assurance that they are in fact true.

Since objective truths are external to the individual and may be checked against outside facts, individuals may claim they know the truth and feel certain that they in fact know the truth about objective facts. Subjective truths are not the same as objective truths, as described next.

Thought And Action: Subjective Truths

Subjective truths relate to one's selfhood, are internal to the individual, and have no objective criteria for judgment. Subjective truths are beliefs and values about concepts and answer the questions of How and Why.

Subjective thinking is not based on a tangible thing that can be touched, but is based on a concept. A concept is contingent upon a specific instance based on mental formulations on a broad scale. The concept of pretty, as the adage goes, "is in the eye of the beholder." Or it can be said that "the ends justify the means," or that "form follows function" which are subjective beliefs or values that are impossible to prove objectively. The question is always, "Do we have the right subjective beliefs or values?"

Objective facts about the How and Why are not available to be checked since these are truths about one's values and beliefs. The subjective truths about values or beliefs about religion, philosophy, art, style, taste, fashion, customs, our likes, or dislikes have no objective truths that may be easily checked to determine good from bad, right from wrong.

Subjective truths are one's beliefs or values that determine the way life's events are prioritized. Subjective truths are not in data, knowledge, or information per se; but, rather in the way that all of these facts and figures are prioritized and arranged based on one's own subjective values. Social institutions especially rely on the subjective truths of How and Why to function properly, as described next.

Social Institutions And Subjective Truths

Social institutions, such as religious institutions, government organizations, business corporations, education institutions, and the stock market all rely on the subjective truths of How and Why to function properly. Social institutions are where thinking human beings are subject to ever changing needs, wants, hopes, and desires and are central to the process of involvement in the organization for its operation.

The subjective truths about How and Why change with different people, in different cultures, and at different historical times. The How of planning a new method, approach, or process in a social institution may be contentious to decide upon and controversial to implement. Consequently, this is why management and leadership are so important in these situations. The Why of decisions or events in a social institution setting concentrates on determining the reasons, purposes, intentions, justifications, and motivations of the people behind the decisions or events which are often unknowable with any certainty; therefore, the whys are frequently left to philosophers to contemplate.

Social institutions can not be brought into the laboratory to have controlled experiments run on them to determine either objective truths or subjective truths. The experiences of individual participants in the social institutions' processes are substituted for laboratory experimentation that is so useful in the physical sciences. Conditions change, times change, the specific people change, and perhaps most importantly the questions change.

The transition from objective fact to subjective concepts occurs based on an individual's values and beliefs. Individuals may well treat all What, Who, Where, and When objective truths as subjective truths, as presented next.

All Truths Are Subjective Truths

All objective truths ultimately become subjective truths to individuals. Objective truths get filtered though subjective truths. Individuals prioritize objective facts and truths. Consequently, the way each one of us prioritizes objective truths or facts ultimately makes them all subjective truths since particular objective truths may now be overshadowed or even ignored if they do not fit one's values or concepts.

Subjective truths concerning one's beliefs or values are used to prioritize objective truths, so in a sense all truths to ourselves are subjective. This is especially evident when humans function in a social institution like the stock market, all truths become subjective truths. Some objective truths become more important than others which can only be answered individually and subjectively. Subjective truths may be further divided into positive subjective truths and negative subjective truths, as explained next.

Subjective Truths: Positive And Negative

Subjective truths, thoughts, beliefs, and values within individuals may be further divided into positive subjective truths and negative subjective truths, thoughts, beliefs, or values. A process or a series of actions is the How of planning one's life to achieve one's goals.

One's life and happiness is open ended and may be defined by incompleteness. Happiness may be described by "How events are occurring in one's life," and ironically perhaps more completely by "How events are *not* occurring in one's life"

Positive subjective truth or thought is that portion of subjective truth that reflects on "How events are occurring in one's life" that one wants to either continue or to change. Negative subjective truth or thought is that portion of subjective truth which contemplates "How events are *not* occurring in one's life" that one might what to include. Therefore ultimately, individuals are responsible for their life through positive subjective truths and negative subjective truths or thoughts by always contemplating "How events are occurring" and could be changed, and by "How events are *not* occurring" but could be included. The overall direction of one's life, or how one is living, is thus individually determined.

Objective and subjective truths, thoughts, and beliefs, plus desires, are the basis for one's decisions and actions in pursuit of life's happiness. So if one changes their objective and subjective beliefs and also change their actions, they may become a different person. Action may be broadened to include both action and non-action which are important to the Life And Happiness Model, a discussion follows.

Action And Non-Action

Action in pursuit of life's happiness by an individual is now expanded to include the possibility for both: 1) action; and 2) non-action. Positive subjective truths relate directly to action while negative subjective truths relate directly to non-action.

The Life And Happiness Model is defined by an individual's thinking and beliefs, objective truths, positive subjective truths and negative subjective truths, plus desires, leading to decisions, determining either one's actions or non-actions in pursuit of life's happiness. The important concept of negative subjective truth or thought relating directly to non-action is a realization of "How events are *not* occurring in one's life," but we may need to include.

Not acting is not the same thing as non-action. Not acting assumes that no awareness is achieved and no thinking is taking place, therefore no decision is reached because not acting assumes a state of ignorance. Non-action presupposes awareness, thinking, and a decision.

In non-action, the thinking by individuals always concerns what will happen or what might happen. The individual passes from a state of ignorance and not acting, to one of contemplation and non-action with doubt in their minds of, "What is going on here?" The eminent Chinese master and philosopher of Taoism, Lao-tzu (604 – 531 B.C.), extensively reflects upon non-action and has a word for it – *wu-wei*. As a result, after considering the possibilities, the best decision may now be for non-action. Investors often use both action and or non-action when participating in the stock market as described next.

Investors Use Of Action And Or Non-Action

Decisions based upon an investor's objective and subjective truths, beliefs, and values, plus desires, determines their actions and or non-actions in pursuit of financial happiness in the stock market. Investors are often attempting to discover what to do and when is the best time to act. While they are thinking, investors are formulating decisions. Investors may decide that more information is needed and decide that non-action is prudent at this time. In this way, non-action is directly related to negative subjective truth.

The prospective investor may now merely observe the stock market without comment or judgment. The best action may be to decide to take non-action. The decision of non-action now becomes the proper action, or simply, non-action may be the best action. It may now be said that there is an element of "action in the non-action taken."

Action may include non-action which is action contemplated but denied. A plan for action may have many parts. Not all of the parts need to be put into action. Only a portion of the plan being implemented may result if the investor decides that the situation necessitates only partial action. Thus the decision to act on only a portion of the considered plan explains that there may be an element of "non-action in the action taken."

The ability to recognize both "action in non-action" and "non-action in action" are important concepts and will help investors comprehend what frequently occurs in the stock market. Lets now add the survival instinct to the Life And Happiness Model to explain how this helps explain human behavior.

Survival Instinct

Some may now ask, "If all it requires to become a new person is to change one's objective and subjective truths, thoughts, beliefs, and values lets believe whatever can be dreamed up and build a utopian civilization." Unfortunately, utopia building is not as simple as just changing one's objective and subjective truths, thoughts, beliefs and values. Human nature has a counterbalance, and that counterbalance is the survival instinct.

All personal objective and subjective truths, thoughts, beliefs, and values are subject to validity since human nature is dependent upon survival. Beliefs put into action are always validated against man's survival instincts.

Important survival issues may include life, liberty, financial, spiritual, social, educational, physical, and emotional concerns. Objective and subjective truths, thoughts, beliefs, and values that are put into action that do not live up to expectations are often quickly discarded.

In a true sense, our identity is grounded in our values and beliefs. Decision and action in pursuit of life's happiness are motivated by a person's needs, wants, hopes, and desires. Therefore, the self is the prime motivation for all of our actions. Thus the importance of Socrates' maxim to know thyself as covered in chapter 2.

The prioritizing of objective facts are established by one's subjective values. Decision and action are never motivated simply by facts, but only after these facts are filtered through one's subjective truths, thoughts, beliefs, and values. Facts may be an excuse for action but only within the context of one's own selfhood, subjective truths, thoughts, beliefs, or values. Lets look at an example of changing objective and subjective truths, thoughts, and beliefs as a result of the survival instinct.

Beliefs And The Survival Instinct: An Example

The following is a story based on fact about Tim, who is vitally concerned about living a long healthy life and consequently in eating a healthy diet. Tim knows that for many years authoritative dietary recommendations have included lowering fat in the diet as a way to lose weight and to live a healthy life.

Dietary recommendations dictate that the consumption of red meat, oils, and fats are to be reduced. Sugar is substituted for fat in food products and they are marketed under the term "lite" to indicate a healthier choice. Based on these objective and subjective beliefs, Tim decides the correct course of action is to cut back on red meat, fat, and oils, and increase lite foods in his diet.

As this is written the Food Guide Pyramid identifies bread, cereal, rice, and pasta as food groups that should be consumed up to eleven servings per day. Consequently, Tim continues to include lite products, bread, potatoes, pasta, rice, cereal, cake, cookies, and sugar in his diet. Foods high in carbohydrates in the diet are not discussed as an issue for over concern in the mainstream dietary literature.

Based on dietary authorities presenting their recommendations on why the low-fat diet is the best, Tim feels confident in his choice of a low-fat diet regimen. The result, over five years, is that Tim gains thirty-five pounds under this low-fat diet and is now categorized under the government's guidelines as obese.

Being overweight is a major cause of heart disease and or type 2 diabetes which are major health problems that are well documented. In 2000, it is estimated that sixty-four percent of Americans are either overweight or obese. Obesity is the second leading cause, behind smoking cigarettes, of preventable deaths in the United States.

When Tim grows concerned and asks why weight is being gained, the answer is – do not eat so much, count calories. Tim, by implication, is told he has lost his self-control. Vowing to do better, Tim starts to count calories and reduce food consumption. But Tim does not lose weight and in addition now feels hungry all the time.

Unexpectedly, eating a low-fat diet is apparently impairing Tim's health. In addition to health worries, Tim is has a forty-inch waist which is a problem for his ego. To survive both physically and emotionally, Tim has to change his dietary objective and subjective truths, thoughts, beliefs, and actions. Since Tim is not happy or healthy, his survival instinct now becomes dominant in his thinking. What is Tim to do? Tim realizes that failure necessitates changing his thinking, beliefs, and actions in order to achieve a healthy weight and for long-term survival.

Being obese is not healthy. Tim's survival instinct takes over because weight gain on the low-fat diet is not expected. Negative subjective truth is employed, what can Tim do differently? Tim now discovers the Dr. Atkins' low-carbohydrate diet. Tim's objective and subjective truths, thoughts, and beliefs change, the desire to return to 170 lbs. reemerges, the decision is made, and the Atkins' diet is implemented.

The Dr. Atkins' diet process is entered into. After passing through the induction phase, the ongoing weight loss phase, and the pre-maintenance phase, Tim is now in the last stage called maintenance. Dr. Atkins' lifetime maintenance diet includes fresh vegetables, salads, fresh fruit, beef, pork, fish, chicken, milk, eggs, butter, and cheese. All lite products, bread, potatoes, pasta, rice, cereal, cake, cookies, and sugar are now excluded from Tim's diet. Happily for Tim, significant weight loss is the result.

Tim now has no problem maintaining a thirty-two inch waist and staying at 170 lbs., all while never feeling hungry. Tim's objective and subjective truths, thoughts, beliefs, and actions, as a result of his survival instincts, have changed and so have his weight-loss results.

The possibility for Tim's long-term survival is greatly improved now that he is at a healthy weight which also helps his ego and self-confidence. Tim looks and feels better. Happily, this is a successful ending to Tim's story. The complete Life And Happiness Model is presented next in graph from.

Life And Happiness Model Graph

The Life And Happiness Model is presented in Graph 12 - 2. The feedback loop from action, non-action and the pursuit of life's happiness back to thinking and beliefs is based on human survival instincts.

Graph 12 - 2: Life And Happiness Model

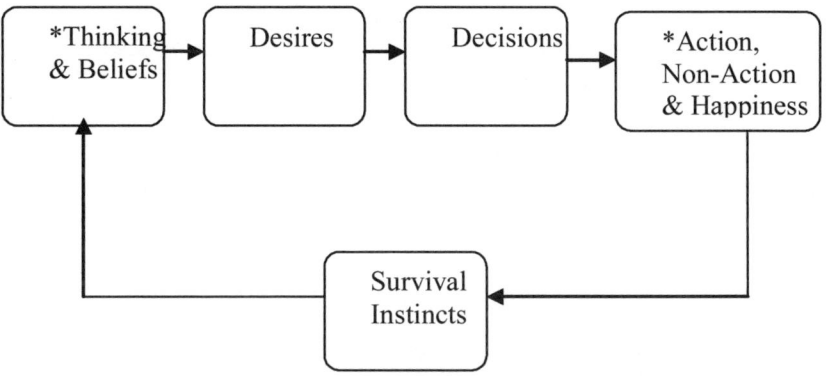

*   What, Who, When, and Where: Objective Truths
How and Why: Positive Subjective Truths & Negative
Subjective Truths

Thinking, knowledge, and beliefs which are dependent on objective truths, positive subjective truths and negative subjective truths, plus needs, wants, hopes, and desires, supports decisions, leading to actions and non-actions to secure one's happiness.

The survival instincts feedback loop allows for individuals to change their thinking, knowledge, beliefs, and values if actions and non-actions are not working as planned in the pursuit of life's happiness. The Life And Happiness Model may be used in the stock market and will help investors better understand the Discounted Capital Market Theory which is presented next.

Discounted Capital Market Theory

The Life And Happiness Model may be used to better understand the Discounted Capital Market Theory in context of investors' objective truths, positive subjective truths, negative subjective truths, thoughts, and beliefs, plus desires, supporting decisions, which leads to both actions and non-actions in pursuit of financial happiness in the stock market.

The Discounted Capital Market Theory is presented, it replaces the Efficient Capital Market Theory which is supported by the Random Walk Theory. The Random Walk Theory is based on the random walk process, and the premise that breaking random news causes stock prices to respond in a random manner much like an American roulette game.

The Discounted Capital Market Theory is founded upon; 1) the Discounted News Theory; and 2) the reality of long-term stock market cycles as a result of political-economic conditions. The overall stock market is expected to be at intrinsic, true, or fair value for much of the time – but not at all times.

Accepting the Discounted Capital Market Theory relies on understanding the premise of the stock market acting as a discounting mechanism. The Discounted News Theory is supported by the expected news discounting process. The first premise necessary for the Discounted Capital Market Theory is the Discounted News Theory, a short review from chapter 8 is presented next.

Discounted News Theory: Premise # 1

Discounting the news is practiced by investors with foresight when newsworthy pronouncements or resulting likely actions or any other expected occurrences, which may effect a company's stock price or the overall stock market, are anticipated in advance.

Expected scheduled news that will effect the stock market has already been fully discounted by professional traders. Expected scheduled news may meet trader expectations and is often why the stock market acts illogically in response to this news. Expected scheduled news may not meet expectations resulting in revised expectations. All expected scheduled news gets incorporated into the stock market on an ongoing basis using the expected news discounting process based on Hegel's Dialectic.

Unexpected news that will effect the stock market is only partially discounted. The most important aspect of breaking unexpected news is the type of stock market that it breaks into – either a weak market or a strong market. Unexpected breaking news, good or bad, in a long-term downtrend or uptrend stock market may have a short or intermediate-term effect; but, the market should continue in its previous long-term downward or upward direction.

The Discounted News Theory is supported by the expected news discounting process and describes how the stock market discounts both expected and unexpected news to look ahead to predict coming political-economic conditions.

The second premise upon which the Discounted Capital Market Theory depends is that the stock market experiences irregular long-term cycles which are dependent upon political-economic conditions. A review from chapters 2, 4 and 7 of the causes and effects of long-term irregular cycles in the stock market are presented next.

Long-Term Stock Market Cycles: Premise # 2

The second premise which supports the Discounted Capital Market Theory is that there are long-term irregular cycles in the U.S. stock market that may take one, two, three, four, five years or more to complete. The stock market over the long-term moves in cycles and may be described in four main stages – downtrend, bottom, uptrend, and top.

The Random Walk Theory is supported by the random walk process which is much like the American roulette game. The stock market differs from the symbolic stand alone American roulette game because the symbolic stock market is dependent upon political-economic conditions which are not random but irregularly cyclical in nature. The symbolic stock market is a consequence of irregularly long-term cyclical political-economic conditions.

The National Bureau of Economic Research (NBER) is the official authority on U.S. business cycle expansions and contractions. NBER's Business Cycle Dating Committee reported that from 1854 to 2001 there have been thirty-two business cycles, the most recent recession or contraction during this time lasted eight months from March, 2001 to November, 2001. The business cycle only partly controls long-term stock market cycles however.

Over the long-term, the stock market does not move up or down simply based on the business cycle. Political factors also play a prominent role in determining stock prices. Significant political factors include government fiscal and monetary policy, lawsuits into stock market or corporate practices, major accounting or business legislation, political unrest in the world, and shifting national agendas. Natural phenomena also plays a part.

Monetary policy is particularly important to long-term cycles in the stock market. The federal funds interest rate, determined by the Federal Reserve Bank, helps shape the interest rate yield curve which may reflect four distinct forms (i.e., normal, steep, inverted, and flat or humped) at various stages in the long-term stock market cycle which corresponds to political-economic conditions.

Long-term stock market cycles are based on the business cycle and political conditions. Political-economic conditions over the long-term determine overall long-term stock market prices which are shown to be irregularly cyclical. The proposition is that the stock market in the past has experienced long-term irregular cycles, and the premise is that the stock market will continue to be irregularly cyclical in the future. The objective is to properly identify these stock market irregular cycles and invest accordingly.

The Life And Happiness Model may be used to better understand the Discounted Capital Market Theory, especially when explaining action and or non-action by investors in the stock market as presented next.

Action And Or Non-Action In The Stock Market

As in the Life And Happiness Model, thoughts and beliefs in the stock market are based on objective truths, positive subjective truths and negative subjective truths, thoughts, beliefs, and values. Subjective truths give priority to objective facts and events. Uncertainty, misgivings, and suspicion determines peoples actions and non-actions in the stock market. Price adjustment in the stock market is the process of traders altering their expectations to probable political-economic conditions. Having reservations brings forth doubt in investors' minds and helps determine their non-actions in the stock market.

Non-actions are as important as the actions that traders take in the stock market. A person's beliefs will counteract not deciding, but only when a conscious effort is adopted. Belief may lead to action, doubt will often lead to delay and non-action. Discounting in the marketplace is determined as much by what the millions of investors do in taking action in the stock market, as well as what they do not do using non-action in the stock market – a discussion follows.

Millions Of Investors' Minds Are At Work

Millions of investors' minds meet in the stock market and the merged group holds almost all of the conceivable opinions, thoughts, beliefs, and values possible to be held by investors anywhere. Individual peculiarities are combined in the stock market to make a composite investor's mind. The meeting of investors' minds produces the foresight that determines how the market discounts coming expected and unexpected events.

The stock market is an extraordinarily complex institution with many trillions of dollars at stake. A large amount of money attracts many excellent minds. Exceptional professional traders may include those trading for their own accounts, hedge fund executives, mutual fund managers, and professional stock investors who have demonstrated over many years an ability to beat the averages (e.g., Warren Buffett). The concentration of money in the stock markets is extraordinary and so are the abilities of the professional stock traders participating in it.

Everything that is knowable, anything ever thought about or expected might happen that is judged to effect the stock market by security traders or prospective security traders are continuously being discounted by their actions and or non-actions in the stock market.

The stock market always wants to look ahead and predict coming political-economic conditions. The stock market may become incredibly inefficient and grossly overshoot intrinsic, true, or fair value both on the way-up at a long-term top and on the way-down at a long-term bottom. When the conventional wisdom in the stock market is either all-up or all-down and the exploring-compensating condition is temporarily suspended, the stock market may be predicting a change in its long-term direction due to changing expected political-economic conditions.

Because the stock market is always striving to look ahead and discounts all expected and unexpected news it may be used as a predictor of the political-economic condition. The definition and formulation of the Discounted Capital Market Theory follows.

Discounted Capital Market Theory Formulation

The Discounted Capital Market Theory definition comes in one version and is based on the Discounted News Theory and the existence of long-term irregular cycles in the stock market due to political-economic conditions.

Discounted Capital Market Theory Definition

The strongest form of stock market effectiveness is achieved. Security prices encompass all past prices, all published information, and all of the information available to investors anywhere.

A presentation and explanation of assumptions supporting the Discounted Capital Market Theory follows.

Eight Assumptions

The Discounted Capital Market Theory is based on eight assumptions. The statements in brackets, listed after many of the assumptions below, are included to give added explanation to these following assumptions:

1) The Discounted Capital Market Theory marketplace includes all large centralized security markets with unrestricted entry which are enormously liquid with extensive trading capital that brings together many millions of participants. [Example markets include: the New York Stock Exchange (NYSE); the National Association of Securities Dealers Automated Quotation (NASDAQ) system; the American Stock Exchange (AMEX); the Chicago Board of Trade (CBOT) where agricultural and financial futures are traded; and the Chicago Mercantile Exchange (CME) where futures and options are traded on interest rates, commodities, stock indexes, and the foreign currency exchange.]

2) The Discounted News Theory describes how expected scheduled news is fully discounted, and unexpected news that will effect the stock market is partially discounted by investors. The stock market is a discounting mechanism using the expected news discounting process. News travels immediately to all market participants.

3) Stocks are partial ownership in real property and/or valuable monetary entities. [The stock market is a symbolic representation of real political-economic conditions.]

4) The overall stock market is irregularly cyclical in the long-term by responding to political-economic conditions. [Due to diversification, investing in the stock market and specifically the S&P 500 Index acts much like the insurance industry. Which individual corporations win or lose within the overall stock market is not as important as the stages of the long-term stock market irregular cycles responding to the systematic factors of political-economic conditions.]

5) Stock market investors exhibit the following range of human behavior: 1) Rational; 2) Non-Rational; and 3) Irrational.

6) The overall stock market pricing closely approximates intrinsic, true, or fair value for most of the time, but not all of the time, using the exploring-compensating condition. [It is only during boom-bubble buying at long-term market peaks during Stage 4, and panic selling at long-term market bottoms during Stage 2, that overall stock market pricing veers appreciably from intrinsic, true, or fair value.]

7) Unsystematic corporate factors, along with the systematic factors of political-economic conditions, determine individual stock prices. [Individual stocks may or may not be at intrinsic, true, or fair value depending on the specific circumstances of each company, regardless of the systematic factors of political-economic conditions extent in the overall stock market.]

8) The stock market is never wrong, individual stocks are only worth what they may be sold for in the marketplace.

The Discounted Capital Market Theory is based on reasoned inference and two premises: 1) The Discounted News Theory which is supported by the expected news discounting process; and 2) that the overall stock market is irregularly cyclical in the long-term by responding to political-economic conditions.

It is believed that the random walk theorists have relied on the following incorrect premise, assumptions and questions to arrive at The Random Walk

Theory which is a poor foundation for The Efficient Capital Market Theory – a discussion follows.

Where Have The Random Walk Theorists Gone Wrong?

The following five reasons are why the random walk theorists may have gone wrong. First, a statement on where the Random Walk Theorists may have gone wrong is listed in italics. Second, the position of the Random Walk Theorist is summarized after each statement from information presented from above and from chapter 2. Third, the *Comment* sections that follows each of the five reasons are used to critique each position taken by the Random Walk Theorists in their support of the Efficient Capital Market Theory.

1) *The random walk theorists have used the wrong premise.* Random Walk Theory assumes all news that comes into the market is unpredictable or random and moves stock prices in an unpredictable random manner as a result.

Comment: The Random Walk Theory makes no distinction for expected scheduled corporate and government agency news that may be discounted by professional stock traders. Random news events causing random stock market pricing vastly underestimates the methods of sophisticated professional traders in the market who use both foresight and discounting the news as a cornerstone of intelligent investing.

2) *The random walk theorists have asked the wrong question.* Day-to-day price movements for individual companies seem to be a random walk process.

Comment 1: Day-to-day movements of stock prices for an individual company are immaterial to long-term success in the overall stock market. Random walk theorists may incorrectly extrapolate the non-predictive power of one day's price movement on the performance of its next day's price movement of an individual stock. Day-to-day price movements may seem random, but that should not be used to make general statements that all prior actions in all equity prices have no predictive ability whatsoever on forthcoming market action.

Comment 2: Statistical analysis of day-to-day stock movements, while interesting, is not germane to the important question in long-term investing. Long-term is the correct planning horizon. Day-to-day stock price movements for individual companies should be ignored as simply the irrational pulse of trading.

3) *Random walk theorists have solved a problem that is too narrow in scope.* Only individual company price stock movements from day-to-day are investigated.

Comment 1: Individual company stock movements from day-to-day are not the same as movements of the S&P 500 Index Nine Month Moving Average Trend Line. The long-term trend is easier to recognize when the daily price movements are smoothed out by using longer duration time units.

Comment 2: The time frame for which stock market price movements should be reported on are collected in monthly units. This will allow investors to get a required panoramic view of an extremely long-term time dimension on the chart being studied. The long-term is the correct planning horizon and using the perspective of monthly data, which smooths out daily price movements, is necessary.

4) *Random walk theorists have overlooked that the marketplace is a result of political-economic conditions which will cause the stock market to be irregularly cyclical over the long term.* The stock market pricing movement is based on the random walk process that equates movements in stock pricing to random chance.

Comment: The stock market over the long-term can not be random process in the same sense that the American roulette game is a random process. The symbolic fair American roulette game is in fact random while the symbolic stock market is a consequence of a real systematic political-economic conditions which are not random but long-term irregularly cyclical.

5) *The Random Walk Theory conceals a proper understanding of the rational workings of the capitalistic system through the financial markets.* The Efficient Capital Market Theory depends on the Random Walk Theory and the random walk process. When using the Random Walk Theory, chance is a rational strategy for success in the stock market.

Comment 1: The Random Walk Theory leads to incomplete and ultimately incorrect beliefs about the U.S. financial system. Deciding that all stock market price movements are random in nature is akin to being defeatist about the stock market. Random market pricing is a misleading belief because studying the stock market, and studying quantitative and qualitative information about individual companies, can be profitable if individuals are astute investors.

Comment 2: Organized security markets in the United States are respected and vital institutions in the U.S. political and economic system. Stock markets serve to raise capital for new and existing businesses which supply services, products, jobs, profits, and taxes so important to the American way of life. Stock market pricing should not be believed to be a random, casual, or haphazard affair. The importance of the Discounted Capital Market Theory is presented next.

Importance Of The Discounted Capital Market Theory

It is reported that the top five ideas, methods, and theories in financial economics includes the:

1) Capital Asset Pricing Model (CAPM)
2) Option Theory
3) Efficient Capital Market Theory
4) Discounting and Net Present Value
5) Value Additivity

The 1990 Nobel Prize for Economics is awarded to Harry M. Markowitz who explains portfolio choice theory; to Merton H. Miller for fundamental theoretical contributions to financial economics; and to William F. Sharpe for the Capital Asset Pricing Model (CAPM) theory which states that financial asset price determination varies proportionally to the expected systematic risk premium of the overall marketplace and not to the unsystematic risk of an individual company.

The 1997 Nobel Prize for Economics is awarded to Robert C. Merton and Myron S. Scholes for their technique when establishing option valuation. Market traders daily use the option theory formula to value stock options and it is the foundation for the extensive expansion of the derivatives markets.

The third important theory listed above is the Efficient Capital Market Theory. The Discounted Capital Market Theory directly refutes the Efficient Capital Market Theory. Resolving this conflict is a prime concern for financial economics.

Understanding the capital markets, demonstrating how stock markets function, and explaining asset pricing formations are fundamental to the capitalistic system. The importance to understanding and teaching the stock market's proper functioning should be a top priority for the financial research community. The following conclusion helps bring together crucial points in favor of the Discounted Capital Market Theory.

Discounted Capital Market Theory Conclusion

The Discounted Capital Market Theory unequivocally contests the Efficient Capital Market Theory. The basic premise of the Random Walk Theory in support of the Efficient Capital Market Theory, that all breaking news causes stock prices to move randomly, leads to a false theories and conclusions about overall stock market price movements.

Statistically testing day-to-day price movements for an individual company is not germane to give the necessary perspective to long-term trends in the stock market. It is a paradox that individual corporate stock prices from day-to-day seem to follow a random walk process while the overall stock market, as represented by the S&P 500 Index, over the super-long-term is a positively correlated time series. This can not be simply explained away by calling this a random walk process with positive drift.

The overall stock market, as represented by the S&P 500 Index, works much like the insurance industry. By collecting publicly traded corporations into a single S&P stock market grouping the unsystematic risk associated with an individual company may be reduced and the portfolio becomes diversified. The S&P 500 Index takes on the characteristics of the overall political economy. Which corporations win or lose within the stock market grouping is not as important as the systematic factors of political-economic conditions. It is expected that if individual stocks are controlled for unsystematic risk and use monthly data, long-term stock trends would also be in evidence for individual stocks.

The Life And Happiness Model is used to make clear the Discounted Capital Market Theory which is the basis for investing success. Because the stock market is always looking ahead, discounts all expected and unexpected information, and incorporates all investor's actions and non-actions, it becomes the long-term leading indicator to the political-economic condition. Consequently, the overall stock market, as represented by the

S&P 500 Index, over the long-term displays both a positively correlated time series (long-term positive drift) or negatively correlated time series (long-term negative drift) as represented by the S&P 500 Index Nine Month Moving Average Trend Line.

Stock Market long-term trends are demonstrated using the S&P 500 Index Nine Month Moving Average Trend Line methodology. Over a thirty-three year period, the S&P 500 Index Nine Month Moving Average Trend Line methodology proves to have been an exploitable opportunity, yielding an eight percent return with all other factors held constant.

The Discounted Capital Market Theory better explains how the overall stock market follows intrinsic, true, or fair value for much of the time, but not all of the time, and that the marketplace is never wrong. The Discounted News Theory and long-term political-economic conditions effecting the stock market are the foundations of the Discounted Capital Market Theory which gives a theoretical basis to the practical ten-step method for investing success found in *The Astute Investor*.

Summary

Mr. Market is put into context so that the astute investor can recognized him when he shows up and therefore take advantage of his emotional ravings and bizarre stock price offers. Mr. Market at long-term market tops or bottoms has disengaged from the overall market's true, fair, or intrinsic, true, or fair value. The time to take advantage of Mr. Market is at long-term stock market peaks or troughs.

The symbolic representations through words, numbers, models, or outlines on a map are not reality or the things themselves. These abstractions (i.e., the map) should conform to the territory (reality). Investors on Wall Street are accustomed to dealing with financial statements (maps) and market pundit opinions (maps-of-maps). Anxiety, uncertainty, and self-doubt about whether the abstractions of maps or maps-of-maps are valid and actually match reality are often in investors' minds.

Thought and action may be defined by What, Who, Where, and When of objective truths which are external to an individual. Objective truths or actions are provable facts that are abstracted from the territory or reality that may be tested and found to be true.

How and Why of thought and action are subjective truths that are internal to an individual. All truths may be defined as subjective truths due to the prioritizing of objective truths by individuals. Subjective truths may either be positive subjective truths or negative subjective truths concerning the "How of events either occurring or *not* occurring in one's life." One's identity is grounded in objective and subjective beliefs and values, and the self is the prime motivation for our actions which determines one's pursuit of happiness.

Objective truths and subjective truths, thoughts, knowledge, beliefs and values, plus desires, leading to decisions, resulting in actions and or non-actions in pursuit of financial happiness defines the Life And Happiness Model's use in the stock market. The feedback mechanism is based on survival instincts which helps rectify the Life And Happiness Model to correspond to our desired results.

The Discounted News Theory explains and validates how the stock market looks ahead to predict expected and unexpected news and is supported by the expected news discounting process. A belief in stock market cycles over the long term based on political-economic conditions is stressed. The Discounted Capital Market Theory is supported by the Discounted News Theory and long-term stock market cycles which are dependent upon political-economic conditions.

The Discounted Capital Market Theory is explained that refutes and replaces the Efficient Capital Market Theory. Areas where the random walk theorists may have gone wrong are presented. Demonstrating how the capital markets function is vitally important and significant in financial economics. The Discounted Capital Market Theory gives a theoretical foundation to the practical ten-step method for investing success found in *The Astute Investor*.

Conclusion

Introduction

THE PRACTICAL BENEFITS of the ten-step method for investing success are highlighted. A synopsis of the Efficient Capital Market Theory critique is presented.

The paradoxes and ironies in the stock market, many as a result of the Random Walk Theory, are reviewed. The basis and conclusions of the Discounted Capital Market Theory: investing foresight; the S&P 500 Index being like the insurance industry; using monthly data for long-term perspective; the Discounted News Theory; and long-term stock market cycles are emphasized.

The Discounted Capital Market Theory being the theoretical foundation of the practical ten-step method for investing success is reviewed. *The Astute Investor* ten investing book firsts are listed.

Practical Benefits

The Astute Investor gives investors what they most need to know and where to find current data on the internet to form their own opinions using the practical ten-step method for investing success which is presented in PART I. Retirement planning using asset allocation is offered in PART II.

The crucial highlights of investing, with examples, in ways that may be practically useful to investors on a day-by-day basis are presented. Investment models are explained along with Website addresses to find appropriate current information and data for investors to run their own models for themselves. The practical benefits presented in *The Astute Investor* rests on a new theoretical foundation, the Discounted News Theory presented in chapter 8, rather then the Random Walk Theory.

In retirement planning, a dollar cost average buy-and-hold strategy for investing in the stock market via the S&P 500 Index is demonstrated to be a superior approach for core investments when investing over the super-long-term for all investors regardless of their volatility tolerance.

Upon retirement, a rebalancing of the portfolio to reliably produce income for living expenses is recommended. The use of fixed-income annuities at retirement are also suggested. A short synopsis of the capital market theory critique is offered next.

Synopsis Of The Efficient Capital Market Theory Critique

The Efficient Capital Market Theory relies on the Random Walk Theory as a conceptual foundation and the random walk process as its premise. Day-to-day random news events straightforwardly moving random day-to-day company stock prices is explained as being too simplistic a premise for the exceptionally sophisticated professional stock market participants who use both foresight and discounting. The complexity of the stock market and those participating in it are summarized from chapters 8 and 12, next.

The Stock Market Is A Complex Institution

The stock market is an exceptionally complex institution with many trillions of dollars at stake. A large amount of money attracts a multitude of excellent minds. The professional stock traders who dominate the action in the stock markets are especially sophisticated about their vocation. The stock market is complicated because professional traders use foresight and discounting the news which often makes the stock market movements seem "illogical," but are readily expected once discounting the news is fully understood.

Millions of investors' minds meet in the stock market and the merged group holds almost all of the conceivable opinions, thoughts, beliefs, and values possible to be held by investors anywhere. The meeting of investors' minds produces the foresight that determines how the market discounts coming expected and unexpected events.

The restrictive assumptions found in the Efficient Capital Market Theory (as presented in chapter 2), of investors always being rational (chapter 5) and investors reacting correctly to breaking news (chapter 8) are misplaced. The Efficient Capital Market Theory assumptions are reviewed to emphasize when they are expected to break down in practice.

Efficient Capital Market Theory Assumptions Break Down

The Efficient Capital Market Theory assumptions are expected to break down at long-term stock market peaks and long-term stock market bottoms. The Efficient Capital Market Theory assumptions are not expected to hold up during peak and trough situations in the long-term cycle of the stock market.

Toward long-term market tops, there is boom-bubble buying by the investing public which brings prices above intrinsic, true, or fair value. At long-term market bottoms there is panic selling that brings prices below intrinsic, true, or fair value. Mr. Market is at work. This creates selling opportunities at long-term stock market peaks and buying opportunities at long-term stock market troughs. Consequently, a sophisticated theory to describe what is actually occurring in the stock market is needed. That sophisticated theory is the Discounted Capital Market Theory.

The Efficient Capital Market Theory assumes that investors always act rationally in the stock market. In chapter 8 it is shown that investors also act non-rationally and irrationally. Investors experience anxiety and stress based on the necessity of using incomplete information and become emotional at times with non-rational hope, fear, or greed. The investing public may become fantastically emotional during boom-bubble buying at long-term stock market tops, and during panic selling at long-term stock market bottoms.

Investors may display irrational influences which they may not be fully aware of in themselves. Investors may have an inordinate need for appreciation and high self-regard, a need for perfection, and experience stock trading addiction. These irrational influences may take precedent over an investor's concern for money.

The Discounted News Theory and Discounted Capital Market Theory better describes what is occurring in the stock market. The current theories explaining what is happening in the stock market, the Efficient Capital Market Theory and the Random Walk Theory, create paradoxes and ironies that run throughout investing. A discussion of these paradoxes and ironies follows.

Paradoxes In The Stock Market

A paradox is a seemingly illogical or incompatible statement, having contradictory positions, that may in fact be true. It has been shown that there are may paradoxes prevalent in the stock market, many created by the Random Walk Theory and the Efficient Capital Market Theory. Those presented throughout *The Astute Investor* include:

Super-Long-Term Paradoxes

The Standard & Poor's (S&P) 500 Index average is at 10 in 1941, and as this is written in 2003 the S&P 500 Index is at 1,050. Over approximately 62 years from 1941 to 2003, the S&P 500 Index's price increase alone – which does not include the S&P 500 Index dividends – compounded at over an eight percent per year growth rate. It is a paradox that individual corporate stock prices from day-to-day seem to follow a random walk process while the overall stock market, as represented by the S&P 500 Index, over the super-long-term is a positively correlated time series.

The super-long-term trend in the stock market is clearly upward and displays a positive serial correlation. The random walk theorists explain this away by saying there is a positive drift in the stock market over the super-long-term that matches the upward trend in the market of approximately a little less than one percent per month. It is not easy to explain away the oxymoron of a random positively correlated time series. Simply saying that there is random walk with positive drift begs the question, since positive drift identification is the looked-for condition for successful super-long-term investing.

The stock market is not random like a fair game of American roulette. The fair symbolic physical American roulette game is in fact random while the upward trend in the overall stock market over the super-long-term matches in general the underlying growth of total corporate earnings. The stock market over the super-long-term is not a random walk process and should not be thought of as such.

Positive drift in the overall stock market over the super-long-term is the explanation of why investors should be in the market – using the S&P 500 Index – if their planning horizon is twenty years or more, since day-to-day stock prices changes are so much extraneous daily chatter and are immaterial to eventual super-long-term investing success.

Leading Economic Indicator Paradoxes

Another paradoxical and even ironic subject involves economists use of 500 common stock market prices as a Leading Economic Indicator (LEI). Various experts in financial economics believe that individual corporate stock prices from day-to-day follow a random walk process and offer no predictive ability whatsoever, while other economists are using 500 common stock prices to help predict future economic conditions.

Either prices mirror all of the information present in the past performance of prices and predicting future stock prices based on prior stock prices is impossible, as under the Efficient Capital Market Theory, or 500 common stock prices may be used as a leading economic indicator to predict the future direction of the overall economy. This is a major dilemma requiring resolution.

The Astute Investor describes the practical ten-step method for investing success which supports using the S&P 500 Index Nine Month Moving Average Trend Line as a leading indicator to political-economic conditions.

The Paradox Of Mr. Market

As the stock market and stock prices advance, the investing public begins to take notice. Paradoxically, when stock prices surge upward faster and faster the more the investing public wants to acquire these very same stocks at higher and higher prices. This forward price momentum may finally result in boom-bubble buying at long-term stock market tops.

Momentum may also happen in reverse on the way down during panic selling at long-term stock market bottoms. Investors may get caught up in the crowd as explained in chapter 5, and begin to fear the imminent danger of losing all their money on an investment and dump their stock at the worst possible time. As prices crash, the less the public wants to purchase these same stocks at lower-then-lower prices. Investors seem to act crazed when getting worked up by a crowd, and only restore their levelheadedness afterward one person at a time.

Mr. Market, as discussed in chapters 2 and 12, is at work here. As presented earlier in this chapter, Mr. Market's arrival is an example of the Efficient Capital Market Theory assumptions breaking down. Mr. Market is to be taken advantage of, but investors should not fall under his spell.

Inverted Yield Curve Paradox

Paradoxically, the inverted yield curve discussed in chapter 7 may fly in the face of common sense. Why would T-Bond investors prefer a lower interest rate on longer-term bonds then on shorter-term T-Bills or T-Notes when seemingly longer-term bonds hold much greater economic and political risk? Why not hold only the short-term T-Bills, which after all pay higher interest rates, with investors having the flexibility to use this money as the short-term T-Bills come due?

The answers to these questions are that long-term T-Bond investors expect that when yield curves are inverted that the economy will slow in the future which will reduce long-term bond interest rates. Long-term T-Bond investors now have the opportunity to invest in long-term T-Bonds prior to the slow down in the economy becoming obvious to most investors which will then result in a sharp reduction in long-term interest rates. The inverted yield curve is predicting a change in the direction of long-term political-economic conditions.

Professional stock traders are expected to posses the same foresight as bond investors when looking ahead and discounting the news, including the news of inverted yield curves associated with political-economic conditions. Thus the paradox of the inverted yield curve works to the advantage of astute investors to help identify long-term stock market tops.

Prices Reacting Illogically To The News Paradox

Paradoxically, stock market price movements are not determined by the news, whether expected or unexpected, but by how investors react to the news. Stock prices are determined by how the many millions of investors sense that news events, either real or expected, may effect the stock market. This becomes a study in human nature.

The Random Walk Theory expects stock market prices to react straightforwardly to breaking news. This premise is not sophisticated enough to accurately explain what is actually occurring in the stock market. Due to investor foresight and discounting the news, it has already been shown in chapter 8 that stock price may react "illogically" when expected scheduled news meets expectations.

In addition, making an assessment and knowing the likely result of the breaking unexpected news is not always straight forward. It takes a while for the unexpected news to work its way through investors' evaluations of what effect it will have on political-economic conditions.

Long-Term Paradoxes

It is a paradox that individual corporate prices from day-to-day seem to follow a random walk process while the overall stock market, as represented by the S&P 500 Index, over the super-long-term is a positively correlated time series. This paradox also follows to long-term movements in the stock market.

The paradox of corporate prices from day-to-day seeming to follow a random walk process while the overall stock market, as represented by the S&P 500 Index, over the long-term is both a positively correlated time series or a negatively correlated time series is presented in *The Astute Investor*.

Identifying both a long-term positive drift and a long-term negative drift through the use of the S&P 500 Index Nine Month Moving Average Trend Line, along with confirming indicators, is demonstrated in chapter 4.

The stock market differs from the symbolic stand alone American roulette game because the symbolic stock market is a result of political-economic conditions. Political-economic conditions do not occur randomly, but over a long period of time and are irregularly cyclical in nature.

The "random walk process" and "prediction," used in the same sentence to describe the same stock price course of action, is a contradiction in terms. A predictive random walk process is an oxymoron. After reading this book it is expected that investors will agree with the predictive use of the S&P 500 Index Nine Month Moving Average Trend Line.

Ironies also abound in the stock market, some due to human nature and some due to the Random Walk Theory – a discussion follows.

Ironies In The Stock Market

Something is ironic when it is completely unexpected. Many ironies concern human nature and non-rational emotions and feelings as described next.

Non-Rational Ironies

The investing public shuns the stock market when it is at its long-term lows. This is ironic since this is the exact time that most investors should demonstrate interest in the stock market and seize the opportunity to invest when prices are at their low point.

Human nature and public investor emotions play tricks and dominate any rational thought during panic selling at long-term market lows or boom-bubble buying at long-term stock market tops. The dramatic emotions of fear and greed may trigger the investor to make impulsive, solely non-rational decisions.

Ironically, investors may feel more emotional when stocks are showing profits then when stocks are in the loss column. Because the investing public tends to sit on losing stocks, the public does not now worry about having to sell their stocks. By not selling, the investor never feels he or she has to face reality and hope that tomorrow may be better than today in the stock market. All impending decision requirements disappear and the investing public may rest comfortably with their paper losses which are conveniently overlooked as not being real losses until finalized.

Once stocks show a profit however, many investors fear finalizing the trade by selling. Investors may become timid and sell too soon and then watch in horror as the stock now zooms upward in price. Or, after a long price increase, the investor may experience the passionate emotion of greed, the feeling of wanting more and more, and not sell at all. The stock price may then turn around and the investor may ride the stock all the way down below their own purchase price, to their infinite chagrin. How the stock market responds to breaking news also creates ironies as presented next.

Discounted News Ironies

Ironically, to make money in the short term on breaking financial corporate news, it is often best to do the exact opposite of what the novice investor thinks is the most logical action to take. The stock price doing the exact opposite of what the novice investor thinks the stock price should do, based on breaking corporate news, is why many investors feel that the stock market is "illogical," and incorrectly conclude that the stock market is not for them.

Illegal insider trading, is an officer of a company buying, selling, or tipping on their stock based on significant non-public information. It is ironic that even when insiders know what the company is doing they can make grave mistakes in the stock market.

Insiders have been known to sit on their stocks when it has become clear to almost everybody else that selling would be the wisest course of action. Knowing how to manage a company is not the same thing as knowing the stock market. In conclusion, having the correct insider news; but, not knowing how best to use this news, is ironic.

Random Walk Theory Irony

The Random Walk Theory is confusing to a proper understanding of the rational workings of the capitalistic system through the financial markets. The U.S. capital markets are a respected foundation of the U.S. political system. As a result, the stock market institution should not be believed to be a random, casual, or haphazard affair that may be described as staggering like an inebriated partygoer in random directions.

The correct premise of the Discounted News Theory to support the Discounted Capital Market Theory better presents the stock market as a sophisticated social institution whose professional participants use foresight and discounting the news for successful investing.

The paradoxes and ironies presented in *The Astute Investor* are fully explained or may be simply taken advantage of by accepting the Discounted News Theory and the Discounted Capital Market Theory. Changing beliefs due to the Discounted Capital Market Theory, plus desires, will lead to new decisions then those based on the Efficient Capital Market Theory. The resulting action or non-action by investors in pursuit of financial happiness in the stock market should now, as a resulting change in theory beliefs, be greatly improved.

Changing stock market actions and or non-actions must now be evaluated using the survival instinct of human nature to determine a theory's worth. The Discounted Capital Market Theory is superior to the Efficient Capital Market Theory, because it is a better determinant of investors' actions and or non-actions for their financial happiness. A summary of conclusions on the Discounted Capital Market Theory from chapter 12 follows.

Discounted Capital Market Theory Summary Conclusions

The Discounted Capital Market Theory depends on the reasoned inference of deriving rational conclusions based on two premises accepted as true: 1) the Discounted News Theory; and 2) irregular long-term stock market cycles as a result of political-economic conditions. To interpret the news correctly requires understanding that economic or corporate news is often anticipated in advance which is called investment foresight as reviewed next.

Investing Foresight

The movement of a stock's price prior to an expected scheduled news occurrence is referred to as discounting the news. The Random Walk Theory's straightforward belief of how news effects daily prices in the marketplace is too simplistic and creates many existing paradoxes and ironies in the stock market. Therefore, the premise of discounting the news is needed to better describe what is occurring in the stock market.

The Discounted Capital Market Theory is explained that replaces the Efficient Capital Market Theory which relies on the Random Walk Theory and the random walk process. The Discounted News Theory follows the expected news discounting process. The Discounted News Theory explains how the stock market looks ahead to predict coming political-economic conditions.

It has already been discussed that the random walk process and the predictive qualities of stock prices as a Leading Economic Indicator should be mutually exclusive. They are currently used in tandem, nonetheless. The Efficient Capital Market Theory assumptions may not be practical over the entire long-term stock market cycle. Mr. Market arrives at these long-term peaks and troughs. Consequently, the assumptions of the Discounted Capital Market Theory better explains practical experience in the stock market.

The S&P 500 Index Is Like The Insurance Industry

The stock market as represented by the S&P 500 Index works much like the insurance industry. By collecting leading publicly traded corporations into a single S&P 500 Index, the unsystematic risk associated with individual companies may be effectively eliminated and the resulting portfolio is then well diversified.

As with a life insurance policy, as long as the risk is spread among all the policy holders, benefits may be paid out even though the specifics of what happens to an actual person at any point in time is unknowable to the company writing the policies. By taking an S&P 500 Index stock market position, investors are assuming the role of the insurance company and spreading their risk using diversification over many corporations and sectors of the economy.

Selecting the S&P 500 Index as a well diversified portfolio effectively eliminates the unsystematic risk of individual corporations. It is assumed that within the S&P 500 Index, one company's failures will be taken advantage of by another company within the stock market grouping and all of these types of pluses and minuses will average out and the stock market average price will be linked to the systematic factors of political-economic conditions.

The S&P 500 Index now takes on the characteristics of the systematic factors of political-economic conditions. Which corporations win or lose within the stock market grouping is not as important as long-term political-economic conditions. It is expected that if individual stocks are controlled for unsystematic risk and use monthly data, long-term stock trends would also be in evidence for individual stocks.

Use Monthly Data For Perspective

Monthly data are instrumental in dampening out the random short-term volatility of day-to-day price movements in the stock market. The long-term trend is easier to recognize when the daily price movements are smoothed out by using longer-term time units The time frame for which stock market price movements will be reported on are collected only in monthly units. This will allow investors to get a required panoramic view of an extremely long-term time dimension on the chart being studied.

Often daily price action represents only frantic short-term movements that are hard for investors to put into the long-term perspective so important to long-term investing. Once the perspective of the monthly data are viewed, it is often easy to see the effect of the normally slow moving political, economic, and world forces that are being played out on stock market prices.

The long-term is the correct planning horizon using monthly data for long-term investing. Daily stock price movements, when investing over the long term, should be ignored as simply the irrational pulse of trading.

Discounted News Theory

The first premise is the Discounted News Theory which describes a stock market that is always looking ahead, discounts fully all expected scheduled news and partially unexpected news, and incorporates all investor's actions and or non-actions; thereby, the overall market through its proxy, the S&P 500 Index Nine Month Moving Average Trend Line, becomes the long-term leading indicator of political-economic conditions.

The Discounted News Theory follows the expected news discounting process, rather than the Random Walk Theory, and is adopted as the foundation of the Discounted Capital Market Theory which gives a theoretical foundation to the practical ten-step method for investing success. Stock markets that demonstrate predictive trends over the super-long-term and long-term time contradict the random walk process for stock movement over these same time frames.

Long-Term Stock Market Cycles

The second premise which supports the Discounted Capital Market Theory is that there are long-term irregular cycles in the U.S. stock market that may take one, two, three, four, five years or more to complete. The stock market over the long-term moves in cycles and may be described in four main stages – downtrend, bottom, uptrend, and top.

Long-term stock market cycles are based on the business cycle and political conditions. Political-economic conditions over the long-term determine overall long-term stock market prices which are shown to be irregularly cyclical. The proposition is that the stock market in the past has experienced long-term irregular cycles, and the premise is that the stock market will continue to be irregularly cyclical in the future.

The Astute Investor Firsts

The Astute Investor offers many investing book firsts. Approximately thirty percent of *The Astute Investor* material has a firm foundation in the referenced classical investing literature. The internet and Websites listed, to locate data to run models, account in importance for an additional ten percent of the material offered. About sixty percent of this book represents new material or material presented in a new context. A summary listing of the many firsts in *The Astute Investor* are:

1) A stock market taxonomy is offered here for the first time which categorizes the stock market for better understanding.

2) This is the first time that the S&P 500 Index Expected Fair Valuation (EFV) Model and where to find updated information on the S&P Website to run the model have been offered in a book on investing.

3) This is the first time that perspective and the use of monthly data for S&P 500 Index Nine Month Moving Average Trend Lines and which specific confirming indicators to indicate long-term stock market trends have been presented in a book on investing.

4) This is the first time an explicit step-by-step real life example to calculate corporate intrinsic, true, or fair value using free cash flow, market value capitalization, bargain values, and margin-of-safety multiples have been offered in a book on investing.

5) Adding the Federal Funds Rate to yield curves and comparing the Fed Funds Rate to the 30-Year U.S. T-Bond interest rate to forecast stock market peaks are offered here for the first time in an investing book.

6) The Discounted News Theory is offered here for the first time as the correct premise to properly explain the sophisticated methods of the

professional stock market traders and as the basis for the Discounted Capital Market Theory.

7) The practical ten-step method for investing success brings together all of the important points to form a systematic approach to evaluate the stock market and individual companies for the astute investor. Real examples are presented. Where to find all of the vital data on the internet Websites to run models are an investing book first.

8) Retirement planning, using asset allocation over the super-long-term with dollar-cost-averaging and a buy-and-hold strategy for core investing in the S&P 500 Index verses corporate bonds, is investigated. What beginning investors learn in this chapter could double their income during retirement. The explanation and use of volatility tolerance for asset allocation determination in retirement planning are presented here first.

9) The Life and Happiness Model is newly developed and presented here first to better explain how proper beliefs yield correct actions and or non-actions for success and happiness in the stock market.

10) The Discounted Capital Market Theory directly refutes the Efficient Capital Market Theory and the Random Walk Theory, and is presented for the first time in a book on investing. The Discounted Capital Market Theory gives the theoretical foundation for why the ten-step method for investing success works in practice.

The goal of *The Astute Investor* is accomplished when novice and advanced investors alike are transformed into astute investors through the knowledge presented here, through comprehensive continued study, and practical investing experience. The knowledge in this book is practical and self-empowering, will help investors feel confident in taking control when investing their own money, and help in building wealth and a secure future for themselves and their families.

Continued Communication

Please visit *The Astute Investor* Website at http://home.earthlink.net/~astuteinvestor to purchase copies of this book autographed by the author, to find answers to the most frequently asked questions (FAQ), for updates concerning changes to referenced Website commands, to contact us, and for additional special offers.

Glossary

FINANCIAL AND INVESTING stock market word definitions may be found at www.investorwords.com, www.trading-glossary.com, or by using the referenced dictionary by Barbara J. Etzel.

Astute Investor. A person who has foresight and is perceptive, discerning, and keenly aware of what information and facts are the most significant in the field of investing. An investor who plans and knows where to locate Website data necessary to run appropriate investment models and how to interpret these models' results for decision making when investing. A seeker of the truth who possesses market vision, investing intelligence, and stock market experience while using the practical **ten-step method for investing success**.

Bargain Value Calculation. The **intrinsic, true, or fair value** for a corporation is compared to the **market value capitalization** to calculate its bargain value using a systematic valuation methodology. If the intrinsic, true, or fair value is greater than the market value capitalization, then the bargain value will be positive. A positive bargain value signifies an undervalued company, and a negative bargain value signifies an overvalued company. The calculated **margin-of-safety multiple** and bargain value for each corporation are rank ordered, highest to lowest values, for comparison to make investments based on the **margin-of-safety** principle.

Basic Net Earnings Per Share (EPS). The Basic EPS figure is a fundamental measure of corporate valuation. Ratio of Net Income (less preferred stock dividends) divided by Total Shares Outstanding. The EPS figure reported after Net Income on the Income Statement [See **Diluted Net Earnings Per Share (DEPS)**]

Basis Points. Used to indicate the different yields available on individual bonds. 100 basis points equals 1 percent.

Buy-and-Hold Strategy. Once securities are purchased during an investor's working career they are held at least until retirement. May be used along with **dollar-cost-averaging** and the core retirement account strategy to save for retirement over the **super-long-term**.

Capital Asset Pricing Model (CAPM). A market portfolio theory which explains that proper market pricing is based on relative security risk to the risk-free rate of return. The model rewards only systematic risk or **market risk** associated with the marketplace, and not unsystematic risk which is related to a specific company. Beta, a measure of market risk, is a result of the model. In efficient markets, the expected risk premium should be directly proportional to beta.

Cash Flow Statement (CFS). Tracks the actual money flow in time through the corporation. The CFS has the following three sections: 1) Cash from Operating Activities; 2) Cash from Investing Activities; and 3) Cash from Financing Activities.

Confirming Indicators. To determine the **long-term** trend in the U.S. stock market, follow the **S&P 500 Index Nine Month Moving Average (MA) Trend Line**. Confirming indicators, although not all required, help substantiate the Stage 1 through Stage 4 **market cycles**.

Contrarian, Being. An investor who desires, at the correct time, not to invest along with the crowd by purchasing good common stocks when prices are low and selling common stocks when prices are high. Investors should not use a **self-selected market adviser's strategy** to being contrarian which is just another form of taking stock tips, but instead use the practical **ten-step method for investing success.**

Corporate Bonds, Callable. Bonds that may be redeemed by the issuing corporation whenever interest rates decline, prior to the maturity date.

Current Ratio. Total Current Assets divided by Total Current Liabilities from a corporation's Balance Sheet. As a general guideline, the Current Ratio should be greater than two.

Debt-to-Equity Ratio. A measure of the capitalization structure of a corporation and whether debt is being used wisely. Total Liabilities divided by Total Stockholder's Equity which are both available on the Balance Sheet. A general guideline is – although this may change with financial institutions or utilities – that most companies want to stay below a debt to equity ratio of 1.00.

Dialectic Theory. The theory presented by the brilliant German philosopher G.W.F. Hegel (1770-1831). In Hegel's system there is a thesis put forth for discussion, then an opposing statement called an antithesis is made, and finally a synthesis is developed that resolves both the thesis and antithesis and settles the conflict. The process then repeats with the synthesis becoming the new thesis. This is the exact process that expected scheduled news makes in the marketplace and describes the **expected news discounting process** which is a continuous and ongoing progression of news anticipation, then the reality of the news, leading to a revised news anticipation by professional stock traders.

Diluted Net Earnings Per Share (DEPS). The denominator for the **Basic EPS** is expanded to include all convertible bonds, convertible preferred stock, warrants, and stock options. If and when these shares are exercised, they would dilute the Basic EPS figure. This is a caution for investors for that possible eventuality.

Discounted Capital Market Theory. The Discounted Capital Market (DCM) Theory has the strongest form of market effectiveness – security prices encompass all past prices, all published information, and all of the information available to investors anywhere. All expected scheduled news is fully discounted and unexpected news that may effect the stock market has already been partially discounted by the marketplace. The **Life and Happiness Model** supports the DCM Theory, all investors' actions and non-actions are included in the marketplace. All objective and subjective truths, beliefs, values, everything that is possible to be known, and everything that is expected to be known about **political-economic conditions** are now included in the stock market. The Discounted Capital Market Theory is based on the **Discounted News Theory** which incorporates the **expected news discounting process**. The premises of **discounting the news** and stock **market cycles** over the **long-term** are emphasized.

Discounted News Theory. The movement of a stock's price prior to an expected scheduled news occurrence is referred to as **discounting the**

news. This explains how the stock market looks ahead to predict coming **political-economic conditions** using the **expected news discounting process**. All news, whether expected or unexpected, has already been either fully or partially discounted by the stock market, by investors' actions and or non-actions in the stock market. The Discounted News Theory supports the **Discounted Capital Market Theory.**

Discounting. The premise is that the stock market is a "discounting mechanism." Stock markets look ahead to what will happen in the future – at a stock market top possibly as much as the next six to twelve months – and reacts based on investor expectations. The discounting premise supports **discounting the news**.

Discounting The News. A prior bidding up or selling down of stock prices by professional stock traders, usually over the short or intermediate term, in anticipation of either good or bad news about a company, economic factors, or political conditions. Discounting the news is also practiced when anticipating government pronouncements or actions or any other expected occurrence which may effect the stock market. Discounting the news is the premise for the **expected news discounting process** which supports the **Discounted News Theory**.

Discount Rate, Risk-Free. The rate at which the expected future **free cash flow** is discounted to calculate the corporation's present-worth or **intrinsic, true, or fair value**. The 30-Year Treasury Bond (T-Bond) interest rate is used as the risk-free discount rate because the 30-Year T-Bond is free of credit risk, exceptionally liquid, and extends over the super-long-term planning horizon.

Dollar-Cost Averaging. Contributing a fixed dollar amount automatically each month to purchase securities. This strategy should never change, regardless of market conditions. May be used with a **buy-and-hold strategy** for retirement savings accounts over the **super-long-term**.

Double Top or Bottom Reversal Pattern. At a market top, two peaks occur on a monthly chart at two separate points in time that look like a upside-down letter W – normally two to six months apart. On a stock chart with almost the same intraday price highs, double tops happen when the S&P 500 Index is rolling over at a long-term market high. At a long-term market bottom, a double bottom occurs on a monthly chart when two troughs that look like the letter W happen on two separate occasions – usually two to six months apart. On a chart with almost the same intraday price lows, double bottoms occur as the S&P 500 Index is forming a base and beginning a overall market upturn. Both are **confirming indicators** to the **S&P 500 Index Nine Month Moving Average Trend Line**.

Due Diligence. Investors are expected to consider properly and thoroughly all possible factors to determine an investment's suitability immediately prior to the outlay being made. This includes investigating the **political-economic conditions** in the stock market, including a company's **intrinsic, true, or fair value**, its **market value capitalization, bargain value, and margin-of-safety multiple**. All **investing** information and data should be judged for accuracy, omissions, and misstatements.

Efficient Capital Market Theory. The theory of the efficient capital market to describe the overall stock market relies on the **Random Walk Theory (RWT)** as a way to represent seemingly random daily movements of individual stock prices. The stock market, says the efficient capital market theorists, is efficient because so many skilled participants who posses a collection of all relevant information are setting prices. Because the participants as a whole know all the relevant information then the market is competitive and true stock market values will always prevail. Consequently, attempting to identify undervalued stocks is pointless because the market has previously priced in information making beating the marketplace unachievable. Results will be as good if stocks for purchase are decided upon randomly, hence the dependence on the RWT. Three versions of market efficiency, weak form, semi-strong form, and strong form of the marketplace are offered along with assumptions.

Electronic tape. A scrolling display, through the trading day, of corporate stock symbols, actual transaction prices, and volume of shares changing hands during the transaction. The scrolling electronic tape display is usually available at stock brokerage offices, on cable television, and on stock market internet Websites. – Also called *tape.*

Expected News. All scheduled news from corporations, from governments, or their agencies. All expected scheduled news, whether meeting or not meeting expectations, that effects the stock market has been fully discounted by professional stock traders using the **expected news discounting process**.

Expected News Discounting Process. Explains how investors with foresight in the stock market constantly look ahead to predict political-economic conditions. This process explains how the stock market operates as a **discounting** mechanism. The recurring scheduled ongoing process of news anticipation, news reality, updated news anticipation is based on Hegel's **Dialectic Theory**. Expected scheduled news does not startle the stock market or professional stock traders because it has previously been fully discounted.

Exploring-Compensating Condition. The exploring-compensating condition technique is used by stock traders to check on whether the stock market is at **intrinsic, true, or fair value**. Investors in the stock market are not always confident of the rightness in the current direction or level of the overall stock market is taking. Investors explore by inquiring, studying, experimenting, and examining the best fit between current market pricing and **political-economic conditions**. Millions of stock market participants diligently search for and intensively pursue the market direction that conforms correctly to political-economic conditions.

Federal Reserve. The U.S. central bank which manages monetary policy: "to promote effectively the goals of maximum employment, stable prices, and moderate long-term interest rates." Creating or withdrawing reserves by the Federal Reserve influences the supply and demand of Federal Reserve Bank balances which adjusts the federal funds interest rate which directly influences **political-economic conditions**. The Federal Reserve sets a target for the federal funds interest rate.

Fixed-Income Annuity. Policies offered by insurance companies paying a lifetime of fixed monthly income. Payment to beneficiaries are based on interest rates as of the time monthly payments begin and will remain constant for the life of the policy.

Forward Price-to-Earnings (P/E) Ratio. Current per-share price divided by the corporation's estimated earnings for the next twelve-month time period. Anticipating the future is the stock market's function, and that is what investors with foresight and vision are striving to predict and estimate. Consequently, the Forward P/E Ratio is more appropriate for use than the **Price-to-Earnings (P/E) Ratio**.

Forward Price-to-Earnings-to-Growth (FPEG) Ratio. FPEG is the forward P/E (diluted) ratio divided by the diluted net earnings per share (DEPS) growth rate per year. An FPEG ratio above 1.00 is poor, below

1.00 is good, and below 0.50 is outstanding. When dividends are considerable, the dividend yield may be added to the DEPS growth rate.

401(k) Plan. A defined, self-directed employee contribution plan set up by corporations to invest tax-deferred income in their employee's retirement account. 401(k) plans are portable and may follow employees from job-to-job. Certain 401(k) plans allow the corporation to match employees' contributions to their retirement plans. Taxes are paid at withdrawal by the employee during retirement.

Free Cash Flow. Free cash flow (FCF) is calculated by adding the normally negative **total capital expenditures** derived from the Cash Flows from Investing Activities portion of the Cash Flow Statement for the year from the hopefully positive Cash from Operating Activities for the year on the **Cash Flow Statement (CFS).** Positive free cash flow (FCF) is considered a benefit for a corporation's stock price because management may then have the option of increasing dividends, buying back their own stock, developing promising new products/markets, or meeting competitive challenges all without the need to raise additional funds from outside sources.

Head and Shoulders Top or Bottom Reversal Pattern. This monthly chart pattern gets its name because at a market top it looks like the head and shoulders of a person's outline on a graph. Three distinctive market peaks during a market top are in evidence. The head is the middle and highest intraday price peak while the left and right shoulders have prices that are approximately equal, but slightly lower in value. For a market bottom, the price pattern is turned upside down. The market bottom head intraday low price trough is the lowest while the left and right shoulder trough price values are approximately equal and not as low as the head's value. Both are **confirming indicators** to the **S&P 500 Index Nine Month Moving Average Trend Line**.

Higher-Highs and Higher-Lows. When the **long-term** trend line is pointing upward during Stage 3: Mark-Up - Uptrend; (see Graph 3 - 3), each wave up on the monthly chart depicts successively higher-highs and higher-low prices until Stage 4: the market top distribution stage is reached. This occurrence is a **confirming indicator** for an up trending **S&P 500 Index Nine Month Moving Average Trend Line**.

Initial Public Offering (IPO). A company's initial stock sale to the general public in the primary market, normally using an underwriter known as an investment banker as a manager. The **Securities and Exchange Commission (SEC)** approves and regulates all proceedings of the IPO.

Intrinsic, True, or Fair Value. An intrinsic, true, or fair value calculation for a company is instrumental for the **margin-of-safety** concept and **value investing**. Based on future yearly expected corporate **Free Cash Flow** (FCF) values which are discounted by the 30-Year U.S. Treasury Bond risk-free rate of return to determine the corporation's present-worth or intrinsic, true, or fair value.

Investing. Proper investing requires **investing foresight** and the most beneficial strategies and analysis leading to suitable evaluation and judgment for purchasing or selling common stocks or fixed-income securities for either capital appreciation and/or predictable income over a many year planning horizon. Investors should prefer high quality securities at proper or reasonable prices which match the investor's scheduled needs. Investors should believe that all relevant factors are favorable prior to making an investment because the power to decline an investment is his or her most cherished advantage. **Due diligence** and the practical **ten-step method for investing success** should be used.

Investing Foresight. Foresight for investors requires them to envision or imagine what will happen in the future based on all the necessary information available to them and then to adequately prepare and properly position themselves for the expected consequences. **Discounting the news** and an awareness of **political-economic conditions** are required.

Japanese Candlestick Charting Technique. The open, high, low and closing values are used to form the candlestick. Solid candlestick bodies show the close lower than the open. White candlestick bodies depict the close higher than the open. The thin lines above and below the solid-or-white candlestick bodies are called upper-and-lower shadows and indicate the high and low price range. Candlesticks are figurative and make stock chart illustrations attractive and easy to understand in one glance.

Keogh Plan. A qualified, self-directed, tax-deferred retirement plan for the self-employed.

Laddered-Bond Portfolio. The rungs of a ladder represents each year when a portion of the notes or bonds in a portfolio matures. An equal amount of bonds are purchased with a spread-out maturity risk due to varying interest rates over the **long term**. As these notes or bonds come due they are rolled over to the next free rung on the bond ladder. In this way notes may be scheduled to mature each year during retirement, thus dampening out interest rate fluctuations.

Life and Happiness Model. Defined by individuals' objective and subjective thinking and beliefs, plus desires, that supports decisions, leading to actions and or non-actions in pursuit of life's happiness. The What, Who, Where, and When of thought and action are defined as provable by **objective truths** which are external to an individual. The fundamentally different How and Why of thought and action are defined as **subjective truths** which are internal to an individual. Subjective truths, thoughts, beliefs, and values within individuals may be further divided into positive subjective truths or negative subjective truths, beliefs, or thoughts. The Life and Happiness Model uses feedback, based on humans' survival instincts, to demonstrate how individuals may determine the best solutions to make them the happiest. The Life and Happiness Model is used when explaining the **Discounted Capital Market Theory.**

Long-Term. In the stock market a period of time lasting one, two, three, four, five years or longer.

Lower-Highs and Lower-Lows. When the **long-term** trend line is pointing down during Stage 1: Mark-Down - Downtrend (see Graph 3 - 1), each wave down on the monthly chart depicts successively lower-highs and lower-low prices until Stage 2: the market bottom accumulation stage is reached. This occurrence is a **confirming indicator** to a down trending **S&P 500 Index Nine Month Moving Average Trend Line**.

Map. The map (abstraction) should conform to the **territory** (reality) to be considered a legitimate map. All maps need constant verification to confirm their validity and to retain legitimacy. Maps should be necessary and sufficient to meet its function and application. The symbolic representation of reality using either maps, models, words, or numbers are never the things themselves (i.e., territories). Investors routinely use maps (financial statements, etc.) or **maps-of-maps** (opinions from experts) on investing, but should always be aware that these are not the actual territories and may not be legitimate.

Maps-of-Maps. Mapmakers should have direct knowledge of their **territory** (reality) and also decide to make a legitimate **map**. If a second mapmaker makes a different map based on the original map, this is making maps-of-maps or an abstraction from an abstraction. Maps-of-maps making is not based on direct knowledge and in addition may be either legitimate or illegitimate. Maps-of-maps creators include **market pundits**.

Margin-of-Safety. The Graham-Dodd-Buffett strategy for their prudent **value investing** style. Purchasing stock at suitable prices, as determined by this sound methodology, should triumph over market adversity in the **long-term**. A positive corporate **bargain value** indicates a stock which is undervalued. A company's stock whose **intrinsic, true, or fair value** is at least twice its market value capitalization has a large enough **margin-of-safety multiple** and is a deserving candidate for purchase based on the **margin-of-safety** concept.

Margin-of-Safety Multiple. A company's stock whose **intrinsic, true, or fair value** is at least twice its **market value capitalization** has a large enough margin-of-safety multiple and is a deserving candidate for purchase based on the **margin-of-safety** concept. The margin-of-safety multiple may be rank ordered from highest to lowest, along with their **bargain values,** to select the most deserving corporate stocks for investments.

Market Cycles. Four main stages in a market cycle over the **long-term** are identified: Stage 1: Mark-Down - Downtrend; Stage 2: Accumulation - Bottoming; Stage 3: Mark-Up - Uptrend; and Stage 4: Distribution - Topping or Rounding Over. Stock markets in the long-term move relatively slowly, monthly data and the **S&P 500 Index Nine Month MA Trend Line** gives the best perspective needed to observe **long-term** stock market trends.

Market Pundit. A so-called expert or investment guru on the stock market or on individual stocks who readily offers rationalizations for stocks being either under-or-over valued, all supported by proffered economic justifications using **maps-of-maps**. A stock market sophist known more for plausible but specious arguments then for being ultimately proved correct. In very limited instances – a seeming authority figure making true but nonetheless unprincipled public statements in an effort to manipulate the investing public to do one thing while the market pundit or his associates are doing something else, all motivated by an expected financial gain.

Market Risk. Risk that may be described as systematic factors of **political-economic conditions** that determine overall stock prices. Market risk uncertainties have a tendency to move most stock prices together and this market risk can not be diversified away regardless of the number of companies or types of stocks in an investment portfolio. Adequate diversification eliminates almost completely all unsystematic risk associated with individual companies. Market risk is also defined as systematic risk.

Market Value Capitalization. Calculated by multiplying the corporation's total number of diluted shares outstanding times the current per share stock price. Used with **intrinsic, true, or fair value** to calculate **bargain value**.

Moving Average Convergence Divergence (MACD). The MACD for the S&P 500 Index displays two crossing moving averages, the MACD (12,26) line and the MACD EMA (9) line. The monthly MACD is effective as a long-term indicator and should be watched closely at the end of each month. The monthly MACD may be used as a confirming indicator for the **S&P 500 Index Nine Month MA Trend Line**.

Objective Truths. Truths external to the individual and answer the questions of What, Who, Where, and When of thought and action. They are provable facts or truths that are abstracted from the territory or reality that may be tested and found to be true. These objective truths may now be tested and consequently individuals may hold these beliefs with assurance that they are in fact true. Objective truths are used to explain the **Life and Happiness Model**.

Outside Reversal Day (ORD). At a stock market bottom, the **S&P 500 Index** makes a new intraday low for the current move and then closes above the intraday high of the previous day on extraordinarily high share-trading volume. At a stock market top, the S&P 500 Index makes a new intraday high for the current move and then closes below the intraday low of the previous day on extraordinarily high share-trading volume. This should be used to confirm a double-top, on the second peak, or double-bottom, on the second trough, of the S&P 500 Index graph pattern. The ORD is used as a **confirming indicator** for the **S&P 500 Index Nine Month MA Trend Line**.

Political-Economic Conditions. The long-term stock **market cycles** are inexorably tied to political-economic conditions. These conditions are defined mainly by long-term business and political conditions that are not random but irregularly cyclical in nature. The stock market is a symbolic representation of not only the real corporate economy, but also everything that impacts on the real economy. For example, political action by the federal, sate, and local governments and agencies that include: the decision to go to war; the policies on fiscal deficits and taxes; currency values; inflation rates; trade laws; decision on the Fed Funds interest rate; **yield curves**; immigration policy; natural events (e.g., earthquakes, hurricanes, a pandemic disease, etc.); world conditions; etc. The ultimate discovery that most investors make in the stock market is that they must examine political-economic conditions, and be able to interpret them to help determine and foresee investment probabilities. Stock market price action discounts **market risk** or systematic political-economic conditions because collectively the millions and millions of investors see more clearly into the future than any one person possibly can. Political-economic conditions are tied to **long-term** stock market stages and are instrumental for the practical **ten-step method for investing success**.

Price-to-Earnings (P/E) Ratio. Current per share price divided by the corporation's **Basic EPS** for a prior period of time. P/E ratios are actual or trailing twelve-month earnings per share divided into the stock price, and are usually reported by the financial media. A stock with a high P/E ratio may signify a faster growing company resulting in the investor's willingness to buy at higher prices the same level of annual earnings. Also called *Actual P/E Ratio*.

Random Walk Process. Movement of a corporation's stock price in the stock market is described in the financial research literature as that of one aimlessly wandering through time as if someone drew by chance a plus or minus number and added that number onto the previous day's closing price. Day to day company stock price movements are seemingly independent from one another and are as random as the flipping of a coin or much like a pure gambling game such as American roulette. Each daily price series for a company's stock being studied seems to act like a random walk process – no cycles are in evidence. The random walk process supports the **Random Walk Theory**.

Random Walk Theory (RWT). The Random Walk Theory (RWT) states that corporate stock prices move randomly, either up or down, and that the prediction of a company's stock price is impossible. The RWT is supported by the premise of the **random walk process**. The RWT assumes that prices are set based on random breaking news information which can not be predicted. Because unpredictable news information comes into the marketplace randomly – it is fully expected that prices respond randomly to this news. The Random Walk Theory supports and is the premise for the **Efficient Capital Market Theory.**

Return-on-Equity (ROE) Ratio. Calculated by taking the annual Net Income (less dividends on preferred stock) located on the Income Statement divided by Total Shareholder's Equity from the Balance Sheet. Investors would like ROE to be a high percentage and improving yearly. ROE is an important measure of management's performance and should be closely monitored when using **value investing**.

Roth IRA. Taxes are paid on the income and the money going into a Roth IRA. However, at retirement, all of the capital appreciation gained in the Roth IRA is allowed to be withdrawn tax-free at retirement. Some income limits apply.

Securities and Exchange Commission (SEC). The federal government board created by the Securities and Exchange Act of 1934 which has regulatory responsibility for the securities industry.

Self-Selected Market Adviser's Strategy. This is the incorrect method for implementing the contrarian approach to investing. Believing that the market is now undervalued or overvalued, based on the financial expert or market adviser's scintillating reasoning (see **maps-of-maps**), the investor decides now is the time to be contrarian and go against the crowd and takes a contrary position in the market. If, as likely, the market moves against the investor, he or she may decide to hold on until the "market comes to its senses" and begins to correctly reflect the investor's "rational opinion." Predictably, this experiment in being contrarian goes awry. Two human behavior traits, opposing the market and pride of opinion, need to be particularly guarded against when attempting to be contrarian.

Standard & Poor's 500 (S&P 500) Index. Includes 500 public corporations selected in proportion to their **market value capitalization**, for their common stock trading liquidity, and industry representation. The S&P 500 Index represents, as this is written, almost 80 percent of the overall U.S. stock market value capitalization of equities on the NYSE, the NASDAQ, and the AMEX stock exchanges. The S&P 500 Index has long been used as a benchmark with which to compare the total returns of other investments, and is a good proxy representative of the overall U.S. stock market.

S&P 500 Index Expected Fair Valuation (EFV) Model. The next twelve months of estimated reported earnings for the S&P 500 Index companies are divided by the S&P 500 Index price resulting in a "S&P 500 Index estimated reported earnings yield." Next, the 10-Year U.S. Treasury Note interest rate is divided by the "S&P 500 Index estimated reported earnings yield" resulting in a S&P 500 Index Value Factor. An expected fair valuation for the S&P 500 Index is calculated by dividing the current S&P 500 Index price by the S&P 500 Index Value Factor. While S&P 500 Index EFV Model is not precise, it will give the astute investor approximate correct forward-looking valuations.

S&P 500 Index Nine Month Moving Average (MA) Trend Line. For the **S&P 500 Index**, the monthly trend line is used for perspective to identify **long-term** trends in the stock market. Because the stock market, over the long-term, moves relatively slowly, the perspective of monthly data are most appropriate to analyzing long-term trends associated with **market cycles**.

S&P 500 Index Two Month Moving Average Trend Line. Helps identify long-term trends in the marketplace. Used as a **confirming indicator** for the **S&P 500 Index Nine Month MA Trend Line** in the stock market.

Subjective Truths. Truths internal to the individual that have no objective criteria for judgment. Subjective truths are beliefs and values about concepts and answer the questions of How and Why. Prioritizing objective truths or facts ultimately makes all objective truths subjective truths since some objective truths may now be overshadowed or even ignored if they do not fit one's concepts. Subjective truths, thoughts, beliefs, and values within individuals may be further divided into positive subjective truths or negative subjective to determine "how events are either occurring or not occurring in one's life" to make us happy. Subjective truths are used to explain the **Life and Happiness Model**.

Super-Long-Term. Twenty years, two decades, or more in the stock market.

Ten-Step Method for Investing Success. The methodology is practical and includes: 1) selecting the correct goal and strategy; 2) identifying **political-economic conditions**; 3) calculating the **S&P 500 Index Expected Fair Valuation Model**; 4) identifying the **S&P 500 Index Nine Month MA Trend Line** using perspective and stock market stages; 5) rational anxiety, non-rational emotions, and irrational influences all counteracted by proper investing character traits; 6) Graham-Dodd-Buffett **value investing** with **intrinsic, true, or fair value, market value capitalization, bargain values, and margin-of-safety multiples**; 7) **yield curve** and interest rate monitoring to identify market tops; 8) news evaluation, **discounting the news, Discounted News Theory,** being skeptical of **market pundits**, and shunning stock tips; 9) avoiding the "**self-selected market adviser's strategy**" to being **contrarian**, and being skeptical of conventional wisdom; 10) investors should then pull all of the information together from steps 1 through 9 to make their own **due diligence** judgments and arrive at their own investment decisions.

Territory. The real world, as one experiences using sight and other the senses, may be described as the actual territory of external reality. Real world experience may be represented symbolically on a **map**. However, maps and or **maps-of-maps** should never be confused with the real world territory.

Total Capital Expenditures. Total capital expenditures are determined by subtracting the purchase of property and equipment (sometimes called capital expenditures), the acquisition/disposition costs or gains from the purchase or sale of subsidiaries, plus the addition of any proceeds from the sale of assets. These accounts are all located on the Cash Flows from Investing Activities portion of the **Cash Flow Statement (CFS).** Total capital expenditures are important when calculating **Free Cash Flow (FCF).**

Unexpected News. Unexpected news is nonscheduled news with only the likelihood of what, who, where, and when the imagined event may take place. The imagined what, who, where, and when of unexpected news events causes some investors to modify both their acts and or non-actions in the stock market. Everything that can be imagined by investors which are determined to effect the stock market are partially discounted by the marketplace.

Value Investing. Buying good securities at a significant discount is the strategy that is expected to triumph over the long-term. Investors should prefer high quality securities at proper or reasonable prices which match their scheduled needs. **Intrinsic, true, or fair value** is a good method for determining a company's present worth and may be compared with its **market value capitalization. Margin-of-safety multiples** and **bargain values** for each stock are rank ordered to identify possible candidates for stock purchase based on the **margin-of-safety** concept. Value investing may be likened to comparison shopping and looking for terrific stock bargains.

Yield Curve. The yield curve is a result of monetary and fiscal policy effecting **political-economic conditions** over time. A normal yield curve for federal funds, T-Bills, T-Notes and T-Bonds occurs during average economic conditions. An inverted yield curve comes about when both money and credit are restrictive and is a good indicator of U.S. economic downturns. If the federal funds target interest rate exceeds the 30-Year T-Bond rate this is a harbinger that the overall stock market may begin to discount a slowdown in the U.S. economy and may be close to peaking.

Zero-Coupon Treasury Bonds. Zero-Coupon Treasury Bonds (Zeros) are purchased at a discount with no interest paid by the U.S. government, but are redeemed at par-value at maturity. The benefit is that all interest is assumed to be reinvested so that the Zeros may be purchased at a deep discount to par-value. There is a disadvantage to Zeros, while no interest is paid until maturity the federal government requires taxes to be paid annually, on a pro-rata basis, as if the interest were actually being paid.

Bibliography

Baruch, Bernard M., *BARUCH: My Own Story*, Cutchogue, New York: Buccaneer Books, 1957.

Bernstein, Jake, *How the Futures Markets Work*, New York: New York Institute of Finance and Prentice Hall Press, 2000.

Cohen, Marilyn with Nick Watson, *The Bond Bible*, New York: New York Institute of Finance and Prentice Hall Press, 2000.

Darvas, Nicolas, *How I Made $2,000,000 in the Stock Market*, New York: Lyle Stuart Kensington Publishing Corp., 1986.

Dreman, David, *Contrarian Investment Strategies: The Next Generation*, New York: Simon & Schuster, 1998.

Edwards, Robert D. and John Magee, *Technical Analysis of Stock Trends*, 8th ed., New York: St. Lucie Press, 2001.

Etzel, Barbara J., *Webster's New World Finance and Investment Dictionary*, Indianapolis, Indiana: Wiley Publishing, Inc., 2003.

Graham, Benjamin, *The Intelligent Investor*, 4th ed., New York: Harper & Row, Publishers, 1984.

Hagstrom, Jr., Robert G., *The Warren Buffett Way*, New York: John Wiley & Sons, Inc., 1994.

Kelly, Fred C., *Why You Win or Lose*, Burlington, Vermont: Fraser Publishing Company, 1998.

Lefevre, Edwin, *Reminiscences of a Stock Operator*, New York: John Wiley & Sons, Inc., 1994.

Livermore, Jesse, added material by Richard Smitten, *How to Trade in Stocks*, Greenville, South Carolina: Traders Press, Inc., 2001.

Loeb, Gerald M., *The Battle for Investment Survival*, New York: John Wiley & Sons, Inc., 1996.

Lynch, Peter, with John Rothchild, *One Up On Wall Street*, New York: Simon & Schuster, 1989.

Lynch, Peter, with John Rothchild, *Beating the Street*, New York: Simon & Schuster, 1993.

Mackay, Charles, *Extraordinary Popular Delusions and the Madness of Crowds*, New York: Barnes & Noble Books, 1989.

Magee, John, edited by W. H. C. Bassetti, *Winning The Mental Game on Wall Street*, Boca Raton: St. Lucie Press, 2000.

Malkiel, Burton G., *A Random Walk Down Wall Street,* 8th ed., New York: W. W. Norton & Company, 2003.

Mamis, Justin, *When To Sell*, Burlington, Vermont: Fraser Publishing Company, 1999.

Mamis, Justin, *How To Buy*, Burlington, Vermont: Fraser Publishing Company, 2001.

McMillan, Lawrence G., *Options as a Strategic Investment*, 4th ed., New York: New York Institute of Finance and Prentice Hall Press, 2002.

McNeel, R. W., *Beating the Stock Market*, Wells, Vermont: Fraser Publishing Company, 1987.

Neill, Humphrey B., *Tape Reading & Market Tactics*, Burlington, Vermont: Fraser Publishing Company, 2000.

Nison, Steve, *Japanese Candlestick Charting Techniques*, 2nd ed., New York: New York Institute of Finance and Prentice Hall Press, 2001.

Norris, Frank, *The Pit*, New York: Penguin Books, 1994.

O'Neil, William J., *How to Make Money in Stocks*, 2nd ed., New York: McGraw-Hill, Inc., 1995.

O'Neil, William J., *24 Essential Lessons for Investment Success*, New York: McGraw-Hill, Inc., 2000.

Oz, Tony, *The Stock Trader*, Oak Park, California: Goldman Brown Business Media Inc., 2000.

Schabacker, Richard W., *Stock Market Profits,* Great Britain: Prentice Hall, 1999.

Schwager, Jack D., *Market Wizards: Interviews With Top Traders*, New York: New York Institute of Finance, 1989.

Selden, G. C., *Psychology of the Stock Market*, Burlington, Vermont: Fraser Publishing Company, 1996.

Tape, Rollo, *Studies in Tape Reading*, Burlington, Vermont: Fraser Publishing Company, 1997.

Tracy, John A., *How to Read a Financial Report,* 5th ed., New York: John Wiley & Sons, Inc., 1999.

Wolf, H. J., *Studies in Stock Speculation*, Burlington, Vermont: Fraser Publishing Company, 1990.

Wolf, H. J., *Studies in Stock Speculation, Volume* II, Burlington, Vermont: Fraser Publishing Company, 1998.

Wyckoff, Richard D., *Stock Market Technique, Number Two*, Burlington, Vermont: Fraser Publishing Company, 1989.

Wyckoff, Richard D., *Stock Market Technique, Number One*, Burlington, Vermont: Fraser Publishing Company, 1990.

Wyckoff, Richard D., *How I Trade and Invest in Stocks & Bonds*, Burlington, Vermont: Fraser Publishing Company, 1998.

Index

A

A.M. Best Company 325
accrual based accounting 62
action 144, 341, 342. *See also* non-action
   difficult 256
   non-rational 145
   rational 144
      investor anxiety 145
action in non-action 342
actual P/E ratio 69, 78
additional crucial factors 181–183
aggressive investors 303, 311. *See also* volatility tolerance
AIG (American International Group) 325
American Association of Individual Investors (AAII 251
American roulette 34

American Stock Exchange (AMEX) 73, 350
annual report 277
Appel, Gerald 102
Aristotle 30, 53
asset allocation 298
   goal selection 299
   mix 299, 312
   model 304
      cash 314
   planning horizon 300
      eight year 315
   risk tolerance 303
   risk vs. expected returns 301
      portfolio returns 301
      stocks 302
astute investor 3, 373
   goal 82

Atkins' diet 344
averaging
   down 132
   up 133

B

back testing 124. *See also* S&P 500
   Nine Month MA Trend Line
balance sheet 61
bankruptcy 58, 243
bargain value 180, 276, 373
Baruch, Bernard M. 226, 236
basic net earnings per share (EPS)
   183, 374
basis points 374
bear market 8
beliefs
   129, 250, 342, 343, 349. *See*
   also Life And Happiness Model
Berkshire Hathaway 167, 306
best time to be in the stock market 64
BigCharts.com 109
Blake, William 247
bond fundamentals 56
   credit risk 59
   interest rates 57
   investment grade 56, 59
   non-investment grade 59
   rating agencies 59
      Dominion Bond Rating Service
      Limited 59
      Fitch Incorporated 59
      Moody's Investors Service 59
      Standard & Poor's 59
   redemption provisions 60
boom-bubble buying
   27, 47, 49, 84, 99, 125, 148. *See*
   also crowd psychology

Buffett, Warren
   160, 167, 170, 276, 284, 305, 349. *See*
   also Warren Buffett's investing
   style
bull market 8
business cycle 85, 348
buy low and sell high 242
buy-and-hold strategy
   243, 318, 374

C

Capital Asset Pricing Model (CAPM)
   354, 374
capitalization rate 177, 281
cash 171
   from financing activities 171
   from investing activities 171
   from operating activities 171, 277
cash flow statement
   61, 62, 267, 277, 374
CBS MarketWatch.com 109
Chicago Board of Trade (CBOT) 350
Chicago Mercantile Exchange (CME)
   350
classic books on investing 9
CNBC 237
CNBC - MSN Money 175, 287
Cohen, Marilyn 57
Columbia University 43, 167. *See*
   also Graham, Benjamin
concentration 23
   portfolio 26
Conference Board 38, 209
confirming indicators
   115, 118, 122, 374. *See also*
   technical analysis
Consensus Index 251

conservative investors
303, 311. *See also* volatility
tolerance
continued communication 372
contrarian, 374
conventional wisdom 242
courage 251
discipline 243
diversification 243
implementation 252, 290
philosophy 242
psychology 249
crowd behavior 249
thinking 257
when to be 255
contrarian approach comparisons
244
financial experts 246
disregarding 248
motives questioned 247
technical analysis 246
The Efficient Capital Market
Theory 245
value investing 244
contrarian investing methodology
257
additional factors 261–262
out of favor industries 258
six steps 258
when to sell 260
corporate bonds, callable 374
couplet 247
coupon yield 57
crowd psychology 149
current interest rates 57
current P/E ratio 69
current ratio 182, 284, 374
custom graphs 114

D

Darvas, Nicolas 236
day-to-day price movements 40
debt-to-equity ratio
65, 182, 261, 284, 375
decisions 345. *See also* Life And
Happiness Model
depreciation 62
Modified Accelerated Cost
Recovery System (MACRS) 62
straight line 62
Descartes, Rene 336
desired character traits 139
desires 342, 345. *See also* Life And
Happiness Model
Dialectic Theory 289, 347, 375
diluted net earnings per share (DEPS)
285, 375
discount rate 193
discount rate, risk-free 376
Discounted Capital Market Theory
329, 337, 346, 375
assumptions 350
conclusions 355
definition 350
foresight 368
formulation 350
importance 354
long-term stock mkt. cycles 370
premise # 1 346
premise # 2 347
Discounted News Theory
227, 288, 370, 375
discounting 69, 70, 289, 376
foresight 71
market bottom 70
discounting and net present value
354

discounting the news 376
diversification 23, 266, 299
   portfolio 24
dividend yield 259, 320
Dodd, David L. 156
dollar-cost averaging 318, 376
Dominion Bond Rating Service
   Limited 59
Dow Jones Industrial Average (DJIA)
   8
Dreman, David 257
due diligence 140, 142, 291, 377

E

earnings before interest and tax
   (EBIT) 183
eBay Inc. 277–278, 292
   bargain value 283
   intrinsic, true, or fair value 277
   margin-of-safety multiple 283
   market value capitalization 283
   ten additional crucial factors 284
economic indicator Index 38
economic indicator index
   paradox 38
Edwards, Robert D. 107
Efficient Capital Market Theory
   45, 246, 346, 354, 360, 377
   assumptions 46
      break down 361
   breakdowns 48
   critique 47
   three versions 46
      semi-strong form 46
      strong form 46
      weak form 46
Einstein, Albert 141
electronic tape 377
English Royal Statistical Society 33

equity fundamentals 60
   management assessment 63
estimated future reported earnings 73
Etzel, Barbara J. 373
expected news 215, 227
expected news discounting process
   217, 218
exploring-compensating condition.
   41, 332, 378
   millions of investor's minds 41

F

fear 142, 144, 145, 147, 153
Federal Reserve
   192, 225, 267, 287, 378
   federal funds rate 194, 225, 267
   keeping a log book 208
   Federal Open Market Committee
   194, 225, 287
   meeting statement 195
   misconception 197
   monetary policy 192, 348
      deficit financing 191
      means for controlling 193
Financial Accounting Standards
   Board (FASB) 62
financial analysis 61
first in first out (FIFO) 61
fiscal and monetary policies 191
Fisher, Philip 162, 168
Fisher's investing style 162
   high potential companies 163
      prosperous and gifted 183
      prosperous because they are
      gifted 183
   interviewing companies 184
   leading companies 165
   operations management 164
   sales organization 164

superior top managements 165
two types of companies 163
Fitch Incorporated 59, 325
fixed-income annuity 323, 378. *See also* retirement planning
insurance companies
    rating agencies 324
    single-premium 325
footnotes 61
foresight 19, 368
    investing 214
    reasoned inference 21
forward P/E ratio 72, 76, 378. *See also* price-to-earnings ratio
forward price-to-earnings-to-growth (FPEG) ratio 378
four main stock market stages 91
    boundary lines 92
    stage 1: mark-down - downtrend 64, 222, 230
    stage 2: market bottom - accumulation 64, 331, 333
    stage 3: mark-up - uptrend 64, 224, 225, 230, 293
    stage 4: market top - distribution 58, 331, 333
Franklin, Benjamin 31
free cash flow calculation 173, 379

G

GARP 261
Gödel, Kurt 141
Graham, Benjamin 43, 156, 330
greed 131, 134, 274
    counteracting greed 134
    optimism 134
    will to believe 135
growth projections
    realistic 162

H

Hagstrom, Jr., Robert G. 177
happiness 345. *See also* Life And Happiness Model
Hegel, G.W.F. 217
Hegel's Dialectic Theory 217, 227
herd mentality 148
high self-regard 150
hope 129
How and Why 339. *See also* subjective truths
Hulbert Financial Digest 238
human nature 128, 273
    common investing behavior 128
    emotional 250
    human weaknesses 130
    investor beliefs 129
    investor illusions 130
    symbols 129
human weaknesses 131

I

illegal insider trading 234
illusion 130. *See also* maps and territories
income statement 61
Incompleteness Theorem 141
indenture 56
inefficient capital markets 84
initial public offering (IPO) 379
inside information 233
insider purchases 261
insurance rating agencies 325
interest 188
    credit history 188
    defined 188

interest rates 77
  10-Year U.S. T-Note 270
  spread 198, 209
  term structure 197
  trends 190
intrinsic, true, or fair value 160, 380
  additional crucial factors 181
  calculation 170
  cash flow statement 170
  discounting free cash flow 175
  first stage 177
  free cash flow 173, 277
  Mr. Market 332
  second stage 177
  total capital expenditures
    171, 387
investing 13, 380
  defined 13, 15
  foresight 19, 368, 380
  goals and strategy 266
  long side 15
  neutral position 15
  not gambling 22
  pitfalls 26
    low-priced stocks 27
    poor timing 27
    promotional stocks 26
  probabilistic approach 19
  seven principles 16
  vision 20
investing character traits 138–
  143, 273, 275
ironies
  discounted news 367
  non-rational 366
  Random Walk Theory 367
irrational influences 149, 275
  need for appreciation 149
  need for perfection 150
  stock trading addiction 151

J

Japanese candlestick graphs 104
  Doji 106
  lower shadows 106
  solid bodies 104
  upper shadows 106
  white bodies 104

K

Kelly, Fred C. 130
Kendall, Maurice 33
Kierkegaard, Soren 338

L

laddered-bond portfolio 380
Lao-tzu 341. *See also* non-action
last in first out (LIFO) 61
leading economic indicator 38, 209
  500 common stock prices 39
life 30
  unexamined 30
  unplanned 30
  unscheduled 31
Life And Happiness Model
  336, 355, 381
  feedback
    survival instincts 336
  graph 345
  survival instinct 342
    an example 343
  thought and action 337
    non-action 341
    objective truths 383

subjective truths 338, 386. *See also* social institutions
What, Who, When, Where, How, and Why 338
thought and thinking 336
premise 337
reasoned inference 337
Livermore, Jesse 236, 253, 323
Loeb, Gerald M. 236
logic 144
long-term 381
Lynch, Peter 63

M

Mackay, Charles 148, 249. *See also* human nature
madness of crowds 148
Magee, John 107, 129
Malkiel, Burton G. 34. *See also* Random Walk Theory
management narrative 61
management's financial responsibilities 64
management's integrity, intelligence, and vitality 183, 286
maps and territories 334, 387
checking the territory 335
maps-of-maps 381
of companies 335
using maps 334
margin buying 133
margin-of-safety 156, 276, 382
calculation 180
for bonds 156
quantitative analysis 157
for stocks 158
intrinsic, rue, or fair value 160
multiples 170, 306, 382
rank ordering 181

value investing 159
market cycles premise 85
market highs 99
market newsletters 237
the internet 237
market stages 91, 271
market value capitalization 179, 383
Market Vane 251
marketing/sales/distribution 183, 286
Markowitz, Harry M. 354
maxims to live by 30
media 248. *See also* news
Merton, Robert C. 354
Miller, Merton H. 354
millions of investors' minds 349, 361
moderate investors 303, 311. *See also* volatility tolerance
Modified Accelerated Cost Recovery System (MACRS) 62
money supply 190
Moody's Investors Service 59, 325
Mr. Market 43, 267. *See also* Graham, Benjamin
arrival 331
at peaks and troughs 333
in context 330
intrinsic, true, or fair value 332
MSN Money 205
mutual funds 322

N

NASDAQ Composite 8, 56, 73, 350
NASDAQ-100 (NDX) 8
National Bureau of Economic Research 37, 85, 124, 209, 348

Neil, Humphrey B. 228
New York Stock Exchange (NYSE) 73, 350
news
　discounting 214
　expected 215, 289, 377
　financial experts 248
　headlines
　　agree 233
　　example 232
　judging corporate 214
　media 230
　nightly 228
　　knee-jerk reaction 229
　　knowing what is important 230
　　recognizing the meaning 234
　　threats 228
　reporting
　　going up or down 231
　scheduled
　　meeting expectations 216
　　not meeting expectations 217
　unexpected 219, 289, 387
nightly business news 228, 239
Nison, Steve 104
Nobel Prize for Economics 354
non-action 341, 342. See also action
　investors use 342
non-action in action 342
non-rational emotions 145, 149, 275
　fear and greed 146
　madness of crowds 148
Norris, Frank 151
novice investors 234, 254

O

objective truths 338, 383

What, Who, Where, and When 338
Omidyar, Pierre 277
Open Information Project 175
open market operations 193
operating profit margin (OPM) 183, 285
operations management 184, 286
Option Theory 354
out-of-favor stocks 249
Outstanding Investor Digest 305

P

panic selling 22, 47, 49, 84, 95, 96, 125. See also crowd psychology
paper loss 151
paradoxes 362
　inverted yield curve 364
　leading economic indicator 38, 363
　long-term 365
　Mr. Market 363
　prices reacting illogically to the news 365
　Random Walk Theory 36
　super-long-term 362
perspective 271
　monthly data 87, 370
　moving averages 87
political-economic conditions 39, 130, 189, 198, 210, 267, 286, 349, 383
　negative 203
　positive 200
　yield curves 198
portfolio asset size 243
preferred stock 58
present worth factors 175, 281
price-to-book value (P/B) 259

price-to-earnings ratio
65, 258, 268, 384
calculation 69
standards 66
historical 67
incomplete 68
interest rates 68
price-to-free cash flow (P/FCF) ratio
259
price-to-sales (P/S) ratio 259
primary market 56
productivity 190

Q

qualified account 324
questionnaire. *See* risk tolerance

R

random walk process 384
Random Walk Theory
33, 49, 245, 337, 384
critique 49
gone wrong 352–353
irony 367
paradox 36
rational action 144, 275
real-estate investment trusts (REIT)
298
recession 348
announcement 94
reserve requirements 193
retirement planning 297. *See also*
asset allocation
20 years vs. 30 years 316
compounding 316
planning horizons 317

401(k) plan 318, 324, 325, 379
at retirement 323
continued equity investment
326
buy-and-hold strategy 318
dollar-cost averaging 318
Keogh plan 318, 380
pre-retirement
Carrie and Cash 318
example 317
two basic strategies 318
return-on-assets ratio 65
return-on-equity (ROE) ratio
65, 182, 285, 385
return-on-sales ratio 65
returns of stocks over bonds 319
risk 24
high 310
low 310
market 24, 382
systematic 24
unsystematic 40
risk tolerance 303. *See also* volatility tolerance
questionnaire 303
semantics 308
risk vs. volatility 306–307
differences 307
semantics 308
separating 309
risk-takers 128
Roth IRA 321, 385
Russell 2000 8

S

S&P 500 Index 25, 73, 385
EARNINGS AND ESTIMATE
REPORT 74, 268

Expected Fair Valuation Model
78, 267, 270, 386
like the insurance industry
25, 369

Nine Month Moving Average
(MA) Trend Line
9, 102, 271, 386
Two Month Moving Average (MA)
Trend Line 9, 273, 386
V shaped bottom failures 93
recession announcements 94
Schabacker, Richard W. 91
scheduled news 216
Scholes, Myron S. 354
secondary market 60
Securities and Exchange Commission
(SEC) 385
Selden, G. C. 149
self-directed retirement accounts 7
self-doubt 144
self-esteem 254
self-selected market adviser's
strategy 252, 385. See also
contrarian
is to blame 254
opposing the market 253
pride of opinion 254
senior bonds 58
senior subordinated debt 58
sentiment indicators 251
share volume 88
at market lows 89
at market peaks 89
upside and downside 90
Sharpe, William F. 354
social institutions 339
subjective truths 339
Socrates 30, 53
stage 1 92, 95
confirming Indicators 115

volume 95
stage 2 95, 117
market bottoms 97
market low turning points 96
volume 96
stage 3 98, 120, 273
stage 4 99, 122
market churning 99
market highs 99
Standard & Poor's (S&P) 36, 72
Standard & Poor's Insurance Services
325
stock challenge 128
stock market. See also maps and
territories
achievement 238
complex institution 360
cycles 256
four stages 90, 382
ironies. See ironies
long-term trends 100
line of least resistance 100
trend reversal 101
never wrong 291
non-action 348
paradoxes. See paradoxes
pricing 83
pundits 382
free advice 231
market gurus 136
shock absorber 86
sophisticated 32
tips 235
for the lazy 236
not always genuine 235
stock market taxonomy 49–51
for proper analysis 52
StockCharts.com 205
stocks top bonds over 30 years 321
subjective truths 338, 386
How and Why 339
negative 340

positive 340
super-long-term 318, 321, 362, 386
symbols 129. *See also* maps and
    territories
systematic 24

T

Taoism 341
taxonomy, stock market 49
    proper analysis 52
    X axis 50
    Y axis 51
technical analysis 9, 107
    double bottom reversal pattern 376
    double top reversal pattern
        108, 376
    head and shoulders reversal pattern
        108, 379
    higher-highs and higher-lows
        107, 379
    Japanese candlesticks 104, 380
        Doji formations 106
    lower-highs and lower-lows
        107, 381
    monthly MA trend lines 102
    Moving Average Convergence
        Divergence 9, 102, 273, 383
    outside reversal day 109, 383
ten-step method for investing success
    386
    analysis results 291
        eBay Inc. 292
        S&P 500 292
        yield curve 293
terrorist attack 221
The Astute Investor
    35, 54, 238, 255, 266, 356, 365
    firsts 371
the media. *See* news

thought and thinking 337
TIAA-CREF 325
time 15, 30
    change 30
    do not squander 32
    is money 32
    is one's life 31
    opportunity 33
    scheduling 31
timing 30
    is money 32
    sophisticated 32
total capital expenditures 171
Tracy, John A. 60
types of investors 137
    impulsive investor 137
    investing at cross purposes 138
    lethargic investor 137

U

U.S. government 190. *See also*
    Federal Reserve
    treasuries 195
unexamined life 30
unexpected news 219, 227
    evaluating 220
    in a strong market 224
        an example 224
    in a weak market 221
        an example 221
unsystematic risks 23

V

value additivity 354
value investing 159, 387

vanity 131, 254, 274
  averaging down 132
  averaging up 133
  margin buying 133
  small profits - large losses 131
volatility 305
  high 310
  low 310
  semantics 309
  total return 314
volatility tolerance 311
  asset mix 312

W

Warren Buffett's investing style 167
  good companies at reasonable
    prices 169
  margin-of-safety 168
what really moves the markets 226
What, Who, Where, and When
    338. *See also* objective truths
will to believe 131, 135, 274
  holding on 136
  hope 135
  market gurus 136
Wilshire 5000 8
Wyckoff, Richard D. 69, 323

X

XYZ Corporation 171

Y

yield curve 197, 286, 388
  dynamic 205
  flat or humped 204
  inverted 202
    an example 203
  normal 199
  steep 200, 287
yield curves in practice
  help identify market tops 206
    an example 207

Z

Zacks 174, 277
Zero-Coupon Treasury Bonds
  322, 388